ENDURING ALLIANCE

ENDURING ALLIANCE

A History of NATO and the
Postwar Global Order

Timothy Andrews Sayle

CORNELL UNIVERSITY PRESS   ITHACA AND LONDON

First published 2019 by Cornell University Press

Library of Congress Cataloging-in-Publication Data

Names: Sayle, Timothy A., author.
Title: Enduring alliance : a history of NATO and the postwar global order / Timothy A. Sayle.
Description: Ithaca [New York] : Cornell University Press, 2019. | Includes bibliographical references and index.
Identifiers: LCCN 2018047435 (print) | LCCN 2018048277 (ebook) | ISBN 9781501735516 (pdf) | ISBN 9781501735523 (ret) | ISBN 9781501735509 | ISBN 9781501735509 (cloth)
Subjects: LCSH: North Atlantic Treaty Organization—History. | Europe, Western—Defenses—History—20th century. | World politics—1945–1989. | Cold War. | United States—Foreign relations—1945–1989.
Classification: LCC D845.2 (ebook) | LCC D845.2 .S29 2019 (print) | DDC 355/.031091821—dc23
LC record available at https://lccn.loc.gov/2018047435

For Nicole, Henry, and Charles

Contents

ENDURING ALLIANCE

THE DANGERS OF DEMOCRACY

NATO Command Post Exercise 5: The first day of the war devastated Central Europe. The Soviet Union detonated eight hundred atomic bombs, while bombers of the United States Strategic Air Command dropped fifteen hundred. After one day of fighting, the Soviet Union had no atomic bombs left, but the war continued. Forces of the North Atlantic Treaty Organization (NATO) clashed with troops of the Red Army and their Warsaw Pact allies. The American bombers continued to pummel Central Europe, then Eastern Europe, then the Soviet Union itself. Day after day, they dropped hundreds of atomic bombs. At the end of the week, the SAC bombers "flew into shattered Moscow." The war was won.

The weeklong simulated war played out in 1955 at the Supreme Headquarters Allied Powers Europe (SHAPE), the seat of NATO's military command. Basil Liddell Hart, a British military historian and strategist visiting SHAPE that same year, thought NATO's military power as demonstrated by the paper exercise was impressive. Nonetheless, he also found the whole process "very disturbing." For the by the end of the war, "the great cities of the West"—with their cathedrals, their parliaments, their museums, let alone their bakeries, their markets, their plumbing and wiring—were destroyed. "Victory," he wrote, had "lost its point."[1]

Liddell Hart was not alone in describing the strategy of the Atlantic Pact as akin to a suicide pact.[2] And yet, allied leaders, speaking through the historical record scattered over more than a dozen archives in Europe and North America,

1

make clear that they built and maintained this pact to keep peace. As NATO's first secretary-general, Lord Ismay, put it, "the business—the paramount, the permanent, the all-absorbing business of NATO is to avoid war."[3]

To ask if NATO deterred the Red Army from marching down the Champs-Élysées or occupying the Channel ports, however, is to ignore just what allied leaders thought the NATO organization and its military force achieved.[4] According to Robert A. Ford, a distinguished Canadian diplomat who served as the dean of ambassadors in Moscow and as an adviser to NATO on Soviet affairs, it was a "myth" that what "NATO had actually done was prevent a military invasion." The real threat to Europe had been the political disintegration of the allies, and this is what NATO had prevented.[5] Ford's analysis was not unique; it was shared widely in the alliance from the 1940s through to the early 1990s. Even the State Department's champions of an Atlantic Pact, men like Theodore Achilles, recalled: "I don't think there has ever been any serious danger of an all out Soviet armed attack west of the East German–West German frontier. The danger has been, and still is, that the Russians can resort to . . . subversion and political blackmail backed by the threat of force."[6]

The great fear of NATO's leaders throughout the Cold War and beyond was not that the Soviet Union or Russia would launch an invasion of Europe. Instead, they feared that Moscow might threaten—even imply—the use of force. The very hint of war might drive citizens in Europe to press their leaders to concede to the Kremlin's demands rather than risk another cataclysm on the continent. Thus what American officials called the "inadequacies and anomalies of NATO, the relative unrealism of the military plans, and the slightly fictional aspects of NATO," were understood on both sides of the Atlantic to be essential components for providing Europeans with an intangible sense of security.[7] This was much more difficult than it might sound, for a constant theme of this book is the nagging worry of NATO leaders that their citizens rejected the very notion of power politics upon which the concept of NATO rested. The allies believed that by signing the North Atlantic Treaty and maintaining NATO—a growing and unruly hodgepodge of councils, commands, and committees—they were insulating themselves, and their citizens, from appeasement and ultimately a war that no one, on either side of the Iron Curtain, wanted.

The democratic nature of allied governments, or some democratic styling of the alliance itself, has long been assumed as the glue that kept NATO together. But the historical records reveal a darker, deeper, and more complex relationship between democracy and NATO. The allies did not maintain NATO because it was an alliance of democracies, but because it offered the best insurance against the dangers of democracy—a fickle electorate that, in seeking peace, might pave the way for war.

Allied leaders built and maintained NATO not simply to deter Soviet military adventures, but to establish what Ismay called a "Pax Atlantica." Like the Pax Romana, the Pax Atlantica was to establish "a period of peace . . . enforced by arms."[8] The North Atlantic Treaty, the NATO institution, and the integrated military commands established a new system of international relations correcting the errors and omissions of the past, and it all rested on a logic that both predated and outlasted the Cold War.

To understand the Pax Atlantica, then, is not to focus solely on the internal workings of NATO councils, committees, and military commands, but to think about the broader pattern of international affairs they lay and preserved. Lord Ismay is said to have quipped that NATO existed "to keep the Russians out, the Americans in, and the Germans down." Many have quoted this explanation for NATO's existence, even if there is no record of Ismay having made the comment. No matter: it is the best explanation of NATO's function. Indeed, we do not have to take Ismay's word for it, for his dictum was repackaged in countless policy documents over the alliance's long history as an explanation of NATO's purpose.

In 1966, American analysts noted that NATO served, first, to ensure that the Soviet Union did not achieve "domination of German and other European resources"—that is, to keep the Russians out of Western Europe. NATO also served to provide "a politically acceptable receptacle for resurgent German military strength" without independence that might see Germany "again run amok"—that is, to keep Germany down. The "principal check" on both German policy and Soviet efforts to dominate Europe was the "U.S. presence"—even if the "particular form of that U.S. presence is secondary, so long as it is assured." America had to be in. Americans and Europeans knew that keeping America in Europe was essential to the other two goals, and that the alliance structure and integrated command helped protect the US commitment from isolationists at home.[9]

Ismay's line, like NATO, survived the fall of the Berlin Wall. In 1990, National Security Council staffers translated the quip into bullet-point bureaucratese, writing that NATO existed

1. to ensure the collective defense of its members against the Soviet threat;
2. to reconcile Germany's legitimate aspirations to regain its sovereignty with Europe's legitimate desires to retain its security;
3. to forge a transatlantic link binding the US to Europe in a durable partnership.[10]

While specific points received varying emphasis over the decades, the allies were consistent in believing that NATO was essential to ensuring these triangular goals.

The Ismay dictum is, fundamentally, an argument about the maintenance of the balance of power in Europe. Buried within the seemingly straightforward sentence, however, is the fact that the most direct threat to any of the three goals lay at the ballot box: a European populace bullied by the threat of war; a resurgent German chancellor; or an isolationist Congress or president.

The public rhetoric of NATO leaders, along with scholars' search for explanations of the alliance's endurance, has obscured the sources of both the gloom within NATO about its future, and the alliance's endurance. The North Atlantic Treaty itself proclaimed the allies' "common heritage and civilisation of their peoples." One need only recall the story told by Lester Pearson upon receiving the Nobel Peace Prize in 1957 to discount this claim. One Christmas Eve during the Second World War, Pearson had tried to drown out the explosions of the London blitz by listening to the radio. Haphazardly turning the dial, he found a station that filled his room "with the beauty and peace of Christmas carols," recalling for him the traditions of the festive season of years gone by. When the carols came to a stop and the announcer's voice came over the radio, the host spoke in German; the carols were being broadcast from the Nazi state dropping bombs on London. Common heritage and civilization, if they exist, are certainly no guarantee of cooperation.[11]

Nor did NATO endure and survive because the alliance or the allies were, in one way or another, democratic either in their membership or operation.[12] There is little to the suggestion that NATO itself operated *like* a democracy. NATO's top political body, the North Atlantic Council (NAC), was not a parliament and did not have majority voting rules, and there was no executive power.[13] As the following chapters make clear, the largest allied states often made their policy in private before bringing it to the other allies in the NAC.

Nor can there be the suggestion that NATO was simply an alliance made up of democratic states. Despite the treaty language and grand speeches about NATO as an alliance of democracies, many officials, like those in the British Foreign Office, believed NATO's "democratic ideology" was "tarnished by autocracy in Portugal and the somewhat authoritarian government in Turkey."[14] Canadian officials negotiating the treaty in 1948 warned the whole idea was "ideologically messy" and that the future alliance would be open to "charges of hypocrisy."[15] Again and again, readers will see that policy makers knew the flowery language of public NATO communiqués to be misleading and often false.

If anything, the practices of democratic government, especially electioneering, ruling minority or coalition governments, and the uncertain longevity of administrations, presented special problems for the alliance. Election campaigns slowed down agreement in the North Atlantic Council and in other forums because politicians were not willing to take strong stands on policy while also on the hustings. The idea that new elections always turned up fresh and talented leaders is far too optimistic. As Dean Acheson remarked, it was a "damned shame that the right 'people' don't turn up in the sheer gamble of politics."[16] The uncertainty of the democratic harvest led to very careful election watching in NATO capitals. The Americans worried that Europeans would elect neutralist, antinuclear, or anti-American governments, while Europeans worried that the people of the United States would find a president on the fringe of the extreme right or left.

Some scholars have suggested the transatlantic relationship rested on a "transnational élite" or an "Atlantic political culture." The idea is that a group of influential individuals, either members of government or those with influence over governments, served as a bridge connecting the allies' values and interests. These scholars point to private social gatherings and meetings where influential officials from the NATO countries met and developed a "basic consensus on transatlantic cooperation and the need for Western unity."[17]

Certainly some, but not all, of the most important officials charged with NATO files met regularly at meetings and conferences of organizations like the English-Speaking Union, Bilderberg, the Council on Foreign Relations, Atlantik-Brücke, and parallel unofficial and sometimes informal clubs. Historians and scholars of these organizations, however, have not been able to identify a direct link between these organizations and policy, and even scholars that study Bilderberg's connections to NATO warn against overestimating the importance of these organizations.[18] Attendance at Bilderberg summits, of course, is no sign of a belief in their effectiveness; McGeorge Bundy, national security adviser to both Kennedy and Lyndon Johnson, sitting in on one such gathering, scribbled a proposed title for future meetings: "Uncle Dean Acheson's Scribble Seminar for Delinquent Youths."[19] Other organizations and lobby groups, like Clarence Streit's "Union Now" and the Atlantic Council, were "just 'pie in the sky'" that officials believed caused "extensive" problems for policy making and "gratuitously create[d] confusion" about policy in NATO.[20]

But an examination of NATO's history from the 1940s through the early 1990s does reveal a critical connection between champions of NATO from both sides of the Atlantic. The great commonality between the individuals involved in the maintenance of NATO—including elected politicians, military officers, and civilian officials—was their understanding of, and often direct experience with, the wars of the first half of the twentieth century. Nearly every individual identified in the chapters that follow suffered the blast of war. And as readers will discover, references to recent wars—and especially the Second World War—were the coin of the realm in argument over NATO policy.

During the Second World War, Dwight Eisenhower had served as supreme allied commander of the Allied Expeditionary Force, and planned for D-Day alongside his British counterpart, Bernard Montgomery. These two men would again work side by side in 1951 as, respectively, supreme commander and deputy supreme commander of NATO forces. "The only real difference," said one retired British officer who saw them working together in 1951, "is that the shooting war in Normandy has been replaced by the cold war in the East."[21] Throughout the Second World War, Eisenhower also worked closely, if not easily, with General Charles de Gaulle, the leader of Free French forces. Their complicated relationship would be reprised in the late 1950s when they were both presidents of NATO powers.

D-Day serves as a touchstone for other, more complicated relationships. On June 6, 1944, General Maxwell Taylor parachuted into Normandy on the instructions of the plane's jumpmaster, Lawrence Legere. General Hans Spiedel, chief of staff to the absent Erwin Rommel, led the Nazi defenses that day. Less than two decades later, in the early 1960s, Taylor was John F. Kennedy's military adviser, and then the chairman of the Joint Chiefs of Staff, with Legere his assistant, studying, among other things, NATO nuclear issues. Spiedel was the commander-in-chief of all NATO troops in Central Europe.

The enmity from the Second World War hardly disappeared in 1945. After the fall of the Berlin Wall, Margaret Thatcher would shudder when informed that Germans were again singing nationalist songs, just as Harold Macmillan had shivered when, at Konrad Adenauer's funeral in 1967, he saw pallbearers wearing the distinctive coal-scuttle helmets of both Imperial and Nazi Germany.[22] West German politicians and officials were well aware of the fear and resentment felt toward them by their continental allies. "Scratch a European and you will find dislike of the Germans," Chancellor Helmut Schmidt told a British colleague. When the Brit demurred, Schmidt, a Wehrmacht conscript who had served on both the Eastern and Western fronts, replied grimly: "You were never occupied."[23]

It is common, and indeed easy, for historians of the post-1945 world to see a firebreak between the postwar world and that which came before. But the men and women of NATO saw no such division. For men like Macmillan, war was not history but their life—or at least a critical part of it. In the First World War, Macmillan had gone "over the top" at Loos and the Somme with the Grenadier Guards. He had his pelvis smashed in one battle, and lay for ten hours in a shell crater, reading a copy of Aeschylus in the original Greek that he kept in his uniform pocket. During the Second World War, Macmillan had a civilian role as political counselor to Eisenhower in the Mediterranean, but this hardly meant he was free from the dangers of war. After a plane crash, Macmillan raced back into the fiery wreckage to rescue a companion. He was burned in the effort, his trademark mustache reportedly blazing with a blue flame.[24] For the whole of NATO's Cold War, under the mufti of the politicians and diplomats sitting around the table of the North Atlantic Council at NATO Headquarters were memories of war, and real scar tissue.

The point of this abridged list of connections between Cold War–era officials and the wars that came before is not to create a theory of historical memory. It is to remind readers that the references to war made in these leaders' claims for NATO's value were not glib analogies. For these men and few women, the experience of war was not abstract, and it fundamentally shaped their understanding of the need for NATO. To understand the allied commitment to NATO, leaders looked less to their contemporary present or future to make their policy, but to the past—their past—to understand the riddles of world affairs and guide their policy.[25]

All of the experiences of NATO officials were different, and some officials came to similar conclusions about the need for NATO based on their study or reading of history, rather than their active participation. But the overarching lesson these officials seem to have taken from their war experience was a belief that peace, however desirable, was not the default human condition. If they were to choose an axiom from the ancients, it would not be Isaiah's suggestion to beat swords to plowshares and spears into pruning hooks, but Vegetius's "Let him who desires peace prepare for war." Indeed, as Ismay would write, "if we are prepared for battle, we will not be called upon to engage in it."[26] Montgomery summed up the unflinching views of allied officials best when he wrote that in the postwar world, the NATO states all "wanted peace above all." But "peace in the modern world cannot be assured without military power, and this costs money. That fact might be sad, but it is true. Peace was, in fact, a by-product."[27]

We know a lot about the origins of NATO and the North Atlantic Treaty. Participants in the early exploratory talks have written excellent, detailed accounts. Other scholars have pored over the historical record: the telegrams, the memorandums of conversation, and the records of the exploratory talks.[28] Indeed, we even know the alcoholic lubricants that helped generate ideas and break mental logjams, be it—on the American side—the Cosmos Club's fishhouse punch, or for British foreign secretary Ernest Bevin, Harveys Bristol Cream. The chapters that follow reveal the continuity of the earliest thinking about NATO through to the debates over NATO's role and purpose at the end of the Cold War.

The history of NATO is a kaleidoscope of domestic politics and national foreign policies, and so no one book could offer a total history of the alliance. Instead, these chapters capture critical episodes that reveal why the allies maintained NATO and why they worried it might disintegrate. Taken together, they point to a remarkable continuity in officials' understanding of NATO's purpose. It was an understanding that crossed the political spectrum and indeed crossed the Atlantic Ocean, but the allies feared it would not cross generations.

NATO's early years were a period of tremendous diplomatic innovation. Like all good creative thought, it was inspired, and the muse was the recent war in Europe. After 1955, however, innovation came to a halt. For allied leaders, it was time for the inglorious but no less essential task of keeping the alliance together. The task would go on, and grow heavier, as hopes for a self-propelling "spirit" of NATO dried up.

NATO's unity was threatened in the 1950s as, outside the North Atlantic area, the allies' interests diverged. The post–Suez crisis Anglo-American rapprochement was Eisenhower's solution to the troubles plaguing NATO: he hoped that close cooperation between London and Washington might serve as a model to the alliance as a whole. The rapprochement, however, created its own problems for the alliance, as de Gaulle launched a lengthy but unsuccessful campaign to reorganize NATO as an instrument of the global Cold War.

In the midst of the struggles with de Gaulle, NATO's attention turned to the simmering crisis over Berlin. In the early 1960s, the John F. Kennedy administration pushed the alliance to develop its own grand strategy, and to use the allies' collective military, diplomatic, and economic strength to deter the Soviet Union from doing anything rash in Berlin. NATO developed a grand strategy—at least on paper. Ultimately, however, the bitterness engendered by America strong-arming ended any hopes that NATO could be transformed into an active instrument of world politics.

As the Cold War crises over Berlin and Cuba cooled, and détente with the Soviet Union seemed possible, NATO's future seemed to be in jeopardy. Allied leaders, however, never doubted the value of retaining NATO: relaxed tensions with the Soviet Union only emphasized the importance of the alliance for containing Germany. The alliance also came to describe itself as a tool for managing the evolving relationship with the states of the Warsaw Pact. The thaw in the Cold War, however, undercut public support for NATO defense spending. The late 1960s mark the beginning of a concern that would haunt NATO for the rest of the Cold War: Would allied governments be willing to pay for NATO's defenses, or would the alliance collapse? This question lingers decades after the end of the Cold War.

Fears of diminishing public support for the alliance became only more acute as the states of Europe sought a unified voice in international affairs. In the 1970s, Richard Nixon and Henry Kissinger worried that the generation of postwar European leaders who had built NATO were being replaced by craven men who would continue to cut defense spending to appease voters. A seeming imbalance in the burdens of defense, plus increasing economic friction between the United States and Europe, threatened an Atlantic rupture. Worried that the emerging European community would take Europe out of harness with American foreign policy, Kissinger threatened—and did—"use NATO to bust Europe" and seriously retard the evolution of a common European foreign policy.

The last long decade of the Cold War emphasized the growing tensions between European domestic opinion and NATO's reliance on nuclear weapons. From the late 1970s through to 1989, debates over the so-called enhanced radiation weapon, long-range theater nuclear forces, and short-range nuclear forces made clear that the domestic consensus over NATO's Cold War strategy was breaking down. Only the second of these three major nuclear modernization programs was successful, leading allied leaders to fear that antinuclear sentiment in Europe might bring NATO to the brink of collapse. NATO's ability to endure longer than the Soviet Union was not as obvious as it might appear in retrospect.

When, in 1989, George H. W. Bush took office, he and his administration believed the alliance was essential. They left office thinking the same thing—even if during that time the Berlin Wall fell, Germany was unified, and the Soviet Union collapsed. For Bush and his advisers, the logic of NATO both as a bulwark against Moscow's influence and as a means of preventing the establishment of a shaky system of alliances in Central Europe continued to apply after the end of the Cold War. The need to salt the earth against a potential reconstitution of Soviet power, and the desire to ensure that the former members of the Warsaw Pact did not seek destabilizing alliances of their own, led to early thinking about the expansion of NATO to the east, and the maintenance of a permanent Pax Atlantica.

What follows, then, is not a bureaucratic history of NATO organs in Paris or Brussels, nor one meant to hive off the history of NATO from the larger Cold War era. Too often, historians reserve NATO as a specialized subject of study, ancillary to some supposed broader relationship between the United States and Europe or bilateral relations between the United States and one ally. This book seeks to turn that styling on its head and to argue that allied leaders on both sides of the Atlantic viewed NATO as the issue of primary importance in both their transatlantic and even global affairs. NATO and the Pax Atlantica, the allies believed, provided the stability and peace that allowed for myriad other complicated non-security relationships between and among NATO allies, and also allowed for the allies to engage with the broader world. When, on occasion, allied leaders had to choose between preserving the Pax Atlantica or pursuing other national interests, they chose NATO. That is why NATO endures.

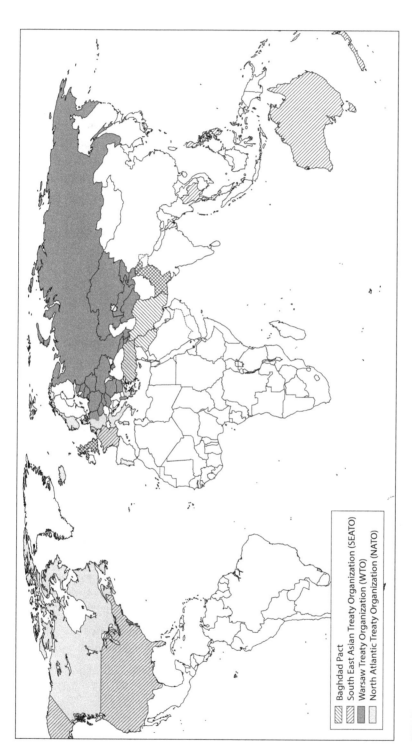

FIGURE 1. Treaty organizations in 1955

Baghdad Pact: Iran, Iraq, Pakistan, Turkey, United Kingdom. SEATO (Southeast Asia Treaty Organization): Australia, France, New Zealand, Pakistan, Philippines, Thailand, United Kingdom, United States. Warsaw Pact (Warsaw Treaty Organization): Albania, Bulgaria, Czechoslovakia, German Democratic Republic, Hungary, Poland, Romania, Soviet Union. North Atlantic Treaty Organization (NATO): Belgium, Canada, Denmark, Federal Republic of Germany, France, Iceland, Italy, Luxembourg, the Netherlands, Norway, Portugal, United Kingdom, United States.

THE SPECTER OF APPEASEMENT

The fear that drove allied leaders to sign the North Atlantic Treaty was not that of a Soviet invasion of Europe. It was the threat of Soviet blackmail: that Moscow might make demands on a government in Europe, and that the citizens of the country in question, fearing a return to war, would insist their leaders accept the Soviet request. The Soviet Union would not go to war, as Ernest Bevin, the British foreign secretary, put it, because it would not need to: "the Russians seem to be fairly confident of getting the fruits of war without going to war."[1]

Bevin had become alarmed by Soviet moves to establish influence in Eastern Europe in 1946 and 1947, the failure of the Soviets to show any interest in genuine solutions to European problems at the Council of Foreign Ministers meeting in December 1947, and an increasingly "tough" line taken by the Soviet foreign minister Vyacheslav Molotov.[2] He wrote to US secretary of state George Marshall that the "Russians"—what many British continued to call the Soviets throughout the Cold War—were "exerting a constantly increasing pressure which threatens the whole fabric of the West." If the states of Europe did not counter this "Russian infiltration," he warned, they would watch "the piecemeal collapse of one Western bastion after another."[3]

In the United States, too, the Soviet expert George F. Kennan warned that the Soviet Union posed a psychological, rather than a military threat. "The Russians," he said, had identified the means to influence and exploit "the vulnerability of liberal democratic society." In 1947, in a speech at the National War College, he warned that the "towers of the Kremlin cast a long shadow." It was "the shadows rather than the substance of things that move the hearts and sway the deeds of statesmen."[4]

Toward the North Atlantic Treaty

Bevin had a plan to prevent this slow deterioration, even if it was a bit fuzzy around the edges. He suggested Paris and London sign a defensive treaty with Belgium, the Netherlands, and Luxembourg (the Benelux countries). This "solid core" might then come to agreements with the Scandinavian countries and Italy. Ultimately, Germany and Spain, too, might come to join this Western union.[5] It would be "backed by the Americas and the Dominions," which he later made clear meant an Anglo-American defense agreement.[6]

Bevin thought such an arrangement necessary to protect gains made by the US-funded program of economic assistance for Europe. Many American officials, like Kennan, had seen the Marshall Plan as the best way of insulating Europe from Soviet pressure. While the economic revival of Europe was crucial, Bevin did not think that, on its own, a better standard of living could help Europeans resist Soviet pressure. A defensive treaty, he argued, was needed to "create confidence and energy on one side," that is, in those parts of Europe outside Soviet control, and to "inspire respect and caution on the other," that is, Moscow.[7] Bevin's belief that a defensive treaty would provide a psychological boost to the people of Western Europe was one of the essential, if perplexing, concepts that would drive NATO forward.

Events in February and March 1948 only seemed to prove Bevin correct. In February, the Czechoslovak Communist Party seized power in Prague—the "Prague coup." The takeover of government, supported by the Communist-controlled police and army, alarmed Western Europeans and Americans alike and caused Washington to wonder whether the coup would stimulate more seizures of power in Europe.[8] As early as 1946, President Truman had argued that the Soviet government was really no different from Russia's czarist government or, for that matter, Hitler and the Nazis.[9] Now, after Prague, parallels between Nazi claims on Czechoslovakia in 1938 and the Soviet-backed coup in Prague obliterated any distinction between Hitler and Stalin. Even German politicians from different sides of the political spectrum agreed the Soviets were "a red-lacquered second edition of the Nazis."[10]

A month after the Prague coup, the Norwegian government warned British officials that they expected an imminent demand from Moscow to negotiate a pact. Earlier that month, Finland had signed an agreement with the Soviet Union that essentially ceded Helsinki's security and defense prerogatives to Moscow in exchange for independence on domestic affairs, a relationship described throughout the Cold War as "Finlandization." During the last war, Norway had been overrun by the Nazis, providing the German navy with wider access to the North Atlantic. A Norwegian-Soviet pact would carry the same strategic threat—perhaps leading to similar demands on Sweden and Denmark, and the making of the Baltic into a "Russian lake."[11] But a "Norwegian defection" from the West to Moscow would also doom any chance for political cooperation in the West, as Moscow picked off states one by one. The result, Bevin said, would be "to repeat our experience with Hitler and to witness helplessly the slow deterioration of our position" until, as a last gasp, "we are forced . . . to resort to war in order to defend or lives and liberty."[12] It was the threats to Norway, rather than simply the Prague coup, that spurred the British and others, including the Canadians, to search for a "bold move" to halt Soviet momentum.[13]

American officials came to echo British fears that the people of Europe might be so "intimidated by the Soviet colossus . . . to the point of losing their will to resist." This, US officials judged, is what had happened at Prague: noncommunist forces that might have stood up to the Communists had there been "any sign of friendly external force" simply did not. The Americans worried, like Bevin, that continual Soviet encroachments would finally force Washington and London to take up arms. Stalin, it seemed, was underestimating the "present temper" of Congress and the American public. If the Soviets pushed their "expansionist tactics," there might be a "forceful American reaction" and a war no one wanted.[14]

Bevin convinced the Americans that transatlantic cooperation could solve the problem. If Washington could offer "concrete evidence of American determination to resist further Communist encroachment," then the people of Europe would not be bullied, and the Soviets would avoid major provocations.[15] After Prague and the Norwegian threats, Marshall recommended to Truman that the United States begin consultations on how to "stiffen morale in the free countries of Europe."[16]

The solid core of Bevin's plan was formed in March 1948 with the Brussels Treaty: Britain, France, and the Benelux states agreed to a defensive alliance and joint military organization. In response, the State Department worked with Senator Arthur Vandenberg to prepare a congressional resolution publicly advising the president to associate the United States with "collective arrangements"—such as the Brussels pact. This provided the political cover for discussion for a new such collective agreement.[17] Within a week, officials from the United States, the United Kingdom, and Canada began a series of "security conversations" to discuss "the establishment of an Atlantic security system."[18] The shape and form of such a system were anything but settled; nor was its membership easily or quickly agreed. The Americans, British, and Canadians did settle on the term "North Atlantic" in an effort to prevent Latin American countries or Australia from asking to join, but they believed the term also gave them flexibility to determine a broader membership.[19]

In the first security conversation in March, the British representatives suggested the primary function of the security system, whatever its name or shape, was to offer "a firm commitment on the part of the US to aid militarily in the event of any aggression in Europe."[20] American military officers on the Joint Chiefs of Staff worried that such a commitment would be biting off more than the postwar United States Army could chew. But officials from both the State Department and the Foreign Office agreed that military capabilities were essentially secondary. The true "objective of the Pact approach was to stop the Soviet Communist advance, and that this would probably be accomplished by the fact of a drawing together of free nations in their own defense."[21] It was not the military power of the pact that would matter so much as the pact itself.[22]

Discussions would stall and start repeatedly throughout 1948. Stalin's decision to blockade Berlin would reinforce the perceived need for transatlantic cooperation. At the same time, however, the British, understanding that a presidential election year was a sensitive time to discuss the United States engaging in its first entangling alliance in a century and a half, carefully dialed back their approaches.[23] But the delays were not owed only to politics. The State Department counselor Charles "Chip" Bohlen and the director of policy planning, George Kennan, both had doubts about the true necessity of a new security system or treaty, and made their views plain. Indeed, their views were likely considered in Moscow, too, as the interlocutor on these matters was the British diplomat and Soviet spy Donald Maclean.[24] Kennan told some of the diplomats visiting Washington that a formal treaty was unnecessary, as it would be "unthinkable that America would stand idly by" if the Soviets made "an aggressive move against any country of Europe."[25] Such arguments meant little to those who remembered events in Europe in 1939 and 1940. What the British, Canadian, and Europeans sought was more than just a unilateral assurance from American diplomats, or even from the president himself. Even at this early stage, the future allies of the United States knew how easily presidents, and their commitments, could change. They wanted an agreement that would survive the transition from one president to the next.[26]

The implication of Kennan and Bohlen's arguments, that the United States did not truly need to be bound to the West Europeans to achieve its foreign policy goals, would forever hang over the alliance. But the greater lesson for the Canadians and Europeans in the delays of 1948 and into 1949 was the primacy of American domestic politics in the formulation of policy. Going forward, the other allies would have no doubt that the politics of presidential elections and the parochial interests of Congress were the most important bellwethers for the American commitment to Europe.

Despite these wrinkles, the Americans agreed to host a working group of diplomats from the United States and their colleagues from Belgium (also representing Luxembourg), Canada, France, the Netherlands, and the UK. The group agreed to a report arguing that the best solution to security problems in Europe was an alliance, and they submitted the report to their governments for consideration. The report argued that while the Marshall Plan had helped improve the economic situation in Europe, a new arrangement was "needed to counteract the fear of peoples of Western Europe that their countries might be overrun by the Soviet Army before effective help could arrive." They noted that while there was no evidence Moscow was planning an invasion, the Soviet Union was maintaining Soviet military strength to "support the Kremlin program of intimidation designed to attain the domination of Europe." They worried that Moscow would exploit the "justified sense of insecurity among the people of Western Europe" and that only a treaty offered a solution.[27] A treaty would transform the United States' relationship with Europe and mark the US as a European power. As Bevin told the French foreign minister Robert Schuman, he, Bevin, was "anxious not to make the same mistakes" as after the First World War, "when the opportunity of getting America right into the affairs of Europe had been lost."[28]

The North Atlantic Treaty negotiated in late 1948 and early 1949 was so obviously directed at Moscow that the drafters joked the treaty's preamble should begin as a letter to Stalin: "Dear Joe . . ."[29] But the diplomats who agreed on the need for the treaty were, in many ways, thinking about the wars of the past. Repeatedly, diplomats and politicians spoke about the treaty as did one Canadian diplomat on the working group: "If a pact along the lines of that currently under discussion had existed in the later 1930's, there would have been no war in 1939, and that a similar pact probably would have prevented the outbreak of the war that began in 1914."[30] Of course, there had been treaties in 1914 and in 1939. But none had included the United States.

In November 1948 Truman was reelected, and the movement toward a treaty, slowed by the American political season, gained momentum. Again, Kennan offered one of his penetrating, if frustrating, analyses of the prospects and limits of a treaty between the North Atlantic powers. Alan Bullock, a historian and biographer of Bevin, is right to say Kennan's memorandum put the case for NATO even better than the treaty itself: Kennan pointed out what all agreed—that the fundamental issue in Europe was the threat of Soviet "political conquest." All the talk about defense coordination was secondary, for "military force plays a major role only as a means of intimidation." Thus any Atlantic pact, focused as it would be on defense and security, would affect Europe's "political war only insofar as it operates to stiffen the self-confidence of western Europeans in the face of Soviet pressures." This was precisely why the North Atlantic Treaty was signed, why NATO was formed, and why president after president and prime minister after prime minister would reaffirm his or her state's commitment to the alliance. But Kennan's argument was frustrating in that it identified a fundamental problem—indeed, NATO's main problem—without a solution: the "preoccupation with military affairs" at the treaty's heart and in the minds of NATO diplomats, officials, and generals, he argued, was "regrettable," for it "addresses itself to what is not the main danger."[31]

In the early security conversations, American, British, and Canadian diplomats had considered how to meet what they knew to be the real threat—what Kennan called "political conquest" and what others called "indirect aggression." Both the Canadians and Americans offered draft treaty language that would refer to protections against a coup d'état, subversion, or even "political change favourable to an aggressor" in an allied state. But the British were dead set against defining the political threat, and the French at the Brussels Treaty discussions had also been against anything that might look like a treaty right to interference in another ally's internal affairs.[32] Looking back in 1952, Theodore Achilles, one of the Department of State officials concerned with drafting the treaty, noted that one of the means by which pro-Communist governments, or even governments with pro-Communist policies, could come to rule was "by parliamentary means."[33] The allies would never find a direct solution to what they believed to be the greatest threat they faced: that the voters in one or more allied countries might elect leaders who in turn would accede to, even champion, policies advantageous to Moscow.

After the November 1948 elections that saw Truman elected president, the diplomats again had to hurry up before waiting. The State Department, with room to operate now that the elections were over, and sensing public opinion in favor of a pact, pushed to accelerate negotiations. Then, in the new year, the Americans hit the brakes. Dean Acheson, whom Truman appointed secretary of state in his new administration, arrived in office only to learn that the Senate had not fully agreed to a treaty as robust as the one envisioned by the diplomats. The primary sticking point was article 5—the most important element of the treaty. The draft treaty declared that in the event of an armed attack on an ally, the signatories "will assist the party or parties so attacked by taking *forthwith such military or other* action . . . *as may be necessary* to restore and reassure the security of the North Atlantic area." This was the real meat of the alliance, but the senators objected to this clause as violating the constitutional practice in the United

States that only Congress can declare war. Put another way, the senators would not sign away their rights to declare war by ratifying a treaty that could compel the United States to go to war. The Europeans and Canadians insisted that the original clause could not be watered down. It had been discussed publicly, and so deletion would be interpreted as a Soviet victory. After some careful maneuvering, Acheson persuaded the Senate to accept a defensive treaty calling for "action including the use of armed force" by allies in case of an attack.[34] This satisfied the allies, although article 5 leaves the decision of how and when to respond to an attack up to individual governments.

The North Atlantic Treaty, signed in April 1949, was a symbol of unity and, more important, of an American commitment to Europe. But the value of the treaty did not go far beyond symbolism. The night before the signing, the US secretary of defense, Louis Johnson, reminded Truman and Acheson that "neither the signing of the Atlantic pact nor any initial U.S. military aid program is going to enable us to hold the Rhine line." Truman agreed, noting that despite the war potential of the United States and Europe, the "Western nations are practically disarmed and have no power sufficient to prevent . . . Soviet divisions from overrunning Western Europe and most of Asia."[35]

Building the Organization

Lord Ismay, NATO's first secretary-general, claimed that the North Atlantic Treaty was not "one of those treaties that you can sign with great pomp, all the photographers taking photographs, gold pens and all that sort of thing, and then put away in the archives of the various F[oreign] O[ffice]s." Instead, the treaty pledged the signatory nations to "collective action, and continuous action," to enhance military and nonmilitary cooperation.[36] After the signing, the allies worked to develop the organizational structure and defense plans for the alliance.[37] But work proceeded slowly and meandered. There was an enormous range of planning and speculation on just how any allied military planning could, or should, be organized. The French wanted a group of allied military planners to be permanently located in Washington—a thinly veiled effort to ensure that the Anglo-American combined chiefs of staff would not be resurrected without French participation. The British wanted the planners in London, where they could replace the organs of the Brussels Treaty.[38] There were larger questions looming in the background: Once NATO's military committees or groups were formed, just what would they plan for?

Both the Americans and the British had initially assumed that NATO military planners would develop a "global strategy." But their thinking changed very quickly when it was clear that the French, too, wanted NATO to be responsible for a worldwide military strategy, and that France expected to play an equal role in developing any such plans. The British and Americans quickly backed away from such a vision, jealous of their own global prerogatives and fearful that the French could not keep secrets.

By the end of 1949, NATO had established a Military Committee, made up of the chiefs of staff of each allied state. The Military Committee had subsidiary groups: five regional planning groups, charged with making plans for the defense of Northern, Western, and Southern Europe, Canada–United States, and the North Atlantic, respectively. A Standing Group, consisting only of American, British, and French officers supported by a small secretariat, would coordinate the regional plans.[39] From early days, the British and Americans would work to keep NATO focused on regional military planning for Europe, while France would continue to press for global planning.[40] The Soviet atomic explosion in 1949 led the allies to expect the Soviet Union would be capable of launching a surprise attack by 1954, and planning proceeded on this basis.[41] Still, on June 15, 1950, Bernard Montgomery surveyed the state of European defense: "As thing stand to-day," if Western Europe were to be attacked, "there would be scenes of appalling and indescribable confusion."[42]

Nine days after Montgomery's dismal prognostication, confusion erupted on the Korean peninsula when North Korean tanks dashed into South Korean territory. The Korean War did not so much change NATO as give urgency to ideas that already existed, especially the interlinked ideas of a centralized command structure and the involvement, somehow, of West German strength.[43]

The fundamental question after Korea, as Dean Acheson told Truman, was not whether Germany should be included in planning the defense of Europe, but how to do it "without putting Germany into a position to act as the balance of power in Europe."[44] Germany, which lay in two halves, was occupied in the west by American, British, and French troops, and in the east by the Soviet Union. At the close of the Second World War, many of the allies who had fought the Nazis wished to see Germany stripped of its potential ever to rearm. By 1950, American thinking had changed significantly, although worry that Germany might once again rise to become a dangerous military force never disappeared.

John J. McCloy, the US high commissioner in Germany, warned in August that a reconstituted German army under German command could give Germany the strength to play off the East against the West, including the option of "ultimately joining the Soviets." The best solution, McCloy argued, was building up a "genuine European army," which would deter the Soviet Union and also "be the best possible insurance against further German aggression."[45]

As American diplomats pondered the idea of a European army, they determined it would need to be connected to NATO, part of a larger command organization, and buttressed with support from Britain and the United States. The American ambassador in London, Lew Douglas, suggested a European army would need to be augmented by three or four divisions of American ground troops and a matching component of British troops. The British and American troops would give the Europeans confidence and protection while they rebuilt their war-shattered forces. He also recommended the appointment of an American general officer to command the force, for this would attach American prestige to the successful defense of the continent. After all, "he who assumes command of an army and the country whose representative wears the toga, is as responsible for defeat as for victory."[46]

McCloy's recommendations for a European army, improved by suggestions from Douglas in Britain and the American ambassador in France, David Bruce, were not based on purely military considerations but on their appreciation of the psychology of European citizens. Much of the American thinking, and indeed that of European officials, was focused on the concept of the "will to fight." Now, in war-ravaged Europe, wrote Douglas, Europeans' will lay "dormant, not because the great majority of the French people and of the German people and of the Belgians and the Dutch prefer communism, but because they doubt that the Soviet hordes can be resisted."[47] The concept of "will to fight" was vague and imprecise. It stood in for the obvious unwillingness of European governments to make the spending trade-offs required for a serious rearmament and defense program. It also represented the fear of European leaders that their citizens would not trust their armies to stand up to Soviet threats. As Paul-Henri Spaak, a former Belgian prime minister and future NATO secretary-general, pointed out in 1951, the armies of Western Europe had been crushed in the last war. "Europeans," he said, "have no confidence in their national military establishments." Only American participation and leadership could provide that confidence.[48]

By the end of 1950, the three-part plan of German integration in a European army, the appointment of an American commander—"on the model of General Eisenhower's headquarters during the last war"—and deployment of British and American troops to Europe was moving forward. Already the United States assumed the end result would be German accession to the North Atlantic Treaty.[49] Truman appointed Eisenhower to serve as supreme allied commander, Europe (SACEUR), a remarkably powerful new position in which he was authorized to deal directly with heads of government and ministers of defense of allied states in peace, and to command their troops in war.[50] The American secretaries of defense and state recommended to Truman that US forces be committed to

Europe to convince the allies that there would be no question of the United States abandoning the continent if war came.[51]

Building the Allied Command Structure

As Eisenhower went about setting up his new supreme headquarters in France, he told his cadre of international officers that NATO was, fundamentally, "not a military organization," nor was it "an organization in government." NATO was "a matter of spirit. It'll work if we generate the spirit."[52] For Eisenhower, as for those who had drafted the North Atlantic Treaty, the very act of cooperation was more important than any specific policies.

But already, at the very beginning of his command, Eisenhower had cause to doubt whether NATO could maintain its spirit. In late 1950 and early 1951, just as Eisenhower was preparing to travel to Europe and as Truman was preparing to authorize the deployment of several divisions of US troops to the continent, a "great debate" erupted in the United States. Men of immense public stature, like the senator Robert Taft and the former president Herbert Hoover, spoke out against sending American troops to Europe. They argued that sending US soldiers to Europe in a time of peace would strip Europeans of any sense of responsibility for their own defense while impoverishing the United States.[53] Less than a year after the US had committed itself to the North Atlantic Treaty, the European allies watched as Americans debated just what NATO meant, in practical terms, to the United States.

The great debate was won by those who advocated sending troops across the Atlantic. The US divisions were deployed to Europe, along with Canadian and British troops. But Eisenhower made clear that the troops were in Europe "temporarily." He and his senior staff believed that in "the long run it will not be feasible to have, in times of peace, large American ground forces stationed in Europe; they will be withdrawn eventually."[54] Off the record, Eisenhower told newspaper editors that US divisions would likely begin to return to America in about three years, once Europe was in "a very fine state."[55] Eisenhower assumed as SACEUR, and indeed later as president, that the United States could, would, and should remove its forces from Europe once the allies rebuilt their armies and reestablished their will to fight.

Upon arriving in Europe, Eisenhower was struck by the "poverty, the extreme poverty of Western Europe."[56] He also found that the American troops being deployed to Europe were not as welcome as he had expected.[57] The two issues were related. Officials like Marshall, now secretary of defense, and Omar Bradley, the chairman of the Joint Chiefs of Staff, recognized that pushing Europeans on military expenditure could undermine the fragile, if recovering, social, economic, and political systems in Europe. In the wealthy United States, more taxation caused by defense expenditures might mean the difference between citizens buying radios or televisions; in Europe, it meant the difference between "white or black bread." The Americans were frustrated that their European colleagues had not convinced their publics of the necessity of sacrifices to strengthen NATO's military power. They resented that European governments had let their citizens think of NATO's defense buildup as akin to "castor oil which has to be taken."[58] But they hoped that, eventually, the Europeans would recover. In the meantime, the United States would not push them to the breaking point.

Eisenhower got to work organizing a command system that could effectively wage war against the Soviet Union in case conflict came, whether by Moscow's wish or by accident. But his attitude, that of the US government, and certainly that of Europeans, was sanguine about the prospects of war. Eisenhower did not

FIGURE 2. President Truman and General Dwight D. Eisenhower walk away from the general's airplane on the snowy runway at Washington National Airport, January 31, 1951. After his appointment as supreme allied commander, Europe (SACEUR), Eisenhower had conducted a "survey tour" of the alliance, visiting each NATO member country. National Archives photo no. NLT-AVC-PHT-(73)3496.

think that the Kremlin wanted war any more than the Western allies. Indeed, by 1951, he thought the worries of European citizens voting directly for "the communistic ticket" in elections had passed. Eisenhower's main worry, and the problem that would cause the greatest concern in NATO for the next four decades, was the Soviet effort to convince the Western Europeans that they had no need for defense and that they should quit NATO and become neutral. "Neutralism," Eisenhower knew, already had "a fairly wide appeal," and it could undo any attempt at the cooperation he thought so crucial.[59]

New Members and New Strategy

Very quickly, then, as Dean Acheson put it, the "bloom was off NATO."[60] News reports continually described NATO council meetings as failures, and the plaintive headline "Whither NATO?" has been with the alliance since its infancy.[61] And yet, in 1951 and 1952, NATO's organizational structure evolved to take its lasting shape. At a North Atlantic Council meeting of the allied ministers in Lisbon in 1952, the allies announced new plans for a military buildup. But they also transformed NATO's organization from an ad hoc meeting of ministers into a council in permanent session with allied delegates, or "permanent representatives." The permanent session of the North Atlantic Council would be chaired by a new secretary-general of the organization, who would also oversee an international secretariat to guide NATO's work and coordinate its committees.[62] One British minister in attendance at Lisbon was the acting minister of defense and Winston Churchill's wartime military assistant, Lord Ismay. Given the hubbub of the meeting, and what he observed to be the alliance's "lack of central direction," Ismay wrote to an American colleague: "This is the first that I have seen of NATO, and thank heaven it's the last." Very shortly after Lisbon, and after Sir Oliver Franks and the Canadian Lester Pearson declined the job, Ismay was—against his wishes—told by Churchill that he would be NATO's first secretary-general.[63]

As NATO evolved, its membership also grew. In 1952, the United States surprised its allied partners by claiming that Greece and Turkey should be allowed to accede to the North Atlantic Treaty. The two Mediterranean states had, in NATO's early years, cooperated with the alliance, but the Americans wished for them to be full members because they were critical to Eisenhower's military plans. The Turks, for their part, had been pushing for membership while also threatening that if they were not permitted to join, there would be widespread neutralism in Turkey "or even a move to compound with the other side."[64] In February 1952, at a meeting of the North Atlantic Council in Lisbon, the allies agreed to invite Turkey and Greece to join, and the alliance as a whole set new force goals: expensive plans to equip and train more divisions of troops for the defense of Europe.

Also in 1952, Eisenhower resigned his post as SACEUR to run for the presidency. His competitor for the Republican nomination was none other than Senator Robert Taft, thus pitting one of the staunchest opponents of the American NATO deployment against the alliance's former commander. Had Taft won the nomination and gone on to the presidency, NATO's history would have been forever changed. As Eisenhower prepared to leave his NATO command in 1952, he issued a lengthy report detailing what NATO had achieved. It is clear that he worried about the commitment of citizens in NATO states to coordinate and maintain their defenses. "Why," he asked, "should there be confusion in the mind of millions of our own peoples as to the basic aims of our defense program, the necessity for it, and the urgent demand for their own individual efforts?" Surely, he went on, once "the truth is understood, once the critical dangers present in the world situation are really known, there will be less complacency concerning our present military situation."[65]

In Eisenhower's own view, however, and indeed in that of those involved with the treaty's signing, the critical danger was of European citizens either voting for Communists or of pressing their leaders to accept Soviet demands in a crisis. While Eisenhower and the other leaders saw a connection between the establishment of a defensive system to create a spirit of cooperation and to protect against blackmail, they found no way to effectively explain to their citizens their real fear: that the citizens themselves would, through their fearful or fickle actions, compel their leaders to give in to Soviet demands and let Moscow dominate Europe without firing a shot.

The prospects for NATO seemed to deteriorate further in March 1953 when Joseph Stalin died. The new leaders in Moscow sent out diplomatic feelers, and officials in both Europe and North America wondered if Stalin's death would usher in a new type of relationship with Moscow. Chinese and Korean agreement to an armistice in Korea contributed to the idea that the Cold War might thaw.[66] The result was a nosedive in support for the defense buildup announced at Lisbon, and a feeling, as Ismay put it, that "NATO was going downhill."[67] If building up a public appetite for defense spending had been difficult when Stalin was alive and war was waged in Korea, it was even more difficult now. Acute budgetary problems in London, in particular, led the allies on a search for a new strategic concept—that is, a new logic, rationale, and plan for how NATO would fulfill its already ambiguous goal.

In 1953, by what one American official called a "magical coincidence," the allies decided that, after fulfilling two-thirds of the troop-level goals set after the outbreak of the Korean War, NATO had all the troops it would need. London, ultimately with the acquiescence of Washington, persuaded the other allies to adopt a strategy and force plan designed to deter the Soviet Union, not to defend Western Europe.[68] The idea, as Montgomery put it, was that the Soviet Union would never contemplate a war with Europe because "they would suffer great damage and much loss of life—equally as great as we would."[69]

This reorientation of NATO's military planning and strategy was made possible by two factors that would affect NATO for the rest of its existence: The first was the need for governments to limit defense spending, and NATO commanders' realization that allied governments would never be willing to pay the money required for a conventional—that is, nonnuclear—force that could defend Europe against a Soviet attack.[70] The dramatic cut to the Lisbon force goals showed that the number of NATO's conventional forces was much less important than the fact that they existed, and that they included US troops. For the rest of the Cold War, the quantity and quality of NATO troops as compared to their Warsaw Pact enemies would be heatedly debated inside and outside the alliance, but it was always a second-order problem compared to the problem of simply ensuring there was a US military presence in Europe.

The second factor was the growing availability of nuclear weapons and the American willingness to deploy these weapons in support of NATO. Even in 1951, NATO had planned to use nuclear weapons in support of a war with the Soviet Union, but both the number of bombs and the strategy for their use were limited.[71] The incredible destructive power of the atom allowed NATO to practice a policy of deterrence, essentially entering into the suicide pact with Moscow described by Montgomery. It also allowed for NATO to claim that it could fight and win a nuclear war with the Warsaw Pact without paying for the deployment of enormous numbers of conventional troops. In 1954, the NATO allies agreed to a new strategy document, M.C. 48, "The Most Effective Pattern of NATO Military Strength for the Next Few Years." This explicit and pronounced emphasis on nuclear weapons in NATO policy—what was called the "new approach," matched the "new look" defense policy of the Eisenhower administration, with its attempt to limit expenditures on conventional forces and increasingly rely on nuclear firepower. The British, for their part, would use the phrase "long haul" to indicate a similar concept of a financially sustainable but robust military policy made possible by nuclear weapons. NATO's "nuclearization" solved problems while creating more.[72]

While the nuclearization of NATO was important for military and economic planning, NATO leaders immediately grasped that reliance on atomic weapons might undercut the unity of the alliance and lessen its appeal to the public. In 1953 and 1954, politicians in the United States and the United Kingdom wondered whether Europeans could stick to an alliance that, if pushed to war, would incinerate large swaths of Europe. Eisenhower's secretary of state, John Foster Dulles, admitted in his remarks to the North Atlantic Council that "it was somewhat unpleasant to discuss the use of atomic weapons," that it "did not lend itself to useful public expression."[73] The British cabinet worried that NATO planning for atomic war could lead to precisely what NATO was trying to prevent: neutralism.[74]

Just as NATO adopted its heavy reliance on nuclear weapons, the issue of German integration came to a head. From 1950 until 1954, talks had dragged on in Paris and in Bonn over how best to establish a European army. The discussion had focused on the French Pleven Plan of 1950, so named after the French premiere. The Pleven Plan envisioned a European Defense Community (EDC), with German military units trained and deployed into the broader force at unit sizes below that of a division. This was an obvious effort to make the German military units useless on their own.[75]

Despite some obvious quirks with the EDC idea, both the British and the Americans supported the plan as the best way to bring Germany into the defensive arrangements for Western Europe. In December 1953, the "Big Three"—the leaders of Britain, France, and the United States—met in Bermuda to hash out their strategy. Ismay, as NATO secretary-general, was invited to attend to prevent any appearance that these three states were dictating policy for the alliance. Eisenhower and Dulles, Churchill and the British foreign secretary Anthony Eden, and the French prime minister Joseph Laniel and foreign minister Georges Bidault agreed that NATO should be guided by the "new look" or "long haul" concept of defense planning, and that critical to this concept was a German role in defense. So convinced was Dulles of the need for an EDC to link Germany to NATO that he warned a failed effort to establish the EDC would amount to Europe "committing suicide."[76]

West Germany Joins the Alliance

Despite Dulles's warnings, and after years of negotiations, the EDC plan was rejected by the French National Assembly in 1954. Instead of having Germany join the EDC, which in turn would be affiliated with NATO, the allies agreed to make Germany a NATO ally like all the others, but with some important differences. In September and October 1954, the signatories to the Brussels Treaty met in London; three weeks later, the foreign ministers of Britain, France, West Germany, and the United States met in Paris. The resulting London and Paris agreements significantly modified the Brussels Treaty and NATO: Britain, France, and the United States agreed to formally end the occupation of western Germany, and

FIGURE 3.   The North Atlantic Council met in ministerial session in Paris, October 1954, and invited the Federal Republic of Germany to become a member of NATO. National Archives photo no. 286-MP-par-06017.

the Federal Republic of Germany (FRG) would now be a sovereign state. What had formerly been American, British, and French occupation forces in Germany would be maintained at the same strength. They would no longer be forces of occupation but defenders of allied soil. And indeed, the FRG would formally have fourteen allies, as the agreements paved the way for the accession of the FRG to the North Atlantic Treaty in 1955. The continued deployment of foreign troops in Germany helped ease worries in Europe of Germany's rehabilitation. To further calm fears in Europe both east and west of the FRG, the new Brussels Treaty limited the types and size of armaments that Germany could build, and Chancellor Konrad Adenauer made a series of unilateral pledges, most significantly promising that the FRG would not build atomic, biological, or chemical weapons on German soil.[77]

By 1955, NATO had taken its essential form: it consisted of a treaty binding the states of Europe and connecting them to the United States, but also an organization and an integrated military command that helped alleviate European concerns about the less-than-rock-solid article 5. NATO had become an international institution, with a staff and a secretary-general and the attendant committees and acronyms. NATO had also realized what historians would come to call "dual containment," in that it had grown to include—even contain— German power, and in turn the newly strengthened NATO was now strong enough to contain any Soviet expansionist designs in Europe. Still, news reports questioned whether NATO had a future; and some wondered whether NATO was necessary now that it had been built, or if it could be put to other uses.

2

THE APPLE CART

In November 1956, Lord Ismay, NATO's secretary-general, telephoned Dwight Eisenhower in a "desperate," tearful mood. Ike knew the secretary-general from the war, when "Pug" Ismay had been Winston Churchill's chief military assistant. Now NATO's first secretary-general was calling to tell Ike, NATO's first supreme commander and president of the United States, that NATO might "be broken up."[1] Ismay's call came amid the disagreement between the United States and the British and French, after the latter two had colluded with Israel to attack Egypt. But it reflected a period of grave uncertainty about the alliance's future.

The main challenge to NATO in 1956 came not from Soviet troops on NATO's borders. Quite the contrary: the great challenge to NATO's survival in the mid-1950s was the absence of an imminent Soviet threat to Western Europe. NATO, seemingly as soon as it had completed its tasks of absorbing West Germany and thus establishing a reasonable military deterrent against the Soviet Union, looked like it might have put itself out of business. Stalin's death, and the efforts by his successors to portray the Soviet government as champions of peace, ushered in a new era of East-West relations inimical to NATO.

As the European empires crumbled and as the Soviet Union began more active attempts to court potential new partners in the developing world, the weight of global crises shifted from Europe to Asia, Africa, and the Middle East. In response, some allied leaders expected NATO to help protect their imperial possessions or aid their colonial struggles. But these issues divided NATO deeply. Some allies, especially the Nordic countries and the Canadians, insisted that NATO had no

FIGURE 4. General Eisenhower, NATO's first supreme allied commander, Europe, and Lord Ismay, NATO's first secretary-general. They knew each other as "Ike" and "Pug." No location or date. National Archives photo no. 286-MP-fra-04433.

responsibility for problems abroad. Critically, Eisenhower and his secretary of state, John Foster Dulles, were unwilling to see NATO's thumb rest on the scales in support of colonial powers. As Eisenhower, speaking of African independence movements, told his National Security Council, "he would like to be on the side of the natives for once."[2]

The American inhibition against using NATO to fight the global Cold War was more than simple moral conviction. Both Eisenhower and Dulles thought that the people of the United States would not support continued participation in an alliance or organization that fought for imperial ends and against independence movements. If NATO tried to fight the crises of empire, American domestic support for the alliance would evaporate, and NATO would crumble, leaving Western Europe as vulnerable to Soviet political pressure as it had been in the late 1940s.

In the Suez crisis and its aftermath, however, Eisenhower saw an opportunity for NATO. The post-Suez Anglo-American rapprochement is well known: Eisenhower and Macmillan rebuilt a "common law alliance" like that between Franklin Roosevelt and Winston Churchill during the Second World War, with the benefits of close cooperation without the rigid formalities of an institutionalized relationship.[3] Eisenhower, however, expected the new relationship to serve as a model for NATO's future. In forging this relationship—an Anglo-Saxon directorate—Eisenhower and the United States saved the alliance from decay, but sowed the seeds of future transatlantic crises.

The Soviet Peace Offensive

Throughout the negotiations over the North Atlantic Treaty, none of the allies believed the Soviet Union wanted war in Europe. Now, by the mid-1950s, they were certain. NATO's deputy supreme commander, Viscount Montgomery of el-Alamein—who as Field Marshal Bernard Montgomery had won great victories against the Nazis in Africa and at Normandy—thought it "virtually certain" there would be "no major war" in Europe into the foreseeable future.[4] American intelligence estimates confirmed the Soviet Union was not planning to use the Red Army to conquer Western Europe.[5]

The change in Soviet tone after Stalin's death in 1953 was dramatic but suspicious. The Kremlin abandoned its threats of war and instead emphasized conciliation with the governments of Western Europe. The Soviet Union signed a peace treaty with Austria and withdrew the Red Army. Moscow issued a disarmament proposal, sent a mission of top Soviet leaders to Yugoslavia, and accepted a meeting with Britain, France, and the United States to discuss European issues. At the same time, the Soviet Union increased its "political action" in European countries, inviting scholars, politicians, and business leaders to visit the USSR.[6] A group of experts on the Soviet Union met at NATO headquarters Paris to discuss the Soviet "peace offensive," and concluded the Kremlin was seeking to "lull, rather than to alarm, the West."[7]

The allied governments remained convinced that the Soviets' "basic purpose" was to "destroy NATO and get foreign forces"—that is, American, British, and Canadian troops—"withdrawn from Europe." Lester Pearson, the Canadian foreign minister and the first NATO foreign minister to visit the USSR, reported back to the allies in 1955 that the Soviets expected NATO would "fall apart" in a period of lessened tension between East and West.[8]

Harold Macmillan, then the British secretary of state for foreign affairs, put it succinctly to the British cabinet: this "Russian peace propaganda is a bit dangerous."[9] Polling data and diplomatic reports from Europe were categorical in claiming that public support for NATO on the continent was waning. This raised "the question of whether continuing reliance can be placed on NATO as the core of U.S.-European policy."[10] The metaphors used to describe NATO in Washington were of decay: The "cement of fear" that had held NATO together was crumbling, according to the State Department; there were "cracks" in the "cement holding NATO together," warned the Operations Coordinating Board.[11] The CIA warned that "some loosening" of the alliance "seems inevitable."[12] The deployment of US troops, it seemed to the Americans, had not stiffened the European resolve sufficiently. General Alfred Gruenther, NATO's supreme commander (SACEUR), privately accused European politicians of being negligent by not encouraging support for the alliance.[13] Eisenhower worried there was a "new feeling growing abroad that NATO may be unnecessary."[14]

Allies everywhere sensed that NATO had failed "to achieve full popular support," and some officials speculated that it was the military nature of the alliance that led to public indifference, even apathy.[15] Here was the disconnect between military means and political ends that Kennan had pointed to in 1948. In an effort to overcome this gap and build up public support for NATO, the allies appointed a committee of three senior officials—the "three wise men"—to try to find more attractive uses for the alliance. Perhaps, as per the special wish of the Canadian delegation to the exploratory talks, the allies could build on article 2 of the treaty that called for greater economic and social cooperation among the allies. NATO's efforts to reestablish the alliance as something more than a military alliance were disappointing. And even before the committee of three could present their report, disaster struck the alliance outside of the treaty region, and far from the North Atlantic.[16]

Keeping NATO out of Suez

The allies had, for the most part, avoided using the North Atlantic Council—NATO's main consultative body—to discuss affairs outside the Western European area. Few wanted to broach thorny and divisive imperial issues in a council designed to demonstrate cooperation. Many of the allies were deeply troubled by French policies in North Africa, both because of anticolonial domestic constituencies and because they believed French actions were embarrassing NATO. The Americans, like Dulles, found themselves simultaneously attempting to prevent the non-imperial NATO states from criticizing the French, while also discouraging the French from raising North African issues. The North Atlantic Council, Dulles believed, was no place to discuss sticky issues.[17]

By the end of 1955, NATO foreign ministers from the Netherlands, Portugal, and France were all pushing for NATO to take a more active interest, and perhaps active policy, outside Europe.[18] These three countries wanted help in Indonesia, Goa and Africa, and North Africa, respectively. But they were joined by non-colonial powers, including the Italians and Germans, who wanted NATO to ensure the Soviet Union did not gain allies in the developing world. The Germans argued, "Wherever one of us loses, all lose."[19] The Americans tolerated this talk, believing it "reflected an attempt to think through other ways and means of giving long-term substance and content to NATO."[20]

In 1955 and 1956, allied foreign ministers believed Soviet activity and influence in North Africa and the Middle East, especially Egypt, posed the greatest threat to NATO. Nearly all the petroleum that fueled and lubricated NATO's armies transited the Suez Canal. More important, the oil and other products from the region provided much of the fuel and energy for Western Europe's recovering, but fragile, economy.[21] In the middle of June 1956, Dulles and his French counterpart, Christian Pineau, agreed that the NATO allies must consult on Egypt's future.

Nothing was coordinated or agreed between the NATO allies by July 1956, however, when the Egyptian leader Gamal Abdel Nasser nationalized and restricted access to the Suez Canal and closed off Egypt's oil pipelines. In the blink of an eye, Europe had become "totally dependent" on the mercy and goodwill of the Arab powers for the lifeblood of its economy. French officials began planning military action to relieve this dependence. The British prime minister, Anthony Eden, suggested that he, along with his colleagues in Paris and Washington, plan a response. Diplomats at the American embassy, on hearing Eden's plan, said they favored such consultations, but suggested broadening the discussion to include other NATO allies.[22]

NATO was Eisenhower's preferred instrument, too—at least at first. In Washington, the president and his advisers thought any intervention, if necessary, would best be done in the "name of NATO."[23] Although it was not Eden's first instinct, he agreed that Britain should take the issue to NATO for discussion.[24] If, as the Foreign Office put it ominously, the crisis over Suez "developed," it was "clearly most important that we should carry the North Atlantic Alliance." The British urged the French to make their case at NATO, too, and hoped the allies would help apply economic and diplomatic pressure on the Egyptians.[25]

The British and French foreign ministers attended the North Atlantic Council meeting in September, and warned they were making military preparations in case Nasser refused to negotiate.[26] Oddly, however, the US delegation to the NAC stayed silent. While in July the president and his advisers had been all for discussing the issue in NATO, by September they were annoyed that the British had played up the meeting as some sort of special session to decide the fate of Egypt.[27]

In the intervening period, Dulles had come to doubt the wisdom of affiliating NATO with the crisis in any way. In August, Dulles had been presiding over a conference of eighteen states in a bid to find a peaceful solution to the closure of the Suez Canal. His primary concern was to prevent the crisis from devolving into a direct test of strength between the United States and the Soviet Union. He now believed it "essential NATO per se should not appear [to] become involved in deciding future courses of action re Suez." If NATO were to play a role, the London Conference would fall apart along East-West lines. Worse, if it were to become public that NATO was "directing Suez policy," the alliance would become a "whipping boy of anti-NATO (anti-white, anti-colonial)" states. Ultimately, he expected, the West would lose the allegiance of several non-NATO states such as Pakistan, Ethiopia, and Iran. It was necessary to make "clear to press and public that Suez is not [a] NATO problem."[28]

Dulles also made sure to remind Eisenhower that the United States had ratified the North Atlantic Treaty with the clear proviso that the treaty "was not to be construed as endorsement of the colonial policies of other NATO countries."[29] The treaty, which had been heatedly contested in the Senate, was still only seven years old. If Congress were to believe that the administration had baited them with an agreement for the protection of Europe and switched it for a global commitment to maintain crumbling empires, the administration would get no more support for NATO.

Meanwhile, in October, British, French, and Israeli officials met secretly in Sèvres, France, and agreed to a plan whereby the Israeli military would invade the Sinai. Immediately after the invasion, British and French forces, acting ostensibly to separate the warring parties, would enter Egypt and open the canal. On October 29, the Israelis invaded. London and Paris issued their bogus ultimatum the next day.

Dulles called October 30, 1956, "the blackest day which has occurred in many years in the relations between England and France and the United States."[30] Lord Ismay, at NATO headquarters in Paris, was, not for the last time, reduced to tears. He warned the council that the rift over the ultimatum represented the greatest threat to NATO since the signing of the treaty.[31]

On October 31 Britain and France began bombing Egypt. In response, Nasser ordered the scuttling of dozens of ships in the canal, rendering it impassable. Days later, on November 5, British and French paratroopers landed in Egypt. Both Dulles and Eisenhower were furious. Dulles complained that the Anglo-French offensive was "nothing but the straight old-fashioned variety of colonialism of the most obvious sort."[32] Eisenhower asked rhetorically, "How could we possibly support Britain and France if in doing so we lose the whole Arab world?"[33]

The United States insisted that the British agree to a cease-fire and present a timetable for withdrawal or Britain would be denied access to the International

Monetary Fund.[34] Harold Macmillan, although a fierce proponent of the British action, understood better than most the precariousness of Britain's entire financial and economic system. In a remarkable about-face, he impressed upon the cabinet that the invasion he had believed so important must now halt.

Dulles wondered how the United States could continue consulting with allies after the British and French had "plunged the 'life line' of Europe into active hostility." So grim were allied relations in November that Dulles had reservations about holding the scheduled December NATO ministerial conference—the semiannual meeting of the foreign ministers of the NATO member states.[35] While seemingly minor, postponing a meeting would have been an act of deep significance in NATO, where symbols of unity reigned supreme. The German foreign minister, Heinrich von Brentano, summed up the mood in the alliance when he said "NATO is dead for the moment."[36]

Getting Over Suez

Soviet tanks helped revive NATO. In the first week of November, the Red Army rolled into Hungary to crush an uprising. While NATO's response to the Hungarian crisis amounted to little more than council discussions about what each country was doing to aid refugees, the Hungarian invasion provided a stark reminder of the strength and proximity of Soviet armor to the capitals of many NATO allies. No doubt because of events in Hungary, Dulles changed his mind and attended the ministerial. What had been a "violent family squabble" over Suez, Dulles told the National Security Council before departing for Paris, was "not one which was likely to end in divorce."[37]

Lester Pearson, the Canadian secretary of state for external affairs, expected that the ministerial in December would help smooth things over, both in discussions within the North Atlantic Council, but "particularly outside" the formal NAC meeting—that is, in the hallways, the cocktail parties, and the dinners.[38] Pearson was right. According to Belgian foreign minister Paul-Henri Spaak, his colleagues met in Paris "more NATO-minded than ever before."[39] In the formal sessions of the council, there was some condemnation of the Suez action, notably from the Scandinavian countries.[40] But Spaak defended the British, French, and colonial powers, which Dulles took as a good sign of rapprochement. Dulles wrote to Eisenhower that there were "no serious fireworks and there is every evidence ranks will be closed."[41]

In Paris, Dulles avoided any meeting with just his British and French colleagues. It was "increasingly difficult," he told Eisenhower, "to maintain the illusion that France was one of the great world powers."[42] Both he and Eisenhower were relieved that neither Pineau nor Lloyd had "asked for a tripartite meeting." He hoped—wrongly as the next years would show—that the problem "is perhaps disposed of for the time being."[43]

In council, Dulles took a conciliatory tone. Rather than look back on the frustrations of 1956, Dulles called on the allies to find, together, "a philosophy of faith, for living and acting, at [this] critical point in our history."[44] Joseph Bech, the prime minister of Luxembourg, lauded Dulles for the "highly successful" meeting and claimed that the "broken China [was] mended."[45]

While NATO's strained relations might have been mended, the same cannot be said for the United Nations—or at least the views of European states, especially Britain and France, toward that institution.[46] By December, the "general sentiment" that Dulles gained from "practically all of the delegations" at NATO was a feeling that the United Nations "was failing" and had fallen into the hands of "new countries." He sensed that the allies wished "to build up NATO as a rival to the United Nations."[47] Spaak told the council that the United Nations was now "bankrupt." Was there any point, he asked, for NATO powers to continue to attend the UN, "only to be in a minority, accorded scant consideration by a majority which included among its members many countries who were without political wisdom"? "Without going to extremes," said Spaak—though he sounded ready to do so—he "wondered under what conditions the United Nations Organization could henceforth fulfill its task."[48] French leaders already deeply disdained the United Nations, which they believed had worked against their interest in North Africa. In Britain, Richard "Rab" Butler, the British politician many Americans expected and hoped would succeed Eden, warned the American embassy that Britain might "withdraw from the UN."[49] Just before the NATO ministerial conference, when the British cabinet discussed their strategy, Lord Salisbury, the lord president of the council, warned Lloyd not to "alienate the U.S. over N.A.T.O.," since, he wishfully projected, they "may intend to build it up instead of [the] U.N."[50]

If the UN did survive, however, the British, French, and others, including the Belgians and Portuguese, wished for NATO to organize itself as a bloc at the United Nations, taking common positions and not—as had happened in the autumn—voting against each other.[51] A few of the alliance's members disagreed. Halvard Lange of Norway, for instance, worried that a common policy would propagate a "myth" that "the defence of colonialism is one of the main aims of NATO policies."[52] Dulles, too, disagreed with the general idea. It was difficult, he complained, "to find and to follow the narrow path between, on the one side, strengthening NATO, and, on the other, avoiding the appearance of 'teaming up' and taking positions in the UN as a bloc."[53] But calls from the European powers were more than just a desire to cooperate at the United

Nations. Many wanted to establish a coordinated, even common, policy toward the world outside of Western Europe.

The 1956 ministerial and subsequent developments reveal that many NATO allies wished for a much greater involvement of NATO outside the European area, not only after Suez, but because of Suez: NATO, it seemed, offered a better hope for coordinating efforts than the UN that had so damaged the British and French. These efforts to closely consult and coordinate policies, however, came not from the United States, but from European states—and not exclusively European colonial powers.[54]

The French had their own opinions about expanding NATO's geographic commitments. The conventional argument holds that the Suez crisis led, in a fairly direct line, to the French withdrawal from the NATO integrated military command a decade later, in 1966.[55] There are certainly connections between Suez and French disillusionment with NATO, discussed in the chapters that follow.[56] Pineau, however, showed no signs of distancing France from NATO at the ministerial. He wanted NATO to address issues of the Middle East and North Africa, and he told Dulles that NATO needed common policies applying to "all four corners [of the] world."[57] Pineau asked his colleagues in the council whether NATO "can be less than worldwide in the geographic limits of solidarity." In response to Dulles and Lange's worries about how NATO might appear to others, he called on them to "recognize the realities of a world which is not as moral as we might wish."[58]

It was remarkable how quickly the NATO allies were to put their differences behind them.[59] Part of the explanation lies in the juxtaposition of the Suez and Hungarian crises. A common enemy and common outrage often cauterized the alliance's wounds. But the extent to which members looked to NATO as a possible solution to their problems outside the European area offers another explanation for the rapid healing. In 1949, just after the treaty's inception, some had worried that NATO might overtake or even mark the end of the UN.[60] Since 1949, NATO had seemed to be a necessary buttress to the UN. By 1956, however, the new argument was that NATO should replace the UN as the fulcrum of Western and global security. Charles de Gaulle would take this idea to the extreme in 1958.

Anglo-American Rapprochement

The Anglo-American rift during Suez had pained Eisenhower, who wanted the crisis "washed off the slate as soon as possible."[61] He acted quickly and graciously to meet with Harold Macmillan, who had replaced the sick and humiliated

Anthony Eden as prime minister. Of all the soldiers and civilians he worked with in World War Two, Eisenhower thought Macmillan the "outstanding one of the British." Macmillan took up Eisenhower's suggestion to conference, and the two met in Bermuda, where the British side could play host.[62]

Macmillan and his officials took every opportunity to put the renewed friendship on display: they filled the main thoroughfares with Union Jacks and star-spangled banners, and there was much military pageantry and other "razzmatazz."[63] The conference itself was casual, and both parties, aware of the need to have and appear to have intimacy, played up their collegiality. Eisenhower and Macmillan acted like old school chums, visiting each other in their bedrooms, sometimes even in pajamas.[64]

The desire for cooperation between Macmillan and Eisenhower was authentic. Neither man thought he could achieve his goals without the other. But the displays of camaraderie, and somewhat subservient tones of Macmillan's presentation—describing Britain, for instance, as the "junior partner"—were carefully calculated.[65] And on policy issues, Britain and the United States were not always so close. They differed over the role of the United Nations, with the British still deeply resentful of the General Assembly's role in the Suez crisis. They also disagreed on the importance of Britain's commitment to keep troops in Europe assigned to NATO. Macmillan, eager to find savings by reducing the British Army of the Rhine, announced a large withdrawal just before the conference and despite last-minute appeals from Eisenhower. Nonetheless, the two struck an important agreement to allow the United States to base intermediate-range ballistic missiles (IRBMs) in Britain.[66]

Eisenhower and Macmillan both thought Bermuda a success and likened it to their intimate relations during the war.[67] All the while, Eisenhower believed that the post-Suez rapprochement with Macmillan was strengthening "the North Atlantic community of nations."[68] There was a growing belief in Washington, born at Bermuda, that "the US-UK relationship is at the core of NATO."[69] NATO might have been dead at the time of Suez, but it had been rejuvenated by Hungary and could be strengthened by Eisenhower and Macmillan's close partnership. For American officials, but especially Eisenhower, relations between London and Washington beat at NATO's heart.

The Anglo-American Axis

On October 4, 1957, the Soviet Union launched a small satellite into space. On its own, Sputnik was a technological marvel. Taken as an indication of Soviet expertise in rocketry, it signaled a capability to launch nuclear weapons that could target the United States. The NATO allies feared that the United States, no longer protected by vast oceans, might dramatically change its Cold War commitment to NATO. Sputnik, and the possible ramifications for the Western alliance, led to the next evolution in the post-Suez Anglo-American rapprochement, wherein Eisenhower and Macmillan would come to see NATO as a key element of their plans.[70]

Less than a week after Sputnik, Macmillan wrote to Eisenhower, asking: "What are we going to do about these Russians?" Had not the time come "when we could go further towards pooling our efforts and decide how best to use them for our common good?" Macmillan claimed his ideas were "very general and abstract." A reference to nuclear weapons, however, indicates what lay at the core of his thinking.[71] Macmillan believed that Britain's "future as a first-class power" would depend on its development of nuclear knowledge, and Sputnik opened the door for the British to press for renewed Anglo-American nuclear cooperation, previously shut by the British atomic spy cases and subsequent Atomic Energy Act in the US.[72]

Eisenhower agreed with Macmillan.[73] He had been bitterly disappointed that President Truman had ended Anglo-American joint staff planning after the Second World War, and remained "very strong for action" of the sort Macmillan had described.[74] Ike and Mac agreed to meet in Washington so that they might begin, in Macmillan's words, to "organize the free world as a whole in the struggle against communism."[75]

Macmillan's letters to Eisenhower stressed that Anglo-American coordination must come first, and then be extended to "those of our friends all over the world."[76] This purposefully mimicked one of Eisenhower's earlier suggestions that while the Anglo-American alliance should be at the core of the free world, "it should also spill out into N.A.T.O. and, quite possibly, into other allied countries of Asia."[77]

Privately, Macmillan and the Foreign Office prioritized Anglo-American coordination far higher than expanding or deepening NATO into anything much bigger than an organization responsible for the military defense of Western Europe. They wished to operate, as much as possible, in secret, to prevent encouraging the jealousies of allies left out.[78] After Suez, they believed that the defense of the West required a "less spectacular approach; and to begin by welding more closely together those countries which have the greatest practical contribution to make," that is, to link more closely Anglo-American policy, particularly by developing "machinery."[79]

The Americans, on the other hand, worried more about the state of America's alliances, like NATO, that Dulles thought were in a "precarious state." Even the British, keen to cut back on their troop commitments to NATO, seemed to "feel dissatisfied with our present alliance."[80] But in Macmillan's letter about the Anglo-American relationship, Dulles saw "an opportunity and a peg for constructive action."[81] Action and results became the key words in planning for another Anglo-American conference. Officials took note of a *Daily Mirror* article warning that "nothing could damage the Western cause more" than another meeting, and another communiqué, "full of flannel, cordiality, and meaningless diplomatic twaddle."[82] Where Bermuda had been seen as an important but largely intangible exercise, Washington must be different.

Dulles had no illusions about Macmillan's motives in coming to Washington. He told Eisenhower that while the Americans wanted to use the conference to "demonstrate our interest in all of our allies," the British sought only to stress the "special relationship." Eisenhower wanted to try and "turn this [British plan] around and work through our alliances to maintain the closest possible contact with the British." He and Dulles agreed that actions taken in Washington could then be "broaden[ed] to the whole alliance."[83]

Livingston T. Merchant, a talented State Department hand recalled from an ambassadorial position to plan for the conference, agreed that the American strategy of building a closer relationship with Britain was in the United States' best interest. But he warned of the dangers in focusing so heavily and publicly on the Anglo-American relationship. Merchant warned that any partnership with Britain to assert "world leadership" will "send shivers down the back of most our allies in NATO." What was worse, if this leadership is not exercised "adequately," the United States could "destroy the effectiveness of NATO." In Merchant's judgment, the primary British goal was not, like Washington's, to establish a broader coalition of powers, but rather "a supreme effort" to "regain their war-time position of exclusive and equal partnership with the U.S." This was not abstract reasoning. What the US and UK would be doing, warned Merchant, was in essence to set up a "NATO Political Standing Group" of just the US and UK. This would deeply upset the Germans, but it would "slay the French."[84]

Despite the prescient warnings from Merchant, Dulles and Eisenhower hoped they could turn the Washington-London axis inside out, from a closed bilateral relationship into the basis of a multilateral, NATO-wide, understanding.[85] This, Dulles believed, would be "a turning point in the organization of the free world." How this maneuver was to be achieved, however, was not carefully considered and, instead, expressed largely in platitudes: the briefing paper Dulles gave to the president before his meetings with Macmillan noted, vaguely, that if they were successful in tightening relations with the British, they "should develop this stronger sense of community with our other allies."[86]

Macmillan was a talented thespian, able to play different roles as required by situation and audience.[87] He did not disappoint in Washington, opening his meeting with the president with a dramatic peroration: "These days may well be decisive for the next few centuries. For several hundred years the Christian West had dominated the world. Now it faced the question of whether that kind of society would be submerged for several centuries by 'Communist Socialism' with Communist Parties working underground as super-governments. It may well happen that what takes place in the next two days can reverse the whole trend."[88]

Macmillan confided in his diary that he had painted "quite a romantic picture." His performance was "practically the last act of [*The Apple Cart*]," the Shavian play in which the Americans tear up the Declaration of Independence, renounce their own sovereignty, but then subsume Britain in a new Atlantic merger. His ultimate purpose in visiting Washington, he had told his cabinet, was to "exploit" any American inclination toward a "merger," all with the goal of reducing British expenditures, especially for the maintenance and development of the British atomic arsenal.[89]

The next day, when Dulles visited the British Embassy to lunch with Macmillan, he brought with him the American draft of a "Declaration of Common Purpose" that would serve as the communiqué for the Washington talks. Macmillan read the document, which indicated the Americans were committed to amending the McMahon Act that limited US nuclear cooperation with other states. Here it was, Macmillan wrote: "the great prize!"[90]

The declaration itself was an important document; it would come to be known also as the Declaration of Interdependence. Its emphasis on a shared sense of solidarity and resource-sharing between the two countries paid homage to all the sentiments Macmillan and Eisenhower had expressed in their replay of the Roosevelt-Churchill correspondence. But to Macmillan, focused so narrowly on the nuclear agreement, this other business was simply "a lot of verbiage."[91]

But the Americans signaled they wanted to continue talking about solidarity between allies. Macmillan, who had shown a penchant himself for this "verbiage" in his letters and speeches to Eisenhower, happily obliged. The record from the Washington talks, like Bermuda, shows that they revolved around big ideas, broad historical sweeps, and grandiose plans for change in the very shape of the system of states, including discussion of union and federation between Britain and the United States, though all pooh-poohed the likelihood of any such major change being presently practical.[92]

Macmillan's tactic of discussing union and then focusing on cooperation in the narrow areas he wanted appealed strongly to Eisenhower's thinking on the organization of the free world. On October 24 Eisenhower summarized for Macmillan what he thought the world needed: "closer union of the United States and the United Kingdom in order to serve better the cause of the free world and its several defense organizations," including NATO but also the Baghdad Pact and the Southeast Asia Treaty Organization.[93] They should do this, said Eisenhower, "almost to the point of operating together under one general policy."[94] He expected such closer union to result largely from vague psychological forces similar to those described by the diplomats who had decided to form the treaty in the first place. Anglo-American comity would, Eisenhower argued, give the "whole free world" a "shot in the arm" and provide "inspiration for the long journey ahead" by demonstrating the benefits of pooling resources.[95]

As it happened, NATO's new secretary-general, Paul-Henri Spaak, was visiting the United States during the Macmillan talks. As Sputnik orbited the globe, "Spaaknik," as the rotund Belgian was privately referred to by State Department officials, toured America.[96] American diplomats worried that the Eisenhower-Macmillan talks would overshadow Spaak's visit, signifying NATO's second-tier status.[97] But in the event, Spaak's visit offered Dulles and Eisenhower their first opportunity to try to transform Anglo-American talks into a plus for NATO. Spaak's meetings in Washington were scheduled to overlap with the Macmillan visit to Washington and give the public and Spaak a sense of connection with what Macmillan called his own "Honeymoon at Washington."[98] Eisenhower told Spaak that the Macmillan talks had not been meant to "forge an Anglo-American alliance, but to strengthen our alliances everywhere and particularly the North Atlantic Treaty Organization."[99]

Before the meetings with Spaak, Eisenhower suggested to Macmillan that at the next NATO ministerial conference in December, each allied state should send its leader as its national representative. Such a meeting of the NATO heads of government might "give a lift to NATO at an important juncture." It would give a "moral boost," he thought, but it would "almost compel constructive thinking and planning in terms of the kind of thinking we had spoken of" in Washington. Eisenhower could not very well invite himself to such a meeting, but if Macmillan could induce Spaak to make such an invitation, he would be "disposed to accede to the suggestion."[100] Spaak did not need any convincing. He issued the invitations.

By the end of the Washington talks, then, Macmillan had received his "great prize." The British and Americans had agreed to a number of practical, coordinated activities, and Spaak had agreed to host a heads of government meeting. But Eisenhower, too, had got what he wanted.

Eisenhower believed deeply in the value of the Anglo-American alliance, but also in NATO; for him, the two were not only nonexclusive, but amounted to the same thing. Eisenhower had said as much publicly when he toasted Queen Elizabeth earlier in October. "At the heart and foundation of all this [that is, NATO]," the president proclaimed, the "English-speaking peoples march forward together."[101] There is little wonder why Eisenhower understood NATO this way. He had played one of the most important roles in leading the predominantly Anglo-American effort to defeat Hitler on the Western front in the Second World War, and his tenure as SACEUR saw him oversee what had been originally a military force primarily composed of "English-speaking peoples." Now, as president, Eisenhower wished to rebuild "much more intimate collaboration between the British and ourselves in the military field." But he wanted this collaboration to occur within the larger context of NATO, within which the United States and the United Kingdom "would have primary responsibility in certain fields."[102]

At the Washington talks, and with the Anglo-American rapprochement generally, Eisenhower had fostered the type of intimate relationship necessary for effective allied relations, and he believed that his cooperation with Macmillan would serve as a model for NATO. He no doubt agreed with a letter Dulles wrote to Lloyd saying that Washington had "laid the ground for even greater things to come."[103] Eisenhower directed his government to prepare for the NATO meeting to be attended by all the heads of government.

Adapting the Anglo-American Model

The purpose of the NATO heads of government meeting, Dulles wrote, was to apply the general principles agreed to between Eisenhower and Macmillan "to a specifically NATO context."[104] Certainly, applying any of the specific agreements between Eisenhower and Macmillan to NATO would be nearly impossible. The president and the prime minister had worked to ensconce machinery and relationships that were necessarily highly secretive: information policy and psychological warfare, covert planning, intelligence sharing, and the exchange of nuclear information. There was little left for alliance-wide consumption. As a result, the focus of American planning for the heads of government meeting was the Declaration of Common Purpose and the call for greater unity among allies.[105]

To complement the traditional bureaucratic process, and to build bipartisan domestic support for Eisenhower's NATO effort, Dulles invited a leading Democrat, Adlai Stevenson, Eisenhower's opponent in both 1952 and 1956, to translate the American basic policy toward NATO—the Declaration of Common Purpose—into concrete actions.[106] Stevenson undertook a thorough study to determine how best to increase NATO's strength "by restoring mutual confidence and enlarging the sense of an interdependent community among its members." He noted that traditional security methods were not the only or the best means to "arrest neutralism" or "restore mutual confidence among the allies and reassure the larger world about Western intentions and capabilities." The "main threat," argued Stevenson, was not military aggression, but "subversion by propaganda, economic bribery and political penetration."[107] Stevenson developed, at length, policy prescriptions for meeting these threats.[108] When it was apparent to him that the administration was not interested in putting these nonmilitary policies into practice, he refused to attend the meeting in Paris.[109]

The simultaneous work done by the bureaucracy was less inspiring. The initial planning document for the NATO meeting stated that the Declaration of Common Purpose had set out to give NATO "a much greater sense of community and reciprocal trust."[110] After much hard work, drafting of position papers, and inter-agency coordination, a "scope paper"—the document that outlined the overall American position for the NATO meeting—stated that, like Anglo-American relations, NATO needed a "sense of strength, unity and confidence."[111] This sense of community played a curious and undefined role: it was American policy to develop a sense of community in NATO, but officials in Washington also argued that a sense of community could overcome policy disagreements between allies. In fact, by the final round of documents circulated in the Department of State, the Americans almost managed to talk themselves out of the need to foster unity, claiming "close analysis indicates that most of the complaints heard about 'lack of unity' within NATO are exaggerated."[112]

But fears about the cohesion of the alliance were not exaggerated; they were felt deeply in Europe, especially Bonn. Chancellor Adenauer told John McCloy that if the treaty members did not find new inspiration, "this would be the end of NATO."[113] Adenauer harbored doubts about American resolve to defend Europe, especially given the Soviet launch of Sputnik, and even entertained a secret French invitation to join with the Italians to develop a nuclear capability.[114]

Adenauer had hardly given up on NATO, however; he wrote Dulles to recommend the alliance offer a "gesture" of "reaffirmation" at its next meeting. He did not want speeches alone but real changes to the alliance. He wanted the North Atlantic Council to have more power and greater propinquity in national cabinets.[115] On the military side, there should be greater standardization of weapons, coordination of logistics, and a deeper integration of military force. "The whole thing," Adenauer said, "should be organized as [the] EDC was planned [with] air and ground combined and integrated force."[116]

Dulles complained about the pressure from the Germans, but settled on two concrete gestures of reaffirmation: an offer to provide European allies with IRBMs and a plan to equip European NATO forces with nuclear warheads.[117] As the heads of government meeting approached, the supreme allied commander, Lauris Norstad, had urged the United States to take up plans for a "nuclear stockpile" whereby it would maintain nuclear weapons in Europe that would, on the president's say so, be released to NATO commanders for use in war. General

Norstad wrote to Eisenhower, a former SACEUR, to encourage him to introduce a NATO atomic stockpile to emphasize "the qualities of solidarity and mutual trust on which the NATO Alliance is based."[118] Dulles especially favored the idea of a NATO stockpile, arguing that "now is the time, otherwise alliances will fall apart."[119]

But as the meeting neared, planning focused not on a particular policy but a single person: the president of the United States. The National Security Council expected that Ike's very presence would "in itself provide a rejuvenation of NATO."[120] Eisenhower discarded initial drafts of his speech, calling for more "hard-hitting paragraphs" and "punchy statements," in an effort to present an image of American "solidarity, cooperation, and vitality."[121] More so than any policy or organization, Eisenhower and all he represented—not only as president of the United States but as the supreme commander of Western forces in both the Second World War and the early Cold War—embodied the spirit of NATO he thought would keep the alliance together.

Eisenhower almost did not make it to the meeting, however; near the end of November, he suffered a stroke. But the president was determined to attend. He flew to Paris with strict instructions from his doctors to keep his hat on during the ceremonies upon his arrival at Orly airport.[122] After the arrival ceremonies, the president was driven through Paris to the cheers of large, adoring crowds. His aide, Andrew Goodpaster, thought the welcome given by the people along the route "was the most enthusiastic and emotional I have ever seen on the part of the French, or think I ever will see. [The i]mpact was terrific."[123]

Because of his lack of strength and problems speaking resulting from the stroke, Eisenhower's speech did not go off as planned. He handed the second half to Dulles to finish.[124] Still, Eisenhower maintained his role as the centerpiece of the conference. At the large formal dinner, he answered the toast by French president Félix Gaillard. On the last day of the conference, Eisenhower even took part in drafting the conference communiqué.[125]

Eisenhower's presence was a boon for NATO, and he and Macmillan agreed afterward that the meeting "was a definite plus for the free world."[126] Marc Trachtenberg has made the case that the atomic stockpile plan was "perhaps the most important policy initiative undertaken by the Eisenhower administration."[127] It fundamentally transformed the capability of NATO forces and undoubtedly helped to build the trust of European leaders in the American commitment to Europe. At the same time, the plan sowed the seeds of a major dispute in NATO with the French. And it was an entirely different approach to transforming NATO in comparison with Stevenson's aborted ideas for nonmilitary solutions.

The allies did reach a secret agreement to instruct Spaak to draft letters to the secretaries-general of the Baghdad Pact, the Organization of American States, and the Southeast Asian Treaty Organization. The letters proposed "simple and discreet arrangements, and suggest[ed] exchanges of information on economic, social, cultural and information problems, with emphasis on free world security."[128] The OAS declined the invitation, but SEATO and the Baghdad Pact accepted. A limited relationship developed between NATO and the Baghdad Pact, including the exchange of study papers and plans for a future coordination of "defence plans" between the organizations.[129]

The main and public focus of the meeting, however, had been Eisenhower and the stockpile plan. Contemporary observers, like one of Eisenhower's special assistants, C. D. Jackson, decried that the Americans had proceeded to the NATO meeting with "what must have been inaccurate or superficial diplomatic intelligence that the one single thing our allies wanted was locally based missiles with atomic warheads."[130]

Already, on December 14, Macmillan was starting to worry that the nuclear promises were not enough to make the meeting a true success, especially after the heightened expectations and press attention given the conference. He faulted Dulles for thinking that the ministerial "could be just a sort of 'jamboree,'" whereby the allies would accept the IRBMs, "give 3 cheers for ourselves and 1 for Uncle Sam and then go home." Macmillan, who had done so much to encourage this line of thinking about unity and interdependence, but offered little concrete vision of his own, found Dulles's vision "foolish ... but Foster has no other ideas at present."[131]

The French Problem

Macmillan himself ultimately decided the heads of government meeting had been enough to satiate the allies; he told his cabinet that "fear of Anglo-US hegemony was dispelled, primarily through private talks."[132] There was a nagging fear in some quarters of the British and American governments that the other allies felt left behind. When the British ambassador to France, Gladwyn Jebb, read the records of the Washington talks early in 1958, after the NATO meeting, he was dumbfounded. Writing after the heads of government meeting, he observed that the Eisenhower-Macmillan talks had focused exclusively on what Macmillan called NATO's "inner core of Anglo-American partnership." In classic British understatement, Jebb said he was "a little surprised" that the outer core of the alliance and changes in Europe were not acknowledged: in March 1957, after all, six European states had taken the monumental step of creating the European Economic Community with the Treaty of Rome. In the Anglo-American talks, there was an "entire absence of any reference" to the European idea, and there seemed no consideration whatsoever of the effects Washington and London's policy might have on the continent. What seemed certain from the records to which Jebb had access was that, informal or otherwise, "an Anglo-American Directorate of some kind has now been created." Jebb knew the enormous benefits of cooperation with the United States, but warned that such a directorate was a "well-known bogey of the French, and indeed, I think of most 'Europeans.'" The NATO heads of government meeting showed, with its lack of concrete results, that an Anglo-American directorate, "flattering though it may be to our self-esteem, will be an insecure basis for our foreign policy" unless it lay within "a rather larger framework."[133]

Jebb's worries were heightened by what he saw in Paris. For the first half of 1958, France seethed as victory in Algeria slipped further and further away. In June 1958, Charles de Gaulle was named prime minister. De Gaulle's ascension was welcomed by London and Washington, if only because it promised some stability after the seemingly never-ending succession of short-lived governments of the Fourth Republic.[134] But many wondered what de Gaulle's return to power would mean for NATO, for he had been an opponent of the alliance in its earliest days.

French diplomats and politicians immediately sought to quell any rumor that de Gaulle's rise to power threatened NATO, but they conceded that de Gaulle did not like some aspects of the organization or the alliance.[135] In June 1958—the month de Gaulle became prime minister (he would become president of France, inaugurating France's Fifth Republic, in 1959)—Eisenhower and Macmillan met again for a series of bilateral talks. Eisenhower, Macmillan, and Dulles all expected de Gaulle would press for a "tripartite relationship" between France, Britain, and the United States. This was no lucky guess; de Gaulle had pushed the idea in 1949, and governments throughout France's Fourth Republic had sought to deepen and formalize the three-state connection.

Eisenhower and Macmillan, however, agreed to deal with France bilaterally or through NATO—they would meet with France trilaterally on only certain subjects, such as Germany. They also agreed that the odd man out of any Anglo-French or Franco-American bilateral talks would be kept "fully informed" of the proceedings.[136]

This approach worried American diplomats, who thought the leaders should take proactive efforts toward de Gaulle, perhaps deferring to his view on NATO military and political policies. It might, they suggested, be time to share atomic energy with France, and resume "Big Three" meetings—that practice whereby American, British, and French leaders had met to discuss world affairs.[137] But

Eisenhower and Dulles, relieved to have been finished with "Big Three" talks in 1956, and Macmillan, still striving to build on the close working relationship with Washington, had no interest in diluting the Anglo-American bond.

De Gaulle was determined to share his views on NATO nonetheless. In June, he complained, separately, to both Macmillan and Dulles, about the alliance, and outlined—if vaguely—his solutions. De Gaulle told Macmillan frankly that he "attached great importance to a reorganization of NATO." The need for reorganization was, first and foremost, related to France's participation in any decision to use atomic weapons. After becoming prime minister, de Gaulle learned that NATO itself did not have any "overall strategic plan known to and approved by the Alliance" for the use of the American or British nuclear arsenal.[138] In one sense, this was true—initiating atomic war was not a NATO, or even North Atlantic Council responsibility, per se. Washington and London had always considered the decision their own. As a briefing note for Macmillan put it, "We hope that our Allies will trust us to use them [nuclear weapons] responsibly."[139] De Gaulle's trust was not so easily extended, however. He would not accept a situation whereby "only the Americans and the British could in fact loose atomic war whenever they wanted."[140]

De Gaulle's next concern was that NATO was "too narrow geographically." He explained that NATO should cover "at least North Africa," perhaps down to the Sahara and even Central Africa. It seemed necessary, from "a strategy point of view" to extend it even further, over the "whole of the Middle East, the Red Sea area, the Arctic and the Indian Ocean."[141] De Gaulle's advisers had apparently convinced him that the North Atlantic Treaty itself would be too difficult to change, for such a change would require unanimous agreement from the allies. Instead, he wanted to "link Morocco, Tunisia, and Algeria in some way to N.A.T.O. without new formal arrangements."[142] He promised to send formal proposals soon.[143]

The British were confused by de Gaulle's plans. Nonetheless, the British had recently reconsidered the benefits of NATO taking greater interest in regions outside the treaty area. Selwyn Lloyd—who passed on de Gaulle's ideas to Spaak—thought it was good that de Gaulle recognized "NATO was affected by what happened outside its present limits."[144]

When Dulles arrived in Paris, de Gaulle told him much the same thing: "NATO is not satisfactory." Even the recent efforts of the United States to revitalize NATO, including the atomic stockpile plan that would equip French forces with nuclear weapons, held "little interest" for de Gaulle. The Frenchman figured that the "disadvantages of having nuclear weapons on French soil," that is, making France a target for Soviet weapons in case of a war, "were not equalized" by their presence, since France would not have complete control over the weapons.[145] After

Suez, the Americans had been seeking to inspire NATO with a sense of unity of membership, and offered ideas for sharing nuclear weapons as a major step in this direction. De Gaulle's preference for closer ties between the three powers and his dislike of the nuclear sharing plan left virtually no common ground on policy between Paris and Washington. And de Gaulle warned Dulles that if there was going to be an Anglo-American intervention in the Middle East, "France wants some participation."[146]

Like the British, the Americans were puzzled by de Gaulle's reference to expanding NATO and inquired about it. Louis Joxe, the permanent secretary-general at the Quai d'Orsay, could say only that "it was difficult to explain de Gaulle's concept in detail and how it could be put into effect."[147] The Americans generally assumed de Gaulle wanted to expand the membership of NATO, perhaps to include at least Tunisia and Morocco, and perhaps even more countries.[148] Dulles, musing about de Gaulle's ideas with his staff, thought that it would be "increasingly difficult" to keep NATO together if it were to include "nations having different political and cultural backgrounds and institutions."[149] De Gaulle had come too late to a problem Dulles had grappled with at Suez.

French officials were not optimistic after de Gaulle's meeting with Macmillan and Dulles. The talks had been superficially pleasant, but this friendliness hid their "negative side." It was obvious that French relations within the alliance were to be limited to either bilateral meetings or meetings of the entire NATO membership—and not privy to the meetings of the newly formed, if informal, Anglo-American directorate.[150] De Gaulle found these limits unacceptable, but they were real and emphasized by events in the Middle East and Asia in the summer of 1958. In July, the Americans landed in Lebanon, and the British deployed troops to Jordan; in neither case was France invited to participate, despite de Gaulle's explicit wish for an invitation to do so. When, later in the summer, the United States edged closer to the brink of war as the People's Republic of China shelled Quemoy and Matsu, de Gaulle became convinced that war on the far side of the world could erupt into a global conflagration. As things stood in the summer of 1958, he had no means of influencing or restricting the use of American nuclear weapons. For de Gaulle, more critical than the crisis in Asia was the festering French wound in Algeria—without a doubt the largest policy concern for French governments in the late 1950s—which continued to worsen without any sign that the allies would aid France.[151]

Ultimately, Eisenhower's willingness to cooperate with Macmillan—predicated, always, on the hope of reinvigorating the alliance—saved NATO from fading into despondency and disagreement in the 1950s. The Anglo-American relationship would remain the most important axis in the relationship for a decade, until the Federal Republic of Germany gained enough power and clout to rival Britain as American's first lieutenant. The Anglo-American model, however, was not ideally suited as an inspiration for an alliance already in place, for it required the other allies to wait for years to build up similar relationships with Washington. Waiting for a common-law relationship to bloom into something more formal was not acceptable to de Gaulle. He wanted a very public wedding.

3

TIED TOGETHER BY HISTORY

In September 1958, the French prime minister Charles de Gaulle wrote out personal letters, in longhand, to Dwight Eisenhower and Harold Macmillan. To
both letters he would attach a memorandum outlining a radical new structure
for NATO. Prompted by the crises of the summer of 1958 in the Middle East
and Asia, de Gaulle had concluded that the Atlantic Alliance, not yet a decade
old, "no longer corresponds to political and strategic realities." NATO should be
revised, he argued, and a new "organization" of the United States, Great Britain,
and France should be established to take "joint decisions" on political questions
of world security and put into effect "strategic plans" regarding nuclear weapons.
These three countries would form a "Permanent Group" and meet in Washington. From there they would divvy up the world into "theaters of operation" covering the Arctic, Atlantic, Pacific, and Indian Oceans.[1]

De Gaulle's memorandum is often recalled as a spectacular outgrowth of the
megalomania that drove *Le Grand Charles*. The wildly ambitious and utterly
impracticable idea of establishing, by fiat, a tripartite directory atop a global NATO
was met—or so the story goes—with a "clear but polite no" from Eisenhower and
Macmillan. Indeed, de Gaulle himself would later claim that he had received no
response to his memorandum, and use the lack of response as a lever to ultimately
pry France from NATO's integrated military command in 1966.

But this barely scratches the surface of the "memorandum diplomacy" that
consumed NATO from 1958 and into 1961. For de Gaulle's memorandum was
neither a bolt from the blue nor a bolt from reality. The rhetoric of Macmillan,

Eisenhower, and Dulles had publicly and purposefully elevated NATO as the primary instrument of Western security, and there had been much talk—if little action—of expanding NATO to address global problems. There is little wonder why de Gaulle foregrounded NATO so prominently in his letter. It would only become clear to the other NATO allies in the years following de Gaulle's memorandum that de Gaulle wanted not necessarily to update NATO—an institution he knew little about and wished to know even less—but to minimize its importance.[2] As the French permanent representative, Geoffroy Chodron de Courcel, explained to his British counterpart, Frank Roberts, de Gaulle had "mixed up two quite separate things, western security as a global problem and the efficient functioning of NATO—the most important but not the only element in western security."[3]

De Gaulle's memorandum was an attempt to create an entirely new structure for global security and to abandon or let wither NATO's integrated military command structure and the North Atlantic Council with its premise that all the allies, regardless of size or power, were equal and sovereign states.

His contemporaries mocked de Gaulle's approach to international affairs, arguing over which previous century better suited his style and ideas. While Harold Macmillan thought de Gaulle "fundamentally an Eighteenth Century figure," Eisenhower disagreed, believing de Gaulle belonged to the "Early Nineteenth."[4] His handwritten letters would earn him the scorn of American diplomats who "could basically imagine him writing with a quill pen."[5] Much of the frustration with de Gaulle was, undoubtedly, due to his inflexible insistence on his own policies, and inability to compromise with the other allies. But the allies' frustration was due, in no small part, to the basic point that the concerns of de Gaulle raised. The expanding Cold War and allied control (or lack thereof) over the use of nuclear weapons were real difficulties for the alliance, and would remain problems for decades. In addition, de Gaulle foresaw serious problems for foreign policy makers that would come from societal change, including growing individualism and declining attachment to national concepts. Long before the crises of malaise in the 1970s, de Gaulle believed, in the late 1950s, that the Atlantic spirit would not motivate the people of France; they needed to be motivated by love of country or they would drift aimlessly.

Just as remarkable as the issues raised by de Gaulle's memorandum, however, was the willingness of his correspondents, Eisenhower and Macmillan, to meet him on many of his points. They were indeed willing to consider radically renovating the Atlantic security architecture. Macmillan, in particular, saw the possibility for a major trade between London and Paris, granting French security wishes in exchange for British economic gains. Such a plan would have gone a long way to resolving the estrangement between London and the European

FIGURE 5. French paratroopers participate in a NATO training exercise at Pau, France, in the mid-1950s. National Archives photo no. 286-MP-fra-06397.

Economic Community that was a nagging thorn in the steady development of European unity. But the solution to this economic problem would have raised an even more worrying concern, for a tripartite directory would have severely damaged that other great postwar goal: mooring Germany to the West.

The Origins of de Gaulle's Memorandum

De Gaulle's memorandum tugged on three loose strands in NATO. Underlying de Gaulle's inherent dislike of NATO was his dislike for military integration, though his worries were largely misunderstood by the allies. In 1948, he had lashed out against the new Western European Union defense organization. It was "fundamentally unacceptable," he said, for the defense of France to be the responsibility of anyone but Frenchmen.[6] By the early 1950s, de Gaulle had opposed plans for an army of European unity—a European Defense Community—that would have seen small units of French, German, and other European soldiers assembled together into larger military formations. He did not think that soldiers fought well for international commanders; French troops would fight to their utmost only if their blood, sweat, and tears were shed in the defense of France. Still, NATO's integrated military command was almost nothing like the plans for the EDC. NATO forces were composed, almost exclusively, of large national units—armies, fleets, air forces—whose top officers would, in wartime, take orders from NATO's supreme command. De Gaulle, however, had made up his mind about integration in the 1950s and believed that NATO operated on the same principles; he worried that NATO was, or would become— as Churchill referred to the EDC plans—a "sludgy amalgam" with no national drive or patriotism to motivate the troops.[7]

De Gaulle disliked the idea of military integration for more profound reasons than the motivation of fighting men. He worried that France needed strong traditions and institutions to keeps its citizens French—that is, to maintain the idea of France as a nation. The tide of communism—both as an indigenous political movement and as a result of Soviet subversion—threatened to challenge this very particular idea of France. De Gaulle believed that there were two institutions in France that could "stand up and defeat Communism— the Church and the Army." The church, he thought, could not be relied upon, perhaps because it was experiencing its own challenges. His foreign minister, Couve de Murville, explained to Home that de Gaulle "feels he must keep the French Army as an integral unit which could be used against the Communists." Surely it was prudent for the leader of a country in which the Communist Party consistently polled about 20 percent to think about the future of his nation.[8] Increasingly, his concerns about integration would get tied up with France's struggle in Algeria.

De Gaulle's worries about the affiliation and attachment of Frenchmen to their nation had corollaries in the worries of American, British, and German officials who, in the 1970s, feared that their citizens were no longer identifying with their state, let alone a grander Atlantic community. But in the late 1950s, these issues were largely in the background. Men like Eisenhower—with his experience as a supreme commander—believed deeply in the need for integrated military commands. Such commands offered a symbol of Atlantic unity. They also represented the only means to effectively defend against modern war, especially in the realm of air defense. De Gaulle's complaints about integration looked to everyone else like a man fighting the tide of time.

Somewhat paradoxically, however, given his dislike of integration, de Gaulle did wish for greater cooperation among leaders on plans and decisions regarding nuclear weapons. Again, to the allies, de Gaulle's wish to participate in "strategic"—that is, nuclear—decision making looked like an effort to increase French glory. Only by the late 1950s was it clear that de Gaulle's nuclear concerns were more nuanced.

For the most part, however, the negotiations surrounding de Gaulle's memorandum had to do with the Cold War outside of Europe. De Gaulle's concerns—while put in his own distinct terms—were not unique. They echoed a swell of sentiment in the alliance that NATO must prepare to battle the Soviets around the world.

In 1958, Field Marshal Bernard Montgomery retired as deputy SACEUR, but not before he had formed—and expounded with his trademark self-righteousness—definitive ideas about the need to reform and expand NATO's military commands. And before Montgomery left his post at SHAPE, he shared with de Gaulle a paper delineating these ideas.[9]

Montgomery had summed up his thoughts on NATO with a quote from Hamlet, declaring grandly to assembled military and political leaders that "the times are out of joint." The NATO allies, he believed, were fixated on "our parish pumps" to the exclusion of other areas—the ones outside Europe, where the security of the West was truly imperiled. NATO needed a policy toward the Middle East, and that "policy must be capable of world-wide application."[10] While French officials found Montgomery's opinions to be "somewhat outrageous," not so de Gaulle.[11] They fit perfectly with his belief that NATO's geography and responsibilities needed to be expanded. Indeed, for those diplomats at NATO who were privy to both Montgomery's thinking and de Gaulle's memorandum, the ideas were indistinguishable. When Frank Roberts, the British permanent representative to NATO, first read de Gaulle's memorandum, he thought he was reading a French translation of an earlier Montgomery speech. The de Gaulle memo, he said, was "pure Monty." It was not a compliment.[12]

The global crises of the 1950s had led many of the allies to search out new purpose and meaning for NATO. After Suez, in the face of both NATO's limitations and what he perceived as the deterioration of the UN, Dulles had begun musing in private about some new means of organizing the "free world," including the dramatic expansion of America's alliances to cover more of the world.[13] Paul-Henri Spaak, NATO's secretary-general, found himself, like Dulles, "rather close to agreeing with the analysis" in de Gaulle's memorandum, for the "Communist threat today is above all Asiatic and African."[14] Macmillan, too, thought de Gaulle had "put his finger on the problem" of NATO's need "to coordinate resistance on [a] world-wide scale" if NATO was not to become a new "Maginot Line."[15]

The German Danger

Dulles, Macmillan, and Spaak all saw parts of de Gaulle's memorandum that were appealing. But Eisenhower thought it was a bad idea from the start. Tripartitism was a threat to the allied unity he sought to foster. NATO's "real strength," as Eisenhower always claimed, lay not in particular policy but instead "rests in our union." Eisenhower would have much preferred if the letter had not been sent, and was not interested in engaging in a discussion of its merits; "the less said about this proposal the better."[16] Looming behind the matter of the memorandum was Germany's future in NATO.

De Gaulle had, deviously, given Spaak a copy of his memorandum, correctly assuming the loquacious secretary-general would promptly share it with the Italians and Germans.[17] Perhaps unaware that de Gaulle would make such a move, French officials had given the Italian and German ambassadors in Paris a watered-down oral account of the memorandum. They were shocked when they learned that de Gaulle had told Spaak, bluntly, that "only major world powers can define a global policy" and that Western policy should and could be determined only by the "three great Western powers."[18] The Italians were "nearly hysterical" and worried that Italian exclusion from a tripartite directorate would upset the delicate political balance in Italy.[19] The problem was even more acute with the Germans. In October, after de Gaulle had written the memorandum but before it was leaked, Konrad Adenauer had met with de Gaulle at Colombey-les-Deux-Églises. The meeting between the two old grand men was deeply symbolic, but the conversation was muddled. De Gaulle did not mention the memorandum per se, but alluded to its ideas. Adenauer likely did not realize that de Gaulle meant to act so firmly on his oft-stated hopes for changing NATO. Ultimately, after learning of the memorandum, *Der Alte* told Macmillan he felt "tricked and deceived."[20]

The American ambassador in Bonn, David Bruce, warned that the Germans were mindful of any signs of discrimination and were already prone to "suspect secret consultation behind their backs." German officials always stressed that there were only two superpowers: the United States and the USSR, and that all other powers operated on a lower tier. By this rationale, the Germans could reconcile their obligation not to build nuclear weapons not as a mark of national discrimination but simply their lot as a non-superpower. But any formal acceptance of something like de Gaulle's directorate would push Germany down to a third tier of state power, below the superpowers and below the level of Britain and France. Of course, any such rankings mattered not in the abstract. What mattered to Germans like Adenauer was whether the German people would be willing to remain in NATO if all they received was shabby treatment as a third-rate member. Bruce warned that if the United States showed any signal of accepting the ideas in de Gaulle's memorandum, there would be "grievous damage" done to German relations with the allies.[21]

Eisenhower tried to render de Gaulle's radioactive letter inert. He wrote a prompt but flavorless reply, implicitly rebuffing formalized tripartitism and hoping that NATO could develop to meet de Gaulle's other wishes. Dulles, too, wrote to Couve, hoping de Gaulle's foreign minister might write a new, clarifying letter that had a chance of acceptance by Eisenhower and Macmillan. But de Gaulle was frustrated by Eisenhower's "bleak and negative" response and thought Dulles's letter "just a blind." The French ambassador, Hervé Alphand, sensed that the lukewarm responses from Washington foreshadowed a showdown with Paris, and warned it was "a sad day for NATO."[22]

Eisenhower surely wished that de Gaulle had not written the memorandum. But by passing the memorandum to Spaak, de Gaulle ensured that it became common knowledge at the top level of all NATO states, and then public knowledge through leaks by offended governments.[23] London and Washington could not turn down de Gaulle flat without causing grave offense. And such offense could have serious repercussions.

Both the Americans and British thought the stakes raised by de Gaulle's memorandum were extremely high. De Gaulle was openly calling into question the postwar Atlantic security architecture, and officials worried he might, if rebuffed, threaten the emerging European economic institutions that had been built up in the postwar world. Britain, while not a member of the European Economic Community, still hoped for de Gaulle's cooperation in building up an alternative "European Free Trade Area." The British were growing acutely concerned by the squeeze that might be put on the British economy by a united and protective European market. Selwyn Lloyd emphasized to Dulles the need to "keep de Gaulle friendly." Macmillan, too, cautioned extreme care; both feared arousing "French hostility" during negotiations for a free trade area.[24]

Macmillan, concerned with Britain's economic prospects, was desperate "not to offend the General."[25] He urged the Americans to deal with de Gaulle's request quickly, insisting that "private tripartite discussions" must "take place pretty soon."[26] Dulles understood immediately that Macmillan might be looking for a grand bargain with de Gaulle. He gave the British a sharp warning that any trade of tripartite talks for de Gaulle's support of the free trade area would end the intimacy of the Anglo-American relationship. Nonetheless, Dulles thought it important to placate de Gaulle, too, and agreed talks should begin soon.[27]

For a number of reasons, then—because of the publicity de Gaulle gave his own personal correspondence, because there was some merit in de Gaulle's diagnosis if not cure, because the British and Americans did not want a jilted de Gaulle to attack the European construction, and partly because they hoped to convince de Gaulle that his ideas were dangerous to both NATO's cohesion in Europe and the West's reputation in the developing world—Dulles met with Alphand for a series of talks, starting initially with talks about talks.[28]

Tripartite Meetings on World Issues

In the last months of 1958 various constellations of French and British, French and American, and French, British, and American officials met to determine what, precisely, it was de Gaulle wanted, and whether these goals could or should be met. The main French idea, Alphand told Dulles, was "strategic military planning on [a] tripartite basis covering such areas as Africa and [the] Middle East as well as political planning." Other NATO allies, he said, "would not be directly involved." As French officials sought to put de Gaulle's grand vision into concrete terms, both the French diplomats and their Anglo-American interlocutors became more and more confused as to whether de Gaulle wanted to change NATO, ignore it, or do away with it entirely.[29] De Gaulle, when he learned that tripartite conversations had begun but were not seized with the substance of his memorandum, noted that things were "not exactly taking the course he originally foresaw," but agreed discussions should proceed. "We will see what develops," he said.[30]

A first round of preliminary tripartite talks began in December. Alphand, obviously uncomfortable and doubting that there was any likelihood NATO could be adjusted as de Gaulle wished, declared nonetheless that the "conditions of global strategy had changed" and that the West's security apparatus had to change with it.[31] He warned that if France did not get the tripartite consultation de Gaulle had requested, "then France has no interests in NATO in its present form" and had the right to "denounce" NATO or seek a revision of the treaty.[32] The first meeting broke up without satisfaction to any side; Robert Murphy, the American deputy undersecretary of state for political affairs, warned the French ambassador that de Gaulle's effort to perfect NATO was making an enemy of the good; the allies, by tinkering with NATO, "could run the risk of destroying or paralyzing what currently exists."[33]

The British and American diplomats pressed Alphand to get clearer instructions as to what de Gaulle sought. Alphand, just as much as the British and Americans, knew that the scope of cooperation de Gaulle was proposing could not simply be declared. The British and American rapprochement had been built slow and carefully, with stops and starts, over decades.[34] Nonetheless, Alphand returned to the next meeting with no answers but more questions sent by de Gaulle: "Is it possible or not on the military level for the three to act strategically in common in case of military conflict anywhere in the world?" Murphy was incredulous—did de Gaulle really want the three states to develop a military staff and formal policy-making machinery to coordinate the global policy of all three states? Alphand conceded that, "if he understood his instructions correctly," this was what de Gaulle wanted.[35] Furthermore, de Gaulle wanted NATO to extend into Africa "at least to the portion of the continent from the Sahara North."

This all worried Eisenhower deeply. To the Americans, it seemed de Gaulle wanted a "complete re-assessment of the entire NATO defense concept" and to "broaden NATO" to include any region where Western interests were at stake. "This," said the president, "was just a little crazy." In Eisenhower's view, NATO had "a specific mission"—deterrence of Soviet military and political pressure in Europe—and the member states needed to "just buckle down and carry it out."[36]

Dulles flew to Paris to see if a personal representation could calm de Gaulle. He promised the general he would return to Washington prepared to undertake a "more substantive exchange of information" and to "discuss thoroughly" the American position on global issues with the French.[37] De Gaulle was not going to settle for any less. He continued to insist to the British that there must be tripartite talks, the North American Treaty must be amended to cover Africa north of the Sahara, NATO's military commands needed to be reorganized, and some method should be found in the "sharing of atomic arms." When Selwyn Lloyd pressed de Gaulle, asking whether he wanted a tripartite organization or institution, de Gaulle replied testily: "if what he said involved institutions then that was what he meant." He wanted ambassadors from the three countries in Washington to "consider political plans for Germany, Iran, [the] Middle East, [the] Pacific, North Africa and Black Africa." It would be, said de Gaulle, an *organisation mondiale*, but if the British did not like the word "organization," it could be a "World Something."[38]

De Gaulle finished by noting that he was "increasingly embarrassed" by American policy. A recent abstention by the United States at a United Nations vote on Algeria "completely proved his point about the need for tripartite agreement on Western strategy." Disagreements over Guinea, too, had been "really tiresome" and made it clear that the "Atlantic Alliance was more and more inadequate." The whole situation, said de Gaulle, "was quite deplorable."[39]

It was under these inauspicious circumstances that Dulles agreed to go ahead with tripartite talks devoted to specific regional areas.[40] These meetings were frustrating for all. The British and Americans were stunned when, at the first meeting, ostensibly to discuss political prospects in the Far East, the French fired off question after question about British and American nuclear plans against China.[41] De Gaulle continued to urge that tripartite meetings be used to discuss "blueprints of global defense."[42] And while the Americans sent military officers to attend some talks, both Dulles and the Pentagon dissembled as to whether the US would participate in plans for global military strategy.[43]

In early 1959, Alphand was recalled to Paris for instructions. He returned with another major announcement from de Gaulle: the French fleet in the Mediterranean would be removed from NATO command.[44] It looked to all involved that de Gaulle's move was a blatant effort to "blackmail" the Americans for tripartite talks.[45] De Gaulle was furious with the allies over their lack of support for France in Algeria. But the withdrawal served domestic political goals, too, for it reassured "integrationists" in his constituency—those who favored Algeria remaining French—that de Gaulle would not "abandon" Algeria.[46]

Norstad thought the French withdrawal was a very serious problem "psychologically and politically," if not militarily.[47] And it was the psychological and political that Americans always believed most important. Undersecretary of State Christian Herter worried the French policy would "give the impression that the alliance was breaking up," and "might even cause the disintegration of the alliance."[48]

Disintegration was no an abstract fear. In 1958, Soviet premier Nikita Khrushchev issued an ultimatum: Britain, France, and the United States must withdraw their garrisons from Berlin within six months.[49] To face down Khrushchev, the allies had to demonstrate they would—and could—stand united. Pro-NATO French officials, who thought the fleet withdrawal a slippery slope, sought to slow down any official notice to the North Atlantic Council that France had withdrawn its fleet.[50] But when de Gaulle learned that official notice had not been given to NATO, he was angry, and the formal letter was rushed to NATO.[51]

American and British diplomats and officials were incensed with de Gaulle in the spring of 1959. They urged their leaders to "have it out" with him and end the tripartite meetings.[52] Herter warned Alphand that formalizing the fleet's withdrawal from NATO would end the tripartite talks and "remove legislative justification for cooperation in [the] nuclear field," that is, the nuclear reactor for a submarine the French had requested and Dulles had promised in 1958.[53] But

Alphand told Herter his threats had been "badly received" in Paris and hinted at the possibility of an escalation of diplomatic tit-for-tat.[54]

The State Department began "stalling actions" on the tripartite meetings, but de Gaulle insisted they continue. Alphand warned that if talks on Africa did not go forward, and if the Americans made a link between the tripartites and the fleet issue, "the General would be furious and there would be a chain reaction."[55] The Americans were not willing to call this bluff. Leaks from Paris suggested de Gaulle was planning a press conference to explain NATO's "shortcomings." This would further erode the appearance of allied unity. It would also be an unpleasant celebration of NATO's tenth anniversary.[56]

In March, Macmillan and Lloyd were back for another series of Washington talks. They concluded that de Gaulle was "capable, any day, of asking Norstad to vacate SHAPE." This would throw the military component of NATO into disarray, and destroy the part of NATO Eisenhower believed most important.[57] The British argued that while de Gaulle was "mad" and should "be handled as a psychopath," it would be counterproductive to get tough with him, and Eisenhower agreed.[58]

The Americans were learning—if the hard way—that it was better for de Gaulle to expound his ideas in a private forum rather than anywhere else, for his public declarations "pose greater danger than that which could be caused by their introduction into tripartite forum." Herter decided it was time "to take [a] more positive approach." He instructed the ambassador in Paris to tell de Gaulle that the French "will find [the] door open in Washington."[59]

The door opened on a series of tripartite talks on Africa. But just as Alphand had sought to make the Far East talks about nuclear weapons, the French representative at the Africa meeting insisted on speaking about military coordination. De Gaulle, he said, wanted to subdivide the world into "theaters of operation in peacetime for wartime use," in order to determine ahead of time who would be the wartime commander for each region.[60] It was necessary, the French argued, that the three countries hold military talks to establish "contingency strategic planning" for military intervention lest the Soviets obtain a "bridge head in Africa itself or on the Mediterranean Basin."[61]

In the five meetings that followed, the French expounded on their ideas for subdividing Africa into "unified military commands" for North Africa, the Sahara, West and Central Africa, and one more "embracing Madagascar and the French Somali Coast."[62] The goal was to make "precise recommendations . . . about the organization of free world defense in Africa, including measures against subversion," which could then be coordinated with NATO plans.[63] All of this looked to Murphy like an audacious, and impractical, global plan for "an eventual general war situation."[64] It also had the whiff of a French effort to cordon off Africa as a French protectorate. The United States simply could not recognize France's supposed "preeminent role in Africa," because the United States had interests there, too.[65]

The tripartites on Africa achieved nothing, but two weeks after the final meeting, the French pushed again. Michel Debré, the French prime minister, told Herter that "the time had come to examine . . . the fundamental problem[s] posed in the Atlantic Alliance." First, there remained de Gaulle's memorandum and its concomitant tripartitism and call for "world-wide common policies." Second was support for France in Algeria; Debré regretted that France had not stressed this before—Algeria, for instance, was not mentioned in the 1958 memorandum—but support from NATO for the Algerian effort was essential for French support of NATO. Third, and finally, was the need for progress in the field of atomic cooperation.[66]

Lack of French cooperation on atomic issues reached a crucial point in the late spring of 1959 while the Berlin crisis smoldered. De Gaulle had refused to accept the 1957 heads of government plan for a nuclear stockpile in Europe, and refused to allow establishment of IRBM bases in France and, even more crucially, the stationing or stockpiling of any American nuclear weapons on French soil. Part of Norstad's plans for defending Europe required the United States to station three wings, or nine squadrons, of F-100s in eastern France to provide support to NATO forces in Germany. To be effective, the F-100s required nuclear weapons. If de Gaulle did not allow storage of nuclear weapons for NATO forces in France, Norstad claimed, the planes were "little more than attractive targets for the enemy."[67]

In the midst of the crisis, de Gaulle wrote to Eisenhower and made clear there would be no agreement on weapons storage in France and that the F-100s would remain unarmed.[68] The squadrons were redeployed. NATO would have to plan its defenses without storing nuclear weapons in the alliance's geographical center. This was much more significant than the fleet action, and prompted Herter to wonder again "whether or not this was likely to signal the beginning of the break-up of NATO."[69]

While the Americans were frustrated over de Gaulle's lack of cooperation on the atomic front, de Gaulle remained upset that his original memorandum had not received the formal reply he expected.[70] Furthermore, the United States had continued to grant visas to Algerian rebels, and when Washington refused to take a strong pro-French position at the upcoming United Nations General Assembly, de Gaulle erupted.[71] It was "inconceivable," he complained, that "the alliance does not extend to all points of the globe where we are face to face with Communism."

If the United States continued to be against France in the United Nations, then the French "presence in NATO would be in question." Instead of "200 jets and the atomic bomb" leaving French soil, it would be "Norstad and the whole organization of the alliance."[72]

Spaak's Intervention

De Gaulle's withdrawal of the French Mediterranean fleet and the refusal to grant atomic storage rights worried the other NATO allies, none of whom were privy to the secret exploratory tripartite talks. NATO's secretary-general took it upon himself to mediate between Washington and Paris. During the 1959 Bastille Day parade, Spaak passed de Gaulle an aide-mémoire describing plans for reconciling the two allies and NATO as a whole.[73]

Spaak had a reputation as a remarkable orator and was known to possess a keen mind. But he read as little as possible and preferred to get his information through discussion with close confidants.[74] According to his deputy, NATO assistant secretary-general Evelyn Shuckburgh, such an approach "goes well usually," though "every once and a while horribly wrong."[75] In his aide-mémoire, Spaak offered a vision of a radically reorganized NATO in an attempt to reconcile his own hopes for NATO with de Gaulle's ideas. He had done so without advice from any military officials or other high NATO officials. And this time, Spaak's approach went horribly wrong.

First, Spaak suggested that NATO establish a "special limited committee," consisting of the NATO states with nuclear weapons stationed on their soil. This committee would be the decision-making machinery for launching nuclear war. Such a plan would deal with de Gaulle's worries and German fears of being left behind. Second, Spaak wrote that he thought Washington would be willing to share atomic information with France as it had done with Great Britain. Finally, Spaak wished to create a series of committees to study and prepare common directives for Africa, the Middle East, the Far East, and South Asia.[76] With these three ideas, Spaak believed he had reconciled de Gaulle's desires while negating the need for tripartism; France could get all it wanted within NATO. With "little or no knowledge of technical military questions," as Frank Roberts observed, Spaak "had jumped in where angels would fear to tread."[77]

The Americans damned Spaak's memorandum as a "disturbing document." The United States would not accept any special NATO machinery for nuclear decisions. Such machinery might deny the United States the time necessary to fire an effective salvo and reduce the Soviet expectations of a definite response. Similarly, global planning committees were unacceptable. It was fine for NATO allies to consult in council as they wished, but the rest of the world would be up in arms if they were to discover NATO was acting as if it was the global over-lord. The worst part of Spaak's memorandum for the Americans was the part on atomic sharing. US policy and congressional attitudes were not in favor of granting France atomic cooperation—Spaak had been "entirely incorrect" in his assessment.[78]

Piling on to the substantive problems with Spaak's memorandum was the signal it offered de Gaulle.[79] De Gaulle, who knew little about NATO and only wished for its continuance if it met his desires, had been presented with a memo-randum by the secretary-general of that very institution suggesting that all of his policies were legitimate and achievable.

Spaak's memorandum would come to naught—that is, beyond muddying the waters—but still the tripartite issue would not die. In September 1959 Eisenhower and the leaders of Britain, France, and the Federal Republic were scheduled to meet to demonstrate their unity. But unity, the Americans worried, would be difficult to achieve with Franco-American relations in the doldrums because of the NATO debates and frictions over North Africa. State Department officials warned that the only area where the United States could give something to France, in the hopes of improving Franco-American relations, was on tripar-titism.[80] Eisenhower continued to mull over the issue, claiming that he had "no objection to conversations, discussions, and even planning so long as there is never any agreement that the majority will rule." He left for Europe prepared to "go pretty far in consultations" with de Gaulle on global issues—that is, "interests outside of NATO."[81]

In Paris, de Gaulle and Eisenhower met privately. In their conversation, they both agreed NATO was necessary and should be maintained. But they differed on what NATO meant. For Eisenhower, military integration needed to be increased, not reduced. He disagreed with de Gaulle's preference for a coali-tion of armies rather than an integrated command structure. After all, Eisen-hower asked, if NATO consisted only of "purely national armies, where would the U.S. put their forces?" De Gaulle countered that NATO, by not covering North Africa, left France torn between responsibilities in the Mediterranean and Africa, and those in Europe. He recited his concern about the American nuclear monopoly, worried that if the United States chose to fight the Soviet Union anywhere in the world, France could end up committed to a war "with-out even knowing it."

Eisenhower then made an important offer. He pledged to de Gaulle that he would "never unleash an atomic war without consultation." Furthermore, he said, "he would be very happy to have General de Gaulle participate with the British Prime Minister and himself in a study of all the problems relating to world strategy in order to attempt to reach decisions taken by joint agreement." NATO issues must still be discussed by all the allies, but other issues could be discussed tripartitely, and even aided by the installation of a direct telephone line between the leaders. The next day, Eisenhower and de Gaulle spent the night at Rambouillet talking in front of the fireplace in bathrobes—a twist on Eisenhower's and Macmillan's pajamas at Bermuda.[82]

Tripartite talks began again after the intimate meeting. The Americans hosted talks on Laos and on arms supplies for Tunis and Morocco and started planning for both military and political talks. The sense of cooperation engendered by these talks seemed to "put to bed" the French-NATO difficulties. British officials, the American Embassy in Paris, and Norstad celebrated warmer French attitudes toward NATO's "knotty problems."[83]

The Americans were pleased and optimistic.[84] But State Department officials noted that the United States had in no way asked France to undo its previous decisions regarding its Mediterranean fleet or the storage of nuclear weapons. And as would soon become evident, very little had changed.[85]

Less than a month after Rambouillet, de Gaulle's diplomatic adviser, Jean-Marc Boegner, told a diplomat at the American Embassy in Paris that their countries were, again, at an impasse. De Gaulle "didn't feel . . . that we had got very far" and believed his memorandum had not been answered. Boegner warned that only "the same degree of tripartitism that existed between Roosevelt, Churchill and Stalin" would satisfy de Gaulle. The general "was not interested in NATO and never would be."[86]

A Concession and a Grand Bargain

If de Gaulle was not interested in NATO, NATO was certainly interested in him— or at least what his ideas portended for the alliance and organization. A month after Eisenhower agreed to increased tripartitism, Spaak called a meeting of his senior staff to discuss NATO's uncertain future.[87] He developed a plan for NATO to act in the "new arena" of the developing world, but his ideas, according to Shuckburgh, were "very undigested and indigestible." Spaak wanted committees made of NATO's "5 Great Powers"—the tripartite three plus Germany and Italy—to create policies for NATO to take toward underdeveloped areas, with a special focus on aid.[88] This plan, if enacted, would have met Spaak's personal goals for NATO, but would not end the tripartite issue: de Gaulle remained uninterested in NATO, while the Americans thought NATO committees would solve nothing. In the words of Robert Murphy, Spaak's ideas were "just nuts."[89] While Spaak's first plan had been a disaster, his second ended any hope that NATO's secretary-general could solve the Gaullist problem. Any real decision on NATO's future would have to come from the summit.

There were no shortages of summits in 1959. In December, the leaders of Britain, France, the Federal Republic, and the United States met once more, this time at Rambouillet in France. In the lead-up to the meeting, American officials expected and told their allies that Eisenhower was going to get tough and tell the general that if he did not come around he would damage the alliance.[90] Norstad assured British diplomats that Eisenhower "was no longer in his old mood of cordiality and amiability, and he was feeling pretty fed up with . . . General de Gaulle and France in particular."[91] Others were not so sure. Gladwyn Jebb, the British ambassador in France, worried that the September meeting, where Eisenhower had not confronted de Gaulle, would repeat itself. Eisenhower would not wish to "spoil that atmosphere of affability and . . . congeniality" that crept into "meetings of the great." Jebb predicted Eisenhower would soften and simply wish that "NATO can, after all, get on somehow even if the French are only, as it were, sleeping members of the alliance."[92]

At Rambouillet, Eisenhower shocked Macmillan and de Gaulle by seeming to grant the French wish. He suggested "the establishment of a tripartite machinery to operate on a clandestine basis with the object of discussing questions of common interest to the three Governments." A group, he said, would meet in one of the three capitals, preferably London, and consist of an official from "the political side, a military figure, and an economist." They would "ensure . . . some agreement between the three Governments on the facts of any given situation." De Gaulle immediately replied that he was "quite satisfied" by this plan.[93]

After the meeting, Macmillan and British officials scrambled. How did Eisenhower think such an organization could be kept clandestine? Were the Americans going to pass nuclear secrets on to Paris? What about nuclear strategy? Would the French be brought in there, too, and if so, "when and how far?" Of greatest concern to Whitehall were the Anglo-American defense talks, agreed to between Macmillan and Eisenhower and planned to begin in March.[94] Would tripartitism somehow jeopardize the Anglo-American rapprochement?

Macmillan's mind, however, had been turning on this issue for months. As prime minister, he had been focused on two problems in external affairs: First was the "cardinal point" of avoiding war. Second was his worry that the European Economic Community—the six—would shut out Britain from European markets. "After all," he said, invoking Napoleon, "we were a nation of shopkeepers, traders, industrialists, and so on. We live by trade."[95] But there was a conundrum. The American security guarantee, achieved through NATO, was essential to stabilizing the global balance of power and thus decreasing the likelihood of war. But NATO, with its informal Anglo-Saxon core, was so unacceptable to de Gaulle that France was likely to continue to reject British plans for European trade unless the British agreed to a policy of tripartitism. Tripartitism, meanwhile, posed a threat to NATO's solidarity and also, possibly, to close Anglo-American cooperation.

But everything changed with Eisenhower's suggestion. Macmillan could now have a discussion with de Gaulle that before would have been "quite impossible without disloyalty to the Americans." He would make a trade. Britain would support de Gaulle on the political front, "encourage him to get the fruits of his famous memorandum, and so forth." In return, Macmillan expected "the greatest practical accommodation that he can on the economic front."

Macmillan, unlike de Gaulle, had a good grasp of NATO's finer details and a sense of the organization's responsibilities and practices. But for him, too, the details were largely irrelevant. In the grand scheme of things, he asked, how important was it "whether a few French fighters are or are not to be put under the command of SACEUR"? Especially, he added, since fighters would be irrelevant in a global war anyway. "As we do not really believe there will be a global war, what is really important is British trade interests."[96] Consequently, NATO could be downgraded, if necessary, in favor of tripartitism.

But just as Macmillan was preparing his barter, things started to go wrong. A day after Eisenhower's comments, Herter, who had become secretary of state after Dulles's death in early 1959, let on that he was completely uninformed of Eisenhower's suggestions for clandestine machinery.[97] The Americans tried to backpedal out of the president's commitment, even denying what Eisenhower said.[98] If the Americans were to forget what was said at Rambouillet, Macmillan thought, it would be "fatal" to both Franco-American and Anglo-French relations.[99]

Herter attempted such a retreat, suggesting a more informal series of "secret tripartite talks" than the "machinery" Eisenhower had mentioned.[100] De Gaulle—via Couve—was unwilling to accept what was clearly a weaker offer than Eisenhower's Rambouillet proposal, and Couve insisted that coordination must be pursued "within the spirit" of de Gaulle's 1958 memorandum. But even the mention of the 1958 memorandum was "especially dangerous" in Herter's view, and he wrote Couve again in an attempt to "sidestep this proposal" while meeting the "substance" of what the French had in mind.[101]

There was no movement toward establishing Eisenhower's clandestine tripartite machinery before de Gaulle, Eisenhower, and Macmillan met again in March 1960 to discuss the ever-present Berlin crisis.[102] De Gaulle had strongly backed the American position, and Macmillan, sensing Eisenhower's willingness to work with de Gaulle, urged Eisenhower "in other words to revive the Rambouillet proposals" when the three met.[103]

Eisenhower—again without any advice or warning to or from his officials—did just this.[104] He told de Gaulle and Macmillan that he "wondered if the cooperation within the working groups"—the ad hoc tripartite meetings—"was a close enough relationship between us." He felt, he said, "that we needed in some way to be closer together at the top governmental level." While there should be "no derogation" of NATO, perhaps the leaders, or their foreign ministers, might communicate more frequently. De Gaulle agreed—this, he said, was precisely what had brought about his memorandum in 1958.

Eisenhower was not "proposing that the three powers set up a directorate to run the world." But the three had special responsibilities as a result "of the last war," and there were "things to be done." He suggested the foreign ministers be required to meet every two months, or perhaps more often; also, the heads of government should meet more frequently. This clearly struck de Gaulle as the way forward. The American translator wrote that de Gaulle said "the world truth was here in this room."[105] That same day, de Gaulle told Eisenhower that it was essential to establish "something permanent" that would exist after Eisenhower, Macmillan, and de Gaulle were gone. After all, de Gaulle said, "With us it is easy; you and I are tied together by history."[106]

De Gaulle's comment about his personal relationship with Eisenhower might have sounded like pomposity, a throwaway grandiosity in a conversation between men of incredible power. But de Gaulle's remark revealed the concern that motivated his memorandum and his insistence on some formal tripartite organization: the need to create structures and institutions in the allied countries that would last when presidents and prime ministers were elected who had not known each other as brothers in arms. Eisenhower believed that NATO, with its integrated commands and spirit of unity, offered the West its staying power; de Gaulle was worried that such a system would work only if the president of the United States was as committed to NATO as was Eisenhower. British and German officials, in the decades to come, would grow more and more worried about the presidential commitment to Europe. But even before the election of the youthful John F. Kennedy, before Lyndon Johnson's obsession with Vietnam, before Nixon's Watergate crisis, and before Jimmy Carter's erratic policies, Ronald Reagan's bellicose speeches—before President Donald J. Trump—de Gaulle knew that the vagaries of American politics would pose challenges to Western security.

Stalled Tripartitism

Macmillan was eager to build on the momentum for tripartitism that Eisenhower had begun at the two summit meetings. He wrote a memorandum for de Gaulle laying out a schedule for frequent meetings of foreign ministers, who might prepare agendas and exchange papers in advance of their meetings. De Gaulle, however, thought this left military and strategic matters unaccounted for. Going back to his 1958 memorandum, he suggested using the NATO Standing Group. The Standing Group was an organ of NATO, formed in its earliest days to provide military advice to NATO, with representatives of what were then NATO's three largest military powers: Britain, France, and the United States. But since its founding, the group had been less and less important; it was resented by the other allies, especially the Germans, who had a reasonable claim to inclusion after their massive military potential was added to the alliance. De Gaulle's suggestion brought the issue back to square one. Because the Standing Group was a NATO institution, and existed in support of NATO as a whole, Eisenhower was adamantly against using it as a forum for tripartitism.[107]

Eisenhower was right to suspect the other NATO allies were worried. The North Atlantic Council's frustrations bubbled over in early June when the Americans told it that the tripartite foreign ministers had met at SEATO and would "continue and develop such consultations" in the future.[108] How could consultation in NATO have any real effect, asked the Belgians, if the tripartite powers reached agreement beforehand? Merely informing the NAC afterward "would be the end of the NATO Council." Perhaps it was "better to be a neutral than an unconsulted ally."[109]

Spaak thought the British and Americans were making a mistake by seeking to placate de Gaulle on an issue for which there was no room for agreement. He asked if anyone really thought that the "facade" of tripartites could make up for American refusal to help France develop nuclear weapons while the Americans continued to aid the British. The Anglo-Saxons were taking positions that would not satisfy de Gaulle but still irritate all the allies. And unspoken in council was the possible effect on Germany.

What bothered Spaak so much was both the appearance of tripartitism and its lack of results.[110] If tripartitism resulted in "a very clear lead to the rest of the Alliance and to the West in general," Spaak said, he would welcome it.[111] But this is not what was happening. Now, with the other allies suspicious but no effective tripartite coordination actually occurring, NATO was getting "the worst of both worlds."[112]

It seemed to the Americans that there was no means to satisfy the French "without a real explosion in NATO."[113] Eisenhower felt stuck; he had "always refused to get into the tripartite thing but what we have now is wrecking NATO."[114] He wrote to Macmillan that "we must find some way to cope with this aspect of General de Gaulle's thinking." Eisenhower suggested offering to hold military talks with France in Washington. While he would not use the Standing Group, he could appoint a US general to meet with the French and British Standing Group representatives.[115] He drafted a letter to de Gaulle offering "wide ranging" military talks "on all subjects of interest to you" and included a section suggesting the three discuss NATO issues.[116]

The Americans showed the British Eisenhower's draft letter, and it threw them into a frenzy. Macmillan was prepared for a trade, but he wanted to be very careful about the effects of tripartism on Anglo-American relations, especially since the "great prize" of nuclear cooperation with Washington had only just been won. Furthermore, as leader of a prime-minister-in-cabinet government, he had to manage the concerns of his secretaries of state and their departments. The Foreign Office was fully converted to the desirability of an Anglo-Saxon directorate. But the Ministry of Defence and the British Chiefs of Staff were especially worried such talks would disrupt "our own special standing with [the] Americans on general defence policy."[117] After an emergency intercession by Selwyn Lloyd, Eisenhower redrafted his letter to limit military talks to subjects "primarily outside the N.A.T.O. area," and the official letter to de Gaulle did not contain the section about NATO and tripartism.[118] Eisenhower, having grudgingly consented to open the door to discuss NATO in a tripartite setting, took London's advice to leave it locked.

The Congo Crisis

Harold Macmillan once told a reporter that the greatest challenge to governments was "events, dear boy, events." Macmillan's quote may well be apocryphal, but it holds true as the explanation for what made negotiating tripartism so difficult. In 1958, Lebanon, Jordan, and China had spurred de Gaulle's call for a tripartite directorate. In August 1960, with Eisenhower prepared to offer tripartite military talks, events in the Congo sent this tentative agreement reeling backward.

In early August 1960 the Congolese security force, the Force Publique, mutinied against its Belgian officers. In response, Belgium rushed paratrooper units to the Congo. There were ominous suggestions from Brussels that the mutiny was inspired by the Soviet Union and might be followed by Soviet military intervention. Congolese calls for Soviet military intervention seemed to mark the Congo as the next battlefield of the Cold War.

Belgian diplomats sought support from their NATO allies, especially the Americans, at the UN. If the Americans did not support Belgium, then the United States was unwittingly "injuring NATO" by giving up what the Belgians claimed to be a "NATO base" in the Congo.[119] While conscious of the risk of a "serious split among NATO powers"—especially between the US and those allies that retained colonial possessions—the US voted to support a United Nations Security Council Resolution (UNSCR) calling on Belgian troops to leave the Congo.[120]

At NATO headquarters, the Belgian representative, André de Staercke, and Spaak—the secretary-general was Belgian, too—called private meetings, and the NAC held emergency sessions to discuss the situation. The Belgians had accepted the UNSCR, but with a specific interpretation: they agreed to withdraw the paratroop forces they had deployed in response to the mutiny. Yet they planned to leave their regular garrison in the country "to ensure the security of the white population" from massacre.[121]

Spaak told the NATO allies that it was essential to agree on the interpretation of the resolution and prepare to take a public stand together. In case the "Russians threatened to declare war on Belgium," there must also be "full and secret prior consultation."[122] But such consultation did not occur. Disgruntled Belgian politicians questioned "the value to Belgium of the N.A.T.O. Alliance" if the allies would not support Belgium in the Congo, and some warned Belgium might abandon NATO and go neutral.[123] But the suggestion that the Congo was important to NATO evaporated quickly, as neither US nor NATO military commanders considered the bases to have strategic value, and even de Staercke admitted "there was no question of the bases being N.A.T.O. bases."[124] By August 1960, however, the United States was making such a significant contribution to a United Nations peacekeeping force in the Congo that its actions won plaudits and heartfelt thanks from Belgian officials. Still, both the NATO and American response upset Spaak; NATO's failure to develop common policies for the global Cold War led him to think about resigning his post, which he ultimately did in April 1961.[125]

De Gaulle was even more upset than Spaak. The Congo crisis was precisely the sort of incident that de Gaulle believed tripartite coordination could have prevented. He bemoaned that the three powers had not "clearly indicated" to the new Congolese government that, while Belgian troops would leave, the Belgian technicians and financial aid necessary for the new state would stay. Such pressure, he thought, would have headed off the crisis. Instead, the Americans had chosen to "hide behind Mr. Hammarskjold"—the secretary-general of the United Nations—and "shirked their responsibility."[126]

De Gaulle had not yet written back to Eisenhower's letter suggesting military tripartite talks when the Congo crisis erupted. He now wrote to say that such talks appeared "too restrictive to bring about joint action." He repeated his call for global coordination and his opposition to NATO's integrated military structure, and called for an emergency meeting of the three heads of government in September.[127] De Gaulle wrote similarly to Macmillan, asking the British prime minister to urge Eisenhower to attend a tripartite meeting of the three. In a pointed reference to the birthplace of the Anglo-Saxon directorate, de Gaulle asked: "Would not Bermuda be the most convenient place to meet, if that would suit you?"[128]

De Gaulle's reaction to the events in the Congo took Eisenhower and Herter by surprise. They thought, initially, that de Gaulle had erred in his letter. Perhaps, rather than the Congo, de Gaulle was upset over Algeria? Neither Eisenhower nor Herter knew how they could have prevented Congolese troops from revolting against their Belgian officers.[129]

Eisenhower gave serious consideration to de Gaulle's letter. He wondered whether it might be practical to divide up the world among the allies, with the French focusing on their Community, the British the Commonwealth, the Germans the Middle East, and the United States "elsewhere." But, he decided, this "geographical division of effort" was not "a feasible scheme."[130] It was also not what Eisenhower believed NATO was or should become. The president was deeply worried by de Gaulle's most recent letter, for it revealed the true depth of the French leader's hostility to NATO's integrated command. Yet how to deal with de Gaulle was anything but clear; the only solution was to "go slow" and talk to Macmillan.[131]

Macmillan thought de Gaulle's call for a tripartite meeting a bad idea. His new foreign secretary, Sir Alexander Douglas Home, the Earl of Home, thought it a "really dangerous thing."[132] With Eisenhower about to leave office, the Americans were not about to make a serious commitment to de Gaulle. Even worse, a tripartite meeting might "stimulate" Khrushchev to take drastic action on Berlin. Most important, Macmillan and Home wanted to avoid saying no to de Gaulle. Adenauer had promised to help resolve the issues of European trade between the six countries of the European Economic Community and those seven potential members of a European Free Trade Area—the problem of "Sixes and Sevens"—and an economic solution remained the British priority. The British hoped that the Americans would turn down the meeting. In such a case, London would get its preference and not be blamed for it. Macmillan urged the Americans to "play it soft" and not reject de Gaulle outright.[133]

Eisenhower offered de Gaulle a meeting of the foreign ministers instead. For the first time, Eisenhower directly took on de Gaulle's arguments. Whereas de Gaulle intimated that NATO was a relic of the past and no longer useful, Eisenhower argued NATO was an entirely new and necessary concept. The "revolution in military strategy" meant that military integration was a must. De Gaulle's suggestions for tripartite cooperation and his rejection of integration in NATO seemed "mutually incompatible." Most important, NATO allowed for an American commitment to Europe that had been "unthinkable" only two decades earlier. It was essential, Eisenhower believed, that American presidents could continue to advertise NATO as a commitment to Europe premised on the equal association of free states, with no titular leaders. For if the American people thought Europe did not want this commitment, he warned, "the historic shift in American policy could again reverse itself."[134]

At a press conference five days after Eisenhower's letter, de Gaulle spelled out his views on a new, confederal structure for Europe that would replace the postwar efforts to integrate the European economy. The Americans were furious with de Gaulle for so blatantly rejecting the current system of European and Atlantic integration and planned to speak out against the idea in council. But the British, on Macmillan's explicit instructions, kept quiet.[135]

In September 1960, the tripartite foreign ministers met at the UN General Assembly with an agenda set ahead of time. The meeting was not a success. The three made plans to meet again at the December 1960 ministerial, but the tripartite meetings, never an effective organ, ground to a halt as a new American president prepared to take office.

The End of de Gaulle's Hopes

Neither de Gaulle, nor Macmillan for that matter, was finished with tripartitism. Just months after John F. Kennedy was sworn in as president of the United States, de Gaulle sent an emissary urging the idea on Kennedy. Jacques Chaban-Delmas, president of the French National Assembly, urged Kennedy to consider the "most complete coordination" between Britain, France, and the United States. The three leaders, through their foreign minister and diplomats, could then implement the directorate's policy "through the natural channel of that member of the Big Three which has the most intimate associations with any particular geographic area." For France, this meant Bonn (no doubt standing in for Europe); for the United States, Tokyo (the Pacific); and for the United Kingdom, "its own area of direct association"—meaning the Commonwealth.[136] The continued elevation of France over Germany was surely not lost on the American audience. De Gaulle's representative left Washington apparently convinced that the Americans' noncommittal response represented private agreement to such consultation.[137]

In the Eisenhower years, Macmillan had hoped de Gaulle could help negotiate between the Sixes and Sevens. By 1961 it was evident that the real peril lay in remaining outside the Common Market. He needed Britain's application to be approved by the Six, and especially de Gaulle. Macmillan sought to gain de Gaulle's acceptance initially by pressing him for a "strong Anglo-French entente."[138] But when Macmillan realized de Gaulle had revived his tripartite idea, Macmillan seized the opportunity to try to solidify a triumvirate.

Macmillan, in correspondence with Kennedy and McGeorge Bundy, Kennedy's special assistant for national security affairs, became an even more strident proponent of tripartitism. He told Kennedy that after NATO came into being, the Western allies had "failed to maintain a sufficient unity either of purpose or organization." It was time for reform and to ensure that France played a full part, for France "is one of the pillars of the Western Alliance." Macmillan attached a series of memorandums to his letter with ideas for a regular system of tripartite consultation in which France had a "natural place." His calls for tripartite coordination on Africa, Southeast Asia, the United Nations, and on the strategic nuclear deterrent echoed de Gaulle's entreaties from the Eisenhower years. He reiterated de Gaulle's suggestion that the three "enter into an agreement for consultation before nuclear weapons are used and for joint arrangements about their use in case of need."[139] Philip de Zulueta, in summarizing Macmillan's arguments, noted that Macmillan's proposal would elevate France to "much the same position over the nuclear as we [the British] have today."[140] Macmillan was willing to push these policies, however, because he hoped Kennedy would "offer something on tripartitism and some review of N.A.T.O." to de Gaulle. In exchange, the French president might "act as a good Free World European" and give up his "insular" policies on Congo, Laos, NATO, and—most important—"European economic divisions."[141] Although Macmillan listed a range of global problems, his diary suggests he saw the bargain as revolving around "Britain's desire to enter Europe on reasonable terms."[142] Macmillan sent his missives to Kennedy in hopes of influencing the president before Kennedy met with de Gaulle in June 1961. Kennedy, however, rejected the idea of a nuclear deal with de Gaulle, limiting hope for any breakthrough.[143]

Perhaps partially because of Macmillan's prodding, Kennedy made a vague offer to implement tripartitism (albeit without a nuclear component). Kennedy told de Gaulle that Secretary of State Dean Rusk and his French and British counterparts "would develop a mechanism for consultations." He suggested the three countries appoint military representatives who might "meet either with three political representatives or, if need be, separately to study and re-examine the strategic situation of the three nations," and he suggested Berlin and Laos as areas that needed study.[144] On his return from Paris, Kennedy stopped in London and told Macmillan that the foreign ministers should "discuss the creation of a tripartite consultative structure which should include some military element."[145] But again, the United States did not follow up on the president's promises, and in 1962 Rusk persuaded Alphand, the French ambassador in Washington, to report to Paris a "basic disagreement in outlook" on the issue of "official tripartitism."[146] Macmillan knew that his "great plan has failed—or at least, failed up to now."[147]

In their June 1961 meeting, de Gaulle told Kennedy that he would soon "call for a re-examination of NATO." NATO, de Gaulle explained, "was first an alliance and second an organization."[148] While he supported the alliance, France needed a "national defence posture"—that is, for French military forces to be organized nationally rather than as part of NATO's integrated organization and command.[149] De Gaulle frequently repeated this distinction between organization and alliance. When, in a conversation with General Norstad, an interpreter erred and said the "Alliance could be weakened and jeopardized," de Gaulle corrected him and said "it would be *NATO*, not the Alliance, that would be weakened and jeopardized; that the U.S. and France had been Allies for a long time and would always remain Allies."[150]

British and American officials complained that de Gaulle did not understand that the alliance and the organization had become inseparable. They viewed his distinction as entirely artificial. They pointed to the development of SHAPE and the role of SACEUR and his integrated military forces.

For de Gaulle, the effects of military integration nearly came home to roost in 1961. All of de Gaulle's talk about the national character of military forces had sounded alien—even farcical—to the other allies. But in April, French officers disaffected by de Gaulle's Algerian policy staged the failed Generals' Putsch to take France by force. Some of the putschists, like Maurice Challe, had recently served in NATO commands. In fact, many in Paris assumed American officers in NATO had assured Challe that the US would support the coup. Making matters worse, members (such as Georges Bidault) of the Organisation Armée Secrète (OAS), the secret paramilitary group that tried to overthrow de Gaulle, were outspokenly pro-NATO. Rumors that the CIA had encouraged the putsch and encouraged the OAS cropped up in France throughout the 1960s.[151]

In separate conversations with Kennedy, Adenauer, and Harold Macmillan, de Gaulle attributed the putschists' actions to the nature of European defense. With Kennedy, de Gaulle awkwardly explained that he did not blame NATO directly, but rather "the state of mind of the generals . . . due to the supranational character of defence in Europe."[152] French diplomats told US officials that de Gaulle believed American officers at SHAPE had encouraged Challe after he told them "a government of pro-American generals would lead to French acceptance of greater NATO integration and other US desires."[153] Of course, it would be silly to draw a straight line between French participation in NATO and the coup attempt—more so since de Gaulle's return to power had not been a sterling example of democracy in action. Nonetheless, McGeorge Bundy was one of the few who recognized that pressing domestic concerns motivated de Gaulle's NATO policy. He scribbled on a legal pad: "why de G is holding back in NATO" and "why not subordinate his army to NATO." "De G.," Bundy answered himself, was in "danger of losing control over Army. OAS show how right he was—Bad elements."[154] Bundy might have added that de Gaulle thought these bad elements had rotted from lying too close in the barrel to NATO allies.

By 1961, any hope that NATO could be reshaped to meet de Gaulle's goals had been smothered. Going forward into the 1960s, NATO would be seeking to deter the Soviet Union while also fighting the infection caused by a member hostile to the organization to which it belonged. De Gaulle's unhappiness with the state of the alliance haunted ministerial meetings until his partial break with NATO in 1966. Other concerns of de Gaulle, especially those about the connection between citizens and their own security, though misunderstood and underappreciated at the time, were harbingers of a future, post-national Europe with rude implications for national defense. By the 1970s, allied leaders had to scramble to deal with the opinion of European citizens—and voters—who saw little connection between themselves and the institutions established to defend them.

4

A PROFOUND BITTERNESS

On July 4, 1962, John F. Kennedy addressed a crowd outside Philadelphia's Independence Hall and proclaimed that he looked forward to a future Declaration of *Interdependence* with a united Europe. The speech, with its promises of Atlantic partnership, community, and commonwealth, is held up as the cornerstone of his administration's European policy. The United States, said Kennedy, was ready to form "a concrete Atlantic partnership, a mutually beneficial partnership between the new union now emerging in Europe and the old American Union founded here 175 years ago."[1] The speech was magnificent oratory, building on the rhetoric that Eisenhower and Macmillan had developed in the 1950s to encourage a spirit of unity between the NATO allies. Many officials in both the Eisenhower and Kennedy administration took the rhetoric to heart and planned for an Atlantic future. They floated ideas to buy "a symbolic piece of real estate" in which to create an "Atlantic District." When the time was right, it could form "the nucleus for the eventual capital of an Atlantic Community." They wanted to draft "Articles of Partnership" and exchange parliamentarians, judges, and other professionals as observers across the Atlantic to breed closer connections.[2]

But the stirring rhetoric of the Kennedy speech, and the Atlantic ideals of some American officials, did not survive impact with the realities of power politics in Europe. In 1961, Nikita Khrushchev and the Soviet Union ratcheted up tensions in Europe by threatening to sign a peace treaty with East Germany and recognize the German Democratic Republic (DDR) as a sovereign state. Such a treaty, Khrushchev argued, would end the rights of American, British, and

French troops to garrison West Berlin and would also crush West German hopes of reunifying Germany East and West. Soviet pressure put Kennedy in a difficult position. He was adamant about not losing face against a Soviet challenge, but his allies were divided. De Gaulle stood firmly with the US, while others wished to avoid conflict in Europe, and possibly to deal away Berlin. For the Federal Republic, whose military contribution to the alliance held the balance of power in the Cold War, Berlin was no bargaining chip.[3]

Up until Kennedy's first year as president, the United States had purposefully kept Berlin issues out of NATO. But in 1961, the United States changed course. Kennedy's double-barreled policy to meet Khrushchev's challenge consisted of negotiation, but negotiation backed up by the threat of war and economic punishment. To be effective, this threat required NATO's military strength and economic clout. Under heavy American pressure, the allies agreed to a series of military and nonmilitary contingency plans. But what looked like a grand strategy on paper was not much more than a series of plans cobbled together by grudging allies.[4]

In the throes of crisis, there was no "partnership" between the United States and Europe. Instead, Kennedy and his administration viewed NATO as a tool of American policy rather than a forum for reaching common cause with allies. While Eisenhower had always believed that NATO's staying power rested in the alliance being treated as an end in itself, this hope wore thin under friction caused by both the Kennedy administration's style and Soviet pressure. Looking back, presidential aide Theodore Sorensen recalled that Kennedy did not "look upon either the Alliance or Atlantic Harmony as an end in itself."[5]

The bruising battles in NATO during the Berlin crisis were fought over the relationship of NATO to American policy. Was there to be a NATO grand strategy for Berlin, of which the United States might very well play the lead role? Or was there to be an American grand strategy for solving the crisis, in which NATO was a mere appendage to American military might? Officials in the Kennedy administration did not consider the former perspective and assumed the latter. And deliberate efforts by the Americans, especially Secretary of Defense Robert McNamara, to use the Berlin crisis to shape NATO's force structure in the image of the new American defense policy only compounded other allies' resentments and suspicions. The Kennedy era marked a turning point in NATO history, replacing the vague but attractive Atlantic spirit of the Eisenhower years with a colder assessment of NATO's role in world affairs.

The Relationship between NATO and Berlin

The Kennedy administration had not come to power intent on crushing the rhetoric of allied unity, or to subordinate the allies to American decision making.

Immediately after Kennedy's inauguration, the new president asked Dean Acheson, who as Truman's secretary of state had signed the North Atlantic Treaty on behalf of the United States, to study American policy toward NATO in hopes of improving allied unity.

Acheson reflected on the era that had come to an end with Eisenhower's departure from the White House. While he knew there were benefits to such close relationships among leaders, he rejected it as a basis for NATO's future. He worried that presidents and prime ministers were too eager to please their colleagues and often went too far in their private commitments; this, he assumed, "was the case with General De Gaulle and General Eisenhower." What was far "safer" was to rely on "full and candid discussion in NATO—even if informally conducted, at first," which would "help to bring mutual understanding among the allies on critical issues."[6] The key to NATO's future, for Acheson, was for the Americans—and surely their allies would follow suit—to "take NATO much more seriously as a forum for consultation."[7]

Acheson argued that the "ultimate goal of the Atlantic nations should be to develop a genuine Atlantic commonwealth" ("commonwealth" was struck through and replaced by "community" on Kennedy's copy of the report).[8] In essence, Acheson was returning to earlier hopes that NATO would become a forum for Atlantic grand strategy. US policy papers had throughout the 1950s described NATO as the "organizational heart of the Atlantic Community . . . capable of making the most effective contribution to the defense of the Free World by wielding political, economic, psychological, and military weapons in the cold war."[9] Before the Berlin crisis struck, Acheson expected that NATO could be used to coordinate all these strands of the NATO member states' power into a NATO grand strategy.

But when Khrushchev stirred up a new Berlin crisis in 1958 and 1959, the Eisenhower administration had avoided seeking out just such an allied grand strategy. NATO's noninvolvement in Berlin politics may seem peculiar, for NATO's very founding was tied inextricably with the Berlin blockade and subsequent airlift of 1948–1949. But even the lessons of that earlier period were not clear to allied officials. American officials held a nagging belief that failure to test the Soviets with armed force—a "probe" against the blockade—had emboldened Moscow and led to the Korean War. When, in 1958, Khrushchev declared an ultimatum that the tripartite powers must withdraw their troops from Berlin in six months, some American officials argued the United States should send a military convoy into West Berlin prepared to fight its way through any military obstacles. The Americans were unsure, however, whether the British or French, let alone the other NATO allies, would participate in such an action.[10]

Beginning in 1958, Secretary-General Paul-Henri Spaak, along with some of the smaller NATO allies, wished to use NATO to coordinate allied policy for

Berlin. The NATO allies could conceivably agree on a solution to the Berlin problem, perhaps by recognizing East Germany. Some allies, like Norway, called for this radical policy out loud in NATO. Others, like the British, only said so privately. The repeated allusions to a recognition—even de facto recognition—of East Germany convinced the Americans that the allies were getting soft. At the root of what the Americans called "softness" was a conviction among European statesmen that their publics would never support military action over Berlin, for fear of war. The West's legal rights in Berlin were, at best, too complex to effectively sway public opinion, and at worst, a "demonstrable sham."[11] The Americans shut down Spaak's effort to make NATO the locus of Western Berlin policy, fearing the effects on West Germany if the allies pressed to abandon the prospect of reunification. Spaak agreed to let the matter lie, but stuck to his fundamental point: Western public opinion would not support the United States "in a conflict the sole purpose of which would be to determine who controls the routes of access to Berlin."[12]

Secretly, however, the United States was pushing military contingency planning into a higher gear. Dulles, at the 1958 NATO ministerial, met with Lauris Norstad in private and recommended that SACEUR "draw up a series of graduated steps which might be taken on the military side, in response to further pressures from the Soviets, for the purpose of demonstrating that we intend at all costs to stand firm."[13] Norstad established a small concealed group of American officers to study military problems related to access to Berlin and quickly expanded this "nucleus" to include French and British officers in a tripartite command organization called Live Oak. Around the same time, the French and British ambassadors in Washington and senior State Department officials established a "Tripartite Planning Group" to serve as an overall coordinating body for the three powers on Berlin policy.[14]

The relationship between Live Oak and SHAPE, and thus NATO, was blurry. Technically, Norstad led Live Oak wearing his hat as a US military officer, rather than as NATO's supreme commander. But Live Oak was staffed by officers from Norstad's SHAPE staff, and if put into action, Live Oak plans would rely on NATO communications facilities. Nonetheless, it was kept secret and physically separate from NATO.[15]

Throughout 1959 and 1960, Norstad and his staff drew up a series of military plans to challenge any blockade of Berlin. Norstad understood these operations would be "political signals, not purely military operations."[16] As a result, he incorporated "a significant amount of bluff" in his owns plans. These plans were based on a tripartite military force and neglected a connection to NATO as a whole.[17] Still, if the military operations went wrong and a battle erupted in Berlin, the NATO states might be compelled to come to their allies' aid. "Much would depend," observed one British official, "on who was first to shoot."[18]

That Live Oak had a tripartite staff did not mean it represented agreement among the tripartite powers. The Live Oak plans troubled Harold Macmillan and his advisers at 10 Downing Street. Macmillan's advisers thought the plans "unsatisfactory" and "aggressive," and "should only be envisaged if N.A.T.O. is ready to undertake global war." They were eager to know when NATO would be "brought in."[19] The US Joint Chiefs of Staff, however, would not take NATO into their confidence, and preferred to keep the planning in Live Oak. Thus, as the British Chiefs of Staff pointed out, "many of the measures could not be undertaken unless N.A.T.O. were prepared for global warfare—and yet N.A.T.O. has not been made aware of the planning, let alone accepted it!" Nonetheless, the British, in the interest of maintaining their close military cooperation with the Americans, continued to participate with the proviso that the plans were made "without political commitment."[20] By the end of the Eisenhower years "a number of plans" had been drawn up "which the U.K. Chiefs of Staff regard as dangerous military nonsense."[21] Fortunately, as the British foreign secretary Selwyn Lloyd wrote in late 1959, "the heat" had "gone out of the Berlin situation."[22]

The Importance of Berlin

The heat was not going to stay out of Berlin. Within a week of John F. Kennedy's inauguration, Secretary of State Dean Rusk warned that Khrushchev would be returning to the Berlin question soon enough. NSC staffers recommended, repeatedly, that the United States develop "imaginative policy planning toward real solutions to Berlin, and possibly the broader situation of Germany itself." Indeed, at the dawn of the Kennedy administration, private US thinking was not significantly different from allied calls for a diplomatic solution to the persistent crisis spot.[23]

But instead of establishing a study of the German problem writ large, Kennedy invited Dean Acheson to undertake a study of possible American responses to a renewed Berlin crisis.[24] It was natural to focus on these plans, since the Kennedy staffers recognized they "come as close as any national security policy to contemplating general war."[25]

Acheson's advice to the president was stark. He was convinced there was no "solution" to the Berlin problem other than total unification of Germany, and unification could never be attained, or so it was assumed, without weakening the Western position—perhaps by the neutralization of Germany. Acheson ruled out any negotiations with the Soviets and called instead for a "bold and dangerous course."[26]

In Acheson's thinking, any of the other instruments of grand strategy, whether diplomatic, economic, or moral suasion, would be ineffective or misunderstood by the Soviets. Military force was the only answer. Where the Live Oak plans had been designed to give policy makers options to call a Soviet bluff, Acheson wanted to take them further. If the Soviets put up "persistent physical interference" on the route to Berlin, they must be challenged by no less than a full "armored division, with another division in reserve." Acheson knew that the British wanted to send at most one battalion, in a probe, and that this small unit would serve only as a test of Soviet determination. But the purpose of Acheson's divisions was not to probe or test the Soviets, but to engage in "a fight over Berlin."[27]

The "purpose of a fight," Acheson argued, would be to force the Soviets to choose between reopening access or to keep on fighting with the risk of escalation. And Acheson expected two more benefits would accrue from the battle: such a fight would "rally our European allies to a unified and determined rearmament program," and have the effect, like the 1948 Czechoslovakia coup and the Korean War, of turning "a liability into an asset, by rallying the alliance into a greater unity and military power." Here was early thinking about how the United States could use the Berlin crisis to build up American and NATO conventional forces to support an emerging US defense strategy that emphasized nonnuclear force. Second, paradoxically, Acheson thought such a "grave conflict in the heart of Europe" might lead to a diplomatic negotiation to solve the outstanding issues of German unification and arms control in Europe.[28] Europeans who knew of Acheson's thinking worried that he was out of touch with the rest of the alliance; nowhere is this more obvious than Acheson's contention that engaging in a either a local or a grave conflict in Europe, unwanted by all of America's NATO allies, would bind the alliance together.

In March, Macmillan visited Washington and received a preview of Acheson's thinking. There is little wonder why he found it "bloodcurdling." First, Acheson believed a battle between American divisions and Soviet troops could remain a "local conflict." This concept of a "sustained fight," without quick escalation to a nuclear exchange, was a significant contradiction to previous American strategic calculation and was at odds with what Norstad believed likely.[29]

When Macmillan and Home, and later British military officials like Chief of the Defence Staff Louis Lord Mountbatten, considered Acheson's plans to use a division-size force, they were still thinking of a probe. They did not understand how Acheson thought a division of armor could move down the autobahn without either stretching into a long, vulnerable column, or—if they were to keep a safer formation in which they would be dispersed on either side of the highway—not complicate the situation by entering East Germany.[30] The simple answer is that Acheson did not conceive of the division as a probe but as a fighting force, and so its transgressions beyond the shoulders of the autobahn mattered not at all.

Macmillan had come to Washington determined not to let Anglo-American disagreements on Berlin ruin hopes of his establishing a "special relationship" with Kennedy. For fear of appearing "soft," Macmillan did not tell the Americans that the British had been working on solutions to the German problem. Nor did he wish to debate the relative merits of military versus nonmilitary countermeasures to any Soviet action. British officials had begun a list of nonmilitary measures that could be taken to inflict pressure on the Soviet Union, only to find that these measures, such as economic sanctions, would probably hurt the UK more than they would hurt the USSR.[31]

Here was the rub for Macmillan: the military contingency plans were considered in London to be simply no good, but if the UK somehow managed to persuade the Americans to drop the military planning, the emphasis would turn to economic embargoes, which would be just as bad. If the British were to argue against both, they would give the Americans the impression that "in a Berlin crisis, we should prefer to do nothing whatever." Although Macmillan and Home raised some concerns over Acheson's plans, they said little during this formative stage of American planning.[32]

Acheson's plans would go on to hold an awkward place in Kennedy's grand strategy over Berlin. Although Kennedy had supported them in discussions with the British, he ultimately decided that Acheson's plans were "too militant." He preferred a peaceful resolution to the crisis; that is, negotiations over Berlin's, and possibly Germany's, future. Macmillan later understood Kennedy's preference, and it comforted him; Adenauer guessed it, and it worried him greatly. In the meantime, Acheson's thinking was the only sustained and organized thought given to Berlin before the Vienna Summit that renewed the crisis in 1961. It also reflected the Kennedy administration's thinking that NATO needed to increase its conventional forces. As a result, Acheson's thinking became the blueprint for the military component of Kennedy's Berlin strategy.[33]

The Europeans Meet Flexible Response

As Acheson worked on his plans for Berlin, however, American pressure on the European allies to adopt a new NATO defense strategy led to transatlantic tensions. Acheson, before studying Berlin, had offered the president a study on NATO. His report reflected a consensus within the administration, held especially by McNamara, that NATO relied too heavily on nuclear weapons for the defense of Europe; the Kennedy administration believed it was necessary for NATO to develop its conventional military capacity to prepare for "more likely contingencies" than an all-out nuclear war in Europe. The American push for better conventional forces was also wrapped up in debates over nuclear strategy, including what would come to be known as "flexible response"—a concept with many permutations and which was held by its acolytes with varying degrees of conviction. NATO military planning had always called for some degree of non-nuclear capability to meet limited military challenges in Europe, but the Kennedy administration made it a centerpiece of NATO policy. The prioritization of preparation for limited war was contrary to American policy and also NATO's strategic concept, which "accorded first priority to preparing for general nuclear war." But more important, it signaled to the European allies that the United States might be willing to wage a war without escalating to strategic nuclear weapons, in the hopes of confining an East-West war to European soil.[34] The European fears launched by Sputnik were hurtling back to earth.

General Norstad, as SACEUR, understood immediately the political costs for NATO of this new American emphasis on conventional defense. One of Norstad's former staff officers wrote to warn him that the "new management at the Pentagon . . . and most conspicuously among them the new technicians from Harvard and Rand who are advising the new magnates . . . miss completely the political and military essence of the Alliance."[35] Norstad, like Eisenhower, firmly believed that ensuring a spirit of unity in NATO was more important than any technical plan for limited war. For military reasons, but also because of the effect such a plan would have on the allies, Norstad directly rejected the notion that preparing for contingencies "short of nuclear or massive non-nuclear attack" was an "acceptable basis for planning."[36]

Washington was convinced that the Soviet Union would not plan to fight a nuclear war, for the cost to them of American bombardment was unacceptably high. Instead, the real problem was a Soviet conventional probe or incursion into Europe, an effort to make gradual military or political gains in Europe by using a level of force small enough that the United States would be prohibited from using their nuclear weapons in response. To deter against this possibility of limited war, the US pushed its allies to spend more on better-quality, if not necessarily more, conventional forces that could meet a limited Soviet offensive.

Acheson and the Kennedy administration misunderstood or ignored the European unwillingness to accept the additional economic and political costs of a conventional force buildup.[37] Part of the Europeans' reason for reticence was undoubtedly that their voters responded better to money spent on social welfare than on armaments. Another was the blow to European "prestige" by their being assigned the "infantry function."[38] But just as important were the logical deductions of Europeans themselves. As early as June 1957, even before Sputnik, an American diplomat had warned Acheson of "schizophrenia" in European strategic thinking. On the one hand, the Europeans were worried that in the event of a Soviet attack, the US might choose to avoid responding with force, so as "not to run the risk of nuclear destruction." On the other hand, there were Europeans "obsessed by the fear that the United States might reply to local aggression carried out with conventional arms, by utilizing nuclear weapons which would inevitably lead to all out nuclear war." The Europeans were, wrote the American diplomat William Tyler, like the man singing "Ol' Man River" in the Broadway musical *Showboat*, "tired of living and afraid of dying." Underlying European fears was the strongly held belief that the "actual military defense of European territory is incompatible with the physical survival of Europe."[39]

Tyler was right. By the time of the Berlin crisis, and indeed for the rest of the Cold War, the European NATO allies could not imagine a situation in which a war in Europe—won or lost—was acceptable. As the German Ministry of Defense wrote in a secret policy document in 1962: "War is not to be any longer a means of policy."[40]

Crafting a Grand Strategy

As transatlantic relations soured under American pressure for Europeans to divert more and more of their budgets to conventional forces, the allies and the rest of the world watched as a band of US-trained Cuban exiles launched an unsuccessful attack against Cuba at the Bay of Pigs. The ill-planned attack was a foreign policy disaster for Kennedy. Eisenhower warned Kennedy the Soviets would be "emboldened" to take action they otherwise might not risk; he was particularly worried they would probe the Americans for weakness in Berlin.[41]

Khrushchev chose to test Kennedy when the two men met for the first time, in June 1961, at Vienna. He harangued Kennedy and blustered about signing a peace treaty with the DDR. Such a treaty would make East Germany sovereign and thus end the right of the United States to keep forces in Berlin. Khrushchev warned that the new nations' borders "would be defended." Any attempt to violate these borders with force "would be met by force," and Khrushchev said the "US should prepare itself for war and the Soviet Union will do the same." The Soviet leader vowed to sign a treaty unilaterally if the USSR and the US could not reach an interim agreement by December. Kennedy had little to say in the face of Khrushchev's tirade, ending the meeting only with warnings of "a cold winter" ahead.[42]

Kennedy launched a major policy review to decide on a course of action. Department of State officials recalled that Kennedy essentially appointed himself "Berlin Desk Officer," and Berlin received the full attention of his White House staff. In May, before Vienna but after Acheson's report, McNamara passed to Kennedy advice from the Joint Chiefs of Staff: if the Soviets were to deny access to Berlin, any solution "must include U.S. and Free World military, diplomatic, and economic countermeasures, on a worldwide basis, in addition to local military action." The JCS urged improving tripartite plans to help execute such a global grand strategy if required.[43]

This thinking—that any response to Berlin would require a range of coordinated instruments—permeated American planning during the crisis. In July, Kennedy's special assistant for national security affairs, McGeorge Bundy, issued a memorandum to Rusk, McNamara, and Douglas Dillon, the secretary of the treasury—representing the arms of the American diplomatic, military, and economic levers of power. The president, Bundy wrote, wished to develop a plan for Berlin that would not simply meet Khrushchev's challenge, but exploit the Berlin crisis "to advance our constructive long-term purposes." He specifically wanted to ensure that a military buildup to meet the Berlin crisis had a "maximum lasting effect on NATO's military posture."[44]

Kennedy also wanted to use the Berlin crisis to develop a sense of "greater Atlantic Cohesion." Berlin, he believed, offered an opportunity to "exploit the felt need for greater inter-dependence which is likely to characterize a period of Berlin tensions and preparation." The renewed challenge over Berlin, the Americans hoped, would lead to increased military and economic cooperation and allow "new steps toward the long-term goal of a wider community" of cooperation in the political field.[45]

This list of goals matched closely what Acheson expected could be achieved by a fight over Berlin. Now, however, the White House hoped to obtain these benefits without going to war. Walt Rostow took the concept and ran with it. Although an economist by training, Rostow was also good at putting political slogans in a nutshell (he had, in fact, designed a bumper sticker for Kennedy's campaign). He urged the president to recast the scenario not as another "Berlin crisis" but instead a "test of the unity, the will, and the creativity of the North Atlantic Community."[46]

The advice of the JCS, Bundy's memo, and Rostow's formulation all pointed to a heady notion that the Berlin crisis would be good for NATO. The allies would build up their conventional forces while at the same time cooperating to coordinate the other instruments of grand strategy. What no one in Washington made explicit was what authority would sit at the top of NATO's grand strategy for Berlin. The United States approached the Berlin crisis as if it were a crisis for Washington alone, with NATO serving as an adjunct to back up some elements of an American grand strategy.[47]

A NATO Role and Allied Worries

As early as July 1961, Kennedy had decided to negotiate with the USSR that coming October, waiting until after the German elections to avoid making German adherence to the Atlantic Alliance a major political issue. It was obvious that most NATO allies would welcome US-USSR negotiations on Berlin and Germany, but that France and West Germany would not. If disagreement broke out in NATO, the Soviets might see this "as an indication of weakness on the Western side."[48] Just how to negotiate over Berlin was hardly agreed upon in Washington, as different elements of the administration battled for leadership.[49] Because of these disagreements between allies and between offices in Washington, the United States did not discuss negotiating positions or timing in the North Atlantic Council.

Other allies, who since the Eisenhower presidency had wished for NATO to act as a diplomatic clearinghouse on Berlin, tried to fill the vacuum. Spaak, now the Belgian foreign minister, continued to advocate a joint NATO counterproposal to Khrushchev. NATO needed to engage politically, he believed, for there would be no NATO military response. He repeated his "grave doubt whether Europe would fight to hold Berlin under present circumstances."[50] Even the Germans were "very, very anxious not to fight for West Berlin," worried there would be little left of Germany afterward. And the British secretary of state for defense, Harold Watkinson, did not think the "status quo is a very satisfactory basis on which to threaten a major war."[51]

In July, the United States finally agreed to consult the NAC on a diplomatic note to the Soviets, but both sides squabbled over how long the council would consider the issue. Permanent representatives were "incensed and discouraged," and it seemed the Kennedy administration's behavior belied its earlier claims to wish to discuss major issues in NATO.[52] The Americans relented on the timing. But Kennedy, exasperated by the inability of parts of his administration to allow him to respond quickly to Khrushchev, was also upset with the delay at NATO.[53]

The Americans assumed the NAC would demand "an exhaustive attempt at negotiations." If tensions increased, "some of the members would be unwilling, in the final analysis, to resort to military action."[54] A frustrated Kennedy asked Acheson, "How do we get it over to our allies to do something?" The former secretary of state assured Kennedy he was "worrying about much needlessly."

"Allies," said Acheson, "will try almost anything to avoid doing anything. We must not appear too eager to negotiate."[55] While recognizing that most allies wanted negotiations, the Kennedy administration did not explain to the council that the president, too, favored negotiations.[56] Instead, the Americans focused on how they might use NATO to win the showdown with Khrushchev.

As part of their grand strategy for Berlin, the Americans wanted to use NATO to coordinate economic sanctions or an embargo against the Soviet bloc in case the crisis escalated.[57] Few of the other allies liked this idea, thinking it would just fuse the Soviet bloc more firmly together. Nor was there an obvious or easy way whereby the allies, with their different legal systems and governments, could effectively enforce an embargo in peacetime.[58] The British complained it was one more example of the Americans "reach[ing] for the sledge-hammer," but did not offer direct opposition for fear of finding themselves in "bad odour" with not only the Americans but also the Germans, who were desperate for nonmilitary solutions.[59] Some of the allies continued to resist the planning, noting that their own trade with the Soviet Union meant the embargo would hurt them, too, but the United States insisted. That the United States, who traded little with the Soviet bloc, would push so hard for a policy that cost them so little, but their allies so much, engendered bitterness from many allies. Ultimately the council agreed that an embargo would be an appropriate response if access to West Berlin was blocked, but not before.[60] This made economic countermeasures a moot point, for if physical access to Berlin was denied, all the focus would be on military options.

Up until midsummer 1961, military contingency plans were still exclusively the domain of Live Oak. The British and most Americans believed the Live Oak plans would be used as probes and political devices for signaling the West's firm intentions to defend their rights in Berlin. Foy Kohler, assistant secretary of state for European affairs, told the British outright that the US was knowingly "taking risks which do not make military sense."[61] Still, British officials close to the planning in Washington believed there to be "clearly another purpose behind these plans." The Kennedy administration, even the "American people," were not "in a mood to take a bad reverse over Berlin." The chairman of the British defense staff, Air Marshal George Mills, warned London that the Americans would first try "everything possible short of large nuclear war" to avoid losing face over Berlin. "Personally," he continued, "I feel that in the last resort they will fight even at the risk of general war."[62]

This worry lingered throughout the Berlin crisis. Lawrence Freedman has captured the American predicament: "Inasmuch as the allies had to be reassured that the United States would not be rash, the Soviet Union had to be persuaded that it just might be."[63] This did not work out in perfect balance. Kennedy's tough talk on communism, the failure at the Bay of Pigs, Khrushchev's diatribe at Vienna, and worries about Kennedy's youthfulness, inexperience, and perhaps inability to control the American military weighed heavily on the minds of his allies.[64] Political opinion polls indicated Kennedy would have significant public support at home if he chose war in response to a new Berlin blockade.[65] Diplomats from both Britain and Canada, two countries that enjoyed relatively intimate relations with officials in the US, privately reported to their capitals that Kennedy was more likely to fight than back down on Berlin.[66]

The British preference in case of blockade had always been for a small, battalion-size probe up the autobahn. If it were turned back, the West should move to an airlift. Now, as Watkinson explained to Macmillan, the British had dug themselves into a hole by participating in Live Oak planning. They had helped develop plans for ground forces larger than a battalion that they "regard as being unrealistic," but now the Americans believed that "all military plans were agreed and feasible."[67] When General Lyman Lemnitzer, the chairman of the Joint Chiefs, told British officers that the United States was "prepared to go the lengths of a real test of strength, up to the point of 'losing a division or two,'" the British grew more worried.[68] Lemnitzer continued to talk tough, arguing that the time had come "for a show down with the Russians."[69] Even the officials of the Foreign Office who usually prioritized agreement with the US above all other priorities thought it time to take the "bull by the horns" and "face up to the Americans even at the risk of a row."[70]

Significantly, Macmillan and his foreign secretary, Home, disagreed with their officials on the need for a showdown with the Americans. If, on one hand, the British were critical of the American planning, it would look like the British were dragging their feet, again playing the "weak sister." On the other hand, if some sort of agreement was reached to take overt military measures, Britain would have to call up troops, move others, and might very well ruin the pound sterling.[71] Macmillan decided it was better to wait. In the coming months, he hoped, the "fiction of the strong man at the White House"—that is, the error of always taking a hard line—would be exploded "when the world sees the dangerous drift to war." Then, perhaps, the British could take the initiative. But now was not the right moment.[72] In the meantime, the British hoped some of the more dangerous American plans, especially a two-division or corps-size probe, would be "shot down" in quadripartite discussions by the French and Germans.[73]

Macmillan's patience paid off. Kennedy came to his own conclusion that military action—likely a probe—would be launched only if West Berlin were directly threatened. Kennedy thus rejected hardline thinking in Washington that even a Soviet peace treaty with East Germany would require American action, and make "general war ... more probable than not."[74] Now, the Foreign Office could happily report that Kennedy finally accepted the approach to Berlin the British had always favored. In return for Kennedy's conversion, the British felt obliged to support his policy. British troops had been banned by ministerial direction from training for operations larger than a battalion. Now, believing that Kennedy had abandoned any real intentions to engage in large limited military operations, Watkinson allowed British troops to begin training and complying with related orders.[75] In addition to the change in thinking about the threshold for war, the Americans made another critical decision: "the whole of NATO should be brought in."[76]

In July, Kennedy informed de Gaulle, Macmillan, and Adenauer that he was willing to negotiate with the Soviets on Berlin. To be successful, however, any negotiations must be accompanied by a buildup of military strength so as to "give such diplomacy a maximum of flexibility" and to ensure that if the Soviets pushed things to the point of war, the West would be prepared.[77] But NATO would need to play a part in the buildup, for the European forces provided the bulk of troops in any realistic war plan. Edward Murrow, the director of the United States Information Agency, warned that the "problem of morale and purpose in Western Europe" remained serious, and that the people of Europe "do not want to fight for Berlin." No one knew if the NATO allies would respond to American exhortations to build up their forces.[78]

Allied Doubts about US Intentions

Dean Rusk presented the president's policy to the NAC and urged the allies to increase their troop strength and call up reserves.[79] But it was what Rusk did not say that rankled America's partners. Before he left Washington, Rusk told the president he was going to Paris with three objectives: to get agreement on a military buildup, to clinch preparations for sanctions, and to bolster the propaganda efforts of NATO concerning Berlin.

Missing from Rusk's list was any intention to discuss the American diplomatic strategy. Rusk and Kennedy had agreed it was best not to discuss the American negotiation position, primarily because of the upcoming Germans elections. The German leaders simply could not be seen as too willing to negotiate on Berlin. Kennedy still wanted negotiations, however, and he hoped that by forcing the Germans to "undertake costly military preparations," it might cause their negotiating mood to "mellow" and help him achieve his goal of achieving a peaceful settlement in Europe.[80] Rusk told the council it was NATO's lack of conventional strength that had led to the Berlin crisis and that only a "calm, sober, deliberate military build-up" could end it. These greatly increased forces would help Khrushchev "to see the trail of powder leading toward general war" so that "he might not strike the match."[81]

The American decision to leave NATO out of one barrel of the double-barreled approach—the negotiation side—while paying such close attention to a force buildup raised eyebrows. Evelyn Shuckburgh detected "longer-term American aims involved" and warned London that "whatever may be arranged in relation to the Berlin crisis will at least constitute a precedent."[82] In Paris, the new NATO secretary-general Dirk Stikker and the organization's international staff became suspicious of American goals in calling for a military buildup. They believed the proposed increase in forces was an effort to implement the Americans' new strategic concept, rather than special action directly related to Berlin. In a remarkable sign of distrust and suspicion between the NATO secretariat and the United States, an international-staff official wrote to Stikker: "It may be that the Berlin crisis, skillfully orchestrated, has not been at all unwelcome to the new military thinkers in the White House, anxious to establish their ideas."[83]

Rusk, in his speech, also revealed the existence of Live Oak and plans to launch a probe of Soviet intentions in case of a blockade, to test whether the Soviets would use force. Although he said the military planning needed to remain restricted to the tripartite powers, he hinted that Live Oak planning would, in future, be coordinated with NATO plans. These imprecise and contradictory statements were variously interpreted and led to later problems. They also left the non-tripartite allies, many of whom had answered Rusk's calls for more troops, "very much in the dark" on contingency plans.[84]

The Berlin Wall

On August 13, 1961, three divisions of Soviet troops formed a ring around Berlin. Under their protection, East German forces erected a barrier around the perimeter of the Western sector of the city, effectively fencing off West Berlin. When the job was done, the Soviet troops retired, indicating to NATO analysts that the new barrier was the responsibility of the East Germans. While some, like Kennedy and Bundy, were privately blasé about the wall, others worried it signaled an escalation of the crisis.[85]

Macmillan, Eisenhower, Kennedy, and de Gaulle would have preferred not to be responsible for Berlin; the Western position there was "untenable," as Eisenhower had remarked.[86] Nonetheless, the Americans were determined to maintain their rights to Berlin, to allay German fears of abandonment. Kennedy felt obliged to respond to the new barrier around Berlin and so ostentatiously reinforced the Berlin garrison, and thus German morale, by sending a battle group into the city overland from West Germany.

FIGURE 6.   American troops and tanks in the afternoon of August 23, 1961, occupy the border sector at Friedrichstrasse, West Berlin. National Archives photo no. 306-BN-100-38603.

The Germans appreciated the troop movement and a high-profile visit from Vice President Lyndon Johnson. The other allies, however, questioned why the battle group was dispatched with such fanfare, down the autobahn, in daylight, rather than at night by train. Kennedy had deeply internalized the lessons of the outbreak of the First World War as portrayed in Barbara Tuchman's *The Guns of August*; he worried throughout his political life about the possibility of Soviet miscalculation leading to accidental war.[87] The other NATO allies feared American miscalculation.

The British, by virtue of their close connections to the Americans, knew more than the other allies and were the most worried. The British Embassy in Bonn was troubled by their American counterpart's insistence that tripartite troops moving into Berlin should be "more forceful and should not hesitate to force their way through against [East German] opposition, even including shooting if necessary."[88] The British learned the American troops were authorized to provide defensive and covering fire for their movements, and the British thought "these instructions seemed likely to turn a dangerous incident into a most grave one."[89]

The British grew more worried when Kennedy appointed Lucius Clay, one of the celebrated figures of the Berlin blockade, to a special position in Berlin. Rusk assured the British that the hard-liner's appointment was only to build morale, and that Clay was outside the military chain of command. The morale Rusk was alluding to was certainly German, not British. When Clay arrived in Berlin in September 1961, he directed military units to build and practice knocking down walls in the German forest. In October 1961, Clay took advantage of a confusing situation to precipitate the infamous Checkpoint Charlie showdown between American and Soviet tanks. The showdown led to "deep disquiet" in the North Atlantic Council and in allied capitals.[90]

In November 1961, when tensions at the border rose once again, the American commandant in Berlin told the British that if the Soviets closed the Friedrichstrasse crossing, Americans troops would immediately tear down the barriers. The British were disturbed because they knew the American commanders, if they chose, could provoke such a closing "and so create the situation to which their plan is tailored."[91] British officials grew even more worried the Americans might purposefully trigger a battle when US officials suggested a plan for "seizing" Soviet or East German personnel from a checkpoint in a "'Commando' type raid." This would put the "onus of taking offensive action"—that is, either by efforts to "recapture" the personnel or by reprisals—on the Soviets.[92]

Rusk and State Department officials assured the British that no American tanks would break down barriers without British "concurrence."[93] The British believed the assurances were given in good faith. But in Berlin, Germany, and Europe, the "American chain of command is so mixed up" that one of the many generals might think he had the authority to undertake a unilateral initiative.[94]

While the British were privy to some of the scrambled nature of American command and control, Norstad would later say it was a good thing the NATO allies did not know the full extent of the confusion. On one day alone, he claimed, he received a number of conflicting instructions from government officials—including three separate cabinet officers—"demanding" he take action he "considered wrong and provocative."[95] Lines of command, control, and communication, especially over the authority of NATO and other ground commanders to use nuclear forces, were blurry.[96] No one knew or agreed on what type of incident would provoke violence, whether that violence would lead to war, what kind of war would be fought, and who—the Americans, the tripartite powers, or NATO—would fight.

Washington, Not SACEUR, Drafts Plans

After the Berlin Wall was erected, Norstad briefed the North Atlantic Council and made explicit the connection between Live Oak plans and NATO. A NATO military buildup was required, he argued, so that NATO forces could defend themselves in case a probe touched off a larger conflagration. For the first time, Norstad provided detail to the allies of the Live Oak plans. But in contrast to Rusk's earlier assurances, Norstad indicated that Live Oak would remain a tripartite command and entirely distinct from NATO.[97]

Just as the NAC was finally learning the particulars of the Live Oak plans, those plans were being reviewed in Washington. McNamara saw holes in Norstad's plans and wished to develop more options in case the Soviets closed off Berlin. He met with the Ambassadorial Working Group—the Tripartite Group's new iteration that included the West Germans—and said "he could not overemphasize the urgency of the situation." In fact, he was "so concerned at the lack of plans that they had begun to plan on their own for N.A.T.O. as a whole." While this might be "inappropriate and in some ways dangerous," they were going ahead with this effort.[98]

The differences between Norstad and the Kennedy administration, especially McNamara, were fundamental. First was disagreement over strategy and whether large military operations in Europe could remain nonnuclear. For Norstad, McNamara's belief that war could be controlled and shaped so carefully confused "the wish with the fact."[99] Norstad believed the conflict would invariably escalate to nuclear war if the Soviets were determined to resist any probe and fighting broke out. In fact, NATO's military planning was such that Norstad would require all the NATO allies to build up their forces as the Americans had requested, *and* prepare to use nuclear weapons, to have a chance of defending Western Europe. McNamara, however, wanted Norstad to expand his plans to allow for corps-size operations in East Germany on the assumption these multidivision groups could engage in fighting short of a nuclear exchange. Norstad resisted, and the disagreement between Norstad and the Kennedy administration led ultimately to Norstad's forced retirement as SACEUR in 1962.[100]

Second, and just as important, was Norstad's perception of his role. Norstad claimed to have learned from SACEUR Eisenhower that there was no difference between the military and political aspects of NATO. Even though he was the supreme commander, any "NATO business . . . was my business."[101] Norstad believed NATO's military plans had to be formed with an eye to what was politically acceptable to the allies, and he warned McNamara to think about how the allies would react to his plans to try to fight a conventional war in Europe.[102] In a testy meeting between McNamara, Rusk, and Norstad that ended with Norstad walking out and slamming the door, the general had attempted to explain to the secretaries "what the Supreme Commander meant in that whole cloth, whole picture," of NATO.[103] The idea of SACEUR playing a special role in NATO—which Eisenhower had originated and Norstad perfected—was not understood by the Kennedy administration whatsoever. Rusk was left to wonder: "How could Norstad have a policy that was a NATO policy? What is a NATO policy? In the end, he has to speak as an American. There is only one American policy."[104]

McNamara was determined to see his plans formalized by NATO's military command.[105] His avenue was the Ambassadorial Working Group—a non-NATO body made up of only four allies. The Americans in the group set it to drafting "instructions" for SACEUR to develop contingency plans for an "integrated . . . general overall strategy applicable on a worldwide scale and perhaps to comprise political, diplomatic, economic, psychological, military and para-military measures." The idea was to present these ideas to Stikker, and for Stikker to have the NAC approve the instructions so they could be forwarded to NATO's military commanders, essentially bypassing the other allies and the NATO organs designed to formulate allied plans.[106]

American Strong-Arm Tactics

When Stikker received the "Draft Instructions to General Norstad, SACEUR," he was deeply disturbed by the document and its implications for NATO. There already existed, after the economic and political debates, "*une amertume profonde*"—a profound bitterness—in council over Berlin and the lack of consultation. He warned that if the draft instructions were presented to the council in their original form, "the results would be disastrous."[107]

The directive instructed Norstad to create a graduated series of military plans for applying increasing pressure to compel the Soviets to reopen access to Berlin. At the same time, because any military action risked "rapid escalation," the plans also had to take account of NATO's overall strategy for any war that might break out.

The graduated plans, laid out in limited detail in the document, ranged from the tripartite powers' Live Oak plans, to "additional military plans" for "broader land, air or naval measures," up to the "selective use of nuclear weapons to demonstrate the will and ability of the Alliance to use them." The "broader . . . measures" that stood between Live Oak and general war were the plans McNamara wished Norstad to develop as official NATO plans.[108]

Within the year the North Atlantic Council would agree to issue these instructions to Norstad, and he would develop plans to meet them. But it was a bruising process. The draft instructions touched Stikker and the council's sensitivities. They diverged from Rusk's statement of August 8 about Live Oak and NATO. The international staff and many allies had interpreted Rusk's August statement as meaning NATO would take over Live Oak planning; this had been Stikker's "bible" on the issue. It was clear from the memorandum that Live Oak would continue in its exclusive form.[109]

Worse, the draft instructions had been explicitly addressed to Norstad as SACEUR. Stikker and his staff did not think it "proper for four governments to give instructions to SACEUR, who is an international Supreme Commander empowered by the 15 nations of the Alliance." There were a number of means by which the Americans could have "suggested" or even "recommended" that SACEUR take up such plans. Instead, the quadripartite powers "seem to speak openly as if they could speak on behalf of all the other members."[110]

Stikker, in an effort to find an acceptable solution, met with the quadripartite powers and helped redraft the instructions. The new draft improved upon the fuzziness about command relationships, but it touched off a battle royal when unveiled in council. The American delegation found their allies were in a "sarcastic fury" and warned of "a great strain on the Alliance which could have disastrous results in an emergency."[111]

The British had gone along with the draft instructions only because the instructions included the proviso that military plans would be enacted only after decisions by governments at the time. This gave Macmillan comfort to continue participating, although British officials believed "we should probably *never* be willing to agree to these operations under any circumstances."[112]

The Germans, too, were wary of the effects of both the instructions and the growing rifts in NATO. The FRG wanted its allies to remain firm in their defense of Berlin, but not at the cost of a ground war that would consume Germany— East or West. The Germans had been willing to go along with the Live Oak planning, even up to the largest plan, a divisional probe code-named "June Ball." But they were deeply worried by the "broader plans" for conventional operations in Germany that would include a six-division assault into East Germany. Any such action, the Germans expected, would generate a counterattack resulting in the Soviets occupying much of Germany. The Germans were essentially brought around to agreeing to the plans by American warnings that it appeared the Germans wished others to fight for them.[113]

The Germans pushed to develop other plans in case of a blockade of Berlin. A strategy of naval harassment and blockade had been considered during the Eisenhower years, but rejected by the president himself as ineffective.[114] In 1961, American officers renewed planning for harassment of Soviet merchant and military ships. The Germans knew these plans would be ineffective but pressed for them as "entail[ing] the least danger of escalation."[115]

The greatest debate in council was sparked by a part of the instructions calling on Norstad to develop plans for the "selective use of nuclear weapons to demonstrate the will of the Alliance to use them." This plan had grown out of the theories of Thomas Schelling, an economist whose writing about bargaining and strategic behavior had made a "deep impression" on Kennedy. Various plans existed for the demonstrative use of a nuclear weapon against Soviet targets to signal that the United States, or NATO, was prepared to use the weapons. The Germans did not wish for the demonstration to take place on German soil. And several of the allies, led by the Canadians, were anxious the Soviets would not understand that the use of nuclear weapons was only a signal, and feared that such a use would touch off a nuclear holocaust.[116]

From Washington, NATO diplomacy was beginning to look like a waste of time. The complaints, questions, and requests for more information from the NAC troubled Rusk and McNamara, who thought NATO lacked "any real sense of urgency." The Americans urged their allies to recognize that the planning was a real test of NATO's usefulness. It seemed to the Americans that the other allies were "unaware that all of us were living in the shadow of a collision."[117] By attempting to use NATO as a component of American strategy, however, the United States had opened up the one question NATO had studiously sought to avoid: How—and why—would NATO go to war?

NATO military plans, since their earliest incarnation, rested on the premise of defense against a Soviet attack.[118] Now, however, the Americans' plans considered using military force not in defense but as "gambits in a psychological contest against the enemy."[119] Military force, though couched in the language of last resort by the Americans, did not mean a last resort before Western Europe was overrun by Soviet armor but the last resort to keep open access to Berlin.

These plans made interpreting article 5 of the North Atlantic Treaty—especially the definition of an "armed attack" on an ally—more difficult. "When," Stikker asked, "does it cease to be an attack and instead the consequence of a miscalculation on the part of some individual country, a miscalculation for which the other members cannot be held responsible?"[120] The decision could not be left only to one country, or "a junta" like the Ambassadorial Working Group, but "new rules have to be developed" for how NATO functioned "in a period of crisis or in time of war."[121]

The draft instructions referred only to "political authorities" as responsible for the decision to execute the military plans, but the council wanted clarification as to who would decide. The Americans in the quadripartite group had hoped NATO members might delegate their authority to the tripartite or quadripartite powers. Few others thought this likely, and the British worried "we are getting into the deep water of political control of NATO and the impracticability of having 15-nation decisions on everything."[122]

Stikker told the council that according to NATO practice, the "political authorities" in the planning documents meant the North Atlantic Council, and so the allies were assured, like the British had been, that governmental decisions would be required to execute the plans. But this did not, at least to the Americans, mean that a unanimous council agreement was required to take action. According to the Americans, the NAC had "never, to our knowledge, formally adopted a rule of unanimity," and Washington did not now want "a rule of unanimity to govern decision on N.A.T.O. plans and their execution with respect to Berlin." The Americans, it seemed, were claiming that it would be Washington, not NATO, who would decide whether or not the alliance went to war over Berlin. The British delegation was shocked both by the American approach and the consequent bitterness in council. They wrote to the Foreign Office: "I suggest the questions the Americans should be asking themselves are: (a) do they want the alliance to continue? And (b) if so, what is the best means of holding the alliance together?"[123]

Telling the Allies What to Do

Dean Acheson had his own answer to the British delegation's point (b). He told Kennedy that the United States had been spending too much time seeking agreement with the allies, when all that really mattered was the "momentum of American decision and action." Furthermore, the United States does not "need to coordinate with our allies. *We need to tell them.*" So much "conferring with Ambassadors" was "a waste of time."[124]

Acheson's words held true. By the end of October, the NAC, aided by Stikker's views on "political authorities," approved the draft instructions and submitted them to the Standing Group, which would pass them on to SHAPE.[125] From October through January, the issue of Berlin lay dormant in the NAC, save for the December ministerial meeting when Rusk and McNamara goaded the allies to build up their forces and face up to the "hard realities" that the crisis over Berlin might result in war.[126] Two days before the ministerial, Home tried to convince Rusk that NATO, like Britain, wanted negotiations on Berlin. Rusk stressed the possible imminence of nuclear war and was "obliged to wonder whether there is in fact an alliance."[127]

In the ambassadorial group, the Americans pressed the British, French, and Germans to accept a "whole series of countermeasures, some of them ineffective or undigested." But the British found it "increasingly embarrassing to raise constant objections," especially in light of American impatience.[128] Buoyed by Macmillan's belief that Kennedy was determined to find a peaceful resolution, the British continued to agree to plans that "took no account of Russian reactions" and might "involve a chain reaction and subsequent loss of control."[129]

In January 1962, the quadripartite powers showed Stikker one of their joint documents, which purported to explain when authority would pass from Live Oak to NATO in the event of conflict. But the document was confusing and seemed incomplete. It stipulated that plans for any operations up to the size of a division would be the responsibility of Live Oak, and that NATO would be responsible for plans larger than a division. If, however, Live Oak sent a battalion-size probe up the autobahn and it was fired upon, NATO might take over. Stikker worried that the plans implied that "NATO countries were being asked to issue a planning blank-cheque to the tripartite powers and might be asked suddenly to take responsibility for operations when they had not participated or even been aware of the planning which left them in this predicament."[130]

Stikker met again with the quadripartite group in Washington and urged it to bring NATO into the planning. He had never heard of the larger Live Oak plans, including June Ball, before the meeting. Only then was it apparent to him just how little he—and the NAC—knew about the full extent of American planning for a NATO war.[131] Stikker again worked to improve the document, but even the new version did not resolve the fundamental problem: the decision to send an armed probe into Berlin, and possibly precipitate a battle, would be taken without most of the allies' involvement. In August, NATO's military authorities replied to the council's instructions from the fall. They distributed the military plans to the council, with a full list of criticisms of each plan.[132] Live Oak existed through to the end of the Cold War.

The Kennedy administration had executed a fait accompli at NATO, and also won the showdown over Berlin. Khrushchev backed off his ultimatums. Kennedy maintained that Khrushchev had abandoned his threats at Vienna because the United States "still maintained a preponderance of military might."[133] And indeed, British officials were left to agree that it had been Moscow's calculations of Soviet weakness that ended the crisis.[134] The lesson for Washington was that strength wins; the corollary was that the strength and backbone of the alliance was American, not European.

The crisis marked the first and only time NATO allies would attempt to use NATO's military strength as a political instrument in a crisis. But the allies had failed to find a means of coordinating the other elements of grand strategy like diplomacy and economic pressure. NATO could not do grand strategy, or could not do grand strategy short of war. And the Kennedy administration was never convinced that the NAC, rather than Washington, could serve as the West's center for strategy and planning.

The Cuban Missile Crisis, unfolding over thirteen days in October 1962, just months after the major row in NATO over Berlin, provided a striking coda to the debate. In that crisis, the United States had, it seemed, used its massive nuclear power to force the Soviet Union to remove nuclear weapons from the island just off the coast of Florida. Both the Berlin plans, and American Cuban policy, had rested on American assurance that they could stare down the Soviet Union in a conflict.

Up until the Kennedy years, it had appeared to the other NATO allies that the United States had been "inclined to consider the North Atlantic Alliance as being almost as much a part of the nation's political life as the American Constitution." A "closer drawing together of the Atlantic community [had been] an unquestioned objective, which appealed strongly to American idealism," even if the Americans had not thought about the implications for their own freedom of action.[135]

But looking back at the crises of Berlin and Cuba later in the 1960s, Patrick Dean, the British ambassador in Washington, believed the Kennedy administration had been convinced that the NATO "allies' role was very marginal" in times of trouble. Vietnam would only drive this point home further, but Dean believed it had begun in Berlin and Cuba, when the "North Atlantic partnership has proved almost entirely useless in this context from an American point of view." British complaints reflected larger fears that the United States had outgrown NATO. While there had always been a gap between the United States and the other NATO allies, the "vast and growing disparity between American military and economic power and that of its allies" was more apparent to the Kennedy administration—or at least better advertised.[136]

Ultimately, the crises of the early 1960s revealed to Dean that the "Atlantic 'mystique,'" the notion that the "closer drawing together of the Atlantic community was an unquestioned objective," had "evaporated."[137] Since NATO's earliest days, allied leaders had premised their participation in the alliance on their own national interest. Still, the idea of an Atlantic community so often adumbrated in speeches had also been apparent in policy and plans. By the end of the Kennedy administration, however, the language of Altanticism had lost its resonance on both sides of the Atlantic. Going into the Johnson administration and beyond, the NATO policies of the allies were understood by all sides to be based on national interest—and little else.

5

THE LIMITS OF INTEGRATION

The Berlin and Cuban crises, in many ways, marked the end of the first Cold War. By 1963, a peace had been constructed in Europe; war was even less likely to be purposefully instigated in Europe than it had been in 1955.[1] The risks of war, made increasingly obvious by the showdown over Cuba in October 1962, were simply too high for Moscow to make another high-profile bet after losing two hands. The Kremlin, humiliated over Cuba, was spurred into a massive program to improve its armaments, precisely to prevent receiving, again, a nuclear diktat from Washington.[2]

And yet, despite the fact that NATO's most powerful state was ascendant in world affairs, American officials remained convinced NATO was an essential component of their national policy. Indeed, American officials surprised their European counterparts with their frenzy for adapting the alliance to ensure its longevity. In the Kennedy and Johnson years, however, the Americans saw NATO not primarily as an element of the Cold War but as an organization for maintaining European stability and a balance of power in Europe that favored the United States. The great fear motivating American foreign policy had little to do, directly, with the Soviet Union, and everything to do with fear that Germany would "return to the bottle."[3]

The Necessity of Integration

The organizing theory of NATO's deterrence—and, if necessary, defense—policy was integration. In war, the armies, navies, and air forces of the NATO allies assigned to defend Europe would come under the command of SACEUR—the supreme allied commander, Europe. In both the First and Second World Wars, supreme command had to be negotiated and assigned in the midst of conflict. For those masters and commanders who had led the defeat of Nazi Germany and gone on to form NATO, supreme command was assumed to be a necessity for any allied war effort. In establishing, ahead of time, a supreme commander and plans for the integration of national war machines, the allies hoped they could prevent a third world war. Integration, also, was the essential means by which German rearmament had been made palatable to the citizens and states of Europe.

William Tyler, an American diplomat and a careful student of European politics, spoke for many NATO officials when, in 1960, he argued that integration remained essential to keeping Germany tied to the West. But nearly since NATO's founding, and increasingly ever after, NATO's deterrent strategy had rested not on the ability to maneuver, reinforce, and resupply the massive conventional forces of previous wars but on the capability to deliver a nuclear strike. And the majority of the nuclear weapons assigned to the defense of Europe were under American, not NATO, control. It was the "great irony" of NATO, Tyler noted, that the United States would not or could not expand integration to the "atomic level." The atomic plane, although the basis of NATO's defense, marked the "limits of integration."[4]

Nonetheless, the year Tyler made his observations on irony, American officials had begun scheming for an integrated nuclear force in NATO. In 1959 and 1960, American planners coalesced around an idea for a NATO nuclear force—what would come to be known as the "multilateral force," or MLF. This group of influential officials, known as the "true believers," or the "Theologians," believed the MLF essential to their twin goals of stifling a return to German militarism and supporting European political and economic integration.[5]

The Theologians were a mix of Kennedy appointees and State Department officials who had worked in postwar Germany, on the Marshall Plan, or on other aspects of the early European integration policy.[6] Not career foreign service officers, they were, as a general rule, unconcerned with the give-and-take of diplomacy. Rather, they concentrated on long-term thinking. In the era of grand designs, these were the ultimate designers.[7]

Their ideas were intertwined with issues of NATO defense policy, nuclear strategy, and the process of European integration. But at heart, their efforts to achieve an MLF rested on fear of a resurgent Germany. This fear of Germany's future was based, quite fairly, on recent history, but did not take into account the contemporary state of German politics or the logical strategic options and possibilities available to Bonn in the 1960s and beyond. A. J. P. Taylor wrote that, in 1848, German "history reached its turning point and did not turn."[8] The Theologians' conviction was that Germany could never turn and must always be contained.

The Theologians believed that NATO, as it existed in the early 1960s, could not contain Germany in the long run, and that if NATO did not adapt, Bonn would strike a deal with Moscow. The Theologians' thinking about Germany and the MLF reveals the great contradiction in the history and rhetoric of NATO. NATO scholars have long argued that NATO survived and endured for so long because of transnational linkages, especially a shared practice of democracy, between states. If democracies make for such natural allies, however, there would be little need to contain Germany. Democracy, in Germany's case, was something to be feared, not celebrated.

Ultimately, the Theologians' efforts to overcome the limits of integration and reshape NATO and its nuclear defenses created a self-fulfilling prophecy of dissatisfaction in Germany. Only gradually did both Kennedy and Johnson throw off the Theologians' advice and accept the anti-MLF recommendations of their National Security Council staff. The presidents came to believe, like their European allies who had lived with the German problem for much longer, that the matter of Germany's role in world affairs would not be solved in one policy stroke, but must be managed indefinitely in NATO.

The Possibility of a Multilateral Force

After Suez and the Anglo-American rapprochement, the Eisenhower administration had struggled to find concrete policies to help cement Atlantic unity. At the very end of Eisenhower's presidency, the Department of State commissioned a study by Robert Bowie, formerly the chairman of the Department of State's Policy Planning Staff, to articulate plans for NATO's future. Bowie's report was no ethereal excursion into a spiritual realm of unity but a hard-nosed assessment of policies he thought NATO needed to be effective in the coming decade.

NATO, Bowie argued, needed to reorganize its defenses to meet the challenges raised by Sputnik, the development of the French nuclear program, and Germany's rapid postwar recovery. He built on an idea previously proposed by Lauris Norstad for a NATO nuclear medium-range ballistic missile (MRBM) force that would operate under SACEUR's control and free from any US veto. Such a force would, in wartime, allow SACEUR to destroy targets farther back from the battlefield, such as the fighter and missile bases supporting a Soviet invasion of Central Europe. But in peace, the effects of such a force would be even more profound. It would reassure the allies and indicate to the Soviets that nuclear force would be available for the alliance's defense without a calculation in Washington whether or not to trade New York for Paris or any other European city. A NATO nuclear force might provide an envelope within which the British nuclear deterrent could one day be wrapped up, along with the nascent French program. Ultimately it would head off any possible desire by the West Germans to develop their own nuclear capacity, since they could be assured their defensive needs would be met by the alliance as a whole.[9] Critically, Bowie's plans did not rest solely on improving NATO's nuclear capability, but included a call for NATO to enhance its non-nuclear, or conventional, forces in Europe so that the allies might resist Soviet attack without having to rely on nuclear weapons.

In the end, Bowie's proposal for a nuclear force without American control was too radical even for the Atlantic-minded Eisenhower administration. But Bowie's report, without the veto-less force, formed the basis of Christian Herter's December 1960 final presentation to his NATO colleagues. He told the allies the United States would assign five Polaris submarines to SACEUR (providing NATO with eighty medium-range ballistic missiles).[10] In the first months after Kennedy's inauguration, the new United States government pledged to uphold this promise, which was significant because it meant NATO commanders would select targets for the nuclear weapons.[11] American officials, if not the president's top advisers, hoped that the assignment of the Polaris submarines would be the basis of a future multilateral force.[12]

In a May speech to the Canadian Parliament in Ottawa, Kennedy provided some more detail on US nuclear policy. The United States, he said, "look[ed] to the possibility of eventually establishing a NATO sea-borne force" that would be multilaterally owned and controlled. The promise of a seaborne force, labeled for a brief time afterward as the "Ottawa Force," was followed with two quick caveats: First, it was up to the Europeans to express their desire and determine the feasibility of such a force. Second, the force was secondary to achieving "NATO's non-nuclear goals," implying that Kennedy expected the allies to get to work building up their conventional forces.[13]

Diagnosing the German Problem

Kennedy's remarks in Ottawa, especially his caveats, reveal that he was not eager to see the MLF take shape. The teeth-pulling required for even a moderate buildup of NATO's forces during the Berlin crisis revealed that Kennedy's prerequisites were unlikely to be met quickly. But the Theologians increasingly saw the MLF as a means to placate what they assumed would be growing German nationalism.

Even before the Berlin showdown, events and personalities in the early Kennedy years conspired to create an atmosphere of morbid curiosity about

Germany's past—and thus its future. The sensational trial of Adolf Eichmann and the publication of William Shirer's best-selling *The Rise and Fall of the Third Reich* brought Nazi atrocities back to the fore of public thinking about the Germans. The Kennedy years were also an era marked by the application of armchair psychology to international relations. In early 1961, Henry Kissinger, a Harvard professor and a part-time consultant on the NSC staff, painted a lurid picture of the Germans for Kennedy. The FRG, he wrote, was suffering "psychological exhaustion" and thus was "a candidate for a nervous breakdown."[14] A few months later, Kissinger wrote to the president's adviser Arthur Schlesinger Jr. to warn that his "nightmare remains that a continuation of present trends will lead to a resurgence of nationalism in Germany and to Soviet-German deals on a national basis, wrecking the achievements of fifteen years of European integration."[15] German diplomats in Washington did little to soothe these worries. American officials filled the gaps in their understanding of German intentions by summoning history rather accepting the present reality.[16]

Kennedy understood that a nuclear Germany would be dangerous. But he did not think this scenario likely. In a March 1962 NSC meeting, Kennedy posed a critical question to his advisers. The Eisenhower administration had made an offer to the NATO allies of a NATO nuclear force, which Kennedy had repeated at Ottawa, for two basic reasons: the first was to "dissuade the French" who did not show any sign of being dissuaded from developing their own nuclear program, and the second was "to deal with the problem of whether the Germans would be stimulated to do the same thing. Since we are clearly failing in our first aim, is it wise to go ahead simply on the ground of dealing with the Germans"? Kennedy worried he was "pouring our money into the ocean in this proposition in order to satisfy a political need whose use was dubious."[17]

Kennedy continued to ponder the interconnected problems of whether or not to aid the French nuclear program and the need for a multilateral force to satiate German desires for a nuclear weapon. In the spring of 1962 he asked the Departments of Defense and State for their opinion. Theologians in the State Department argued against helping the French nuclear program, largely because they feared the effects on Germany. It was "unrealistic," wrote Henry Owen, "that over a period of time German politicians could resist the temptation to exploit the issue of US nuclear discrimination against Germany." Compounding this problem was the Theologians' belief that Germany's desires were insatiable. "The only arrangement likely to prevent German pressures for a national program would be . . . a genuinely multilateral program" akin to the "approach and proposal that Secretary Marshall extended in the economic field in 1947."[18] But the State Department's advice to Kennedy was peculiar in that it offered no suggestion that other factors, like Soviet threats, public opinion, or ongoing diplomatic efforts, could thwart German desires for control.

FIGURE 7. President John F. Kennedy observes the firing of a Polaris missile by the submarine *Andrew Jackson* aboard the USS *Observation Island* off the coast of Florida on November 16, 1963. National Archives photo no. KN-C30560_a / 6816403.

It was, oddly, the Pentagon that gave more credence to diplomacy. Defense officials maintained that NATO worked along a "fairly well established pecking order of national power and prestige," which "runs, after the U.S., the U.K., France, Germany, Italy, the Low Countries." As the top country gained a nuclear capability, so the next in line would desire one for motives "largely, and vaguely, political." Nonetheless, "In light of Germany's special history and position," they argued, the process would likely stop with France. Perhaps some Germans would be unhappy and feel discriminated against in this case, but the Pentagon believed that the opposition of the other NATO allies to a nuclear Germany would inhibit a nuclear choice in Bonn.[19]

These positions set the terms of the debate for the rest of the Kennedy admin-istration and beyond. The Pentagon argued that a German desire for nuclear weapons was a moot point because of the international political pressure on Germany. The State Department insisted German domestic political pressure for a nuclear weapon must be taken for granted, and that no level of international pressure could halt German development once the domestic demand had grown to a certain size. Neither side would budge.

Kennedy's special assistant for national security affairs, McGeorge Bundy, broke the deadlock. Siding with the Pentagon, he wrote Kennedy that "the danger of heavy pressure for a German national nuclear deterrent is *not* the central jus-tification of our current policy" of not aiding France. The real issue for the Ger-mans, he wrote, was that they wanted to be assured of a quick and sure nuclear defense. "The truth is that the existing arrangements please them very much."[20] These arrangements had been spelled out by Robert McNamara at Athens in May 1962, when he had revealed, for the first time in detail, the awesome nuclear firepower available to the president, and thus NATO.[21]

The allies were impressed by McNamara's presentation. Kennedy, too, was so "impressed with the abundance of nuclear weapons available for the defense of the Alliance" that he wished to force an end to discussion of the MLF at NATO. He instructed America's top diplomat at NATO, Thomas Finletter, to make clear that NATO had no military need for the MLF. If, however, the Europeans insisted on such a program, the United States would pay its share but not finance the whole project. Finletter, who thought the MLF the right idea, dutifully told the allies that they could expect to pay most of the billions of dollars such a force would cost. The allies were unhappy with the American move to back away from their own plan for an MLF. Finletter, though he had carried out Kennedy's instruction, was discouraged, believing that now, without a multilateral force, the "Germans will reach [a] point of despair" and would "move, surreptitiously at first and then openly, to create their own nuclear force."[22]

The next week Rusk visited Europe, and he, too, grew increasingly worried that Germany was seeking its own national nuclear force. In London, the British told Rusk they saw no such desire; in fact they were sure the promise of more consultation and the dramatic details presented at Athens had removed any pres-sure from Bonn on the nuclear front. Nonetheless, Rusk persuaded the British to participate in a joint study to determine whether France and Germany were involved in the clandestine production of nuclear weapons.[23]

The British and American embassies in Bonn and Paris ferreted about for evidence of Franco-German cooperation on nuclear weapons, but found no evi-dence to suggest the Germans were producing anything. In reasoning through the absence of any such cooperation, both the American and British embassies were "convinced that, at present, balance of advantage for FRG lies in existing, openly known arrangements stemming from NATO membership and US possession of nuclear deterrent." Although there was the "intangible factor" of Germany following "pure nationalistic motivations," it seemed the Germans would continue to guide their policy by "their relationship with US and NATO."[24]

But Rusk came to a strikingly different conclusion in Bonn. He wrote to Kennedy that his visit "removed any doubt I might have had as to the inevitable growth of German pressure for nuclear weapons unless there are multilateral arrangements in NATO or Europe or unless there are significant steps toward disarmament in this field." Adenauer had "asserted in the most positive terms" that his 1954 declaration renouncing production of nuclear weapons was not permanent. It had been made, Adenauer said, under the conditions of the time, and that even John Foster Dulles had offered the legal maxim *rebus sic stantibus*—that the declaration was valid as long as circumstances remained the same—as a means of interpreting the chancellor's pledge.[25]

Rusk interpreted Adenauer's refusal to repeat the chancellor's already existing renunciation of nuclear production as evidence that the renunciation had no substance. And he ignored that Adenauer had refused only in response to a request from him, Rusk, to reiterate his voluntary pledge as part of the American push for a nonproliferation treaty. While it might not have been apparent to Rusk, it was obvious to Defense Department officials that Adenauer would not unnecessarily forfeit one of Bonn's strongest cards in any eventual negotiation over German unification. Strauss had made this argument to Rusk seven months before. Still, Rusk could not see the connection between renunciation and reunification.[26]

On the same trip in June 1962, Rusk met with Gerhard Schroeder, the German foreign minister. Schroeder assured Rusk the relationship with the United States was "the cornerstone German foreign policy." Schroeder wished for Rusk to understand that Germany was "not politically as healthy" as the United States. As a result, the US would "need occasionally to show more understanding for Germans than Germans sometimes do for [the US]." Schroeder's humble plea was really a clever effort to implore Rusk to look at the larger picture of German's domestic politics and Germany's awkward geography. But Rusk, and the Theologians, missed the nuance.[27]

The perspective of Britain's Lord Home, foreign secretary in a country whose elites and general public had no sympathy for Germany, contrasted sharply with Rusk's. Although Home had roughly the same information as Rusk, he found little to worry about. Indeed, he sought to assuage his American counterpart. The British, said Home, had determined from recent discussions with their German counterparts that the FRG was "quite satisfied, at least for present," by American promises to share more information about the nuclear deterrent with their NATO allies. Rusk disagreed, telling Home again how Adenauer had left him impressed that they wanted "to reserve their position" on nuclear questions.[28] A few weeks after returning to Washington, Rusk wrote to Finletter that he was "prepared to see us lean quite hard on the political importance of multilateral force, in view of the impressions of German attitudes which I formed in Bonn."[29]

Crises Reinvigorate the MLF

Rusk's worries might have amounted to little had not political events on two islands—Cuba and Britain—intervened. October proved serendipitous for proponents of the MLF. The world was transfixed by the drama of the Cuban Missile Crisis, with its attendant nuclear possibilities. The United States had agreed, as part of the crisis's resolution, to withdraw NATO MRBM squadrons in Italy and Turkey. No sooner had Kennedy sought to shut down discussion over MRBMs for NATO than he found a gap to fill in its nuclear planning. Without laying any preliminary groundwork, American officials switched gears, suggesting a multilateral seaborne force might be launched on a test basis, in the Mediterranean, breathing life into the nearly extinguished plan.[30]

The next month, in November 1962, McNamara prepared to cancel the development of a new missile, the "Skybolt." The cancellation created an embarrassing crisis for Macmillan by revealing the extent Britain's nominally independent nuclear capability was truly dependent on America. The solution to Macmillan's political problems, agreed to at a meeting with Kennedy at Nassau, was the American sale of Polaris missiles to Britain.

Kennedy and McNamara's decision to sell the missiles ran counter to the American policy of encouraging Britain to renounce its independent deterrent. The Theologians and many other American officials judged the sale a bad idea. Walt Rostow summed up the emerging consensus that the sale of Polaris missiles would put de Gaulle and Adenauer in a difficult position. He urged Kennedy to push the multilateral force as an opportunity for the other allies to increase their say in nuclear affairs. This was the only means, he told Kennedy, to "avoid Germany either turning away from the West or acquiring a national nuclear capability."[31]

The Theologians got their way. The Anglo-American Nassau agreement, reflecting its rushed nature and Macmillan's shrewd negotiating skills, actually included plans for two NATO nuclear forces. One, Macmillan's preference, was for a "NATO nuclear force," which came to be known by various names, including the Inter-Allied Nuclear Force. It was predicated on the coordination of national deterrents. The next two paragraphs of the agreement, however, called for a "multilateral NATO nuclear force"—essentially the MLF—something Macmillan hoped would fall through.[32]

This multilateral force had been intended as a sop to the French and Germans, excluded from Nassau, but there had been no planning for follow-through with either Paris or Bonn. The Americans hastily schemed to offer the sale of Polaris to France, too, both to help with American balance of payments and to placate de Gaulle in his requests for US assistance to the French nuclear program. But de Gaulle attacked the Nassau Agreement and announced he would not buy Polaris missiles. In the same announcement, de Gaulle refused to accept the proposed British modifications to the Common Market, effectively ending negotiations for Britain's accession to the EEC.[33]

After Nassau, Undersecretary of State George Ball flew to Paris and announced to the NAC the Anglo-American agreement was the first step toward an MLF for NATO.[34] But others—including other Americans—doubted anything much had changed. Eugene Rostow, the dean of the Yale Law School and Walt Rostow's brother, found the claim that Nassau could "reunify the Alliance . . . a bit Alician"—as in, worthy of Wonderland. An American proclamation, made without any allied input beyond Macmillan's, was hardly a coup for NATO solidarity. Even the Germans were wary. They worried that the creation of a NATO nuclear force might lead to reductions in the deployment of tactical nuclear weapons, and actually diminish the American commitment to Europe. They might have sensed, correctly, that McNamara believed the MLF was a lever with which he would press the Germans to increase their conventional forces.[35]

The British worked to delay the MLF, and instead put emphasis on the Inter-Allied Nuclear Force. British officials and politicians rejected the Theologians' claims of an acute German nuclear problem and thought the MLF might spur a demand that did not currently exist. And given de Gaulle's hostility, it might also foreclose any future dialogue with France over entry into the Common Market. The question, in London, was how best to sink the American project, not how to make it float.[36]

The Question of Adenauer's Successor

The Theologians' fear of a German resurgence reached a fever pitch as Adenauer prepared to resign the chancellorship in 1963. Adenauer had carefully handled relations with the West since the days of the postwar occupation, and Western officials considered him a bulwark against both the extreme left and right. As Ball put it, the United States "simply had no experience of a Federal Republic freed from the Old Fox's iron discipline." He thought Ludwig Erhard, Adenauer's most likely successor, had no political convictions and was weak and thus easily manipulated by a "residuum of dark forces moving beneath the surface."[37] Finletter agreed. He urged Washington to push forward with the MLF "in order that they [the Germans] may be fully enmeshed in the Alliance machinery."[38]

Because of its Rube Goldberg organization—with various schemes for weighted financing and control, none of which was ever agreed to with any finality—the MLF was hardly an ideal solution. Even Walt Rostow conceded that it might "seem odd to create such an elaborate structure merely to solve the problem of Germany's nuclear role." But, he claimed, it was precisely because of this apparent oddness that the MLF had so much to commend it. The "truth is," he explained, "that most of our creative innovations in European policy since 1945"—Rostow listed the Marshall Plan, NATO, the Schuman Plan, and the Common Market—"have been more or less directly the result of efforts to solve aspects of the German problem." The MLF, he argued, was just one more "multilateral formula" on the "familiar and reasonably distinguished track" of tying "Germany tightly to both Western Europe and the U.S."[39]

The Theologians assumed Germany wanted its own nuclear capability. Rusk clearly believed this. And Rostow argued that if the MLF failed, the Germans would believe "some kind of national effort is the only feasible answer."[40] Ball told Kennedy that it was "no good saying that Germans do not want atomic weapons," for "even if that were true today" it would not be in the future.[41]

Ball's conviction rested entirely on historical precedent. He admitted as much. If "the world learned anything from the experience between the wars," Ball wrote to Kennedy, it was that ganging up on Germany would not keep the FRG to its 1954 self-denying promises. If Germany were discriminated against, it would succumb to a "festering resentment," as it had after Versailles. The West, he argued, pointing to German rearmament in the interwar period, "cannot afford to make the same mistake twice," and so Germany must be "tied institutionally to the West."[42]

Rostow, too, relied largely on what he called "historical analogy." He argued that if the MLF failed, contemporary German centrists would be, like Chancellor Brüning in the last years of the Weimar Republic, torn between a left hostile to rearmament and a right wishing to renounce Germany's promises—back then Versailles, now Adenauer's 1954 promises. This, argued Rostow, was America's chance to ensure Germany did not lose moderate German leadership.[43]

The Theologians' greatest worry was that West Germany might engage in "a game of maneuver between East and West that would play havoc with the delicate power balance."[44] This echoed, or perhaps drew from, similar anxieties espoused by Jean Monnet. Monnet, from 1959 until 1963, had warned his

American friends repeatedly of the danger that the "Germans and the Russians will one day get together again." Any German feeling of discrimination on the nuclear issue would "be the opening wedge to permit the Soviets to leverage Germany into its camp."[45] So focused were the Theologians on historical allusion that they ignored both strategic logic and current diplomatic and intelligence reporting and analysis.

Reporting on German Desires

The Theologians found themselves almost always arguing against the information received from American diplomats abroad and the analysis provided by the American intelligence community, including even the State Department's own Bureau of Intelligence and Research (INR). Early in Kennedy's term, the INR judged that it was "unlikely" Germany would withdraw from NATO. It had "essentially no alternative to an exclusively pro-Western policy course" and relied heavily on the US security guarantee. The INR's analysis is a classic geopolitical assessment, but the conclusion was supported by specific evidence. The analysts noted that whenever NATO unity was threatened by French "hypernationalist policies," the FRG "exerts all its influence to counteract such pressures and to preserve the NATO security system." At the same time, there was "no evidence" that the USSR was prepared to offer any concessions to Germany that might entice it away from the alliance.[46]

Throughout the Kennedy years, the INR doubted that the FRG would leave NATO, let alone reach some kind of accommodation with the Soviet Union. Certainly, the INR wrote, the FRG's industrial might and its geographic position gave it a "capacity to embark upon a potentially disastrous independence in foreign policy." But it was precisely because of this capacity—and the German understanding of the risks inherent in any such policy—that Bonn adhered so closely to NATO and the alliance's American leadership.[47]

In a lengthy report, the INR analysts considered "the Specter of Rapallo"— a reference to the interwar Soviet-German condominium. Worries of "a new Rapallo" cropped up in newspapers and the idle chat of diplomats. An especially pervasive rumor told of "vaguely defined 'German industrial circles' with a fatal attraction toward the USSR."[48] This attraction was thought to mirror the *Drang nach Osten* of the German past, and rumors of its prevalence were encouraged by the stresses of the Berlin crisis and the difficulty of forming a new West German government after the 1961 elections. But the INR argued that the bonds upon which *Drang nach Osten* had been based "have been eradicated by the sequences of Nazi depredations, spreading Communist power, and mass migrations during and after World War II; today only a *Drang nach Westen* offers any prospect for the re-establishment of German influence on a worldwide scale." Ultimately, according to the INR's assessment, Bonn remained "firmly convinced" that the Federal Republic "had no useful alternative to the policy of intimate association with the West."[49]

The INR's assessment matched the impressions of other US analysts. By April 1963 the American Embassy in Bonn told the State Department that the German press was treating the MLF as a dead issue with little prospect of materializing. After all, only 7 percent of the population was in favor of the FRG having its own nuclear force.[50] When Ray Cline, who headed the Central Intelligence Agency's Directorate of Intelligence, visited Germany in 1963, he found that the Germans were "not clamoring for nuclear weapons, either control of ours or possession of their own." German citizens in their forties and fifties, he observed, were "savoring the pleasures of material comfort and absence of immediate military danger." These men and women had, after all, lived through the depressions, the Second World War, and the deprivations of the early postwar period. "None of the people who are going to be running things in Western Europe through most of the 1960's," Cline wrote Bundy, were "inclined to battle for 'independence' or for NATO or for anything else if they can help it." In fact, the German leaders had such an interest in keeping the United States in Europe they would "go along with almost any NATO rigmarole which will please us." And putting up with rigmarole was precisely what Cline estimated the Germans were doing with the MLF. They saw the whole idea "as a kind of charade which we are playing for our own benefit while pretending we are responding to a European demand (which does not yet exist) for control of nuclear weapons."[51]

In 1964, Alistair Buchan, the influential director of the Institute for Strategic Studies in London, looked back on the Kennedy-era debates over the MLF and marveled how the MLF had such staying power in Washington despite the lack of evidence supporting its rationale. "To my mind," he wrote unequivocally, "the Kennedy Administration created a purely theoretical model about German demands upon its allies and about the conceivability of Germany deciding to acquire national nuclear weapons if they were not satisfied."[52]

Sinking the MLF

Albeit theoretical, the model had highly practical results. In 1963 Adenauer told Kissinger that he would never have requested a force such as the MLF. "However," Kissinger recorded Adenauer as saying, "once the United States had proposed it only one answer was possible for the Federal Republic." Germany, he said, "would join the multilateral force in order not to lose contact with America."[53] Adenauer's comments confirmed the worst fears of the MLF's opponents. Kennedy's advisers, like Arthur Schlesinger, had come to worry that as the United States "raised the possibility of German participation, any German government will have to make nuclear noises."[54]

In 1964 Martin Hillenbrand, America's chargé d'affaires in Bonn, reflected on the evolution of the MLF. What initially had been only a "gimmick" had gradually become "a political cause which, with our usual enthusiasm, we began to push very hard indeed and to vest with all sorts of emotional connotations." The Germans, he said, did the same thing, and the project generated its own momentum.[55]

Adenauer's succession and the domestic struggle for power in 1963 turned Bonn into "a morass with everyone ready to cut everyone else's throat."[56] Almost immediately on becoming chancellor, Erhard came under attack from Adenauer and the right wing of the Christian Democratic Union/Christian Social Union (CDU/CSU). Looking to shore up his flank, the chancellor sought to move forward on the MLF, no doubt because US support for the force suggested it could produce quick results. Thus Erhard advocated for the MLF, although his support was mild, and he left the heavy lifting to his foreign minister, Gerhard Schroeder, and defense minister, Kai-Uwe von Hassel. As the German ministers attached themselves more thoroughly and publicly to the MLF, some Americans worried that abandoning the MLF now would undercut their staunch allies in Bonn.[57]

The Theologians had created a self-fulfilling prophecy. Now Ball could point to the right wing of the CDU/CSU as indicative of a "strong stain of resurgent German nationalism."[58] Denis Healey, the new British secretary of state for defense, suggested to Ball that it was the Americans who had stimulated the German desire to participate in the MLF. Ball's response was to wrap the project in the mantle of earlier transatlantic programs: "every constructive post-war step that had been taken in Atlantic arrangements had been controversial. This was an essential aspect of progress."[59]

The NSC staff pointed out that while now the Germans were publicly in favor of the MLF, they had not been as recently as 1961 and 1962. There had been "no great pressure within the German Government and no pressure at all from any segment of the German public for closer German association with strategic nuclear weapons." The Germans themselves were only for it because of "rather certain strong proponents of the MLF within the U.S. Government."[60] Henry Kissinger, who frequently traveled to Europe and had many contacts in Germany, told Bundy the MLF was only a significant policy issue in Germany because "Erhard and Schroeder at our urging have staked their prestige on it." The Americans now had to navigate "between the shoals of excessive pressure for a version of the MLF which is becoming less and less acceptable in the rest of Europe," still only supported by part of the CDU, and "abandoning individuals who have staked their careers on an American project."[61] NSC staffers went to work formulating plans for "de-fusing" the MLF.[62]

By late November 1964, the forces aligned against the MLF were overwhelming. The USSR and France were adamantly opposed. A deeply reluctant Great Britain constantly offered modifications that were unwelcome to the Germans. The Germans themselves were divided. The MLF put strains on the Italian governing coalition. In the United States, the American military, except for the navy, were against the plan, and it had virtually no support in Congress.[63] Prominent commentators on American foreign affairs like George Kennan and Walter Lippmann lambasted the idea. There were more than enough reasons for national security adviser Bundy to recommend that "the U.S. should now arrange to let the MLF sink out of sight."[64]

By the end of 1964, President Lyndon Johnson seems to have grasped the essential paradox at the heart of the MLF as a solution to the German problem: "We seem to be unable to initiate a course and bring it to success. And often enough our policy seems circular."[65] McNamara argued that the time had come "to have done with this issue, either by action or by blowing the whistle."[66] But White House officials under Bundy understood things would only worsen if the MLF came to a "dead-stop labeled 'failure.'"[67] Bundy advised the president that if he were to go "full steam ahead" with the MLF, he would face confrontations with Congress and de Gaulle, and there was "a possibility of defeat." If, however, the United States backed off and went "half steam ahead, there will probably be no MLF, but it will not be your fault alone."[68]

The president accepted Bundy's advice and issued a national security action memoranda (NSAM) forbidding government officials from encouraging the MLF without his authorization.[69] Inside the government, the Theologians were muzzled. Finletter, in Paris, was considered a "particularly important target" of the NSAM.[70] To ensure the allies knew of his decision, Johnson showed the NSAM to *New York Times* reporter James Reston, who published an account of the policy.[71]

German supporters of the MLF were surprised by Reston's revelations, but immediately understood it signaled the abandonment of the MLF. Schroeder, in particular, felt "let down." George McGhee, who had been in Bonn for almost two years, described the atmosphere as the worst he had encountered during his ambassadorship. This current crisis in American-German relations, he wrote, had been "set in motion by events emanating from the US, which led to a genuine misunderstanding" of American intentions to proceed with the MLF.[72]

Erhard himself had sent "high level, secret German political signals" to Washington hoping Johnson would relax pressure on the MLF before Germany's

September elections, and this was a further motive for Johnson.[73] The MLF had become a source of tension between Germany and France, and Erhard had worried that the debate over the MLF might affect the elections. By May, the entire German cabinet, save for Schroeder and von Hassel, was "convinced that the MLF was dead and, at this stage, undesirable."[74] Given the strains the MLF was putting on Franco-German relations, Erhard, opined David Klein of the NSC, "is probably the most relieved politician in the Alliance not to have the MLF on his shoulders."[75]

Still nursing his hopes for the MLF in the autumn of 1965, Ball waged a duel of memos with Bundy for Johnson's attention. Ball went on at length about the interwar period, warning that a "frustrated and neurotic Germany is quite capable of making a deal with the Soviet Union on terms catastrophic to the West. The Germans did it at Rapallo in 1922 and again in 1939." Germany might easily become the "prey of its own Teutonic fantasies," and the United States "cannot afford another psychotic Germany."[76] But Bundy, finished with the MLF, wrote to the president saying that the United States, and by extension NATO, should instead improve consultation about nuclear weapons rather than provide Germany with nuclear hardware. Bundy's memo killed the MLF.[77]

The Nuclear Planning Group

In the MLF's place, the allies established the most trusted of NATO solutions: a committee. Some American officials, recognizing the MLF was fraught with potential pitfalls, had looked for "something to fall back on" in case the initiative collapsed. McGhee, writing from Bonn, agreed with many in Washington that improved consultation and exchange of information in NATO, like that promised at Athens in the Kennedy years, should be encouraged as "a hedge in our efforts to solve the nuclear problem which originally inspired the MLF."[78]

In May 1965, McNamara suggested NATO establish a temporary "Select Committee" of defense ministers to discuss NATO nuclear issues.[79] All allies would be welcome to receive the reports from the committee, but the Select Committee would have restricted membership. There was lots of haggling in NATO as to who would sit on what committee, and how many allies would participate.[80] In the end, the Select Committee, now "Special Committee," established three working groups, one each for studying communications, data and intelligence, and nuclear planning.[81] The idea of the committee and its working groups was, according to the American permanent representative, to "work out ways of holding practical consultations at government level about our whole nuclear strategy . . . within the framework of the alliance."[82]

The purpose of the committee was, broadly, to inform the allies about nuclear policy, but the main targets were German leaders. The American goal was to use the committee "to make FRG status in nuclear planning evident to all without national nuclear force."[83] This appealed to the British, who saw an opportunity to establish "tripartite machinery" whereby the US, the UK, and the FRG could discuss nuclear issues. The three defense ministers were "already in the process of establishing an 'inner group'" to discuss nuclear policy that quaintly came to be called the "dinner club."[84]

This setup suited the FRG, too. Bonn had no desire to establish a separate and formal tripartite group like the one de Gaulle had called for. This would offend and worry both Germany's allies and the Soviet Union. By forming a committee in NATO, Bonn, London, and Washington could avoid any charges that they were excluding their allies. Still, the obvious prominence of the three powers worried NATO's newest secretary-general, Manlio Brosio, who feared the committee portended an "alliance within an alliance." McNamara did not disagree with as much as steamroll over Brosio. For him, the primary issue was the exchange of national views, whether in NATO or not.[85] McNamara told officials in Washington that he "approved trilateralism as a substitute for NATO as a means of concerting power." The Special Committee was the example of how this would work: he "was prepared to have any number join [the committee] but use a tripartite group to coordinate and run it behind the scenes."[86]

With the collapse of the MLF in 1966, McNamara moved to make the Special Committee a permanent committee at NATO, to be known as the Nuclear Planning Group (NPG).[87] After some careful maneuvering in the State Department, Dean Acheson persuaded Dean Rusk to sign off on the idea, somehow avoiding George Ball.[88] By the end of the year, the NATO allies had agreed to establish the NPG, and McNamara wanted to "drive it forward fast."[89] He pressed to ensure that the NPG meetings were substantive and insisted that the conference table used for the meetings be so small that only defense ministers could have a seat. He encouraged his colleagues to discuss matters freely rather than rely on "some canned words" their staffs had prepared.[90] The NPG got down to work discussing issues related to tactical nuclear weapons doctrine, various new nuclear munitions, and a host of other issues.[91] The promises of the NPG allowed for a soft landing after the collapse of the MLF.

The Root of Difference

Reporting from both American diplomats and intelligence analysts supported the White House decision to end the MLF project. In December 1965, the CIA reported that "one point . . . on which all responsible German leaders are agreed is that at present, legal, political and moral considerations rule out either German manufacture of nuclear weapons or the acquisition of an independent national nuclear complement." There remained "widespread public indifference in Germany to the nuclear sharing problem," despite the Theologians' prognostication that the end of the MLF would stir up a hornet's nest in Germany.[92] The embassy in Bonn agreed that it knew of "no responsible political leader in Germany of any party, any known private group, or any discernible body of German opinion, that considers it desirable for the Germans to have an independent nuclear capability." While this did not mean Germany could be excluded from an important role in nuclear defense, there were overwhelming legal, political, and geostrategic reasons for Bonn to refuse to develop German nuclear force.[93]

The State Department remained riven by bitter divisions, especially between Washington officials who had been pro-MLF and their diplomatic counterparts in the field who had seen the idea cause so many problems in the alliance. At a meeting of American ambassadors to Europe in 1966, George McGhee railed against the MLF as "a major disservice to Germany. [The Theologians] have stimulated fears of Germany throughout Europe—both East and West."[94] When one Theologian disagreed, McGhee continued his diatribe: "This is a dead issue. It should never have been raised. Congress doesn't want it, the President doesn't want it. The idea of an alleged German demand for nuclear weapons is a straw man. It is not real. The only people who believe or care about the issue are Von Hassel and Schroeder. Erhard doesn't care. He wishes it would go away. We should really bury this one!!"[95]

The Theologians had understood nuclear weapons purely as a matter of prestige and as a political device. Officials in the National Security Council, the Pentagon, and especially in Germany believed there was more to nuclear weapons. Certainly, they were important for prestige. But they had two other important functions: first, for the defense of Germany, and second, as a possible bargaining chip over reunification. These American officials, along with the German counterparts, recognized that the American nuclear guarantee to Germany was part and parcel of NATO. A German attempt to gain its own nuclear capability, or even a strident effort within NATO to assert German control, could result in one or more of the following: Germany becoming once again a pariah in Western Europe; the collapse of NATO; and the Soviet Union deciding it was necessary to move against an independent Germany before the Germans could, again, invade the USSR. German officials knew they had simply too much to lose from pushing for a German finger on the nuclear trigger. The German public, on the other hand, was showing its growing distaste for and uninterest in power politics—a change that would soon come to present a whole new range of problems for NATO's survival.

The MLF saga reveals the allies' continued interest in using NATO to tie Germany to the West by limiting its military power and thus its capacity for war or diplomatic maneuver. Manlio Brosio, NATO's secretary-general during the latter part of the MLF debate, outright said that "NATO has a double purpose: defense against the Soviet threat and provision of a framework for Germany in Western Europe."[96] In fact, American Embassy personnel from Norway, Denmark, the Netherlands, Italy, France, and the UK all reported that their host countries viewed "the containment of Germany as the primary purpose of NATO."[97] In 1965, the INR wrote that the alliance, though formed to resist the Soviets, "has become equally important as a political system . . . for handling the 'German problem.'" NATO, the INR argued, was promised a long life, as long as it continued "to serve the political functions regarding West Germany which the latter's neighbors wish it to serve."[98]

Fear that the German body politic remained a serious potential source of political instability, and that the FRG needed to be contained just as vigorously as the Soviet Union, would ultimately outlast the Cold War. The MLF crisis, however, reflected a dual fear, held by allies on both sides of the Atlantic, that the Germans might either elect a revanchist government or one that would lay down its arms to the Soviet Union. By the end of the 1960s, fear of a resurgent Germany was all but extinguished, replaced by fear that Germans not only did not want their own nuclear weapon, but wanted no nuclear weapons on their soil whatsoever: denuclearization. The battle over the MLF was only one stage in a series of nuclear-political crises in Germany that threatened to destabilize the alliance up until 1989.

6

THE NEW TRIPARTITISM

While NATO officials fretted and finagled over the decline of the MLF, far more important changes, with longer-lasting effects for NATO, were afoot. In 1966, Charles de Gaulle believed that France could safely renounce the North Atlantic Treaty. He was only convinced at the last moment by his officials that such an action might invalidate the 1954 Brussels Treaty that allowed French troops in Germany and provided a system for integrating, and thus controlling, German military power.[1] De Gaulle ultimately decided to settle for the less serious but still significant step of withdrawing French forces from NATO's integrated military command and kicking NATO troops out of France. The allies responded by jury-rigging a new system of committees, withdrawing troops and aircraft from France, and adapting military defense plans.

Before the French withdrawal, the United Kingdom had been the NATO ally most akin to the Gaullist vision of the alliance. Harold Macmillan, after all, had been eager to accommodate French wishes if it would result in Britain gaining access to the European Economic Community. But with de Gaulle's challenge to NATO, the British government saw an opportunity to transform the burden of NATO membership into a crown of laurel. London shocked the other allies by leading the charge to maintain NATO's status quo in face of the French withdrawal. This was a careful British calculation. It was designed to cast Britain as the "good ally" as a demonstration to the other states of Europe, and especially Germany, that Britain was worthy of entry into Europe. This British defense of NATO, along with emerging closer cooperation between Bonn, Washington, and London on nuclear matters and a concerted US-UK-FRG effort to manage changes to NATO's defense posture after the French withdrawal from the military command, established an informal pattern of tripartite cooperation in NATO.

On the heels of the Gaullist challenge, however, came a greater challenge to NATO's existence. Economic and political problems in Bonn, London, and Washington threatened to reduce the Anglo-American continental commitment and unravel NATO's defenses. The "offset crisis" of 1966–1967, because it challenged the domestic political and financial basis on which NATO rested, posed a bigger and more difficult challenge to NATO than did de Gaulle. Ultimately, American, British, and German officials negotiated a three-way agreement to solve the financial issues. It is unlikely that these negotiations would have been successful if not for the emerging pattern of tripartitism engendered by the French withdrawal. Either way, British officials at the time recognized that the "offset crisis" and resulting Anglo-American-German negotiations had rebuilt "NATO around the core of a special, close-knit, Anglo/U.S./German relationship."[2] The negotiations that prevented NATO from unraveling were deeply upsetting for the other allies, who believed that de Gaulle's directory—with Bonn replacing Paris—had finally been established. Even more troubling, and only glimpsed at the time by the allies, was that the political and economic challenges of the offset crisis were harbingers of the internal challenges NATO would face for the rest of the Cold War.

De Gaulle Post–Missile Crisis

The Cuban Missile Crisis of 1962 was, according to European observers like Jean Monnet, a "turning point of history" and revealed American "military superiority."[3] Kennedy's response to the missiles in Cuba, and the apparent Soviet capitulation, revealed the massive disparities in power between the United States and the rest of the world, including its European allies. It was American supremacy, rather than polycentrism or the rise of a new Europe, that was the true shape of world affairs in the 1960s. Indeed, a few years after Cuba, the senior British diplomat Patrick Dean would look back on the period and write that only one moral might be drawn from the state of world affairs: that "the United States has so outdistanced its allies in power and resources . . . that all the rest of us including France have assumed the dimensions of pigmies in American calculation of true power relationships in the world."[4]

It was in this world of overwhelming American power that de Gaulle saw an opportunity. After Cuba, he explained to the British ambassador in Paris, Pierson Dixon, it was now clear that the Americans and "Russians" would not "attack the other," and "it did not seem to him that there was much danger of war."[5] He had told Chip Bohlen something similar enough that Bohlen concluded de Gaulle "tends to regard the Cold War as over."[6] He could now ignore the Cold War alliances and begin to build a new Europe with France at its center.[7]

De Gaulle would make much of the argument that France could not rely on the United States for its nuclear protection as his reason for withdrawing from NATO. But this was a clever ruse, leaving American diplomats complaining that it was not "possible for a woman positively to prove her virtue."[8] In fact, de Gaulle's policy of withdrawal from the alliance in the 1960s was premised not on a belief that France *could* not rely on the United States, but that war was so unlikely it *need* not. Even by April 1966, when the Quai d'Orsay scrambled to draft a paper providing some policy rationale for de Gaulle's decision to withdraw from NATO's integrated command, French officials argued that the Cold War had "reached climax at Cuba," and after 1962 the Soviets had "abandoned more and more any idea of a military clash with the West or of military blackmail."[9] As British officials recognized in 1964—too late for Macmillan's hopes—de Gaulle's assumption that "major war can be excluded" meant he was now "free to play politics without restrictions."[10]

British Decisions after the French Veto

When, in 1962, Macmillan had conceded that a tripartite deal would never materialize, he sought to persuade de Gaulle to allow British entry into the European Economic Community in exchange for bilateral Anglo-French defense arrangements, including nuclear cooperation.[11] This plan would bring France into the upper echelons of world power; the unspoken quid pro quo would be French acceptance of the British application to the EEC. Macmillan had become deeply convinced of the need for Britain to join Europe. If de Gaulle spurned the British application, Macmillan told advisers, Britain's response would be, "at least," to denounce the Brussels Treaty, thus destroying the legal basis for Britain's continental commitment to NATO, "and at the most extreme might involve reaching an understanding with the Soviet Union."[12] But when de Gaulle did veto Britain's application, Macmillan did nothing of the sort. Rather than isolate Britain, Macmillan told Kennedy it was de Gaulle who should be isolated.[13]

In early 1963, immediately after the veto, all British officials involved in formulating Britain's next moves believed that NATO held the answer for British policy problems. Consequently, NATO's preservation took on new importance in London. Macmillan and his private secretary, Philip de Zulueta, agreed that the UK should act to prevent de Gaulle from consolidating his plans for

Europe. But beyond this negative aim, Britain should also seek to "unite a wider Europe and to make her into a powerful and equal partner with the United States in the Atlantic Alliance." Britain needed now, more than ever, to demonstrate a British commitment to Europe in hopes of making another future bid for membership.[14]

The cabinet committee established to deal with the fallout from the veto also argued the main emphasis of British policy "should surely be here," in NATO.[15] Dixon, writing from Paris, agreed, believing that the British commitment to NATO would "symbolize the opening of a campaign in favour of the British approach to Europe." At NATO, Britain could maintain links with the Belgians, the Dutch, and especially the Germans—the "ones who really count."[16] No longer would British officials talk seriously of trading NATO in a bid to join Europe. Instead, NATO became an instrument for improving conditions for a future application to join the EEC. "The main effort to thwart General de Gaulle," explained Edward Heath, "must be made in NATO."[17] Here was the beginning of the Anglo-German rapprochement, what the CIA would later dub London's "sudden awareness" of the importance of the rest of Europe.[18]

De Gaulle's Attack on NATO

In the shadow of de Gaulle's veto, British officials began to brainstorm how NATO could help in the service of Britain's European goals. At the same time, however, France began to push NATO further away. In the spring of 1963, de Gaulle moved to disassociate the French fleet from NATO, as he had done with the Mediterranean fleet in 1959. During the earlier withdrawal, the European allies had acceded quietly to de Gaulle's decisions; now, the French permanent representative came "under heavy fire" from the Belgians, Dutch, and Germans. The other allies thought the French military explanations "specious" and worried what motives lay behind de Gaulle's maneuvers.[19] In early 1964, de Gaulle withdrew French naval officers from NATO's naval headquarters. The timing confused the allies, who could not tell whether this was merely to tidy up the fleet withdrawals or a sign of more to come. It was the latter.

Next, de Gaulle began to prohibit French officers seconded to NATO commands from participating in major exercises. Since these exercises tested how well commanders could receive political guidance in case of war, the French absence suggested the "beginning of the break up of integrated staffs."[20] These withdrawals were all carefully choreographed, accompanied by French officers making "violent little scenes in public."[21]

The French coupled their moves in NATO with a publicity campaign. French officials started telling their European colleagues and the press that de Gaulle had never received a reply to his 1958 memorandum. The Johnson administration declined to publish Eisenhower's correspondence that would have revealed the attention Eisenhower had given the issue. De Gaulle met with his European colleagues and harangued the Americans, claiming he was "violently opposed to the blatant American imperialism now rampant in the world." He told the Italians that he would "continue to 'attack' and to oppose the United States in Latin America, in Asia, and in Africa." He also fretted, aloud, that France's continued membership in NATO might draw France back into Vietnam, though of course he would have known from his own experience over Algeria that this was untrue. All of de Gaulle's efforts were connected to his plans for formal bilateral treaties, rather than an alliance en bloc; he told the Italians, for instance, he wished for a formal Italian-French treaty. When the Italians asked about the implications for NATO, de Gaulle replied: "NATO, blah, blah, blah . . ." and changed the subject.[22]

The British Connection

Harold Wilson's British Labour government that replaced the Conservatives in 1964 scrambled to resist de Gaulle's private and public campaigns against NATO. Some diplomats proposed waging a propaganda campaign against de Gaulle, but they canceled their plans when they realized they would easily play into French hands. Denis Healey, secretary of state for defense, at first took up combative language in public, branding France a "bad ally," before feeling obliged to withdraw his remarks.[23]

By the terms of the 1954 Brussels Treaty, Britain had agreed to maintain seventy-seven thousand troops on the continent. But by claiming economic hardship, London had gained the begrudged consent of the allies to reduce British obligations to fifty-five thousand troops, and it hoped to whittle down this number yet further. British officials knew that raising France's record as a NATO ally would highlight these British reductions, along with London's opposition to the MLF, the doing away with conscription, and disagreements with a number of American proposals for NATO-wide economic sanctions against the Soviet Union. One Foreign Office official did not even need to finish the phrase: "People in glass houses . . ."[24]

The British saw an opportunity to play up Britain's commitment to NATO—not to advertise Paris as a bad ally, but London as a good ally. The juxtaposition was increasingly beneficial to Britain, as the French warned they would soon "propose [the] abolition of NATO for which they would like to substitute loose alliances."[25] These warnings coincided with a separate battle, waged by de Gaulle in the European Economic Community, against plans for greater economic integration. Observers on both sides of the Atlantic worried de Gaulle was seeking to generate crises, in both NATO and the EEC, to force the European allies to accept his plans. John Tuthill, the American ambassador in Brussels, worried that de Gaulle would condition "Europeans, like Pavlov's dogs to follow his will," and that if the EEC fell apart, so would NATO.[26] The other five members of the Six shared Tuthill's fears, and they believed the corollary of Tuthill's prediction, too: if France withdrew from NATO, the EEC could not survive. All of a sudden, the Americans noticed, de Gaulle had put some "starch" in the back of the Five.[27] They too, would turn to NATO to save their European construction.

In June 1965, a number of permanent representatives to NATO—the American, Belgian, British, Dutch, and German ambassadors—met in private to hear a remarkable suggestion. André de Staercke, the Belgian representative and a close associate of Belgian foreign minister Spaak, urged the allies to "get together in secret to formulate contingency plans for facing up to the challenge from de Gaulle." The Europeans were worried that de Gaulle would soon begin to blackmail the European allies. According to Spaak, the "only effective means which the five would possess for calling the General's bluff would be to be able to show that Britain was ready 'to take France's place in the E.E.C.'" Henry Boon, the Dutch representative, agreed, and suggested that a renewed British commitment to joining the EEC would be a means "not only of frustrating General de Gaulle's destructive purposes towards Europe and NATO but also . . . of bringing Britain into the Common Market." Shuckburgh pointed out that the reality might be more complicated, but the conversation marked "quite a significant development."[28]

In London, senior Foreign Office officials saw "an obvious attraction in profiting by the upheaval caused by de Gaulle to re-establish our political position in Europe." It was not yet time, perhaps, to reapply to the Common Market, but Britain could bide its time and focus on NATO—the "defense field." Britain would become the "pivot around which the other European allies rally" in their opposition to de Gaulle, and "step in to take a lead in the rescue of NATO from the shambles which will occur" if de Gaulle withdraws from the alliance and forces NATO troops and institutions from France.[29]

The need for British patience was made starkly apparent as the Americans began to lose theirs. After French officials started hinting de Gaulle might withdraw from NATO, Johnson's secretary of state, Dean Rusk, lost his cool. He told allied officials that if de Gaulle wanted to leave NATO, the United States "too could develop alternative defence policies." British officials recorded that Rusk threatened "retargeting [Strategic Air Command] to cover Western Europe as well as the Satellites in the Soviet Union!"[30] This was a toxic argument. If the

United States were to keep it up, it would undo all the assurances about nuclear defense that lay at NATO's core. British officials worried that US officials were "falling into the trap that General de Gaulle has prepared for them."[31]

Rusk represented an emerging strain of thought in the Department of State that wished to force a confrontation with de Gaulle over NATO in a bid to have French voters turn him out.[32] The British and Europeans, however, wanted no such showdown. Instead, the British suggested the other allies "should go ahead with what was essentially a public relations exercise, as if we were sure that NATO would continue to exist."[33] Lyndon Johnson would ultimately agree and settle on this approach.

The British repeated their mantra and tried to persuade the State Department to maintain the "calm assumption that whatever France does, NATO will continue."[34] The State Department was anything but calm. Officials feared they could not sit back while "the Alliance is sliced up like salami." Dean Acheson, once again invited to take a lead role in providing policy recommendations to the president, planned an offense against de Gaulle. He wanted to strip France of the US security guarantee provided for in article 5 of the North Atlantic Treaty, even if de Gaulle did not renounce the alliance. Acheson, along with Ball and Rusk, saw this is as another way of uniting French voters against de Gaulle. Johnson, on advice of McGeorge Bundy, avoided making a decision.[35]

The one thing the advisers did agree on was the importance of the German position. Since at least 1964, the French had been conducting propaganda efforts out of their consulates in Germany, seeking to convince the Germans that the FRG was being treated as an American "satellite" and that Germany's proper place was beside France, rather than the unhealthy, Anglo-Saxon-dominated Atlantic Alliance.[36] Bundy worried that de Gaulle would try to black-mail the Germans, or offer them terms to resolve the EEC crisis, if Bonn agreed to "diminish" its relationship with NATO. The "best hope" to avoiding a total collapse in NATO, Bundy believed, was "to stiffen Erhard's spine" by engendering closer cooperation between Washington, London, and Bonn.[37] Like the Anglo-American relationship after Suez, the Americans were now planning to build an Anglo-German-American understanding at the heart of NATO "to which other NATO members could subscribe."[38]

France Exits and the British Step Up

On March 7, 1966, de Gaulle penned letters advising all the allied leaders that France would no longer "place her forces at the disposal of NATO."[39] France did not withdraw from the North Atlantic Treaty, but soldiers in France not under

French command would have to leave France. In the letter to Bonn, he explained that the French troops in Germany, currently there under NATO auspices, would remain under "residual occupation rights."[40] The State Department, especially Acheson, urged Johnson to withdraw the collective defense protections of the treaty and "fling down the gauntlet to de Gaulle."[41]

Acheson's letter raised hackles from officials in the NSC and Department of Defense, who thought the hard-line approach made little legal or military sense and was just "plain silly."[42] The other allies, too, wanted the Americans to do nothing "unnecessarily nasty to the French," in case the French retaliated against the EEC.[43] Francis Bator, the lead NSC staffer on the issue, advised Johnson that if the situation escalated, America might be "blamed by some Europeans for splitting Europe." Johnson ultimately accepted the advice of Bator and Robert Komer to write de Gaulle a softer letter with a "golden bridge" making clear France was welcome back in the integrated command at any time.[44]

Johnson later explained his method for handling de Gaulle with a baseball analogy: "I get out of the box when he starts winding up."[45] He avoided falling into the trap, as Rusk had nearly done, of a hysterical Franco-American showdown that would only have suited de Gaulle's hand in Europe and in France.

FIGURE 8.   German president Heinrich Lübke encourages Lyndon Johnson and Charles de Gaulle to shake hands. Johnson and de Gaulle were in Bonn for the funeral of former West German chancellor Konrad Adenauer. Bundesarchiv, B 145 Bild-F024624-0004 / Gräfingholt, Detlef/CC-BY-SA 3.0

Given his preoccupation with Vietnam and domestic politics, Johnson was wisely avoiding a showdown because there was no way to win, rather than thinking he was winning by avoiding a showdown.[46]

By stepping out of the batter's box, Johnson allowed the British to step up to the plate. The British cabinet was not happy with de Gaulle's decision, as making up for the French troop withdrawal would be both expensive and have "a disquieting increase in the relative importance and standing of Germany within the Alliance."[47] Wilson and his cabinet had, briefly, hoped to take advantage of the crisis to refashion the alliance on a "more economical basis"—that is, to achieve the further withdrawal of British Army of the Rhine (BAOR) troops from the continent.[48] But Healey warned Wilson that the British should not immediately consider major reductions of forces on the continent, for this would be a "body blow which might complete the work of destruction begun by de Gaulle."[49] Other officials warned, too, that Britain needed to "consider our attitude to NATO" carefully, for it would be interpreted by the Europeans "in close relation to our future attitude to the EEC."[50]

Instead of seeking to change NATO, British officials took charge in a bid to maintain the solidarity of the NATO allies. This was crucial, for there was "softness under the surface" of the fourteen other allies. The Benelux countries worried about the Common Market, Germany was concerned about its relations with France and East Germany, and the Canadians were focused on Quebec. But the British drafted a "Fourteen Power Declaration" of unity, and they convinced all the allies to agree to it, committing them to work together to maintain NATO's operations.[51]

The British declaration served as the rallying point for the tedious negotiations that resulted in the new committee structure allowing NATO's work to proceed. By the end of 1966, the NAC officially agreed to implement new "constitutional" arrangements: The fourteen would sit together as the Defense Planning Committee and discuss military issues, while the full fifteen members, with France, would sit as the NAC to discuss nonmilitary issues.[52] NATO's physical headquarters would leave France for Belgium: the North Atlantic Council and international staff would be reconstituted in Evere, on the outskirts of Brussels. The Belgians insisted that SHAPE, an obvious target in nuclear warfare, be located a significant distance from Brussels, and it was relocated from Rocquencourt to Casteau, near Mons, with a new highway built to link Brussels and Mons.[53]

Diplomacy and French Troops in Germany

The American Embassy in London reported their surprise, and that of the other allies, that the British were "so militant and so energetic about NATO at this time."[54] The Americans concluded that the British were "'stand-patters' par excellence so far as the Alliance is concerned—they do not want it to change."[55] But this analysis missed the mark. The British had been looking to modify NATO for years. They were still desperate to achieve some saving on defense expenditures, but they also recognized that Britain needed free access to European markets. Although the Wilson government had entered office in 1964 with few European sensibilities, a number of economic difficulties in 1965 conspired to revive British interest in the Common Market.[56]

The connection was apparent to the Europeans just as it was to the British. Indeed, Spaak and a number of European officials told the British that after de Gaulle's actions, "if the political will in Europe to have us in had not been very strong before, it certainly was now."[57] The foreign secretary and another member of Wilson's cabinet, George Thomson, both wished to use the crisis to press the Five to invite Britain to join the EEC. Wilson avoided making a direct link between the issues, but Britain's defense of NATO allowed London to play the role of good ally the Five wished to see.[58]

The Germans, for their part, also played the role of good ally. Even before de Gaulle's withdrawal, but after the Germans saw the writing on the wall, Secretary of State Carstens put down a record of sixty theses to guide German foreign policy. Carsten's conclusions on NATO in this Luther-like document are clear: "We have a great interest in the preservation of NATO in its present form— not only for safety but also for the sake of our German policy." As Germany served NATO, NATO—and especially the American commitment to Germans' security—served Germany. "This was the only basis for German policy."[59]

The Germans worked to reassure their allies that they would not follow France out of NATO. This was critical, in Bonn's eyes, both to protect the German position in Europe but also to reassure the Soviet Union that Bonn had no desire to constitute its own independent army or otherwise threaten the USSR.

When de Gaulle announced that France would withdraw from the military command, the Western European allies feared Germany might take advantage of de Gaulle's maneuver to free itself of its obligations. At NATO, when word of de Gaulle's decision was explained by the French representative, the Dutch, Danish, and Luxembourger representatives all argued that "their governments had only participated in Germany's entry into NATO on the basis of very carefully contributed commitments and self-denying declarations by Germany in Paris agreements of 1954." If the French action led the Germans to believe they were free of these commitments, there would be "deep and violent reactions in their countries."[60] Minor German diplomats fed these fears with "hipshooting reactions" and claims the French action "would free FRG from its post war limitations on freedom of action in the military field."[61]

But the ultimate test of German intentions in this case was their actions. The focus was on French forces that had been stationed in Germany, the Forces françaises en Allemagne (FFA). The FFA, including air force units and two divisions of ground troops, were assigned to NATO and were armed with American nuclear weapons. When de Gaulle declared that French troops would no longer be under NATO command, the United States withdrew their nuclear warheads. This rendered the French forces less military useful than they had been before, and their military value—even when nuclear-equipped—was a matter of debate. The FFA's withdrawal from NATO command would be a pain, but not an insurmountable military problem.[62] It was far more important as a litmus test of German policy under such circumstances.[63]

The Germans were extremely unhappy and uncomfortable, squeezed between NATO and Franco-German rapprochement. De Gaulle's policy of withdrawing from NATO and trying to maintain troops in Germany also threatened to undo Germany's security policies and ultimate hopes for reunification. Just as bad, de Gaulle had suggested he would use postwar occupation rights to justify a continued French presence in Germany—something clearly humiliating for Bonn.

Still, German officials took a long view of the situation. It was preferable for the Germans to have French troops, even token forces, in Germany. From a military point of view it was better than no troops at all. And some French troops were committed to Live Oak plans, which the Germans wished to remain multilateral as a symbol of the West's commitment to Berlin. Perhaps most important, French troops represented an "important symbol of Franco-German collaboration."[64]

De Gaulle issued an aide-mémoire to Bonn, and a series of minutes crisscrossed from Paris and back. But the German position, made clear by Schroeder in the Bundestag, was that "the agreement of 1954 which ended the occupation and permitted Germany to enter NATO constituted an indivisible whole." This agreement, on which the deployment of not only French but also British and American troops in Germany was based, was the basis of Germany's negotiating position with France. The effect was to avoid a Franco-German negotiation and instead represent it as one involving all the signatories of the 1954 agreements— a NATO-France negotiation.[65] In practical terms, the Germans could not have responded to a French bilateral treaty offer. The FRG had no military forces not committed to NATO, so they could not "make good their end of the alliance"; since NATO commanders effectively acted as Germany's high command, the Germans had no general staff to plan with the French.[66] The French challenge over FFA revealed that the 1954 agreements had worked. More important, Germany wanted them to work. Allied officials in Bonn could report that Germany "has no desire for [a] national army."[67]

The diplomacy regarding the FFA was coordinated in informal tripartite meetings in Bonn. Schroeder and Carstens started meeting with Frank Roberts and George McGhee, the British and American ambassadors. Schroeder explained the basic German approach: the "French departure from NATO meant that the fifteen must become fourteen" and that "the four became three," and the relationship among the three "remained as firm and strong as it had been between the four."[68]

The three allies, as they worked, were careful to keep the other NATO allies updated and passed them copies of their working papers and documents. Indeed, the German attitude to the entire episode was nothing if not careful. This was a well-practiced art for German diplomats in NATO, who, with only minor exceptions, did their utmost to appear committed to the alliance and the organization. As Carstens had noted before, Germany's security and broader foreign policies relied on NATO. But as much as German foreign policy experts looked to their relations with the West, they were also carefully attuned to noises from Moscow. German Soviet experts in the spring of 1966 understood that the Soviets, like almost all other observers, realized de Gaulle's moves gave Bonn choices: perhaps to raise the FRG's profile in NATO, but perhaps to break free of their obligations and limitations. The Germans were worried the Soviets would think Bonn was going to "withdraw German forces from NATO, increase their size, and become more active in the nuclear field."[69] The Germans had every interest to signal this was not their intention. Both for their security and to ensure others felt secure, Germany remained committed to the alliance so much so that Dean Acheson could report that the FRG "on the whole behaved extremely well in the last few weeks and had shown considerable good sense and moderation."[70]

The haggling with France continued, leading to a negotiation between NATO's SACEUR, Lyman Lemnitzer, and the French chief of staff, Charles Ailleret, that provided a satisfactory agreement for coordinating NATO and French troops and ensuring they had necessary access to tactical nuclear weapons.[71] But just as important, the FFA negotiations had demonstrated that the essential decisions for NATO's defense rested on tripartite lines, and that—if handled delicately and well—this was not intolerable to the other allies. But even the three did not operate in perfect synchronization. In the midst of the negotiations, the United States announced that it was withdrawing fifteen thousand specialists from American forces in Germany to help train more soldiers for Vietnam. And although the Americans eventually replaced the soldiers man for man, they were substituted with greener troops.[72] State Department officials regretted this decision, and the practice, as "badly handled," for it raised the prospect of further American unilateral withdrawals and Washington's growing prioritization of the war in Southeast

Asia over the defense of Europe.[73] In the months after de Gaulle's withdrawal from the NATO command, a British financial crisis and a German political crisis, combined with the possibility of further American troop reductions, threatened to undo the whole agreement that underpinned the stationing of British and American troops in Germany.

The "offset crisis," by challenging the very basis of the defense of Europe—the Anglo-American continental commitment—was a greater threat to NATO than de Gaulle's withdrawal.[74] Historians have hailed the trilateral negotiations that resolved the crisis as "an example of successful intra-Alliance crisis management."[75] Paradoxically, however, the negotiations that prevented NATO from unraveling were deeply upsetting for the other NATO allies, who believed that de Gaulle's directory—with Bonn standing in for Paris—had finally been established.[76]

The Origins of the Offset Crisis

In 1965 and early 1966, Britain's economic problems were acute enough to compel a search for savings. Michael Stewart, the British foreign secretary, explained to the Americans that the obvious place for Britain to save money was in Germany, but that the British saw a political point to keeping the troops there: they wanted a "link with the Common Market."[77] A British defense review ultimately concluded that Britain would maintain its forces in Germany as long as it could "find some further means of lightening" the balance-of-payments burden.[78]

The review, however, was too optimistic. British ministers took a harder and harder line as to what they required from the Germans to maintain the BAOR in Germany. Until 1954, British and American troops in Germany had been armies of occupation, and Bonn had paid their costs. After the 1954 agreements and Germany's accession to NATO, Washington and London paid, and Bonn offset some of the British and all of the American balance-of-payments costs by purchasing arms from both countries.

In Chancellor of the Exchequer James Callaghan's spring budget speech, he stated that the UK would now require Germany to pay a 100 percent offset—that is, to make arms purchases from Britain totaling the full amount of foreign exchange incurred by maintaining the BAOR. In July, Prime Minister Wilson upped the ante, insisting that Britain would withdraw troops from the continent to make up any gap between British costs and German purchases. This set the stage for an economic tug-of-war between London and Bonn, with NATO forces as the rope.

In July Britain faced another currency crisis, no less disastrous for being a regular occurrence in the postwar era. American officials, including Secretary of the Treasury Henry Fowler, worried that the Wilson government would cut "back on defense East of Suez *and* in Germany." British military presence in the East, like the enormous naval base in Singapore, allowed the United States to focus its efforts on Vietnam.

Just as important, the British presence "East of Suez" helped maintain the Johnson administration's argument that the Far East was an important geopolitical concern for the West. McNamara considered the British presence there "absolutely essential" and worried that "anything which will smell of a British pull out will fatally undermine our domestic base on Viet Nam." McNamara's preference was for the British to substantially cut back their troops in Europe and spend the money on Asia.[79] But the British, especially Healey, put the emphasis on maintaining British forces in Germany. Otherwise, the inroads made by the British performance as the good ally during the "French defection" would dissipate and thus "jeopardize support for UK European policy."[80]

Nonetheless, economic conditions in Britain increased public pressure for Her Majesty's government to reduce troops in Germany. The pressure gauge spiked in Washington, too. In August, Senator Mike Mansfield introduced a resolution calling for a reduction of US forces in Europe. Mansfield and other American senators, for a host of reasons, which included the balance-of-payments problems, the growing costs of the war in Vietnam, and the belief that the Europeans—especially de Gaulle—were not playing a full role in NATO, wished to reduce American deployments to Europe. The White House feared that Mansfield's resolution represented the opening wedge in a split between Europe and the United States. Any sign that America's partners would reduce their efforts in NATO—as the British were threatening—would drive this wedge deeper. The pressure from Mansfield continued throughout the year and picked up again in January 1967; Johnson recognized the difficulty of persuading Congress to support NATO if the Europeans were not seen to be doing their fair share.[81]

When the Germans learned the British would press hard for a full offset, they got their backs up. The German defense minister, Ulrich von Hassel, had no sympathy for London, especially after British politicians had benefited from the politically popular move to end conscription while Germany maintained compulsory service. Moreover, the Germans had their own troubles. There were still fourteen million West Germans displaced by the war, many of whom relied on government assistance. German social legislation linked pension payouts to cost-of-living increases, and there was nothing that could be done, so von Hassel claimed, to keep those costs down. As a result, the Germans refused to meet the British offset gap, especially not at the level of 100 percent. If the British could reduce the costs of their current troop deployments by a third, the Germans would pay for half; but the fewer British troops in Germany, the less Germany would pay.[82] The British wanted the Germans to purchase more arms—and increase their offset coverage—even if the BAOR was going to shrink somewhat. Possibilities of a straight Anglo-German agreement were clearly nil.

But the Germans were also unable to meet their offset agreements with the US. McNamara reported to Johnson that the Germans would maintain only an "austere" defense budget and would devote more expenditure to social welfare. This left a budget "totally inadequate" to pay for the qualitative improvements McNamara insisted were necessary to the German military. Nor would it be nearly enough money to make the purchases required to cover the offset costs for both Britain and the United States.[83]

This worried the Americans, who noted that the Germans were ignoring the connection between the British threats and possible ramifications for NATO. The fates of the three governments' economic and defense policies were so intertwined that rash action in one capital might collapse the alliance.[84]

Trilateral Talks

American officials urged the Germans to solve the offset problem on their own. Washington hoped, unrealistically, that Bonn would impose a new tax and use the income to buy more American arms. Johnson's advisers agreed that the president should give Erhard a "hard push on offset," with troop reductions as an implied threat. Some Americans warned that Erhard had little room to operate. German diplomats urged the Americans to stop "stop linking money and troops," fearing it would polarize German domestic politics.[85] McNamara, however, wanted Johnson to insist on the Germans meeting the total offset with weapons purchases in the US. This was so unlikely that many in the State Department assumed McNamara was setting the Germans up to fail so he could reduce the number of American troops in Europe.[86]

By the end of August, nobody thought Erhard could meet the offset, and Americans worried that the economic strain was giving "the impression that NATO is falling apart." Johnson's adviser Francis Bator thought it a "poor trade . . . to take serious risks with stability of German and alliance politics, and hence with our security position in Europe, in order to make marginal gains on our balance of payments." By the end of the crisis Bator had developed a strategy to gain important economic concessions from Germany. Still, he and Johnson believed it essential to avoid the appearance of "the financial tail wagging the security dog."[87]

American insistence achieved little in Bonn, and Erhard did not offer a plan to satisfy either Washington or London. The British were still signaling they would cut back some troops. The Americans sought to keep the British from going to the North Atlantic Council and winning agreement on a BAOR reduction, as they had done in the past. Such a withdrawal, the Americans worried, might trigger a "progressive unraveling of other NATO ready forces as Belgium and Holland follow the example of the British." Domestic pressure for Johnson to bring home American troops would spike. Officials who, during the MLF crisis, had argued that Germany would not seek nuclear weapons or an agreement with Moscow had rested their case on the strength of NATO. But if NATO were to unravel, the Germans would have a "far greater interest in national nuclear weapons to secure themselves" than before.[88]

There had been never-ending talk of crisis in NATO before. But the offset crisis raised the possibility that the leaders of NATO states would find the continental commitment unserviceable in light of their domestic politics. NSC staffer Edward Hamilton wrote a memorandum about this "ripeness for disintegration." He could picture, in the future—perhaps only two years hence—the United States and Europe politically and economically isolated from each other, Britain weak and bankrupt, and the Germans "dangerously unsettled, with a strong anti-American flavor." The North Atlantic Treaty might remain in effect, the North Atlantic Council might continue to meet, but the "de facto collapse of NATO is not at all inconceivable."[89] Bator, too, warned Johnson that taking a hard line with Erhard could lead, in only a few years, to a "disintegration of our postwar security arrangements in Europe."[90]

Bator and Hamilton both believed the solution to the economic and troop problem in Europe had to be achieved by the three powers working together.[91] A trilateral negotiation would have the advantage of "fuzzing up and rendering more palatable" any reductions that had to be made, while—critically—wrapping the reductions in the robe of consensus and allowing each capital to point to multilateral agreement. Johnson, Wilson, and Erhard could argue that the other allies were doing their part and that they, in turn, should reciprocate; the political, as well as the economic, costs of NATO could be spread among the allies.[92]

Johnson agreed with his advisers and sent letters to Wilson and Erhard warning of the potential "unraveling in NATO" and the need for tripartite agreement.[93] British diplomats and officials, who had initially wanted American support in their negotiations with Bonn, were now wary. Because the British had only 50 percent of their foreign exchange costs covered by German purchases, and the Americans had bargained for 100 percent, London feared any tripartite deal would leave peanuts for the UK. Still, the British worried that reducing British troops would be disastrous for British policy. The British might lose their vaunted position in the NATO command structure, which mattered for prestige but was also considered a critical element for containing Germany.[94]

The three parties agreed to talks in principle, but the Germans and Americans wished to delay until Erhard visited Washington in October. British officials accepted the delay but warned that negotiations of some sort needed to get under way quickly to give the prime minister a credible excuse in Parliament to prevent an immediate announcement of troop withdrawals.[95] The "clock," warned the British, "is ticking."[96]

When Erhard arrived in Washington in October, State Department officials warned Johnson the meeting might determine the "political future" of not only Erhard but also "that of German-American relations and NATO itself."[97] That future did not look bright. The Americans knew, through intelligence sources, that Erhard would reject demands for future offsets. But they were surprised when Erhard also reneged on the current German agreements. The FRG could not meet its 1965 or 1966 year promises to place $1.35 billion in military orders, to be paid by the end of 1967. Erhard wanted to stretch out those payments. What would happen after the current agreement expired at the end of June 30, 1967, was anyone's guess.[98]

Ambassador McGhee warned that Erhard's inability to pay was not a bluff but the product of a genuine political bind. Somehow, the United States and the Germans had to find an agreement whereby US combat forces would not leave Europe in significant numbers. Otherwise, McGhee provided a list of fourteen negative domino effects, including the unraveling of NATO and the disintegration of American influence in Europe and a return to isolationism. "History would record it as the ebb point—the beginning of an American withdrawal from Europe."[99]

Although the Americans were frustrated with Erhard, they looked for ways to prop him up politically. Johnson would offer assurances, never made to Germans before, that he would not fire nuclear weapons located in Germany without German consent. He would agree to enhance NATO's nuclear consultative mechanisms, including, if need be, a new tripartite group. But on the issue that mattered the most—offset—the Americans maintained their hard line that the shortfall must be met, in full, by weapons purchases. Johnson took the McNamara line, refusing to allow Germany to provide its offset in other ways, for instance by buying US bonds.[100]

About the only positive result from Erhard's trip was agreement to trilateral meetings. The Johnson-Erhard communiqué proclaimed a "searching reappraisal to be undertaken by US, UK and FRG of the threat, force levels, burden sharing, and financial problems results from troop deployment in FRG."[101] Johnson wrote to Wilson explaining that these trilaterals could "help us hold off the pressures on each of us . . . to do things which would badly damage NATO and the Western position in Europe." The three powers would put NATO "on a more sustainable basis."[102]

The US Reexamines Its Commitment

The task of the trilateral negotiations, according to Walt Rostow, was no less than to give "the Alliance a new foundation for the next decade."[103] The three allies would together study and agree on questions about the Soviet threat, the strategy to deter it, how to share the burden, and how to alleviate pressures on the allies' balance of payments. The three powers would then take their report to NATO and get approval from the allies.

To the other NATO allies, this plan smacked of de Gaulle's directorate. Manlio Brosio, NATO secretary-general, was shocked "the responsibilities of NATO . . . would now be subject of a tripartite reappraisal outside the NATO framework."[104] While Rostow might have thought the United States was laying the foundation, others thought the tripartite efforts signaled "rather bleak" prospects for NATO, and was perhaps the alliance's "valedictory" effort or its "requiem."[105] The British, eager to get some satisfaction on offset but also not wishing to offend the other members of the EEC, sought to appear like good allies and finish the trilateral talks before the December ministerial.[106]

Johnson chose John J. McCloy, the "chairman" of America's fabled "wise men," a financier who had served as the high commissioner in postwar Germany and an influential adviser, as the lead American negotiator for the trilateral talks. He proved to be an excellent choice when he brought Germany back to the negotiating table after a political crisis in Bonn. But his appointment was controversial; both McNamara and the British would try to have him removed because they feared he would be too soft on the Germans.[107]

McCloy's first task was to determine just what America's continental commitment should be. He did this by interviewing key administration officials. Since McCloy had strong opinions about the importance of Germany to the United States and the importance of NATO to the West, he was not likely to recommend doing away with the alliance or the organization. Still, his preparations for the trilaterals were one of the few concerted efforts to think through the American commitment to the North Atlantic Treaty in nearly two decades.

Llewellyn "Tommy" Thompson, one of America's foremost Sovietologists, told McCloy that if the Soviets "ever had a chance safely to destroy us, I have little doubt but that they would do so." Still, ever since the Cuban Missile Crisis, the Soviets had opted for defense rather than offense in their military strategy, and would probably like to reduce their own troop strength in Europe. Thus the Soviet threat "is not such as to require large American forces in Europe from a strictly military point of view." In fact, Thompson thought, the Soviets might respond to a small American withdrawal with a troop drawdown of their own. Nonetheless, the United States must take into account two intertwined risks: The troop reductions would have a psychological impact on the Europeans, who might weaken their own commitments. This would then tempt the Soviets "into some dangerous venture."[108]

Chairman of the Joint Chiefs of Staff Earle Wheeler offered McCloy a similar diagnosis. Wheeler argued that without NATO, Europe would be "too tempting" for the Soviets. But containing Germany was just as important. A Germany not tied to the West, Wheeler warned, might attach itself to the Soviet Union, creating a duo that could overwhelm the West. Or, if Germany were to set out on its own, it would be "putting us back where we were in 1913 and 1939." Wheeler urged against significant withdrawals that would undermine NATO, since the West must have some way of deterring the Soviets and containing Germany. If NATO, as a means of dual containment, were to disappear, the United States would, "like Voltaire's God immediately have to invent another."[109]

McCloy opened the first meeting on October 18 declaring that the three allies would "consult fully" with their NATO partners before taking any decisions that might affect the alliance. But contradictorily, McCloy said also that the "trilateral discussion" was "intended to center the attention of NATO on the present military and political situation." "NATO," in McCloy's usage, really meant the three. And the trilateral powers formed working groups on "Warsaw Pact Capabilities," "NATO Capabilities," and the "BOP [balance-of-payment] Impact of Stationing Troops," all areas that had ostensibly been NATO's domain in the past.[110] After the meeting, McCloy would visit the North Atlantic Council to try to exorcise "the ghost of tripartite directorate," but this did little to calm concerns of other allies that a new tripartite group had replaced NATO as the nerve center of Western defense.[111]

Karl Carstens, the German negotiator, left the meeting knowing the Germans were in a difficult situation. He and McCloy had agreed that the issue of NATO's future and the trilateral negotiations were primarily political, rather than military. If there were withdrawals, and "the European people's confidence in the alliance's protection should be shaken, there would be severe repercussions." Failure to support the US would only bolster those, like Senator Mansfield, calling for reductions. Carstens urged Erhard to do what he could to offset the American presence in Europe, but he all but ignored the British dimension.[112]

At the next meetings, on November 9 and 10, the three disagreed whether NATO's force posture should be based on an assessment of the Warsaw Pact's intentions or, instead, its capabilities. George Thomson, who represented the British in the trilaterals, argued that the Soviets had fundamentally changed their purposes and objectives, and so NATO could safely reduce its armaments. The Germans thought otherwise, arguing that weakening NATO would be fatal. Anticipating the arguments made by Richard Nixon and Henry Kissinger in a similar crisis in 1973, Carstens warned that the "NATO countries would hardly be willing and able to step up their forces in the short term." Once NATO began to dismantle its military strength, it would be slow and difficult to rebuild. McCloy supported the Germans, arguing that any change in Soviet policy was only the result of NATO's military strength.[113]

Despite these disagreements, the three allies agreed to a six-point minute that laid out a fundamental basis for NATO troop strength. They agreed that NATO needed to maintain both nuclear and conventional forces, including tactical nuclear weapons to deter Soviet aggression, but that strategic nuclear forces constituted the "backbone" of NATO's military capabilities. On foreign exchange issues, however, they remained in deep disagreement on even the basic math of how much the troop deployments cost.[114]

The Collapse of Erhard's Government

After the first trilateral meeting, political crisis struck in Bonn. Erhard's governing coalition broke apart. Carstens told McCloy that the Germans could not now agree to a package by the December NATO ministerial, and probably not even in January, since it was uncertain what new coalition would emerge in Bonn. The clock in London was still ticking, however, and without some assistance, Wilson's position would fall apart, and the pressure to unilaterally withdraw troops would be unbearable.

McCloy sought to shore up support for Wilson's domestic political position. He told Johnson that the British presence in Germany was the "symbol and rallying point around which we can hope to rebuild a genuinely collective security system," and it was essential for Britain to be a part of any burden-sharing agreement.[115] If the Americans could help unhook Wilson from his deadline for troop announcements, the German government could have time to form and make critical decisions. The White House staff drafted a letter for Johnson to send to Wilson: "Would it help if I placed in the United Kingdom in the near future £35 million in orders?"[116] It would and did; Wilson committed to a delay of six months.

The Americans had bought time but no solution. Because of the collapse of the German government, there was little hope of making any progress at a third trilateral meeting on November 25. In fact, the three powers were able to reach further agreement on military strategy, and to agree to a number of common appreciations of Soviet intentions that stressed the unlikelihood of general war but the need to maintain allied military power to prevent Soviet blackmail.[117]

There remained no agreement on the more critical issue of foreign exchange. McCloy, trying to get the others to think about alternative solutions, suggested a new style of offset that went beyond arms purchase to include central bank cooperation. Already, McCloy and the Americans were trying to find a way to adjust the "over-all international financial system" to help maintain American troops in Germany.[118] These were the seeds of the solution to the trilateral negotiations, but agreement was a long way off.

It was impossible to move forward while Erhard struggled to rebuild his coalition. On December 1, he resigned. McCloy's responsibility was now to persuade the new German government to continue the talks. In mid-December he met with the new chancellor, Kurt Georg Kiesinger. Kiesinger was now the CDU/CSU leader, and he had built a "grand coalition" with the Social Democratic Party (SPD). McCloy assured Kiesinger that Johnson was committed to the defense of Europe, but the chancellor could promise nothing so early in his tenure.[119]

Franz Josef Strauss, Kiesinger's new finance minister (and formerly Adenauer's minister of defense), resented the American pressure for offset. He claimed that all he heard from the United States was, "Unless we get our offsets, we will go home and sacrifice you to the Russians."[120] This stood in for only part of the growing bitterness of some of Kiesinger's cabinet toward the United States. Strauss especially (but also the new chancellor) was growing more and more worried that the American effort to achieve a nuclear nonproliferation treaty was "a sign of a new pattern of world organization being worked out secretly together—and imposed—by the two super powers."[121]

While the Germans were frustrated with the Americans, their position toward the British only hardened. Foreign Office officials worried that if the new German cabinet took an explicit decision that they would pay no offset whatsoever, the British cabinet would have no reason to wait for the conclusion of trilateral talks before deciding on withdrawals.[122]

The British Foreign Office knew that if Britain made a full withdrawal, it would "reverse [British] policy since [Ernest] Bevin" and "destroy NATO and thus prejudice the defence of Western Europe and the British Isles." A partial withdraw would lead to the "same consequences, but in lesser measure." In various reports and briefings, the British officials warned that full withdrawal would be "fatal for our move to join the E.E.C.," and that even partial withdrawal would "antagonize . . . E.E.C. members."[123]

The Germans, under pressure from British and American diplomats in Bonn, were persuaded not to take a precipitate decision, and the new government in Bonn agreed it would continue the trilateral talks begun by its predecessor. The trilateral talks were out of limbo but seemed nowhere close to producing agreement.

Showdown in Washington

Erhard's fall in late 1966 had put off a major showdown between McCloy and McNamara over US policy in Europe and the best way to maintain NATO in the long run. But the showdown came early in the next year. McCloy wanted the US to get what it could from the Germans in terms of offset but "eat the difference" and not make significant troops cuts. McNamara thought that the current level of American deployment to Europe was expensive and unnecessary. He worried that any gap in offset would be unacceptable to Congress, and so recommended "preventive surgery" of cutting more than a division from Europe to put the American continental commitment on a more sustainable basis.[124]

In January McNamara made his move. He drafted a lengthy memorandum for the president and circulated it in Washington. It contained a detailed case why the exact number of NATO troops in Europe would have no significant effect on the Soviet strategic calculus. There were now enough NATO troops, armed with enough tactical nuclear weapons and backed up by hardened and dispersed American strategic nuclear weapons, that Europe's security was assured. In fact, fewer troops would do just fine. Containment of the Soviet Union, McNamara argued, had not only succeeded but had encouraged "certain organic changes" in the Soviet Union and among its allies. What looked like growing independence of the Eastern European countries and the Sino-Soviet split left the Soviet leadership "beset with complications which did not exist when NATO was created, nor even 5 years ago." Containment may still be necessary, but the Soviets could now be contained with far fewer US troops.

McNamara's solution was to "dual-base" a large number of fighter aircraft and ground troops. One-quarter of the aircraft and one-third of the ground forces would always be stationed in Europe, with individual units rotating between Europe and the United States. Once a year, the full wings and divisions would be on the continent for training as a unit and to keep "highly visible NATO strings." In a crisis or war, the full complements could be dispatched across the Atlantic.[125]

Earle Wheeler, the chairman of the Joint Chiefs, rejected McNamara's analysis, arguing that cuts of such "magnitude . . . would impair the security of the Western World." The general, along with McCloy and officials in the State Department, thought the Europeans would sense the crumbling of the American security guarantee and be susceptible to Soviet blackmail. McCloy warned Johnson the plan would undermine German confidence in the United States, and he vigorously opposed McNamara's proposal.[126]

McNamara and McCloy's positions were poles apart. McNamara believed that the dual basing could be done "without traumatic psychological impact in Germany, in NATO or in the United States."[127] McCloy believed that the dramatic action would cause the allies—and no doubt the Germans in particular—to hedge their bets and "cast worried glances in the direction of the Soviet Union." NSC officials thought McCloy's warning too dire, even "nuts!" To them, the far more realistic scenario, though just as fatal to NATO, would see Bonn turn away from Washington and exclusively toward Paris.[128]

The president's advisers met to make their case to Johnson. Francis Bator prepared a scorecard of the key players' positions, lining up McNamara against the JCS and McCloy, with Rusk somewhere in the middle worrying about Atlantic politics. Bator agreed with Rusk that the real issue was not the military argument—McNamara's logic was unimpeachable. Bator did not necessarily subscribe to McCloy's "Wagnerian German nightmare," for "1967 is not 1914 or 1933." He feared, instead, a repeat of the Skybolt crisis, with the Americans making a unilateral decision that led to political crises for the allies and bad blood in the alliance. Bator favored a middle course of dual-basing one division, rather than two.[129]

It was clear to Bator that 100 percent offset would not be forthcoming from the Germans, and that linking troop reductions with payments from Germany would backfire badly. What the United States required was cooperation with the allies on new financial steps and perhaps some "sort of rules" that would get the "world on to a dollar standard" and limit American vulnerability to a continued balance-of-payments deficit. Perhaps, in the solution to the NATO crisis, the US could become "banker to the world."[130]

Johnson himself believed he would eventually have to cut some forces and provide "dollar outlays" to keep the British from cutting theirs. Cognizant of Bator's allusion to Skybolt and accusations that the United States was "dominating" Europe by making unilateral decisions, while trying to protect his position in Congress, Johnson planned to "move slowly" until he was clear as to what the British and Germans would do.[131]

Johnson started to build support in Washington for rotating one division in and out of Europe. He told the congressional leadership at a breakfast that

American "troops are in Europe to protect vital national interests. They are not there to do anybody a favor." Johnson defended NATO and the maintenance of American troops in Europe, citing the need not only to balance the Soviets but also to protect Europe from blackmail and ensure the "wrong political tendencies"—German neutralism, revanchism, or nationalism—did not grow. The military and political security situation in Europe was such, he said, that he would not have considered reducing the American troop strength if it were not for congressional pressure.

Still, it was up to the Germans to decide what levels of procurement they wished to undertake, and the British and Americans "should deal with the remaining balance of payments consequences . . . by cooperation in the management of monetary reserves." What the United States and its allies were doing, said Johnson, was moving away from the "old rigid offset concept" that had covered the costs of British and American commitments to NATO. The new plan moved toward "close and permanent cooperation on the monetary field" that would protect the American gold stock. This would be a "stabilizing policy" and "very much in [American] long run interests," for in the last decade other countries had converted their reserve dollars to gold at an increasing rate. But rather than telling London and Bonn what the United States would do, Johnson would avoid making a final decision and instead propose that the US would dual base one of its divisions and one air wing.[132]

McCloy thought Johnson was making a mistake and told him. NATO needed a "clear note on the trumpet" from the United States, not an invitation to collaborate on a multilateral solution that looked like American indecision. He wanted permission from Johnson to tell the Germans and the British that Johnson preferred "not to do any cutting" if a solution could be worked out. Johnson hit back, blaming McCloy, McNamara, and Rusk for not doing their "job with Congress" and leaving Johnson exposed. Although he would prefer the one-division rotation, he feared that pressure from Congress for more significant cuts would make that impossible. "Ultimately," Johnson told McCloy, "we will be very lucky if we do not have to cut 2 divisions."

Johnson told McCloy to tell the allies that "we've got to get together and see what we can do," meaning that the problem could be solved only by a three-way agreement. A unilateral or bilateral fix would not work. If the Germans could come up with something to help the British, then maybe the United States "could hold the line" and help keep the British and American forces assigned to NATO in Europe. But the American position, and Johnson's position with Congress, were ultimately dependent on whether and how the Germans and British helped solve the matter of offset. "The third brother," Johnson explained in his down-home way, "just can't hold it together by himself."[133] McCloy, Johnson said, needed to find out what the other brothers would put "in the family pot." But before the meeting wrapped up, Walt Rostow mentioned something that had gone unsaid by McCloy or Johnson, but that was clearly the basis of Johnson's—and Bator's—thinking. The "sleeper" issue in the negotiations, said Rostow, was that the United States might get a "good money bargain with the Germans" that would "help stabilize the monetary situation and provide protection for the dollar."[134]

These ongoing discussions in Washington had delayed the tripartite talks. The British sensed that the Americans would try to use the talks to make international monetary arrangements that suited the United States. This interested them very little, for they desperately needed German purchases—the "rigid old offset" system Johnson wanted to do away with. And in early March, Kiesinger was not fully convinced that the British commitment to stationing troops in Germany as part of a NATO force was necessary for Germany's security or keeping the American contribution to NATO on the continent. Neither London nor Bonn was looking toward a multilateral solution.

Balancing Bonds and Troop Withdrawals

McCloy met with both Wilson and Kiesinger, both of whom maintained a hard line. Wilson said he would not make any concessions to Germany. Moreover, after having "stuck our neck out when France had weakened the Alliance," Britain was now being treated unfairly. Britain had saved NATO then; now Britain needed help. Kiesinger worried that no matter what he did, the British would reduce their troops, and so would the Americans.[135]

The political cover provided by NATO, however, helped break the logjam. It was clear to all the allies that Britain's financial situation would compel some level of British reduction. In a private conversation with McCloy, Thomson, the British envoy, suggested a means of framing this reduction that would take the pressure off the other allies. He suggested that the British could delay their cuts and then present them as part of a trilaterally agreed reorganization. This would avoid it seeming as if the British reduction was the direct result of offset negotiations. But, Thomson warned, if there was no German offer on offset at all, withdrawals would be "massive," perhaps more than half the BAOR.[136]

McCloy then met with the Germans, who still claimed they could "tolerate any Anglo-German failure" to come to an agreement. But, McCloy insisted, the Americans could not. McCloy told them it was "utterly unrealistic" to think that the Americans could maintain their position in Europe if the British were withdrawing on a massive scale. If the Germans gave no quarter to the British, the British withdrawal "would therefore be followed by an American reaction that would gravely endanger the German security position." The Germans, McCloy made clear, had to find a way to support the British, or the Americans would leave. Still, the Germans were reluctant to agree to any formal offset agreement.[137]

The solution to the problem of British reductions had been to wrap up the troop cuts in multilateral agreement; the Americans believed the same formula could work for the balance-of-payments problems. The American idea, Walt Rostow told the British, was a "global solution" that "secured German participation in a solution of world liquidity problems."[138] There would be three stages to the plan: In the immediate short term, there must be found some way of relieving the balance-of-payments pressure. The Americans would allow the Germans to neutralize some of the foreign exchange costs by buying bonds. This would not help the British, however, who needed cash purchases. But perhaps the German relief at not having to meet the full American offset with arms purchases would free up Bonn's money for London. In the medium term, the United States would build a "club of gold-abstainers" who would promise not to trade the dollars they held for gold. In the long term, the allies could work out a means of "underpinning the reserve currencies." The British would be bailed out with a massive multibillion dollar loan from the Americans, Germans, and others that would allow London to pay off its debts and get its house in order.[139]

This plan would bring the Americans great gains. The British privately railed against these "grandiose American monetary ideas," believing that they represented, like the MLF, more "American grand schemes to solve all known problems."[140] They did not like lumping together "defence and world liquidity," and they knew that the Americans were using the crisis to try to solve "a number of wide financial problems."[141] Ultimately they would go along because they needed to find some solution to their foreign exchange costs before things got "completely out of control."[142]

The Germans agreed that the Bundesbank would buy enough bonds to neutralize more than half the American foreign exchange costs of keeping troops in Germany. Critically, they promised not to convert dollars to gold. This essentially put them on a dollar standard. The Germans agreed to work to get other Europeans to agree (though it would be an obvious nonstarter in Paris), and the United States lobbied the Canadians and Japanese to join the club of abstainers. In Washington, the implications not only for defense but for government spending were enormous. Bator told Johnson that now "we won't need to worry much about our deficit, as long as it does not get completely out of hand."[143]

Now with all the parties committed to finding a multilateral solution, the British and Germans shared their tentative "magic numbers"—that is, the minimum the British required in order to avoid massive cuts, and the maximum the Germans could come up with in offset. The difference was small, but there was a difference. As one State Department official remarked, "we are, almost literally, within $40 million of preventing really serious damage to NATO."[144] Bator warned the president that the gap, if left unfilled, would lead to a "UK-FRG collision and massive cuts in the BAOR." Johnson would then face pressure to make unilateral withdrawals, and this would begin the "unraveling process." Most important, perhaps, the "chances of getting German help on international money will nosedive."[145] Johnson told his advisers to find a solution; perhaps the Germans and Americans could split the difference. He declared "he would not see NATO go down over $40 million."[146]

Kiesinger, ultimately, was convinced of the need for a solution and carried his cabinet on a commitment to buy bonds, abstain from buying gold for dollars, and provide some offset for Britain. At the final trilateral meeting in late March, the Germans came up with more money for Britain than expected, and the Americans made new military orders to keep British foreign exchange costs very low. The British agreed to withdraw only one brigade—about five thousand men—from the continent. But they surprised their partners by springing a plan to redeploy RAF forces, too. Still, the British agreed to avoid any major reduction or to seek, once again, to alter their commitments under the 1954 agreement.[147]

Johnson was thus able to hold back demands for larger reductions, and the US and Germans entered an agreed minute that the US would rotate one division and some fighter jets—far fewer than McNamara had hoped.[148] Publicly, the Americans presented their plan as one resting on "military logic," rather than financial arguments. They claimed it was a multilaterally agreed decision, rather than an American "cut."[149] On Capitol Hill, Mansfield called the plan "an encouraging start" and "enough for the time being."[150]

"All in all," Bator told Johnson, "we have avoided what could have become a major crisis in our Atlantic relations." Bator pushed hard to convert the solution into a permanent structure. He prioritized the next steps: first was the German pledge not to trade dollars for gold, second was the German purchase of American bonds, and third was the need to avoid "large-scale, helter-skelter" troop cuts.[151] The Americans, who had begun the trilaterals to build a new foundation for the alliance, had used the discussions of NATO troop strength and expenditures to achieve their own national financial and economic goals.

The trilateral meetings—despite the economic benefits for the United States—had preserved the Anglo-American commitment upon which NATO rested. But the three had kept everything secret from the other NATO allies during the critical decision-making period in March for fear that leaks or debates in the North Atlantic Council might scuttle agreement. But leaks came anyway, likely from the Department of Defense. The aggrieved allies first learned from the

New York Times and the *New York Herald Tribune* that the British and Americans had decided on their force adjustment plans—affecting the very basis of NATO's defense—long ahead of any NATO-wide meeting. If the NATO allies did not make allied strategy and force plans together, what was NATO for?[152]

The Gaullist challenge and the offset crisis offered closely related and nearly simultaneous challenges to NATO. De Gaulle's crisis was more easily resolved because it revolved around national positions and national interests. But the roots of the offset crisis were far more complex, for they lay largely in domestic political problems: pressure from the Senate in the United States to reduce expenditures and balance-of-payment costs in Europe, difficult choices in the United Kingdom over how to justify defense costs in an era of financial strain, and political pressure on German politicians to spend more on social services and avoid defense spending increases. This coincidence of events challenged the domestic consensus in Washington that the United States should maintain a large continental commitment to Europe indefinitely. Eisenhower, as early as 1955, had sensed the domestic consensus supporting NATO had begun to fray; it was now beginning to break down in all the allied countries. For the rest of the Cold War, the allies would be unable to maintain constant defense spending, and instead seek ways to avoid drastic cutbacks that might instigate a chain reaction and the collapse of the alliance.

7

AN ALLIANCE FOR PEACE

In 1966, the former secretary-general Paul-Henri Spaak proclaimed NATO was "one of the few organizations which has ever achieved complete success. It had never had to resort to military force to protect the North Atlantic area."[1] And yet NATO's success was paradoxical. Adam Yarmolinsky of the Department of Defense articulated the assumption held by so many officials in this period: "The problems of the NATO Alliance are not the result of failure but success."[2] The more secure was Western Europe, the less secure was NATO. It was conceivable that NATO could put itself out of business.

Toward the end of the decade, hopes for greater relaxation of tensions between the East and the West—détente—appeared to be both the fruits of NATO's success and the seeds of its demise. Both the crises begun in 1966—de Gaulle's withdrawal from the integrated military command and the threat of the collapse of the Anglo-American continental commitment—were symptoms of this larger paradox. Robert Komer pointed to the absurdity of the situation when he asked: "Is the price of re-uniting NATO re-uniting the Sino-Soviet bloc?"[3] Komer was not suggesting this policy. None would have wished to piece back together a Communist monolith. In the crises of the 1960s, the NATO allies had continually determined that NATO was essential not only because of the latent threat of Soviet military or political pressure, but as an organization that allowed Germany to play a major role in world affairs without needing to develop its own general staff, nuclear weapons, or capability for independent military action. Although all the NATO allies, even the Germans, believed it to be true, they also believed that public claims that NATO contained Germany might, in turn, undo German support for NATO.

In the late 1960s, neither the Cold War nor the threat of Germany once more going berserk in Europe offered politicians a viable argument for the continued support of NATO. Nor were the Americans likely to trumpet too loudly that in turn for their continued support of the continental commitment, Washington had extracted from its allies a temporary dollar standard.

Instead, the allies set out to provide a new face for NATO in a world where the alliance looked obsolete. The allies hoped to link NATO to the emerging fads of the late 1960s: improving "East-West relations" and the spirit of détente. The primary effort to give NATO a new public face was a chaotic study on "the future tasks of the alliance" proposed by Belgian minister of foreign affairs Pierre Harmel. Informally, the study was known as the "Harmel Exercise" and the final paper christened the "Harmel Report." Scholars have held it up as an important event that transformed NATO from a purely defensive organization into one that justified its existence on the two pillars of defending the West and encouraging détente with the East. The Harmel Exercise was in itself a mess, regretted by most participants, and nearly jettisoned several times. Its primary purpose, in which it narrowly succeeded, was to give allied politicians a new argument for supporting NATO and the defense spending required of allies even when hopes of détente made this spending seem frivolous.[4]

Questioning NATO's Role

For many foreign policy observers, the idea that NATO could improve East-West relations was counterintuitive. NATO, according to the famed American diplomat and scholar George Kennan, was "a device for avoiding political compromise rather than for facilitating it."[5] And Kennan's thinking had its official champions. In 1959, Robert Komer circulated what he called a "variant" of an earlier plan, drafted by Kennan, for America's disengagement from its "outworn European policy." Komer wanted the United States to negotiate with the Soviet Union to withdraw troops from Germany. The withdrawal would "create a fluid situation in which the life expectancy of the GDR would increasingly decline."[6]

A few years later, in 1963, Arthur Schlesinger Jr. warned Kennedy that the Soviets were more likely to negotiate a European settlement and German reunification "with a non-NATO Western Europe than with NATO."[7] The same year, the deputy director of intelligence at the CIA, Ray Cline, drafted a document for the Director of Central Intelligence John McCone envisioning a diplomatic settlement in Europe. The "McCone Plan," foreshadowing de Gaulle's ideas, argued that the United States would be better off abandoning NATO and relying on "conventional bilateral diplomacy to keep Germany, France and the United Kingdom individually balanced against one another and collectively balanced against the USSR."[8]

Komer's, Schlesinger's, and Cline's plans all offer tantalizing glimpses of how American presidents, if holding greater confidence in the possibilities for negotiation with the Soviet Union, might have chosen a more dynamic policy in Europe. They also all suggest that any such negotiation over Europe would require the end of NATO. The United States, and all its NATO allies—even de Gaulle—were unwilling to risk the stability of Europe without the stabilizing influence of the North Atlantic Treaty.

But by the mid-1960s the NATO allies could no longer ignore that significant and growing exchanges across the Iron Curtain had created a new dynamic between East and West. From 1953 to 1959, trade between NATO countries and the Soviet bloc had more than doubled, representing a higher rate of trade expansion than either inter-European trade or world trade. Throughout the 1960s, the increase continued at "phenomenal" rates.[9]

To try to gauge the importance of these exchanges, the NATO allies formed an ad hoc working group to study East-West trade. The allies in the group espoused a range of contradictory opinions over the implications of trade. They worried that in the short term, a concerted Soviet economic offensive would allow Moscow to exploit differences between the Western allies, or between the West and other allies like Japan. NATO economic analysts pointed out that the West's sales of machinery and technical knowhow to the East was benefiting the economies of the Warsaw Pact countries more than the West. Some allies were comfortable with this, while others were not. The Americans were the most militant in ensuring NATO allies not send the Soviet bloc items that might be put to military use and "bolster up its aggressivity."[10]

But all the NATO allies agreed that in the long term, trade with the Soviet Union was desirable. US officials also argued that improved economic relations with the Soviet bloc would "help to stimulate pressure for change within the Communist system, and thus to promote evolutionary tendencies."[11] While the Americans still hoped they could use trade as a tool in their dealings with the USSR, they believed the NATO allies could "seek to establish meaningful communications with the Communist regimes, and thereby hope to influence their long term orientation." This would be only "a long term change," and there was "no reason to be sanguine over the possibilities." Moscow would be clever enough to prevent any bloc country from developing a political vulnerability by trading too much with the West. But the allies all hoped to encourage a "tendency for the political cohesion of the Bloc to diminish" and ultimately its fragmentation.[12]

The British, for their part, did not think of trade as a tap that could be turned off and on. London always prioritized trade over Cold War politics and export controls, and this led to rows over exports to Communist countries in the 1960s. The British argued that since Stalin's death, the Soviet Union had shifted more to a consumerist society than its leaders intended, and would continue to shift, for "the appetite grows with eating: the Soviet and satellite peoples will want the rise in living standard to continue and will certainly resist, as far as they can, any abrupt reversal." This would put the onus on Soviet leaders to adapt to their society's wishes, and avoid taking risks or increasing tensions that might result in war. It was surely right, the British delegation told its NATO allies, to "foster such tendencies," and to develop exchanges that would "expose the whole range of those who influence policy in each country to the contagion of Western thought and experience." That the West would need more and more markets and supplies for its own economic growth was certainly part of the British argument.[13]

In trying to make sense of the debates at NATO, the Germans noted two broad arguments for economic trade, regarding which the British and Americans offered the most outspoken positions: First that economic relations offered an "opportunity for exerting political influence and for a gradual easing of the conflict between east and west." The other view was that economic relations were simply a "political weapon" that the East used better than the West.[14]

Because of the bitterness caused by efforts to coordinate an economic embargo during the Berlin crisis, the roller coaster ride of the British Common Market application, and the alliance's focus on defense issues and particularly the MLF, the North Atlantic Council and the allies took few further steps on the matter of East-West trade. Instead, NATO recommended that a group of experts produce a study of economic measures NATO might take to "loosen the ties between the USSR and the various satellites," and there was a conference of national officials to discuss such steps. The experts did a better job of highlighting differences between allies than finding agreement. Some allies wanted to coordinate and target national economic policies to try to pick off Communist countries "who showed signs of emancipating themselves from the Soviet bloc."[15] Others, however, were reluctant to envisage politically motivated trade discrimination and preferred to encourage trade for trade's sake.[16]

Ultimately, the private economies of the NATO countries made coordination nearly impossible. Some specific financial exchanges, like British credits to the East Germans, complicated the FRG's efforts to apply carrots and sticks to the East German regime. The countries of the Warsaw Pact were moving to greater participation in international organizations and global economics in the 1960s, applying to the General Agreement on Tariffs and Trade (GATT) and the IMF, and making use of the UN Economic Commission for Europe (ECE). NATO did not, could not, and would not work to manage East-West trade, even if trade offered the most likely means of inserting information and ideas behind the Iron Curtain.[17]

With no agreement in NATO, the allies took their own steps to build relations with Eastern Europe, both by encouraging trade and by reaching out for small but symbolic bilateral diplomatic contacts. In 1964, the French foreign minister visited several Warsaw Pact countries, the British invited Alexei Kosygin and later Andrei Gromyko to visit London, Turkey received a Soviet parliamentary delegation, and the West Germans continued their policy of resuming contacts with the states of Eastern Europe. The Canadian government undertook a concerted effort to develop trade and exchanges with the Soviet Union and its satellites, both to increase sales of wheat and to try to plant the seeds of change in the Warsaw Pact. Johnson, in his State of the Union address, called for an exchange of visits between the US and the USSR. In December, at the NATO ministerial, many of the allied foreign ministers celebrated these growing contacts with Eastern Europe and called on each other to encourage détente between East and West.

This proliferation of contact, however, had worrying implications for an organization whose public raison d'être was the defense of Western Europe from a manipulative Moscow. Brosio warned the allies that as contacts with the Soviet Union increased, the NATO allies "should seek the widest possible consensus as to the objectives to be achieved, the practical possibilities of achieving them, and the methods by which they are to be pursued." It was "essential," he argued, that the NATO allies avoid competing with each other, for the Soviets might "play one of us off against the others."[18]

Instrument of Détente

As the improvised and unorganized contacts across the Iron Curtain multiplied, the allies considered how they could use NATO in this new environment. To a surprising degree, the thoughts of officials in capitals beyond Paris merged with General de Gaulle's ideas about détente. The French leader's plan for rapprochement with the Soviets represented, at its core, a belief that the Soviet Union was simply Russia by another name, a state in a world of states that could be bargained with like any other.

While the British had put on a public show of saving NATO from France, Harold Wilson, like Macmillan before him, found much to agree with in de Gaulle's judgment on international politics. Even if the French president was uncooperative and his methods potentially dangerous, "not all of his ideas are wrong." In fact, several were sound: Wilson agreed with de Gaulle that there would be no war in Europe, and as a result, the "NATO powers" ought to seriously try to promote détente. Since there "is really no danger from the East," there was little if any need for "continuing with the weight of armament on both sides of the Iron Curtain."[19] Wilson put these ideas in a note to his foreign secretary, and eventually in a letter to Lyndon Johnson. The crux of his thinking lay in his question: "What have we armed for, if not to parley?"[20]

American diplomats reported similar opinions throughout the continent. Ridgway Knight, the American ambassador in Belgium, claimed that the Belgians desired "détente and a workable long-term *modus vivendi* with the Soviets." The Europeans believed their safety was achieved, and there was widespread consensus the Soviets "no longer threaten Europe."[21]

The leaders of Europe no longer viewed the Cold War as an ideological battle. But this did not mean the end of power politics in Europe. Even if they wished to pay less for defense, the Europeans still wished to maintain the NATO alliance and the American commitment to Europe. They debated just how many troops NATO required, but they always agreed that some forces were necessary for fostering a détente. And the congenital European worry of a resurgent Germany never abated. Neither, therefore, did support for an integrated military system. For Wilson, NATO was necessary as the "only tolerable context for West German defence."[22] The British remained convinced in 1966 that the "forces of German irredentism" needed containing.[23]

The Cold War had provided the easy rhetoric for NATO. Balance-of-power politics and the threat of allies turning again into enemies were much more complicated public relations issues. But after de Gaulle's attack on NATO, American diplomats kept hearing of a "widespread feeling that if NATO is not to disintegrate, it must find some rationale beyond military deterrence." American officials started to consider recasting NATO as an instrument for encouraging peace rather than preventing war. So what was NATO for? The "inevitable" answer, Americans officials decided, was that NATO would be a tool for attaining a formal European settlement.[24]

Dean Acheson, prompted by de Gaulle's withdrawal to brand NATO with a "new purpose," argued that the alliance should find "a resolution of the major European problem left from the last war—the separation from Western Europe and the continued division of Germany."[25] State Department officials sought to put Acheson's ideas into policy terms, suggesting NATO do more to encourage trade and cultural relations with the East and thus lessen distrust, to focus on arms control measures, and to encourage contacts between West and East Germany. Immediately, though, these officials also formed a lengthy list of impediments to NATO's taking any central role. German issues were the domain of the four powers (the US, USSR, UK, and France), not NATO. France now opposed

any political role for NATO whatsoever, making any unanimous policy or statement moot. The German Hallstein doctrine, in which the FRG refused to recognize any country that recognized East Germany, was a major impediment to
any NATO country's efforts toward the East. And the Americans had for years
encouraged systems to prevent trade with Eastern Europe, such as the Coordinating Committee for Multilateral Export Controls (COCOM).[26]

Still, the Americans sensed that NATO needed a new identity to survive
détente. They continued to search for what Knight, in Belgium, called a "political reason for NATO." By this, he meant one that could be easily marshaled in
domestic political debates. Americans like Knight did not want to transform
NATO for the sake of it, but only to insulate it from change, and to help "retain
the essential military strength which the organization provides."[27] Harlan Cleveland, the American permanent representative to NATO, provided the negative
corollary to Knight's prognostication. He warned that the United States had to
prevent the emerging "impulse to seek a broader detente" from getting "out of
hand." Too much focus on improving exchanges with the Soviet Union could
leave individual NATO allies exposed but also totally undermine the rationale
for maintaining military strength. "The problem," he warned, "must somehow
be contained by defining it and coming to grips with it."[28]

Détente, the Americans worried, might run away from the United States.
Zbigniew Brzezinski, a scholar of Eastern European affairs on the State Department's Policy Planning Council, argued that the United States needed to control
the pace of détente and promote the "evolution of the Communist camp" rather
than succumb to any pressures to do away with both NATO and the Warsaw Pact.
NATO, in Brzezinski's eyes at least, came to be seen as an instrument for winning
the peace that would follow the Cold War. The partnership between the United
States and Europe, embodied in NATO, was the essential precondition "for building world order on the basis of closer collaboration among the more developed
nations, perhaps including eventually some of the Communist states."[29]

American officials could only dream of a NATO that outlasted the Warsaw
Pact if NATO kept its political and military cohesion. In the 1970s, American
officials would argue in detail how a weakened NATO would lead to Soviet political blackmail in Europe; in the late 1960s, they were content to simply argue that
NATO's strength was the source of Soviet quiescence. US diplomats believed that
covering NATO in the language of détente would provide a sugar coating for the
increasingly bitter pill of paying for NATO's military structure, and that it was
essential for the US to prove it took détente seriously.

This thinking motivated Johnson's advisers to press him to make a major public pronouncement on America's policy toward Europe. His staff crafted a speech
intended to foster American goals of improving US-USSR relations, while also

playing catch-up with the European allies who were already far ahead in improving their contacts with Eastern Europe. On October 7, 1966, Johnson declared that it was time "to make Europe whole again." His speech laid out an argument for overcoming the "bitter hostility" between the opposing alliances in Europe. But he also made a strong case for maintaining and strengthening NATO, albeit a "modernize[d]" NATO which would consult on East-West relations.[30]

A month after Johnson's speech, the FRG's new foreign minister, Willy Brandt, told his colleagues at the NATO ministerial that his government would "not be bound by the rigid theology of the Adenauer period" on relations with Eastern Europe. This removed one of the main barriers to East-West exchanges.[31] Kiesinger's "grand coalition," even before Brandt's accession to the chancellorship in 1969, had opened new possibilities for East-West exchange. But it was not universally celebrated. Brandt's ideas were "exhilarating to some and disquieting to others." The perennial worry that Germany would shift into neutralism or perhaps into alignment with Moscow gave weight to the American argument that détente was dangerous and needed coordination.[32]

Domestic Origins of the Harmel Report

It was an attractive sound bite to argue that the NATO allies would consult each other on the complex range of East-West relations. But through the rest of 1966, the United States did little more than rely on slogans like Johnson's "building bridges." Harlan Cleveland, writing from NATO, warned that the United States could no longer "afford to stick to generalities" when talking about these relationships. American officials needed to pause and get an "intellectual grip" on what a broad approach to détente would mean. Détente, and relations with Eastern Europe, was a "dangerous business," and Cleveland wanted a careful analysis done of what NATO or the NATO allies could do before developing a new "pack of initiatives."[33]

Before a thorough and searching study of a NATO strategy for East-West relations could be undertaken, however, domestic political events intervened to force the allies' hand. While many of the NATO capitals had been thinking of how best to adjust NATO to changes in the Cold War, the Belgian minister of foreign affairs, Pierre Harmel, put the issue squarely before the North Atlantic Council. The NATO foreign ministers agreed "to study the future tasks which face the Alliance, and its procedures for fulfilling them, in order to strengthen the Alliance as a factor for a durable peace."[34]

That the exercise came from Belgium, the new home of NATO headquarters after its eviction from Paris, was not a coincidence. The resolution was a creature of Harmel's own private office and rested on his government's domestic political needs to make the relocation, and continued Belgian defense spending, more palatable to an electorate that saw NATO as "an organization of the past."[35]

There was little enthusiasm from any of the allies for the Harmel study, and they begrudged its necessity. Few wanted to generate any more animosity with Paris. The British wanted any study of NATO to avoid discussing economic issues, for doing so might confuse their negotiations with Western Europe, while the Americans initially refused to discuss the "German question"—on which any discussion of détente and the new realities of Europe obviously hinged. Neither the Germans nor the Americans wanted to discuss military matters, especially while they were in the final stages of the trilateral talks. Not much was left for discussion. After the NAC adopted the Harmel Resolution, the other allies found it depressing that the Belgians wanted the other allies to do the hard work of giving the proposal substance. All the allies knew was that Harmel hoped to see NATO "increasingly assume a political character and become '*une alliance pour la paix*.'"[36]

Still, many of the allied governments shared the Belgian government's political needs. What the Americans complained were "fuzzy, but nonetheless real" desires to "reexamine and reformulate Alliance goals" were in fact quite explicit on the continent.[37] The Italian Socialist Unified Party had pledged its support to NATO, but only on the condition there was an "evolution of the alliance." A failure to effectively redefine NATO would be a big boost to the Italian Communist Party.[38] The Norwegians expected a major debate on NATO in their legislature, the Storting, in the upcoming year, and it was imperative that the government be able to explain "that the Alliance and détente were not contradictory."[39] The Danes, the Dutch, the Canadians, the Italians, and the Norwegians all claimed, like the Belgians, that they needed a "more active and political" component to NATO to help maintain NATO's "defence machinery."[40] The Americans also had their political needs. They saw a review of NATO as a possible weapon with which to "combat the ever-present pressure of isolationism," as exemplified by Senator Mike Mansfield's calls for troop reductions.[41]

While in some cases the allies fretted over specific domestic political debates, there was a broader fear that NATO would lose its appeal as young Europeans who did "not remember why we got into an Atlantic Alliance to begin with" reached political maturity.[42] It was necessary to convince a voting public that otherwise might not "automatically accept that [NATO] should continue indefinitely after 1969."[43] NATO's future—and, insisted the generation that had fought in the Second World War, peace in Europe—rested on the allies convincing their citizens "that NATO can play a constructive role in East/West relations if the détente develops."[44]

There was a broad enough consensus that the Harmel Exercise was necessary—that NATO needed a new image acceptable to the voting public—for the study to go forward. Just what, precisely, the Harmel Exercise would accomplish, and how, were secondary. The permanent representatives, jealous of ceding national prerogatives to an international organization, moved quickly to ensure that national delegations and not the NATO staff controlled the study.[45] The allies agreed, after much haggling, that an ad hoc group of national officials organized into an overarching "special group" would oversee the work of four working groups or subgroups. Rapporteurs were assigned to the subgroups, and they would write a report to the special group of their subgroups' discussions. The special group would draw on these reports to write the final Harmel Report.

East-West relations, the prospects for détente, and a possible European settlement were the responsibility of subgroup 1. Since any European settlement would revolve around Germany, the allies agreed it was necessary to have a German play a leading role. Still, "no one was willing to leave it to the Germans alone," according to Walt Rostow, so the group had both a German and a British rapporteur. Subgroup 2, led by Paul-Henri Spaak, dealt with interallied relations, especially those between North America and Europe. Foy Kohler, a foreign service officer who served as US ambassador in Moscow during the Cuban Missile Crisis and had much experience dealing with the NATO allies, was the rapporteur for subgroup 3 on security and defense policy. Subgroup 4, on problems outside the North Atlantic area, was a hot potato that ultimately fell in the lap of a Dutch professor named Patijhn.[46]

The results of subgroups 2 and 4 were insignificant. The allies created subgroup 2 to discuss European-American relations with the expectation Britain would soon join the Common Market and that transatlantic relations would undergo fundamental change. De Gaulle's May 1967 veto ended this prospect. Spaak led the subgroup with considerable gusto but also his traditional controversy, and his papers had to be rewritten and were essentially written off.[47]

Subgroup 4 had offered hope to Americans who saw it as "part of the continuing process of re-engaging Western Europe's interest and sense of responsibility on a world-wide basis." They hoped that current consultations and Harmel "will help get some motion on concerting policies for the Mediterranean and the Middle East. Next year we might be able to direct Allied interest to more distant geographical areas such as China."[48] Canada and Italy both backed out of the rapporteur job. All the allies could read between the lines. The Canadians, for example, when interviewed by NATO officials as part of the working group's research, "were prodigal with examples of American invitations to consult which were, they said, in fact invitations to align along the American position."[49] In the shadow of Vietnam, the idea was dead on arrival.

A Report Meant to Keep Allies in Step

The real substance of the Harmel Exercise was in subgroups 1 and 3, which considered, respectively, East-West relations and defense policy. Kohler, who chaired subgroup 3, and Adam Watson, the British co-rapporteur of subgroup 1, cooperated as they produced their reports. At the outset, Kohler told Watson that while there was no "Webster definition" of détente, he hoped the Harmel Exercise would help the allies come to some consensus on what Soviet objectives were in pressing détente and what Western attitudes should be.[50]

Finding common ground was challenging. There was no agreement between NATO allies, not even between officials in national capitals, on what détente was or whether it existed at all. One NATO official tried to catalog the conundrums: If indeed the Soviet threat had diminished, as so many believed, what was the cause? Were the Soviets less powerful now? Or were they simply counterbalanced by force? If so, did NATO itself provide a counterbalance, or were the Soviets simply deterred by American nuclear power? Was Moscow reticent because of the Sino-Soviet rift, or because the cohesion of the Warsaw Pact was less than previously? Or had the Soviets themselves "radically changed their minds"?[51] The responses to these questions could have dramatically different consequences for NATO by influencing whether it needed to maintain its troop strength, reduce troops, or even continue to exist.

The questionnaire that Watson distributed to the members of his group posed some of the choices: "Is *détente* an end in itself? Or is it rather to be seen as a means to an end, the end being a European settlement and disarmament?"[52] In the working group, discussion turned toward the philosophical. Helmut Sonnenfeldt, an American representative on Watson's subgroup, argued that it was "not possible to define détente in real life" because everyone had his own definition.[53]

Although there was no official agreement on détente's meaning, a consensus emerged that the purpose of détente—and by extension the emerging purpose of NATO—was to achieve a European settlement. This had been the major thrust of Johnson's October 1966 speech, and American officials like Eugene Rostow continued to argue that "beyond deterrence and détente, the objective of the Alliance is to create conditions in which the division in Europe could be healed."[54] Brosio and the secretary-general's staff also used this language that Johnson had employed in calculated response to what Americans thought Europeans wanted. Brosio started referring to the "principal task of the Alliance" as "achiev[ing] a stable settlement in Europe."[55]

This notion, however, received little support from the American officials and diplomats, especially Kohler, who actually shaped the Harmel Exercise. They no doubt agreed with their president that relaxing East-West tensions was good for the United States, if handled carefully. But they were not optimistic. At the spring 1967 meeting of American chiefs of mission in Europe, the Sovietologist Tommy Thompson "stated flatly that detente doesn't exist," and none of his colleagues disagreed.[56]

Kohler himself thought Moscow was using détente to further Soviet interests, hoping to relax "tensions selectively, to weaken the cohesion of the Alliance, divide the states of Western Europe, and in particular, to isolate the Federal Republic and open differences between Western Europe and the US." Moscow's long-term objective was to "reduce US influence in Western Europe and eventually remove the US presence from the continent" by making NATO "no longer relevant."[57] He could point to continued improvements in Soviet weaponry, especially missiles, as evidence of their true intentions.

Kohler worked throughout the Harmel Exercise to emphasize the need for "defence and solidarity" and to play down "freewheeling bilateralism."[58] Kohler's final subgroup report argued that NATO members' security "rests on two pillars": first, the "maintenance of adequate military strength and political solidarity to deter aggression and other forms of pressure," and second, "realistic measures to reduce tensions and the risk of conflict, including arms control and disarmament measures."[59] The special group gave the concept of two pillars a prominent place in the final Harmel Report. But there should be no assumption of equality or equivalence between the pillars in the minds of allied officials. Détente was always, and would only be, a possibility derived from a continued and consistent maintenance of NATO's military strength.[60]

The Americans had effectively done their job in using the Harmel Exercise to warn their allies of the risks of détente. They seemed to have convinced Brosio of the harm in trying to change NATO too much in response to hopes that Soviet interest in exerting influence on the continent had ended. Indeed, by spring 1967 Brosio feared that efforts to adapt NATO might "weaken the Alliance and perhaps disintegrate it altogether." He started bombarding the subgroups with papers and oral advice stressing "the Soviet political threat."[61]

The British, for their part, disagreed with the United States on the security situation. They continued to believe, as Thomson argued during the trilaterals (and as had McNamara), that the security situation had changed significantly as a result of changes in Soviet thinking. Still, the Foreign Office thought it "impossible to state the political purpose of NATO . . . related to the *détente* without at the same time restating the military purpose of it which made the *détente* possible."[62] Whether because of US urging or their own analysis, the European allies largely agreed that whatever they said publicly about NATO's new role, NATO's military structure remained important and necessary. "Western Europe and its institutions," reported one of the NATO international staffers, "will survive as long as the Soviets tolerate it." They tolerated Western Europe now because of the presence of Americans troops and American nuclear weapons. "Therefore, NATO commitments must continue."[63]

Still, Kohler's attention to arms control and disarmament was of consequence. Kohler argued that NATO should be expanded to include a permanent arms control and disarmament committee. Kohler and State Department officials were opposed to "any reductions of forces by anyone, including the United States, in Europe." Although the trilateral exercise had prevented any unilateral withdrawals in 1967, the Americans wished to establish a more enduring process for managing, and ideally preventing, any troop reductions unmatched by the East. A committee on arms control and disarmament, however, would provide assurances to the Americans that they could help control reductions, even while NATO publicly appeared to be an institution with a new goal of achieving mutual force reductions with the Warsaw Pact. This modest idea to expand the NATO machine was considered the most constructive aspect of the whole Harmel Report.[64]

Before the four subgroup reports could be synthesized to produce the official Harmel Report, the exercise reached its own state of crisis. The allies complained about the chaos of the subgroups and drafting process, and it was unclear whether the allies could produce a valuable final product. Important officials involved in the project, like Bob Bowie, Zbigniew Brzezinski, and John Barnes of the Foreign Office, all thought it would have been better had the Harmel initiative not begun at all.[65]

Throughout the study, French officials had let the "wheels" of the Harmel Exercise turn, "always, however, holding a spanner poised for dropping between them."[66] As the rapporteurs presented their papers, de Gaulle dropped the wrench. The French claimed great offense in these efforts to charge NATO with responsibility for political or diplomatic affairs. Nearly a decade after his revolutionary memorandum, de Gaulle had completely reversed his stance: NATO was only a military alliance and had no responsibility for coordinating anything but the defense of Europe. Couve spoke "violently" to Brosio to this effect. Because the French were upset, the Germans were ready to throw the entire project overboard rather than open another rift with France. The British, anxious to protect their application to the Common Market, wished to avoid any major battle with

Paris. To keep the peace, they were willing to jettison the "expendable" reports of subgroups 2 and 4, which had particularly offended France.[67]

Still, the domestic political needs that necessitated the study kept it going. The allies agreed the "Harmel Exercise could not just terminate in empty space," or NATO's public image would be even worse off.[68] The Americans were the least deterred by French objections and supported the study once it got started. They worried that if the French scuttled the Harmel Report, it would strengthen those in Congress calling for the return of American troops from the continent. The allies were keen to have a final report before the December 1967 ministerial meeting, one that they could agree upon with great fanfare. They also needed something that the French could agree to. The allies kept redrafting the final report—an amalgam of watered-down rapporteurs' reports—under the looming pressure of what verged on the "almost complete failure of [the] Harmel exercise as a public presentation of future tasks of [the] alliance."[69]

Delegations admitted that the final report was "somewhat indigestible" for the public and journalists, but it was trotted out at the December ministerial. The allies were content that the public document, which claimed NATO rested on two pillars—deterrence and détente—portrayed the alliance as "forward looking and actively seeking a political settlement in Europe."[70]

The study of East-West relations was very confusing for the East. One Soviet diplomat told an NSC staffer that he was "genuinely puzzled as to why such apparent effort could yield so innocuous a result."[71] Anatoly Dobrynin, the Soviet ambassador in Washington, asked Walt Rostow whether the report was "an operational decision or a statement of intent? Are we expected to respond now?"[72] Like so much of the NATO machine built up in the 1950s and 1960s, the Harmel Report had been about relations between allies, not policies toward enemies.

Soviet Intervention in Czechoslovakia

NATO had established a new Situation Center at its headquarters in Belgium, to monitor crises and ensure allied preparedness. In the middle of the night between August 20 and 21, 1968, the Situation Center was quiet. At 2:09 a.m. the Associated Press put out a "flash" report on its wire service announcing that Warsaw Pact tanks were rolling into Prague. The Situation Center remained quiet. The one teleprinter was out of order. Although several national capitals were aware of the invasion, they did not inform anyone at NATO. At 3:15 a.m., the duty officer at SHAPE, eighty-five kilometers away, called his colleagues at the Situation Center. Only then did the Situation Center rouse NATO's senior officials. The officials did not arrive at the center until 4:15 a.m., and the NATO delegations were not advised of the conflict until 5:00 that morning.[73]

NATO's Situation Center was set up to receive information from SHAPE but also from national ministries. It was to collate this information and distribute it to all the national delegations, allied capitals, and major NATO commanders. But the allies had not alerted NATO when they learned of the invasion; the national intelligence authorities on which NATO relied for its intelligence had not passed on word; and NATO's radar network had failed to spot Soviet aircraft entering Czechoslovakia. For the first twelve hours of the crisis, NATO headquarters "functioned almost entirely on press reports."[74]

NATO officials did have warning that the Soviets were preparing some sort of response to the Czechoslovak dissidents. As early as April 1968, SHAPE had started including reports on Czechoslovakia in its weekly intelligence report. In May, NATO's Situation Center started issuing "special bulletins." But there was "no single assessment" that had predicted an invasion, and "NATO had no tactical warning whatever" of the invasion.[75] Instead, like the night three Red Army divisions had moved around Berlin to cover the building of the Berlin Wall, NATO had proved unable to recognize Warsaw Pact military actions in the heart of Europe.

The Prague Coup of 1948 was one of the main catalysts for forming the alliance in the first place; twenty years later, Soviet actions in Prague and Czechoslovakia persuaded the allies to ignore the provisions in the treaty allowing them to leave the alliance after 1969. While the allies worked hard to maintain détente despite Soviet actions, the invasion suggested it was imprudent to guess at Soviet intentions; the Military Committee urged the allies to realize that NATO's plans "must consider the enemy's capabilities for military courses of action rather than an estimate of his possible intentions."[76] As Rusk told the cabinet in Washington, the Soviet decision to take military action "indicates that the Soviets are either changing their basic attitudes or are nervous and fearful and therefore dangerous."[77]

In a sense, then, the West was back to where it was at the start of the Cold War: containing the Soviet Union and waiting for it to rot from the inside out. NATO remained essential to contain the Soviets, to contain the Germans, and—now that the collapse of the Soviet empire was at least conceivable—to control the dissolution of the Warsaw Pact. But there was one difference. The NATO allies' discussions of NATO's future after Czechoslovakia did not hearken to the old tropes of an Atlantic mystique. Gone were the references to community, values, culture, and heritage; no longer was it simply assumed that the NATO allies operated together because they were bound exclusively by intangibles. They no longer argued that the values they celebrated were inherent only to North Americans and Western Europeans; not when Czechoslovaks were revolting. They knew that NATO was necessary to maintain the Pax Atlantica, and that they would benefit if this order was maintained and expanded. Once again, the NATO allies considered how best to adapt NATO to meet changes in the world and at home, especially the need for Europe both to have a greater voice and carry more of the burden in the alliance. NATO's post-Czechoslovakia diplomacy was, like past diplomacy at NATO, hard-nosed and based on national interests. Now the allies did not pretend it was anything else.

Adding Stability to NATO's Tasks

The increase of Warsaw Pact troops in Czechoslovakia was problematic from a strictly military point of view, for it moved more troops closer to NATO and shortened the warning time available in case of mobilization against the West. The allies did not believe the Warsaw Pact would attack NATO directly, but they envisioned a number of scenarios that could lead to war. Belgian general Baron Charles de Cumont, chair of the NATO Military Committee, had worried that units—perhaps even whole divisions—of Czechoslovak troops might retreat or be forced across their borders into Bavaria or Austria. It was unclear how NATO would react, who would manage the refugees, and who would disarm these soldiers, who, after all, belonged to the Warsaw Pact. The Department of State sent out a "flash" cable to the NATO mission and all NATO capitals to ensure American forces and its allies avoided any border incident that might open a new conflict.[78]

If the Soviets took further steps to crush dissidents in Eastern Europe in an effort to "nail down the status quo," warned John Leddy of the State Department, there was a possibility of greater violence. General de Cumont told the council the Soviets could move again, and it was especially "disquieting . . . that the Russians had now tasted blood." There were rumors the Soviets might move next on Romania.[79] A move against Romania, either by invasion, Warsaw Pact maneuvers meant to bring Romania to heel, or perhaps a coup d'état against Nicolae Ceaușescu, might touch off a frontier incident between Romania and Hungary. It might also be preparation for a move against Tito. If so, American officials expected the United States would "engage in military support operations for Yugoslavia."[80] Maybe the Soviets would move on Austria. Or Finland. Or Berlin. Or perhaps the East Germans would rise up again, creating a humanitarian catastrophe, refugees, and great confusion. For the rest of the Cold War, the Czechoslovak invasion would worry allied officials as a possible model for the expansion of Soviet control beyond the Warsaw Pact.[81]

After 1968, the allies could no longer ignore violence in Europe, even if it was not directed at NATO. As John Leddy put it, "aggression anywhere in Europe is of concern to NATO."[82] The prospects for violence in Eastern Europe were increasing and might "spill-over" into the NATO area.[83] The pressure for liberalization created a situation now "more precarious than it had been during the days of Stalin." The NATO allies, even French officials who had been sanguine about prospects for peace in Europe, worried about the "dangers of explosion."[84]

Czechoslovakia convinced the NATO allies that the Soviet Union's empire had started to fall apart. The chairman of NATO's committee of political advisers wrote that the "gap between rulers and ruled in the Eastern Europe satellites" was now widened to the point where "more people than ever will be watching for the day of change," not only in the satellites, but "in the Soviet Zone and elsewhere."[85] Of course, the willingness of the Soviets to use military force to maintain their empire would likely cause dissidents to act more cautiously. But dissent would build. The invasion of Czechoslovakia would embitter Czechs and Slovaks, certainly. But Hungarians, Poles, and East Germans would not forgive their own leaders for partaking in the invasion. British and French officials expected that after 1968, "the Soviet Union and the Socialist system generally in Eastern Europe would almost certainly be subjected to violent upheavals."[86] The possibility—perhaps unannounced, but likely violent—of the collapse of the Soviet satellite system gave sharp meaning to American arguments of 1967 that NATO was necessary not only for the Cold War but for its aftermath, too.

Of course the Cold War did not end in 1968, or quickly after. In fact, those who had hoped in 1967 that a European settlement could be arrived at quickly had their hopes dashed, and there was much backtracking. French officials, like Jacques Andréani, head of Eastern European affairs at the Quai d'Orsay, admitted to his British colleague that "the French had been wrong about their assessment of Soviet intentions." All around Europe, officials like Andréani were coming to "a darker and more pessimistic view."[87] Although de Gaulle still wished to carry on with his policy of détente, even he conceded publicly that the USSR had "not separated itself from the policy of blocs," a separation essential to his vision of Europe without NATO.[88] The allies did not expect the collapse of the Warsaw Pact or the Soviet system of control to be imminent. But when it did come, and they believed it would, the results might well be violent and dangerous for all of Western Europe. In either scenario, there would be no easy and "agreed solution of European problems." Accordingly, the British Foreign Office assessed that "NATO should expect a long future."[89]

The Politics of the Post-Czechoslovakia Buildup

Immediately after the invasion, Kiesinger called on his fellow leaders to hold a NATO summit meeting to demonstrate cohesion. Of all the allies, officials in

Bonn were most concerned by the actions in Czechoslovakia, for it put Soviet troops on the Bavarian border and alarming images of Soviet tanks in Prague, not so very far from the FRG, on German televisions. American officials believed Kiesinger's call reflected a broader "European opinion" that had "moved sharply in the direction of traditional US policy goals of promoting the integration of Europe and the strengthening of NATO."[90]

American officials recognized the invasion could be much more powerful than Washington's exhortations for Europeans to improve their conventional forces. It was the "Russians," in Czechoslovakia, who "stopped the rot and underlined the fact that NATO must be preserved."[91] The Soviet actions ended, for the time being, the drawdown of NATO defense budgets. The Belgians and Canadians had been moving toward unilateral force reductions, but these were put off in light of the crisis. The Americans wanted the Europeans to do more; the secretary of defense, Clark Clifford, wanted to "use the crisis" to push the allies, especially the Germans, on their defense budgets, troop quality, and ability to mobilize in an emergency.[92]

The Americans let the crisis sink in to European cabinets and chancelleries. They refused to attend a summit, or to move up the regular December ministerial meeting. The Americans did not wish to use NATO to make any declaratory statement, preferring that the condemnation of the invasion occur in the UN. They had not pressed for any alert of NATO forces. When a heightened alert finally did come, a month after the invasion, the Germans thought this was far too late. The German permanent representative at NATO complained that NATO's reaction to the crisis was "inadequate or non-existent."[93]

This was a deliberate policy set by Lyndon Johnson. Moving slowly was a dangerous game; Henry Cabot Lodge, the US ambassador in Germany, reminded Washington of all the old fears that if NATO ignored Germans' security worries, Bonn would be in "a mood of pessimism and of accommodation towards the USSR."[94] But Johnson had not forgotten the years of difficulty in trying to get the Europeans to contribute more to NATO's defense posture. The British and German stinginess during the trilateral negotiations had put this into sharp contrast. In Czechoslovakia, he saw an opportunity to press the Europeans to contribute more troops to the alliance. American ambassadors in NATO capitals told their hosts that the United States would agree to an early meeting only if the Europeans stepped up their contribution to NATO.[95]

While the Germans were frustrated with the American position, the British had a sense that the United States was "trying to make our flesh creep." They correctly assumed that Washington was trying to instill fear in London, Bonn, and perhaps Paris and others of "the dangers looming up for NATO if Europe does not do more for itself, for their own national motives."[96] Throughout

NATO's first two decades, the United States had been ambiguous and confused about what role it wanted Europe to play in NATO. Eisenhower, Kennedy, and Johnson had always wanted the European states to pay more of the costs of defending the continent, but they had all shied away from anything like a European bloc, or caucus in NATO. In nuclear policy the United States had never accepted the possibility of anything but an American finger on the trigger. And when "the chips were down," recalled one permanent representative, thinking about Cuba, and perhaps Berlin, "all NATO could do was hold its breath while Washington took whatever steps the president and his military advisers deemed appropriate."[97]

American policy in 1968 was not to browbeat its allies, but to force them to fill a vacuum. US officials sought to nourish the growing European entity, and—most tangibly for the Americans, pick up some of the costs paid by the United States. After previously insisting on setting NATO policy in Washington, the United States now sat silently and waited for the Europeans to form their own views, hoping to spark European initiative. Ultimately, Rostow told Johnson, France might "come back into the European and NATO family," and Britain would join Europe. This would strengthen NATO. But it would also be the "basis for a carefully scheduled decline in U.S. forces in the years ahead."[98] The Americans pressed carefully, and slowly, and some believed the best way to maintain NATO was to dramatically change it by accepting—even pressing for—an explicit European foreign and defense policy.[99]

The Europeans agreed to seek increases to their defense budgets, and the regular ministerial meeting was moved to November, from December. Afterward, American intelligence analysts judged the European response to Czechoslovakia as "more promise than performance," for there were no dramatic increases in European defense expenditure. But the European allies started to discuss the possibility of a new European Defense Community. There was a growing conviction in Washington, London, and Bonn that the Europeans needed to concert their defense efforts: in his memoir, Harold Wilson recalled the "twin lesson" of Czechoslovakia, that NATO was necessary but so too was "the greater unity of Europe, so that the view of Europe as a whole could be more strongly concentrated on any threat to freedom."[100] Denis Healey persuaded his European colleagues to establish an informal "Eurogroup" of defense ministers to find a means whereby Western Europe could "play a more active role than in the past."[101] Even de Gaulle seems to have reconsidered the EDC he had so loathed in its earlier incarnation; the CIA obtained records of de Gaulle's ideas for a new European defense entity.[102] Perhaps a united Europe, enlarged to include Britain and others, would lift some of the burdens from NATO's shoulders. Or—as the next chapter shows—perhaps it would make things much, much worse.

The Czechoslovakian crisis helped the allies solve the problem of NATO's twentieth anniversary. After all, 1969 was the first year that the signatories could give notice to abrogate the North Atlantic Treaty. For years, Soviet propaganda had cleverly portrayed the year 1969 as the "end" of NATO, and the NATO allies had never found a viable way to contradict this myth. At the November ministerial, the allies announced that Czechoslovakia had made it necessary to consider the North Atlantic Treaty one of "indefinite duration." Even this language reflected hard bargaining between allies.[103] None wished for NATO to disappear, but none were willing to rely on the language of the Atlantic mystique, or the sonorous language of the treaty, with its suggestion that the allies were natural partners because they shared a "common heritage and civilization," to justify NATO's continued existence. By the end of the decade, there was little political gain to be had by trumpeting NATO from the hustings. Instead, Denis Healey thought the allies' attitude reflected the lesson taught by Hilaire Belloc's poem "Jim," about a boy who had slipped his nurse's hand and been eaten by a lion at the zoo: "best to keep ahold of nurse for fear of having something worse," as Healey put it.[104] Prudent advice, but not the stuff of inspiration.

8

BUSTING EUROPE

In May 1971, Richard Nixon's secretary of defense Melvin Laird traveled to Europe to meet with his NATO colleagues. They were a glum bunch. In a private meeting, Helmut Schmidt, the German minister, told Laird he was worried by the "anti-military attitude of the German people, particularly the young." Fearing antinuclear and anti-NATO repercussions, the German government would stall NATO plans to improve the defense of German borders by pre-positioning small nuclear mines. Schmidt feared that if discovered, the mines would trigger a "pacific movement in Germany" that would damage NATO further. At the same time, the German government was under parliamentary pressure to reduce troops. Laird left Schmidt, and moved on to meet with the British minister, Lord Carrington. "I'm like Helmut," Carrington told Laird, "I'm depressed." Anyone could see "the world looks awful," he sighed, and yet "no one is worried."[1]

Carrington was describing the public mood, not that of NATO officials. Indeed, during Nixon's presidency, the leaders of NATO's states all worried about NATO's future and whether they had begun to lose the Cold War. What Carrington was describing, and what Laird reported to Nixon, was a citizenry in Western Europe looking for any means to cut defense spending, "apathetic about national defense and indifferent to NATO's role in preserving peace in Europe."[2]

The greatest threat to NATO in the Nixon years was not friction between the national interests of the allied states, but that the citizens of NATO states would simply reject the necessity of the alliance. Kissinger and Nixon, along with their European partners, foresaw an apocalyptic scenario whereby voters, and thus legislators, in both Europe and North America would reject the need for defense spending and troop deployments. They worried that cuts in one country—any country—might force a domino effect in all allied capitals. In Washington, domestic incentives to cut costs on the defense of Europe only grew as it seemed the European Economic Community would become an economic adversary of the US, and as Europeans experimented with ideas for an independent foreign policy that played, to Nixon's and Kissinger's ears, in an anti-American key.

Ultimately, however, fear of NATO's impending collapse was rooted in distrust between generations, not states. Lord Cromer, the British ambassador in Washington as of 1971, summed it up by explaining that the current ruling generation was the "last to have experienced the significance of the Atlantic assertion as exemplified in the latter part of World War II." Successive generations would not recognize that peace rested on Atlantic security cooperation—ironically, this was obscured by NATO's success—and "as a consequence may be more easily lulled into misplaced complacency."[3]

Three years earlier, the CIA had observed the emergence of a "generation gap" in NATO countries. Younger people were dismissing "traditional patterns of political activity, and the historic rivalries among nations," as "obsolete, artificial, and irrelevant."[4] The gap was apparent in Europe, but worse in the United States, where Cromer observed a "rejection of history and its lessons for mankind."[5]

Richard Nixon and Henry Kissinger shared Cromer's worries. They believed Western youth were unconscious of—or worse, consciously rejected—the fact that their present opportunities, prosperity, and very security rested on the careful management of military power. In the spring of 1973, Nixon and Kissinger launched the last great effort to organize Atlantic relations before the end of the Cold War. They hoped to appeal to a new generation by reinvigorating transatlantic relations with a clarion call similar to George C. Marshall's call for a postwar European recovery program. More important, they also wanted to lock future governments on both sides of the Atlantic into a system that could not be easily cast off by a new generation of voters. Henry Kissinger's famous speech kicking off the "Year of Europe" was no simple public relations event, but an attempt to reach a strategic reckoning between the United States and Europe.

The "Year of Europe" was plagued by myriad difficulties and misunderstandings. The Europeans misinterpreted the speech as an opportunity to try to develop a common foreign policy independent of Washington. This was, in fact, one of Nixon and Kissinger's secret fears, and they worried it would lead to the end of NATO and result in the Soviet domination of the continent. They responded by smashing the Europeans' fledgling attempts to coordinate a European foreign policy. Nixon and Kissinger believed they had to destroy European policy to save the Europeans—and the United States—from Soviet depredations.

FIGURE 9.   President Richard Nixon attends a meeting of the North Atlantic Council at NATO Headquarters in Brussels, February 1969. National Archives photo no. WHPO-0370-11.

Fears of Détente and *Ostpolitik*

A year before Nixon was elected, NATO issued its Harmel Report, solemnly observing that the alliance was now committed both to the defense of its members and to encouraging détente. But Lyndon Johnson's diplomats had pushed a conservative definition of détente that Nixon maintained: American policy toward East-West relations was aimed at "making the present security system in Europe more stable—not at replacing it."[6]

Détente was an amorphous concept. It was not clarified by Moscow's public calls for an end to confrontation while the Red Army rapidly built up its military strength. In the Soviet smile of the 1950s, the Allies had seen deviousness. In the détente of the 1960s and early 1970s most NATO leaders, like NATO's secretary-general Manlio Brosio, believed Moscow was seeking "to weaken, divide and finally demolish NATO."[7] Despite their skepticism of Soviet intentions, the NATO allies worried détente would gain a momentum of its own. The British prime minister James Callaghan worried that even the beginning of strategic arms limitation talks (SALT) would generate an "unjustified euphoria" in the public at large and lead "rapidly to relaxation of the vigilance and cohesion of NATO."[8]

Kissinger warned that the Soviets did not even have to outsmart the NATO allies at the bargaining table to be successful. The very existence of armaments talks and peace conferences would help to "sustain a mood in Europe" that considered defense spending less and less important. The Soviet call for a European security conference, the "idea of alternative security organisations," implied that NATO had become unnecessary.[9] It was a tool the Soviets had used before, and that Mikhail Gorbachev would use again later in an effort to undermine the very notion that NATO was necessary. If the Soviets played their hand carefully, they might be able to create a public climate that favored an American withdrawal from Europe, ultimately "chang[ing] the balance of power in Europe" to favor Moscow.[10]

As always, the German problem weighed heaviest in that balance. Willy Brandt, the first chancellor in the FRG from the Social Democratic Party of Germany (SDP), along with his foreign policy adviser Egon Bahr, were committed to *Ostpolitik*—an effort to improve German relations with both the USSR and the Soviet satellites. Ultimately, Brandt and Bahr wished for the demise of the bloc system and the removal of both NATO and USSR troops from Europe, but in the meantime they acknowledged their eastern policy "was only possible on the basis of the NATO alliance." Theirs was a careful game that required NATO for the foreseeable future; timing was everything.[11]

The other allies worried that Brandt and Bahr were unleashing forces they could not control. Kissinger, Nixon, and British officials worried that *Ostpolitik* might "engender euphoria" in the Federal Republic, and Brandt would be "sucked into more and more concessions" to Moscow to keep *Ostpolitik* alive.[12]

A German problem might quickly become an American problem. Kissinger, alert to the transatlantic flow of ideas between both legislators and political activists, worried that the rejection of NATO in Germany would "give ammunition to our own détente-minded people here at home." The result would be a mutual encouragement between anti-NATO Germans and isolationist Americans fueling each other's protests.[13] And if the Germans rejected NATO, and the Americans rejected their troop deployment to Germany in turn, Bonn would feel compelled to move closer to Moscow, and the Soviets might compel the Germans to agree to "shoehorning us"—the Americans—"out of Europe."[14]

As in the debates over the multilateral force in the 1960s, Rapallo was on the lips of officials and politicians concerned with German policy in the 1970s.[15] American Department of Defense officials went as far as to worry that *Ostpolitik* might lead to the "disintegration of the Alliance" and the "same power vacuum" that forced the US to intervene in two World Wars.[16]

The more nuanced and realistic worry was not of a return to the dark days of Imperial or Nazi Germany. It was, as British foreign secretary Sir Alec

Douglas-Home put it, that Brandt would sup with Moscow and "not use a long enough spoon."[17] The devil was in the details of domestic politics, not diplomacy.[18]

New Soviet Weapons and Old Soviet Tactics

While détente seemed to make NATO politically vulnerable, the other pillar of the alliance, its defense, was starting to crumble. It was clear in the late 1960s that a Soviet crash nuclear program would cause the US and the USSR to be, by 1975, roughly in strategic parity. In such a scenario, the United States could no longer confidently rely on its nuclear weapons to deter the Soviet Union, for the USSR could, in turn, strike back at the US. The idea of a "nuclear umbrella in NATO," Nixon concluded less than a month after his inauguration in 1969, was "a lot of crap."[19]

After the development of NATO's military command structure, the deployment of American troops to Europe, and the addition of the armed forces of the Federal Republic of Germany in the 1950s, the Soviets had limited their threats of armed confrontation as a tool of their politics in Europe; after Berlin and Cuba they had all but stopped. But with parity, Kissinger worried the Soviets might again attempt to use the threat of armed confrontation to "extend their political influence in Western Europe."[20]

George Kennan and other contemporary analysts of international affairs rejected the idea that the Soviet Union could or would use the threat of military attacks, especially nuclear blackmail, against Western Europe.[21] But NATO politicians did not think it unreasonable. Georges Pompidou, the French prime minister, worried that if and when Tito or Mao died, the Red Army might make a "camouflaged advance" into either Yugoslavia or China, similar to that against Czechoslovakia in 1968, but with much higher stakes. There was "a series of moves the Soviets could make below the threshold of a war," allowing them to encircle NATO Europe while remaining confident NATO had no credible military response to such actions.[22]

The British and Americans saw similar avenues for the Soviet Union to exert political influence in Europe. Burke Trend, the secretary to the British cabinet, worried that if NATO's credibility waned, Communist influence in France and Italy would grow, and Bonn might strike its own bargain with Moscow.[23] Nixon believed that the Europeans, and especially the Germans, would "make a deal with whoever is Number One" in terms of military strength in Europe. Today it was Washington; soon it could be Moscow.[24]

And Washington's power seemed to be slipping away just as the Soviet Union was flexing. In the early months of Nixon's presidency, Kissinger commissioned studies that put NATO's chances in a war with the Soviet Union at "50–50," but only "if we're lucky."[25] The only solution, all else remaining equal, was an increase in NATO conventional forces and a continued US commitment to maintaining, even increasing, conventional capability in Europe.[26]

But all else was not equal. As Kissinger later recalled, geopolitical pressure in the Nixon years called for troop increases, while domestic political pressure called for defense cuts and withdrawals. NATO's conventional forces were not increasing, and the allies were all seeking ways to reduce their troop numbers.[27]

To Americans like Thomas Moorer, the chairman of the Joint Chiefs of Staff, failure of the NATO allies to dramatically improve their conventional forces meant they must be "living in a dream world," ignoring the strategic realities brought about by parity.[28] But European leaders believed that winning a conventional war in Europe would have results not markedly better than losing one. Nixon's fellow leaders, pointed out some NSC officials, "reflecting quite accurately the sentiments of their constituents, are not interested in making nuclear war more rational or conventional defense more feasible—they want to make war in Europe impossible."[29] The American troops in Europe assigned to NATO, the Europeans believed, rendered war impossible, not because the Americans would fight and win a conventional war, but because the American public would force their president to unleash nuclear hell on the USSR if US soldiers came under Soviet attack. An attack on European soldiers provided no such guarantee. In the final analysis, American officials believed that if they did not provide such a guarantee, the states of Europe would drift "towards the Russians," resulting in the "Soviet domination of Europe."[30] Later, Nixon and Kissinger would argue that they could not allow American troops in Europe to be seen as hostages. But in the age of approaching parity, that was already their fate.

Presidents from both parties had understood this most fundamental role of US troops in NATO Europe. But increasingly, both Americans and Europeans worried that the American ability to maintain a commitment to Europe was beyond the power of the president. In 1968, outgoing secretary of defense Clark Clifford warned the allies that the "most pressing problem confronting us both today in this regard is the problem within the United States." Congress was increasingly convinced that the defense of Europe was "now primarily a European problem." The "men in the Congress," he said, "sense the public opinion and the public mood. They are politicians, and they have read their mail." Their letters, in the midst of Vietnam, said no to foreign entanglements.[31]

Officials in Washington saw this creeping congressional threat to NATO grow in the 1970s. Anyone who thought the United States could maintain its forces in Europe at current levels, warned the Department of Defense, was ignoring "certain political facts of life."[32] French, German, and British officials all thought the domestic backlash against the Vietnam War and the Cambodian incursion in particular would undercut Nixon's commitment to Europe. Furthermore, they worried that "radicals"—antiwar protesters—in Europe would paralyze their own governments. All feared the Soviets would take advantage of political uncertainty in NATO countries and find "appeasers" who would press for accommodation with Moscow.[33]

Kissinger worried that NATO might fall apart without Moscow even having to lift a finger. He assumed that if Congress truly grasped the dangers of parity it would turn sharply against NATO. He could hardly explain to Congress that American forces were deployed to Europe as hostages, and yet he knew that careful analysis would show that a more rational explanation for the American deployment—conventional defense—would reveal that NATO was outmatched. If the United States government was unable to confidently claim that its troops in Europe could fight and win a war, Congress would call the troops home.[34]

Indeed, Congress had been calling for such a return for years. During the Johnson years, Senator Mike Mansfield had resolved to cut American troop deployments in Europe. By 1970, Mansfield told British diplomats he would now get his cuts, as "Congress is in an anti-military mood."[35]

Nixon and his secretary of state, William Rogers, appealed to the Europeans for political help in Congress to fight Mansfield. Already, the Eurogroup—an informal grouping of European NATO allies, formed in the late 1960s—had been searching for means to shore up Nixon's position in Congress. The Eurogroup responded to American entreaties and sought to help solve some of Nixon's domestic problems. They developed a list of short-term measures that helped Nixon battle congressional claims that Europe was doing nothing in its own defense. But the "Europackage" was nothing more than a stopgap, and the Europeans quickly fell short of their promised contributions. No one on either side of the Atlantic believed that the limited European efforts could long forestall congressional challenges to NATO.[36]

Threats to NATO from Congress

In May 1971, Mansfield launched his major challenge to Nixon and to NATO: in an amendment, he called for a 50 percent reduction of US forces in Europe. The "brutal fact," Kissinger told his staff, was that such a reduction would cause Europeans to "seek nuclear autonomy or . . . move in the direction of Finland or possibly do both things simultaneously."[37]

Nixon fought hard against Mansfield. He told Republicans and Democrats alike that NATO was the "blue chip" at the center of American policy. Only by keeping Europe stable could America respond to the massive shifts in world affairs and the rising strength of countries in Asia, Latin America, and the Middle East.[38] This was no mere political posturing. Nixon believed that American military power, even if only in garrison, stabilized Europe and gave him the "diplomatic wallop" necessary for his ambitious policies toward the USSR and China.[39]

The White House drummed up support from some of the old Democrat grandees of NATO's past to make the case that NATO was worth defending. They warned that if the US cut troops now, it would lose any leverage in negotiations aimed at getting matching cuts from Moscow.[40] But the strongest case against troop cuts was also the one allied officials had always been wary of making in public: if NATO fell apart, the FRG would be untethered from the West. It was the Germans, Nixon told a group of assembled elder statesmen, who posed "potentially the most difficult problem in the heart of Europe." The German problem motivated Democratic and Republican statesmen alike to take to the airwaves and the telephones to save NATO.[41]

Congress defeated the Mansfield amendment, but the issue was hardly dead. Senator John Stennis, who voted against Mansfield, warned Kissinger "this is really not over . . . it's a deep undercurrent among the people."[42] The European allies wondered whether Nixon could fend off isolationist pressures indefinitely. British officials warned that Nixon's political decisions now had to be made against the background of an interminable list of domestic problems: "fears of slump; continuing preoccupations with Vietnam; balance of payments worries; black power; the egghead–silent majority gap; the generation gap; the crime wave; urban blight; a disquieting degree of military indiscipline; Congress increasingly hard to control; and so on."[43]

In 1971, Nixon had defeated Mansfield by trotting out "the old war-horses of the Cold War," but this hardly seemed a sustainable solution to the generation gap in the US.[44] Just as Nixon and Kissinger had feared that Brandt would become beholden to his voters who wished for rapprochement with the East, America's NATO allies worried that Nixon would become "a prisoner of circumstance," unable to hold off the growing domestic political pressure for troop cuts and retrenchment.[45]

Alone, the problem of isolationist sentiment seemed difficult but manageable. But by the middle of 1971, as British accession to the European Economic Community loomed larger, it seemed that the isolationist wave might mix with an economic protectionist sentiment in the United States, forming a combustible combination with explosive results for NATO.[46]

Connections between Economics and Defense

Richard Nixon and Henry Kissinger carried on the American tradition of public support for European political and economic integration. But both men harbored qualms about the implications of European integration for NATO, fearing that Congress would refuse to put American blood and treasure on the line to defend Europe if the Europeans were economic adversaries.[47] Nixon, sensing that Congress would not tolerate a "too passive attitude" in trade negotiations between America and Europe, had let the decidedly undiplomatic secretary of the treasury John Connally be America's primary spokesman for economic diplomacy.[48] In May 1971, Connally stunned the allies by openly calling into question the future of the Atlantic alliance.

Speaking to a bankers' association in Munich, Connally reminded the Europeans that the United States might have easily retreated into "Fortress America" after the last war. Instead, Washington had financed a "military shield"—NATO—that covered both America and Europe. Now, he said, after twenty-five years, "legitimate questions" arose over how to pay for the shield. As Europe benefited from a global economic system supported and defended by the United States, Washington had "the right to expect more equitable trading arrangements." Connally's speech, though the text itself hardly reads like dynamite, was explosive in NATO. The United States government, for the first time, was making a link between trade arrangements and the defense of Europe. Implicit in Connally's remarks was that the United States might demand economic concessions from Europe in return for military protection.[49]

NATO allies, especially in London and Bonn, understood immediately that the transatlantic economic issues Connally raised were not "merely a matter of trade policies," but of defense policy.[50] For decades, American presidents had refrained from linking Atlantic economic relationships with security relationships, while full-throatedly supporting European integration. What had changed in the American calculations? "The Americans," wrote the head of the North American Department in the FCO, "have suddenly woken up to the economic monster which is being created in Europe."[51]

The US Might Go Its Own Way

Connally's speech came amid a wave of transatlantic tensions. American arms negotiations with the Soviets caused anxiety and mistrust in Europe; SALT looked to Burke Trend like "the Americans may be thinking in terms of doing a deal direct with the Russians, over the heads of Western Europe." All the indications in London were of "something going on" between Washington and Moscow, behind

NATO's back.[52] A few months after Connally's speech, Nixon announced that the United States would no longer convert US dollars to gold, raising "very real fears of an international trade war" between the NATO allies.[53] Before the year was out, Nixon surprised the allies again by announcing that he would visit the People's Republic of China next year.[54]

NATO's newest secretary-general, the Dutchman Joseph Luns, worried that NATO was losing all importance next to Nixon's summit diplomacy with America's Cold War enemies. An American agreement with the Soviet Union on the nonuse of atomic weapons led to further doubts and estrangement. And the Europeans increasingly doubted American good faith in plans for "Mutually Balanced Force Reductions," which looked like "a device for a quick, politically motivated US troop cut" connected to the upcoming presidential election.

The allies worried that radically shifting public opinion could compel a future president—or even Nixon himself—"to withdraw troops from Europe willy-nilly."[55] When, in the 1972 presidential campaign, the Democratic candidate George McGovern proposed to reduce US troops in Europe by 50 percent over a three-year period, Europeans wondered if Nixon would be the last pro-NATO president.[56] Even less-drastic withdrawals, Pompidou assumed, would force Bonn into either a policy of nuclearization or into the arms of the USSR. Helmut Schmidt himself believed US reductions would weaken the little remaining "resolve the German people have in maintaining an adequate defense establishment."[57] It was in these grim early months of 1972 that Laird visited Europe and met with the other NATO defense ministers; he found the mood in Europe so bad that "we may well be witnessing a fragmentation of the Alliance."[58]

The Value and Danger of Europe

The allies waited anxiously to see if Nixon would repeat Connally's link between economics and security. Nixon, privately, knew there was "obviously a link between economics and political-security issues," but he faced down pressure from Congress and some of his own administrators who wanted him to make that link explicit.[59]

Nixon's conviction was that the economic relationship between the United States and Europe was about far more than "horse-trading" over "soybeans and cheese." It was about the question of Europe's position "vis-à-vis the US and the Soviet Union." If Europe and the United States could not agree on a trade policy acceptable to Congress, NATO would "come apart." But if the Americans pushed too hard, demanding economic concessions for security, the Europeans might believe the US was not committed to the defense of Europe and so turn east. The dissolution of NATO, Nixon warned, would leave Europe as "an economic giant but a military and political pigmy." Without the political protection provided by NATO, "the USSR will encroach on [Europe]. It will not be in the traditional way but a new-style invasion."[60] None of the NATO allies would have disagreed with Nixon's diagnosis, but there was no obvious cure to the isolationism and economic protectionism that threatened to undo the alliance.

Lack of a clear American policy for solving the transatlantic puzzle was, as Kissinger put it, just one more "price of Vietnam."[61] Over the winter of 1972–1973, Nixon was outraged by the NATO allies, especially the Germans and Canadians, who criticized American policy in Vietnam. The criticism stung Nixon and caused him to reconsider his approach to NATO. What he had always considered an "alliance of interest and friendship" was now predicated solely on balancing national interests; in a bit of Nixonian hyperbole he swore there would be "no more toasts, no more state visits" with European countries.[62] Still, Nixon did not doubt that NATO was crucial to American interests.[63] When Kissinger warned the British of Nixon's frustrations, he told Burke Trend that "all his life," Nixon "had been a NATO man." "In the longer term," Trend replied, "it is terribly important he should go on being one."[64]

By early 1973, the Europeans began to doubt whether Nixon was strong enough to save NATO. They worried, as Edward Heath put it, about the American public getting "worked up on [E]EC trade."[65] If the growing isolationist attitude that Cromer had identified were to merge with the economic protectionists in Congress and form an "unholy alliance," America's commitment to NATO would be in danger.[66] The Europeans were desperate to avoid any overt "linkage" between the transatlantic economic and defense relationships.[67]

Kissinger, however, thought the connections between security and economic relations could no longer be ignored. What was required, he told a group of senior advisers, was "some philosophy for the next three or four years which would encompass economic, defense and arms control policy" rather than allowing these negotiations to run separate, uncontrollable, courses.[68] Some of Kissinger's advisers warned that such a grand reckoning was practically impossible; others warned that such an obvious bartering of trade for defense would signal that the United States did *not* think NATO was indispensable, and as a result, "the Europeans would turn more to the USSR."[69]

Nonetheless, Kissinger, supported by Nixon, moved forward with a plan to reorder Atlantic relations. Not only would such a reckoning come at the expense of European integration—this was precisely the point. By March 1973, Nixon had become convinced that "European unity will not be in our interest, certainly not from a political viewpoint or from an economic viewpoint." In the immediate postwar decades, Nixon wrote Kissinger, European statesman had been "people that we could get along with." Now, political trends revealed that Europe would, in the future, be led "primarily by Left-leaning or Socialist heads of government." Germany, especially, would be pulled further and further to the left by its own internal politics. The upshot of this new trend was that in economics, politics, and eventually "even the military field," Europe would be "in increasing confrontation with the United States" rather than helping form "a united front against Soviet encroachment." If the United States did not act now to counter European unity, "we will create in Europe, a Frankenstein monster, which could prove to be highly detrimental to our interests in the years ahead."[70] Nixon and Kissinger set out to save NATO by damaging the emerging European entity.

Kissinger Launches the "Year of Europe"

Only a sense of anxiety and looming crisis can explain why, on April 23, 1973, Kissinger launched the "Year of Europe" with an ill-prepared speech to the annual luncheon of the Associated Press. Undoubtedly, both Nixon and Kissinger would have preferred more time to execute their plan. But in the spring of 1973, they needed to act urgently. While Nixon was hardly planning on resigning over Watergate, it was clear that the crisis brewing in the United States would limit his political capital. They also wished to activate their plan before France, the European state most likely to resist a new grand design, took the rotating presidency of the European Community.[71]

In his speech, Kissinger called on the NATO allies, along with, awkwardly, Japan, to agree to "a new Atlantic Charter setting the goals for the future." The charter would be a "blueprint" that would explicitly link and solve the interconnected problems of trade, finance, and defense.[72]

Some reporters initially heard an echo of George Marshall's speech ushering in the European Recovery Program. But this was a generous comparison. Nearly everyone, including many American officials, bristled upon reading the speech. Both Heath and Brandt would later write that it seemed a hasty mistake. No allied governments or publics had been prepared for the speech, nor had American embassies or State Department officials in Washington been consulted in advance. Kissinger's own staff had been busy with the Vietnam peace settlement and Soviet leader Leonid Brezhnev's visit.[73]

Nonetheless, the NATO allies understood that Kissinger's speech was an attempt at "linkage," an effort to wrap up negotiations over trade and defense in "one ball of wax."[74] Brandt and his officials heard an ultimatum, and the British were wary. Kissinger, Trend advised Heath, was "inviting us, in effect, to subordinate the economic interests of Europe to the political exigencies of Washington—a risk against which we have clearly to be on our guard."[75]

Still, now that the Americans had launched their project, it could not be rebuffed. The best solution, and what the Europeans assumed the Americans wanted, was for the European Economic Community, just recently enlarged from six members to nine, to discuss a response among themselves. Here, the Europeans thought, was a process that would help move Europe toward a common foreign policy—precisely what Nixon and Kissinger wanted to stave off with their "Year of Europe."[76]

Following his speech, Kissinger entered into a series of bilateral meetings with NATO foreign ministers, telling them that his goal was to "anchor the Atlantic Alliance" and "give it a new emotional basis." He warned that the American people needed "some reason to believe" in NATO and the Atlantic relationship, and so did the Europeans. Otherwise, he said, "erosion is inevitable. Europe will drift."[77] Kissinger was confident that the Europeans, even the French, would agree to a new Atlantic Charter, and Nixon and his advisers expected the drafting process would culminate in a presidential trip to Europe.[78]

But the Year of Europe screeched to a halt in the summer of 1973. At a NATO meeting in June, Michel Jobert, the French minister of foreign affairs, railed against the idea of linking economics and defense. He warned that trying to negotiate the relationship between the two would undo NATO. "Nous avons une bonne Alliance: gardons-la," he said: We have a good alliance; let us protect it.[79]

Kissinger, who thought he had gained Jobert's agreement to the concept of a new charter, was furious. Still he pressed on. In early July, Kissinger distributed draft Atlantic Declarations to the British, the French, and likely the Italians and other allies. He did so with an injunction that the recipient countries not tell anyone else they had seen the American papers, and that they should communicate about the drafts bilaterally. Likely in an effort to sow dissension in the European Community, Kissinger told Jobert that the British had been given a draft declaration, exposing the British for keeping a draft from their French partners.[80] ("Declaration" had replaced "Charter" as the preferred document title in the late spring.)

The Europeans, sensing Kissinger's efforts to divide and conquer the nine, agreed that one representative, the chair of the committee of European foreign ministers, would be Europe's point person in negotiating the declaration with the United States. The Danish foreign minister, Knud Borge Andersen, was appointed to represent Europe. This, it seemed to the Europeans, was the logical result of the movement toward European unity.[81]

Kissinger supposedly once asked: "What is the phone number of Europe?" In July 1973, the Europeans gave Kissinger the proverbial phone number. That the call was to be answered by the Danish foreign minister was not acceptable. On July 30, 1973, Kissinger exploded in a meeting with British officials. Even in an administration known for its emotional outbursts, Kissinger's was still remarkable. He found the European plan "incompatible with our relationship, even insulting." The Europeans, he accused, were turning the search for joint principles into a formalized, almost adversarial negotiation, and "using it to help European unity." Kissinger made clear that the president's trip to Europe was now unlikely. Later, when the Europeans implied the president might sign a declaration alongside European foreign ministers, not heads of government, the trip was doomed.[82]

Kissinger "confessed that his speech had been . . . one of the worst mistakes that he had made." He had wanted an Atlantic Declaration in a bid "to penetrate American consciousness," to confirm an emotional connection to the defense of Europe that could override lesser concerns about trade and money. The effect of the European response had been the opposite, and the result was a series of frosty letters between Nixon, Heath, and Brandt.[83]

Kissinger told the British how much it bothered him that the Europeans expected "unconditional American nuclear guarantees" through NATO, yet treated the transatlantic relationship as a negotiation between two distant parties.[84] "How," Kissinger inquired, did the Europeans "imagine that the deterrent would be reliable if the ties of sentiment that alone gave it credibility were not there"?[85] British officials chalked up Kissinger's outburst to his failure to listen to American diplomats and deep dysfunction in the American foreign policy establishment, and put the blame on Watergate.[86]

The British misunderstood the calculations that motivated Nixon and Kissinger's project. The Year of Europe was never, solely, about public relations and public agreement to charters or philosophies, nor was it about the emotions or personalities of leaders. Nixon's brooding and Kissinger's emotional explosions submerged their deeper, analytically based fears about the future of Europe and the strength of NATO's defenses.

The Defense Component

Nixon and Kissinger wanted to use the Year of Europe to design a pattern of transatlantic relations that would prevent trade wars and the collapse of NATO.

But they also wanted to fundamentally reshape NATO to provide for the long-term defense against Soviet political pressure on the European states.[87] Indeed, only by considering this element of the Year of Europe does American policy toward Europe as a whole make sense.

By 1973, Nixon's concerns about strategic parity and increases in Soviet conventional strength were deeper than ever: intelligence reports revealed to him that "the Soviets are going all out."[88] He told Heath that if the Soviet Union did some "huffing and puffing" anywhere in Central Europe, "they would not now be seriously deterred by the threat of United States nuclear retaliation."[89] Kissinger warned the allies that if NATO was not prepared, "some younger, more ruthless Soviet leader would test us, and the alliance would fall apart."[90] The Soviets would always be on the lookout for ways to undermine NATO and threaten its unity. But the states of the West, including the United States, simply did not have the political will to respond to a Soviet challenge, say, over Berlin.[91]

Kissinger frequently invoked the history of the World Wars to make his point. In the First World War, Kissinger recalled, French soldiers had been rushed forward by train to meet invading German armies. But the West of the 1970s was not the West of the 1910s or the 1940s. "Western governments, given their domestic structure, will never be willing to send troops to the front by the Gare de l'Est, or however they used to do it."[92]

NATO, in Nixon's and Kissinger's eyes, was the only solution to the lack of political will in the West. Kissinger's staff drew up ideas for integrating US and European forces "into a single fighting force" with combined logistics and national specialization that could efficiently and effectively repel a Soviet conventional attack.[93] Kissinger also wanted NATO's North Atlantic Council to "organize itself better," replacing its "legalistic approach . . . by a strategic approach which concentrated on the big issues."[94]

Ultimately, however, the American solution to strengthening NATO's defense was a reorganization predicated on conventional forces. But when Secretary of Defense James Schlesinger told his colleagues that NATO should prepare itself to fight and win a conventional war, the result was a disaster. By suggesting he "envisaged a long conventional phase in any European conflict," Schlesinger "added fuel to the flames of concern about the readiness of the United States to use nuclear weapons in the defence of Europe."[95]

The Americans continued to urge their allies to improve their forces, promising that it would take only a little more effort and a little more money for NATO to have the defense it needed. But as Carrington warned Schlesinger, if Western governments were told that NATO was not too far off from meeting the Soviet effort, then what little support remained for defense spending in Europe was just as likely to collapse. Overall, "all Western governments," Carrington warned, "had to recognise that defence expenditures were unpopular, particularly to the younger generation who tended to regard as meaningless the whole panoply of NATO and the military confrontation."[96]

Given the American pressure, both in the broader call for a Year of Europe and regarding improvements to NATO's defense posture, the Europeans quietly considered whether they should hedge their bets by establishing a European defense identity.[97] Heath, in Britain, sought to engage Pompidou in a program of Anglo-French nuclear sharing—the necessary base of European defense. But as one French official put it bluntly, the "problem was the Germans." As always, the problem was not today's chancellor, and not today's German government, but rather that "one could not be sure about the future." "Herr Brandt," Pompidou said, "was not eternal. It was salutary to remember that only ten years had separated Herr Stresemann from Adolf Hitler."[98] An Anglo-French nuclear program might alienate the Germans, pushing them away from the NATO organization that was essential to tying Bonn to the West.

Nor were Brandt or the Germans interested in any new organization for European defense, especially anything that would require more German defense spending. Already, the German cabinet faced "the opposition of young people, and their teachers and professors as well," who thought Germany spent too much on defense.[99] At the same time, German *Ostpolitik* rested on the peace and security provided by the American guarantee to NATO. The Germans feared a European defense effort would weaken the American commitment, circumscribe Bonn's bargaining power, and lead German opinion to "look towards the East."[100] The Europeans, just like Nixon and the NSC staff, concluded that there was no alternative to NATO.

The Europeans gambled. They believed that Nixon could overcome the challenges he faced in Congress and in American society at large, and that NATO could survive in its present form. They had come to believe that Kissinger's speech had been an effort to blackmail Europe into increasing its defense spending, and that if Europe held firm, Nixon would find a way to preserve NATO. After all, Jobert told Kissinger, "everybody had their parliament."[101]

Thus the Europeans made their twin decisions, or essential nondecisions: They would continue to work as a European unit in their approach to the Atlantic Declaration, using the so-called Year of Europe to build a pattern of common European foreign policy making. They also refused to put any significant effort into changing NATO strategy or to provide significantly more resources for defense.

These actions convinced Nixon and Kissinger of their worst fears: the Europeans were taking a "free ride" on security, using NATO as a shelter so that they could build up Europe while avoiding the hard decisions about defense resources and their own relationships with one another—especially with Germany.[102] Nixon and Kissinger thought the Europeans were making an enormous strategic mistake. The Europeans evidently believed that they could, by taking cheap shots at Washington and distinguishing themselves from the US, build a domestic political consensus in Europe for a common foreign policy. But this would so alienate the American people and Congress that the president would be forced, politically, and against every one of his geopolitical instincts, to turn his back on Europe. The Europeans, unprepared to defend themselves, would fall prey to Moscow.

Nixon and Kissinger Move against Europe

Nixon and Kissinger decided to call the European bluff and "bust the Europeans."[103] In August 1973, they agreed to break Europe by threatening to reduce the American commitment to its defense. "Mr. President, the Europeans will be on their knees by the end of this year," Kissinger promised. Nixon, incensed with Europe, went further, saying "we don't have to stay Henry." The United States may have to keep troops in Japan and Korea, Nixon argued, but not Europe. When Kissinger tried to soften this extreme statement, Nixon replied: "No, nobody even in Europe." Was this a rhetorical extreme? Kissinger knew the president's position on Europe—that it was in the American interest to keep it tied to the US through NATO. He tried again to soften the president's position, saying that while Europe "cannot exclude us from their deliberations and expect us to give them an undiluted nuclear guarantee," it was "certainly not going to come to that point." Nixon replied: "Right. Right."[104]

Instead of making an outright threat to leave Europe, the Americans took a number of important but limited actions in an effort to keep "Europe from developing their unity as a bloc against us."[105] Kissinger considered, but ultimately rejected as too dangerous, the idea of building up a German-American alliance to separate the FRG from France and its other European allies. The Americans, wounded by Britain's unwillingness to act as their Trojan horse in Europe, tried to limit British interest in European cooperation by threatening their special intelligence relationship.[106]

The key moves were in the arena of nuclear politics. Kissinger planned to threaten Anglo-American nuclear cooperation, increase Anglo-French friction, and simultaneously remove the possibility of Anglo-French nuclear cooperation that was assumed to be the necessary basis for a European defensive organization. Kissinger knew that if the United States kept "the French hoping they can get ahead of the British," it would encourage the French to maintain their independent deterrent, ultimately limiting the prospect for a European defense capability beyond NATO.[107] Kissinger wanted to make the French "drool" by suggesting increased assistance to the French nuclear problem. Still, he planned only to give them information that "looks like a step forward but doesn't give them anything yet."[108]

This was hardball diplomacy, and it produced results from the French.[109] Simultaneously, in Congress, pressure for troop cuts in Europe was relieved as "mutual and balanced force reduction" (MBFR) talks with the Soviets chugged along. Senators were convinced that if they waited, American troop cuts would come with a balanced Soviet reduction. Watergate was creating unpredictable political incentives for Nixon, but the "orgy of isolationism" seemed to have run out of steam.[110] Cromer wrote from Washington on October 2 to say Atlantic relations now enjoyed a "more favourable climate." "A modicum of rejoicing is therefore in order."[111]

The rejoicing was not to last long. Just days later, Egypt and Syria launched a surprise attack on Israel. The October War, which quickly entangled the superpowers, ushered in another crisis in NATO. To Washington's frustration, several NATO allies immediately warned the United States that their air bases were not available for any non-NATO actions—that is, American support for Israel.[112]

Relations frayed further after the allies rejected a request from Donald Rumsfeld, the American representative, for NATO to "coordinate or harmonize a set of policies" to respond to Soviet involvement in the Arab-Israeli war.[113] The European allies were furious with the suggestion. Rumsfeld's speech seemed "couched in the kind of language which I imagine the Russians customarily use at meetings of the Warsaw Pact."[114] With transatlantic relations already roiled by restrictions on American use of allies' bases and Rumsfeld's speech, the crisis reached fever pitch on October 25, when the United States Strategic Air Command went on alert, and the NATO allies were informed only after a significant delay.[115]

In the midst of the crisis, Nixon was so upset with the lack of European cooperation with American diplomatic efforts that he told Kissinger that just one more vote from a NATO ally against an American resolution in the United Nations would be the "end of our NATO relationship. . . . I will go further, I will comply with the Mansfield [amendment]." Nixon, having clearly lost his temper, said: "The hell with them. We'll just get our boys back home."[116]

The war ended before Nixon felt compelled to take any action over US forces in Europe. But the Americans believed that the Europeans had let them down. Such weakness did not suggest a united Europe could be a useful diplomatic partner for Washington, but the opposite: another adversary. Worse, Kissinger's fears had come true. The Europeans had seemed to use the crisis to build up European unity by taking anti-American positions. He was particularly aggrieved by newspaper articles in Europe suggesting European leaders were "facing the President down" over the October War. To American officials and to allies, Kissinger excoriated NATO: "I ask myself what in God's name is this alliance."[117]

Paradoxically, the frustration of the October War only convinced Kissinger and Nixon how crucial it was they maintain the alliance. They decided it was time "to be tough" with the Europeans. There would be a *"quid pro quo"* for everything, and "no longer a free ride." Kissinger prepared to attend the upcoming NATO summit meeting in December, with instructions from the president to "lay it out cold" to the Europeans in an effort to shock them back to a full consideration of the importance of NATO. "There will be screaming," Kissinger promised.[118]

At the December NATO meeting, Kissinger maintained his tough talk, telling an aide he wanted "to hit [the allies] in the eyes."[119] Kissinger and Jobert sparred during the meeting and afterward. In a restricted, post-dinner exchange with his British, French, and German colleagues, Kissinger told them bluntly that they were trying to build European unity "against the U.S." and claimed—in what seemed a nod to American code-breaking skills—that the United States had "ways of learning how your ambassadors are reporting." The conversation was sharp and testy. Home told Kissinger "I hope you won't think that the Nine are organizing their policies against the United States," but Kissinger replied, "That's just what I think."[120]

Remarkably, Jobert, who at the NATO meeting had railed against American policy, pivoted the dinner conversation to his concerns about "Russian power." Kissinger agreed, saying that "it's hard to believe we are arguing as we do. After all, there are 45,000 Soviet tanks between the Elbe and the Caucasus." "And 20,000 planes," Jobert added.[121] Jobert's acknowledgment of the Soviet threat indicated an increasing French suspicion of Soviet intentions and disillusionment with détente.[122] The NATO allies, as frustrated as they were by elements of the transatlantic relationship and flaws in their partners, believed the common defense was as essential as ever.

A few weeks after the summit, Nixon told Cromer that the "Soviet Union still has one goal—to Balkanize Europe. So the U.S. must play a role in Europe." While the British "may have to say things in Britain and I may have to say things . . . Henry has put out some unfortunate statements—we all get emotional." Still, one only had to "look at the world. In terms of the world balance, you [the British] can't hold by yourselves. The French can't, Germany can't. NATO is enormously important because it makes the Soviets act more responsibly."[123]

Growing Soviet capabilities only convinced Nixon further that he and Kissinger needed to continue attacking the emerging European foreign policy. Their next move was at the 1974 Washington Conference on oil and energy, which the Americans used to separate France from the British and other Europeans. In a speech, Nixon told the delegations that "security and economic considerations are inevitably linked, and energy cannot be separated from either." This was Nixon's first public connection between security and economic matters, and he intended it as "a shot across the bow" of the alliance.[124] Nixon, thrilled by the conference and the divisions it created between European states, called Kissinger to say it had "taught an important lesson to the European community." They learned they "can't gang up against us and we can use it now, we can use it on trade, security, with everything else." At the time and since, the link between the energy conference and NATO was obscure, but Nixon believed it was a "historical breakthrough, people will see it later, Henry, and by God, it was a hell of a thing."[125]

The Primacy of NATO over Europe

Since Kissinger's "Year of Europe" speech, the idea of two declarations of principles, one to be signed by the European Community and the United States, the other to be signed by the NATO allies, had limped along. When the French pushed for a declaration of Atlantic principles predicated on a united Europe—the Knud Borge Andersen episode redux—Kissinger planned to cause the declaration to fail. He wanted to show the Europeans that the United States would never accept a negotiation in which Europe presented America with an agreed position, and to impress upon the European allies, especially London and Bonn, that they must choose Atlantic over European forums.[126]

Kissinger insisted to his staff: "I would rather break the European community than have it organized against the U.S." In March 1974, in the North Atlantic Council, Kissinger announced that the United States "could not be expected to give a multilateral defence guarantee [to] countries refusing any organic connexion with the United States." The NAC, though it had lost its key place in the diplomatic constellation, remained a forum where etiquette and manners reigned supreme. For an American secretary of state to announce to the council that the whole basis of NATO was so flimsy was extraordinary.[127] But privately, Kissinger admitted to other American officials that the United States was "a long way" from "ever thinking about withdrawing forces from Europe." Instead, the US was "tak[ing] on Europe to save NATO and to keep our forces there."[128]

Kissinger's remarks to NATO were the opening thrust in a series of efforts to convince the Europeans that it was "dangerous" to cross the United States. The United States, he said, had "never gone for the jugular" with the Europeans, but perhaps now it was time to "huff and puff and steam and show them that when we say we want a stronger NATO, we mean it." He planned to "scare the hell out of" the Europeans by getting the NATO allies to agree to a NATO declaration of principles, and then refuse to sign.[129]

Nixon and Kissinger ultimately settled on a less extreme strategy: They would continue to link economics and security in public, and also put the onus for a NATO declaration on the Europeans. At the same time they would work to strengthen NATO as the primary forum for transatlantic relations, including by sharing more intelligence with the NATO Military Committee.[130] The United States, Kissinger declared, would "counter Europe by using NATO."[131]

Nixon's remarks to the Executives' Club of Chicago on March 15 served as the linchpin of American efforts to bust Europe. He carefully planned his remarks, making them part of a question-and-answer session that would allow him to be blunter than in a traditional speech. Kissinger urged that the timing was right, and Nixon agreed. "OK, Henry," said Nixon; "I'll hit them even harder than you did—for the ladies."[132] In Chicago, Nixon concluded the answer to one question with "an observation for our European friends." He said: "Now, the Europeans cannot have it both ways. They cannot have the United States participation and cooperation on the security front and then proceed to have confrontation and even hostility on the economic and political front." And, he continued, if the Europeans were not willing to sit down and discuss the necessary cooperation, there could be no meetings of the heads of government of the West.[133]

The Europeans understood the speech was "shock treatment" against French efforts to shape a European policy with an "anti-American slant." Harold Wilson's new British government in London, and Brandt's government in Bonn, were wary of cooperating with the French if it meant any lessened American commitment to Europe.[134]

Days after the speech, Kissinger told German diplomats that, in regard to his request for an Atlantic Charter—what had now become plans for a NATO Declaration of Principles—"there would be no further US initiatives of any sort." He was prepared to drop the idea of a declaration if the Europeans so wanted. Otherwise, he would be pleased to hear from the Europeans as to how to proceed. A week later, Kissinger met with Brandt, and it was obvious that American pressure had "a major impact on the Germans."[135] Through back-channel sources, Kissinger learned that the French were "becoming very consillatory [sic]" and that the Germans "have said they will never again sign anything without full consultation with the US."[136] Wilson, after meeting with Kissinger, made clear that his government would be nowhere near as pro-French as Heath's.[137] Kissinger was confident "this European thing will work out okay. They are pissing in their pants."[138]

The events of March revealed that the United States' view of Europe had undergone a "significant shift." As one British official put it, for decades the Americans had thought of European unity as a "good thing," a "reasonable price to pay for putting an end to the historic divisions and rivalries in Europe." But Washington's conceit had been "only intellectual and theoretical" and did not survive any European effort or policy not totally aligned with US interests. Now, the US was prepared to oppose any European policy the Americans deemed harmful. Washington clearly had had no reservations taking action that "might lead to the emasculation of the political consultation among the Nine" and weakening any trend toward integration.[139]

At the end of March 1974, allied officials got down to work on a NATO declaration. They returned, first, to the American draft declaration—which the British planning staff found a "mixture of euphemism, cliché, half-truth and empty promise." In a developing theme among the non-American NATO allies, the British saw in the American draft something "more reminiscent of a Warsaw Pact Declaration than of a statement by the members of the Alliance."[140]

As delegations waded through the American text and considered their own, the French astonished everyone with their draft. In what would become the "Declaration on Atlantic Relations," adopted by the alliance in June 1974, there was a nod to the importance of US troops—the sine qua non for the Americans. But it also acknowledged the value of the French nuclear force. The Americans, aware the draft was "basically very Gaullist sort of thinking," nonetheless expressed satisfaction and withdrew their own draft. The end result of the Year of Europe, in NATO at least, was a continued commitment of the United States to the continent.[141]

In Ottawa in May, the NATO foreign ministers met for a debate free of the acrimony of earlier sessions. Kissinger "dominated the proceedings," emphasizing by word and deed his determination not to neglect European interests in American-Soviet relations.[142] This assured the Europeans, but also served to reinforce Kissinger's efforts to upgrade NATO as the primary forum for transatlantic discussions.

Weeks later, on Nixon's suggestion, the NATO heads of government met in Brussels to sign the Atlantic Declaration and celebrate NATO's twenty-fifth anniversary.[143] The meeting also allowed Nixon to meet with his colleagues before traveling to Moscow for a meeting with Brezhnev. His visit to NATO thus offered another signal that the Americans would not trade in the alliance for a new bilateral relationship with the USSR.[144]

In Brussels, Wilson told Nixon that the "work that had gone into [the declaration] had made people concentrate their thoughts on the importance of

NATO."[145] What seems like a benign comment was indeed quite profound; for the allies had all looked into an alternate future without NATO and determined it would be uninhabitable. But by 1974, six months after the end of the Year of Europe, NATO had not improved the underlying contradictions and difficulties that had made the Nixon era such a difficult one for the alliance.

The allies found no solution to the problems posed by pressure for détente or the need for a new defense strategy, let alone the contradictions between defense and détente. In Ottawa, Kissinger had argued that "détente was no substitute for the alliance," but, "nevertheless, if only for reasons of Western public opinion, it was essential to continue to work for real détente."[146] NATO had not agreed to, nor really considered, a rethinking of its military strategy. At the time of the heads of government meeting, the British and Dutch were both considering defense reductions that the allies worried might be contagious. Meanwhile, Soviet forces, especially strategic forces, continued to grow at a worrying pace.[147]

The whole summit occurred in the shadow of Nixon's growing infamy. Over twelve hundred pages of White House transcripts had by then been released, making him the focus of the world's media.[148] At Brussels, the other heads of state mattered little as the press focused solely on Nixon. Legend held that over five hundred Secret Service agents were deployed to Brussels, and the motorcades and barriers protecting Nixon made travel for the other heads of government nearly impossible.[149] The dominance of the president, but also his fallibility, had never been clearer.

Indeed, the political health of many of the allies was in doubt. Fragile parliamentary majorities governed in a host of capitals. They suffered from domestic inflation and anxiety about oil supplies. The United States was wracked by more difficulties than Cromer could have predicted in the earlier years. Nixon would resign only two and a half months after the NATO summit, in the midst of what contemporary observers described as a constitutional crisis unparalleled since the Civil War.[150]

Neither in the United States nor in any of the European states had NATO inspired its citizens with a new vision or philosophy of Atlantic relations. Instead, during the Year of Europe and the era of Nixon, the allies ended up fighting a rearguard action meant to stave off potentially critical challenges to NATO, rather than creating a project for the future. In the process, the Americans had knocked down some of the very hopes that European leaders had for providing their citizens with a sense of direction and purpose in international affairs, something to interest youth and prevent pressures for nihilism or neutralism. When Callaghan visited Bonn in March, he found the German vice-chancellor Walter Scheel and Brandt both "anxious to provide an ideal which the youth of Germany can work towards." They had hoped it might have been the idea of Europe; it was surely not going to be the NATO Declaration.[151] With the European idea busted, at least for now, Schmidt worried about "what would happen to the next generation of Germans if there were no European ideal to follow."[152] The drift of the newest generation of voters from NATO would grow more dramatic, and more dangerous, in the years to come, and the Americans would be watching German public opinion with growing concern in the 1980s. The relationship between NATO and a European foreign policy and defense identity, too, remained fraught. For the rest of the Cold War, and indeed even after the collapse of the Warsaw Pact, American officials would work to ensure that the Europeans did not construct a military organization or policy that would compete for resources with SACEUR's plans for the defense of Europe.

9

LEADERLESS MEN

The doomsday prophecies foretold by the allied leaders during the Vietnam era, in which allies on both sides of the Atlantic warned of a collapse of the alliance based on changing social mores and the rejection of power politics, were only half right. For the last decade of the Cold War, there was not a virulent anti-NATO sentiment in the United States or Europe strong enough to challenge the alliance directly. But from 1977 through until 1989—the last long decade of the Cold War—allied governments worried that NATO itself was on the verge of collapse as more and more Europeans came to oppose NATO's nuclear weapons.

The allies had believed for decades that the Soviets sought the "denuclearization" of Europe: the removal of the nuclear weapons that NATO relied on to counterbalance the Soviet superiority in conventional forces. NATO's cohesion, ultimately, rested on the availability of these nuclear weapons. Without them, Congress would force the withdrawal of US troops from the continent, for no president could insist that forces remain in Europe unprotected by advanced weaponry. With the American commitment in question, the Soviets might use their military superiority to threaten and cajole European governments into taking Moscow's line on questions of foreign policy, and Germany might adopt a neutral, if not pro-Soviet, policy. Such a prospect was bad enough; the only thing worse would be if Germany reacted, as after Versailles, against this imposed neutralism and adopted an aggressive military policy. This time it might have nuclear weapons, and the Third World War would be much shorter than the first two.

If Europe was denuclearized, the pillars of safety and security in Europe would collapse. This was gospel for allied officials from all the large NATO powers, but never something they preached in public. The antinuclear sentiment of their citizens, allied officials realized too late, was the legacy of decades of advertising NATO as an alliance of values and common heritage, rather than as an instrument of defense and deterrence.

In the late 1970s and 1980s, NATO planned to modernize a number of its short- and intermediate-range nuclear weapons systems in Europe. In response, Europeans chained themselves to fences of military installations, camped out around nuclear bases, and took to the streets in the hundreds of thousands to demonstrate against proposed missile deployments. This antinuclear sentiment was partly the product of a genuine appreciation of the weapons' potential horrors. It was also, in some instances, encouraged and funded by agents of the Warsaw Pact. But it was fueled by the apparent inconsistency, even hypocrisy, between NATO's nuclear modernization programs and the alliance's public offers of arms control negotiations. This antinuclear sentiment grew dramatically in the Cold War's last decade. By 1989 it seemed the political pressure on NATO governments to negotiate away NATO's nuclear weapons had become irresistible.

Growing Fear over Soviet Power

On November 2, 1976, Americans went to the polls to vote for their next president. During the internal political and social unrest caused by the Vietnam War, the allies had worried that Nixon would be the last pro-NATO president, and that Americans would turn to the fringe—either the right or the left—for their next commander-in-chief. Gerald Ford, who had acceded to the presidency on Nixon's resignation, had maintained Nixon's pro-NATO policies. But on that November day in 1976, the allies wondered whether their worst fears had come true.

Jimmy Carter, who beat Ford, was hardly the Europeans' preference for president. The German chancellor, Helmut Schmidt, had gone so far as to make public his preference for Ford. The other NATO allies worried that Carter's campaign-trail promises to cut US defense spending and his commitment to nuclear disarmament would weaken the alliance.[1]

While Carter had campaigned on defense cuts and the abolishment of nuclear weapons, the Soviet military had continued its rapid military buildup. On the day of the American election, NATO's supreme allied commander, General Alexander Haig, stood before NATO's Military Committee and announced that NATO was at a "watershed." The Red Army, Haig warned the allies, now posed an "unprecedented threat," for Moscow had enough force to support an "imperialist phase in Soviet foreign policy."[2] Although the Kremlin had been a champion of disarmament talks in the 1970s, allied officials believed negotiations were Moscow's "smoke-screen" for efforts to alter the "co-relationship of forces"—that is, the balance of military power—in Europe. The allies had worried about changes in the Red Army's doctrine and equipment earlier in the decade, especially the increased number of battle tanks. But the deployment of new Soviet nuclear weapons systems, the "Backfire" bomber and the SS-20 missiles, both capable of delivering nuclear payloads on Western Europe, elevated NATO's sense of alarm.[3]

As ever, the NATO allies did not imagine Moscow was planning to invade and occupy Western Europe. But they still thought the Soviet buildup extremely dangerous. "The problem," wrote Britain's longtime permanent representative to NATO, Sir John Killick, "is in fact the possible use of the existence of superior military force for purposes of political pressure."[4] Nixon and Kissinger and their European contemporaries had, at the start of the decade, argued that the Soviet Union would use its military power to extort, blackmail, or otherwise pressure Western European governments. This analysis did not change by party affiliation or political spectrum. By 1977, a Democratic secretary of state in the United States, Cyrus Vance, and a Labour prime minister in Great Britain, James Callaghan, agreed with their Republican and Conservative predecessors that the Soviet Union's goal was to increase its military strength as a means of gaining influence over Western Europe.[5]

Just two months into the Carter administration, the president received a comprehensive review from his national security team explaining that the Soviet goal was to force the "departure of US military presence and politico-economic influence in Europe," and to see the continent divided into a "loose constellation of states." With the Soviet Union as the strongest power among them, Europeans would be "amenable to Soviet foreign policy initiatives and positions." To accomplish this goal, the Soviets would burnish their "peace-loving" image, pose as the champions of accommodation in a bid to weaken the West's cohesion, all the while building up their military forces.[6]

The Kremlin's desire to expand its influence in Europe was not a new problem. Officials in Britain saw the same political power games of Russia's czarist past. NATO had successfully managed this threat since 1949, however, and the Policy Planning Staff suggested that the danger of the "Russian menace" needed "to be kept in proportion." It would be "perfectly manageable," they argued, "by a united West."[7]

But more and more, Killick warned his masters in London, allied unity could not be taken for granted. Growing public indifference toward matters of the alliance and outright disgust with nuclear weapons made it increasingly difficult for NATO governments to maintain a concerted plan of defense and deterrence. To keep NATO together, Killick wrote, it is "going to be a damned expensive business—in terms not only of arms and men, but of political resolution."[8]

Why did Killick and other NATO officials think the costs of keeping NATO together would be so high? First of all, acute domestic problems, many brought on by oil shocks and economic crises, preempted the attention of politicians in the 1970s. These politicians also had to grapple with a tremendous assortment of new and challenging problems, ranging from environmental movements to the emerging threat of non-state terrorists. Apprehensive British diplomats wondered whether governments truly had the capacity to respond to the myriad challenges of the era. According to Robert Sykes of the Foreign and Commonwealth Office, writing to a colleague in 1976, it was now "virtually impossible" for ministers "to concentrate—in the way you and I can remember in the past—on the larger East/West security issues," except in reaction to events.[9] Less than three years after penning this note, Sykes was shot dead by Provisional Irish Republican Army terrorists, one emblem of the emerging challenges to order in Europe.

There was little political capital left over for grand designs in foreign policy. The Carter administration came into office sworn not to try another grand unifying event like Kissinger's failed "Year of Europe." Because politicians and the public were focused on so many domestic and economic problems, there hung, everywhere, "a large question mark over the future of the defence effort."[10] Governments had little time or inclination to educate their publics about the necessity of nuclear weapons, particularly when Carter himself had called for the weapons' banishment. And yet, the fundamental tenet of military planning and alliance cohesion—nuclear deterrence—remained unquestioned in the halls of NATO.

The Neutron Bomb Fiasco

The Carter administration began, like so many of its predecessors, convinced that the buildup of European conventional forces was the silver bullet solution to both the Soviet challenge and the need to reduce nuclear armaments. But, also like those who had come before, Carter and his advisers soon learned that the European allies were unwilling to sacrifice popular social welfare programs to increase defense spending to any degree that would lessen NATO's reliance on nuclear weapons.[11]

Zbigniew Brzezinski, Carter's national security adviser, quickly accepted that the "current political environment" made it impossible for the allies to raise enough conventional forces to "maintain territorial integrity"—that is, not be overrun—"if deterrence failed." He proposed that the United States reconsider its war plans and prepare a "stalemate" strategy for Europe. In Brzezinski's new strategy, NATO troops would fall back in front of a Soviet attack, ceding part of Europe before taking up defensive positions and looking to negotiate a political resolution. Although Carter and US officials maintained publicly that the United States and NATO would be prepared to fight and defend Europe, they believed no such thing. The Americans had to keep the "stalemate strategy" secret, to maintain what they euphemistically called the "distinction between declaratory strategy and actual capability."[12]

Brzezinski's strategic theorizing might have mattered little had it remained secret. But in the summer of 1977, PRM-10, the National Security Council document that reflected Brzezinski's thinking on the stalemate strategy, was leaked to the press. Brzezinski was quoted as personally favoring a "sacrifice" option that would cede a third of the FRG to the Soviets.[13]

The government in Bonn, and especially the FRG foreign minister Hans-Dietrich Genscher, were outraged by this apparent American perfidy. The FRG had decades earlier pushed NATO to adopt a "forward strategy" that would see NATO troops meet Red Army advances at or before the German border. Brzezinski's stalemate or sacrifice option was against Bonn's strategic interests and military thinking. But the real problem with PRM-10 was political: Genscher warned that a German public in doubt of American protection would not support Germany's continued commitment to NATO. Bonn could not justify remaining in NATO if the alliance's plan was to sacrifice the FRG. Already, SPD representatives were arguing that PRM-10 cast doubt on the basis for NATO, and Genscher worried that "left political forces" would use the controversy to press Bonn to make "considerable concessions" in disarmament negotiations and elsewhere in the FRG's dealings with the USSR.[14] The Carter administration's fecklessness on European defense seemed to fulfill the worries of half a decade earlier, when Europeans had begun to wonder whether the political and social turmoil of the Nixon years would lead to the election of presidents who were uninformed, or uninterested, in the defense of Europe.

Another leak in the summer of 1977 would further bedevil NATO. In June 1977, Walter Pincus of the *Washington Post* broke the story that the US was developing a "neutron killer warhead."[15] The warhead, which came to be known by the dramatic sobriquet "neutron bomb," was an enhanced radiation warhead (ERW) that the Americans, along with the other allies, had already agreed necessary to modernize NATO's nuclear armories. The controversy over the weapon foreshadowed just how NATO might be stripped of its nuclear defenses under dual pressure from domestic antinuclear groups and Soviet propaganda.

NATO's plan to adopt the ERW had developed simply enough and, purposefully, without much fanfare. In 1976, the US secretaries of state and defense informed the allies that Washington planned to modernize the tactical nuclear warheads stored in Europe. This would allow the US to field fewer weapons, for the newer weapons would provide greater destructive capability. Such modernization, the secretaries argued, was crucial to ensure Congress did not put pressure on the White House for the withdrawal of nuclear weapons from Europe. The terrorist attacks on the 1972 Munich Olympics had made Congress skittish about the security of American nuclear weapons in Europe, so the fewer warheads, the better. Still, Congress also insisted the American forces on the continent be equipped with weapons that would give them a fighting chance in war. The allies accepted these arguments but, critically, assumed there would be no public discussion of the modernization. The ERW, they expected, would be "integrated quietly with the rest of the theater nuclear posture."[16]

The ERW differed from NATO's existing nuclear artillery in that a higher proportion of the energy output from the explosion was radiation, rather than blast or heat. This made the weapon more effective for incapacitating Soviet tank crews while also causing less collateral destruction. As the British defense secretary put it, if the proposal had been reversed—that is, if ERWs were already deployed and NATO had proposed to replace ERWs with the weapons NATO currently stockpiled—there would have been, "rightly, an enormous public reaction to the introduction of weapons, which would kill more people as well as greatly expand the area of collateral damage to property, to achieve the same military objective."[17]

Despite this logic, the Pincus story set off an intense and emotional public reaction in Europe against the ERW. Germany, as the most likely site of a Soviet tank attack, was also the obvious deployment area for the weapons and became the scene of greatest outrage. Members of the ruling SPD, including Egon Bahr, Willy Brandt's former adviser, railed against the proposed weapon. The Soviets, too, used the ERW, "as an all-purpose stick with which to flail the US" in speeches and in the press. Who but fat cat capitalists would wish to destroy humans but leave property intact? Soviet diplomats increased the pressure on Bonn to refuse the ERW by warning senior members of the SDP—the party with its fortunes most closely tied to *Ostpolitik*—that if the Germans accepted the weapon on their territory, USSR-FRG relations would deteriorate.[18] There could be no quiet modernization now.

The military benefits of the ERW were obvious to the allied planners, and the value of the weapon seemed validated by Soviet concern about its possible deployment. Military and civilian officials in key NATO countries—Britain, the

United States, and the FRG—were all in favor of deployment of the ERW. But the political calculations in allied capitals were not so straightforward.[19]

In Washington, Carter knew that cancellation of the weapon would expose him to criticisms of weakness from the political right. The left, meanwhile, thought the weapon violated Carter's campaign position against nuclear weapons. The Americans decided that the best option was to press the allies for a quick agreement to deployment of the ERW so as to finish with the matter before Congress adjourned in late October.[20]

But what suited Carter's political situation only made trouble for governments on the other side of the Atlantic. David Owen, the British foreign secretary, worried that an early agreement to ERWs would cause severe political strain in the Labour Party. Already, the British press was alive with stories of the "neutron bomb," and he worried that if the Callaghan government agreed to the ERW just before the upcoming Labour Party conference, the government would be in for a rough ride. It was essential, Owen concluded, to "avoid, or at least to damp down, renewed controversy over nuclear weapons." Callaghan agreed and asked Brzezinski for more time to get the British public—and his own party—on side. The Germans, too, wanted a delay. The leak had allowed both antinuclear activists and Soviet propagandists to get the jump on the German government. Schmidt's government needed time to "educate public opinion" before any announcement was made on ERW production and deployment.[21]

The Soviet efforts—both bald public propaganda and a private whispering campaign—continued apace. Brezhnev penned letters to all the NATO allies inviting them to reject deployment of ERWs to Europe. Allied officials thought Brezhnev's actions clumsy and that Soviet propaganda was "forcing NATO's hand on ERW deployment," for the alliance could not possibly accede to Soviet pressure by not deploying the weapon.[22]

In Bonn, London, and Washington, diplomats began to tell one another that if the ERW was going to go forward, the political costs—those actions that might incur domestic backlash, such as arguing for the weapon, or deciding on its production and deployment—would have to be shared between the allies. This strategy, of using NATO as cover for politically unpopular decisions, would ultimately be employed by the allies when they agreed to field longer-range tactical nuclear forces in Europe in 1979. But in 1977, the allies suspected that these burden-sharing requests were nothing but veiled attempts to foist the political price onto another ally.[23]

The Americans proposed to consult the NATO allies on whether or not the United States should produce the ERW. Schmidt objected. The US had never before consulted with its allies on whether to produce a particular nuclear weapon, let alone in public. He concluded that this was Carter's ploy to reduce pressure from his left flank in Congress by having the Europeans ask for the ERW.[24]

Schmidt, however, saw an opportunity. What if the Americans built the neutron bomb, but did so specifically as a bargaining chip to trade for a reduction in Soviet forces? The ERW was an antitank weapon, so why not promise to scrap the ERW if the Soviets limited the number of their tanks in Europe? The Americans did not like the ERW-for-tanks trade, but Carter finally agreed to produce ERWs with the hope of bargaining them against other Soviet nuclear weapons. He hoped that such a trade might help set the stage for a broader agreement "to prohibit production of all nuclear weapons."[25] This notion, that NATO could modernize its nuclear weapons in order to create conditions to better negotiate on arms control with the Soviet Union, would also live on past the ERW crisis.

Early in 1978, the Americans presented their NATO allies with a three-pronged approach to cover each of the allies' political flanks: the United States alone would make the decision to produce the weapon. The Europeans would then agree to its deployment in Europe. Finally, NATO, in a bid to demonstrate the alliance's commitment to arms control, would offer to trade the ERW against Soviet weapons. In the American formulation, the arms control trade would be the ERWs for the Soviets' new SS-20 missiles.[26] The Americans wanted the allies to agree to the specifics of this three-pronged approach by March 23, and the NATO diplomats got to work to meet the timeline.[27]

In London, Callaghan and Owen remained wary of touching off a nuclear debate in Britain before the next general election. Nonetheless, Callaghan was "prepared to ride it out politically" if Carter made a clear decision in favor of production, even if it meant a "major row with the left wing of the Labour Party."[28] In Germany, too, Schmidt faced opposition inside his party, but he worked to build consensus for the ERW. The governments of the smaller West European allies, especially the Dutch and Danes, faced significant public opposition to the deployment. But by March 20 American officials reported that the last holdouts had agreed to the US plan in NATO.[29]

Carter assembled his national security team for discussion that very evening. But ahead of the meeting, NSC officials learned that Carter's position had shifted against the weapon. They sent Brzezinski a memorandum warning that if the president reversed his position on the ERW now, it would, "without any doubt, damage our authority and standing with the Europeans" and "raise questions about whether we know what we are doing and our basic competence." Just as bad, it would be an admission that "a Soviet-backed propaganda assault can force decisions on us that do not fit the facts." It would look to the world like either a "sign of weakness or as American moralism running rampant over real security needs and concerns."[30]

Carter, in the meeting, said he wished he "had never heard of this weapon." Although the allies had come around to the American three-pronged approach, Carter decided he wanted still more explicit support from Callaghan and Schmidt before going ahead. This seemed politically impossible for either man, and Brzezinski interpreted Carter's reservation as an effort to cancel the ERW.[31]

The Germans were "surprised and angry" by Carter's delay, as it allowed more time for leaks and Soviet propaganda to chip away at the delicate domestic consensus each leader had formed to support the ERW's deployment.[32] The British advised Deputy Secretary of State Warren Christopher that cancellation of ERW would have a "disastrous impact" on Carter's "credibility and hence leadership in the Western world."[33] Privately, the British cabinet committee charged with nuclear policy thought Carter had shown "considerable incompetence" while also offering "a substantial propaganda victory for the Russians."[34] Schmidt was outraged the president would back out of the ERW plan after gaining "complete agreement" among the allies.[35]

After the Pincus leak, the allies had had to scramble to reach an agreed position in favor of ERW. Now they needed time to present a unified position against the weapon. But another leak, this time by Richard Burt of the *New York Times* on April 4, gave the American line that Carter had delayed the ERW decision because he could not rely on his allies.[36] A few days later, the Americans officially announced Carter's decision to defer production of the ERW.

The leak to Burt led to acrimonious debate in the Bundestag and attacks on first Schmidt, then the Americans, in German newspapers and magazines. Franz Josef Strauss, the CDU leader, wrote that ERW marked "the first time that an American president has openly and visibly lain down in front of a Russian Tsar." "Unpredictable Carter" was singled out for opprobrium by the German press, and Genscher was quoted as having called Carter a "religious dreamer."[37] Schmidt survived the crisis but was increasingly vulnerable on his left flank.

NATO, British officials feared, was now led by "a President who is too often ruled by the heart rather than the head" and who "cannot effectively administer the United States as a whole." Washington, noted German official visitors, was filled with "leaderless men"—senior American officials—"openly whispering their incomprehension of the President's change of front." Worst of all, the Germans assumed this was not simply the result of Carter's ineffective leadership, but emblematic of a "sea change in American affairs" caused by Vietnam, the shift of power from White House to Congress, and "a lessening of will on the part of the Americans in foreign affairs which has led to a decline in their leadership."[38] Without consistent leadership from the United States, other allied governments were buffeted between what they believed to be NATO's strategic demands and their publics' antinuclear attitude.

Arms Limitations and the Erosion of Trust

The hard feelings over the ERW bungle were both cause and symptom of European, and especially German, concerns about American policy toward NATO defense and arms control. In the Nixon years, the European allies had worried that Moscow would seek to compel Washington to bargain away NATO's Forward Based Systems in SALT. But by the late 1970s, European worries had both changed and grown more acute.

SALT had focused only on US and Soviet strategic systems and had not touched on nuclear weapons systems in Europe. But in the meantime, the USSR had introduced tremendously powerful nuclear weapons in the "gray area" between battlefield nuclear weapons and the intercontinental strategic systems that could target the US from the USSR, or vice versa. While the SS-20 missile and the Backfire bomber could not reach the US, they could wreak massive damage on Western Europe, and the Europeans considered them "strategic" weapons just the same. SALT, the Europeans realized, had done nothing to limit Moscow's capability to destroy Western Europe by either nuclear or conventional arms, and only worked to strip the United States—and thus NATO—of the ability to hold the USSR hostage for an attack on Europe.[39]

In October 1977, Helmut Schmidt set out these concerns in a speech to London's International Institute for Strategic Studies. Arms talks between Washington and Moscow, he said, would "inevitably impair the security of the West European members of the Alliance vis-à-vis Soviet military superiority in Europe." He called for parallel negotiations to limit the disparity of military power in Europe that so favored the USSR.[40]

Privately, Schmidt worried that if the Soviets continued their buildup of theater weapons, the USSR would reverse the "arms balance" in Europe within ten to fifteen years. If the balance tipped, the SS-20 and the Backfire would "be used to blackmail Mediterranean countries, the Middle East and so on"—no doubt he meant Bonn, too.[41] Schmidt already felt the pressure of Soviet strength, complaining that he was compelled to "speak softly to the Russians." American officials, too, observed an increased German "attentiveness to Soviet concerns . . . a form of Finlandization."[42]

Arms control was an attractive option to Europeans who were beginning to wonder whether the Americans believed in the alliance any longer. If the Soviets pointed their SS-20s at the FRG, Schmidt said, he "had to go begging" to the French, the British, or the Americans and "ask them to produce a counter threat." He thought the allies might only move against the USSR if Moscow first fired nuclear weapons on Germany. He trusted his NATO contemporary colleagues, he said. Nevertheless, "One had to consider," he told Callaghan, "the possibility that a Eugene McCarthy or a Barry Goldwater might one day become President of the United States."[43] British officials, too, were scarred by the president's action over ERWs when Carter had backed down after "a failure of nerve or by guidance from the Southern Baptist God," neither of which portended positively for European security. The Germans did not trust Carter; the British grew wary.[44]

Schmidt and the Germans continued to insist that the West had to try to find a way to limit the Soviet theater nuclear capability via negotiations. Negotiations might lead to the withdrawal of Soviet weapons, but commitment to negotiations would also be politically essential to get some domestic agreement on any plan to deploy new nuclear weapons—arms control and modernization were always flip sides of the same coin. The only way to hold negotiations on gray-area weapons systems was, first, to build something to trade; so began the search for what Schmidt called "the Western pawn."[45]

Nuclear Modernization

Just as Schmidt was formulating his new approach to arms control, NATO officials were again considering how best to upgrade and modernize NATO's nuclear capabilities. With the increase in Soviet theater forces and the increasing obsolescence of NATO's existing strike aircraft, European strategists feared a "gap" in the NATO deterrent that would leave the allies unable to respond to each type of Soviet escalation without themselves pushing conflict to general war.[46]

As a solution, the Americans offered to provide NATO commanders with more submarine-launched ballistic missiles (SLBMs), for these weapons had long range and were not nearly as vulnerable as aircraft. But the European officials came to agree that it was essential that NATO's ground forces, not US submarines, have the capability to launch long-range theater nuclear forces (LRTNF) that could strike the USSR.[47]

In discussion at NATO, the chairman of the Military Committee warned that the deployment of LRTNF in NATO Europe, rather than SLBMs at sea, could be justified only "on political rather than on military grounds." But it was the political implications of the weapons' location, the German delegation pointed out, that mattered most. It was critical that such weapons be "visibly present in Europe so as to reassure domestic public opinion and to demonstrate the reality of the deterrent to the Warsaw Pact." Strengthening NATO's long-range theater nuclear forces, they claimed, was "very important for political and for psychological reasons."[48]

Schmidt, too, believed that the matter of LRTNF was one of politics, not military strategy. The real problem with the Soviet buildup was that it "publicly emphasises NATO's growing inferiority" and would "be perceived as weakening the West's political resolve to resist Soviet pressure in a future European crisis."[49] And the other allies worried, as they had for nearly a decade, that a German public that doubted NATO's commitment could encourage Bonn to move closer to Moscow.

But Schmidt's worry about his public's resolve was only half the problem. The other half, an issue present to varying degrees in all the allied capitals, was the growing popular aversion to nuclear weapons. Already, more than half of NATO's theater nuclear forces were based in Germany. While German officials knew it would make sense to station LRTNF in Germany, they also insisted, firmly and repeatedly, that the FRG could not be the sole site of NATO's new LRTNF. Schmidt's own party had an antinuclear wing, one whose power had been obvious in the ERW debate. He feared the upheaval caused by a new weapons system would create domestic political problems as well as make Bonn the "sole target for pressure from the Soviet Union."[50]

Thus the paradox, never effectively enunciated by the NATO allies, but at the heart of their analysis: NATO governments, especially Bonn, believed that the presence of a nuclear deterrent in Europe would reassure their citizens and reduce domestic political pressures to kowtow to Moscow's demands in a time of crisis. At the same time, reliance on nuclear weapons was a political liability, and so NATO governments shaped their policy and rhetoric to minimize the public attention given to the deterrent. NATO's nuclear weapons, allied officials believed, were crucial to protect their citizens—but those same citizens would punish governments who sought to deploy them.

All the European allies expected a NATO decision on nuclear modernization would cause political heartache. The Germans hoped that any new deployment of LRTNF could be managed in an "evolutionary" manner. Pershing missiles already in Germany might be upgraded so they could strike the USSR. This would be preferable—and less dramatic—than introducing a whole new weapons system, such as cruise missiles. Other European countries, including the United Kingdom, would receive cruise missile batteries. Governments expected opposition, but did not appreciate how controversial these deployments would become.[51]

Despite the looming political problems, NATO officials concluded that the alliance needed LRTNF, just as they had agreed NATO needed ERWs. But the ERW consensus had broken down at the very top level of allied leadership. To avoid another such catastrophe, Carter, Schmidt, Callaghan, and the French president Valéry Giscard d'Estaing arranged to meet in Guadeloupe in January 1979. The meeting's focus on NATO's gray-area systems was kept secret from the Soviets and from the other NATO allies. The leaders knew that any positive decision regarding LRTNF required the support of the whole alliance, and that the issue was "vital for the future both of NATO's strategic posture and political relations within the Alliance." But like the critical meetings over Berlin in the Kennedy years and the offset and strategy negotiations of the late 1960s, the largest NATO allies believed it was essential to reach agreement among themselves first.[52]

Photos of the Guadeloupe summit show smiling leaders and suggest pleasant Caribbean weather. But records of the meeting reveal clear strains between leaders. Carter told the others that he was willing to upgrade NATO's LRTNF in order to gain the leverage required for negotiating away the Soviet SS-20s. But, he said, the "onus was on the Europeans who were worried about the SS 20s"—that is, the Germans. If they wanted negotiations, they needed to accept the missiles. Schmidt, however, stuck to his earlier condition that Germany would accept the LRTNF only if "at least one other European NATO ally did so also," not to include the United Kingdom. Carter, surprised and disturbed by Schmidt's intransigence, warned the chancellor that "if Germany was not prepared to take the necessary measures to defend herself it was difficult to see why others should do so on her behalf."[53]

Schmidt refused to budge. For the Germans, the deployment of nuclear missiles that could strike the Soviet Union would be a "watershed" moment. It would open Schmidt to accusations from Moscow of warmongering. But if Bonn could present the deployment as a concerted NATO effort to meet the Soviet challenge and, more important, to encourage arms limitation talks, Schmidt might be able to cobble together enough support at home for the deployment. The West Germans, Schmidt's foreign policy adviser told American NSC officials, "need help to do the right thing" and move forward with LRTNF.[54]

American officials, albeit slowly, came to agree with Schmidt's concern that the "gap" between Soviet and NATO theater nuclear capabilities "could expose Europe to nuclear intimidation by the Soviets during a crisis." In 1962, amid the Cuban Missile Crisis, the overall strategic weapons gap had favored the United States, helping John F. Kennedy prevail over Nikita Khrushchev. Now, the Americans agreed it essential to prevent such a gap in Europe, "to ensure that we do not suffer a 'Cuba-in-reverse'—from which we might not recover."[55]

In the spring of 1979, a specially formed "high level group" of NATO's Nuclear Planning Group concluded, formally, that LRTNF deployment in Europe was necessary. To accommodate Schmidt's needs, NATO planned to upgrade the Pershings in the FRG and to deploy ground-launched cruise missiles in the UK, Italy, Belgium, and the Netherlands. But striking agreement between allied governments in private was perhaps the easiest part of what came to be called NATO's Dual-Track decision. Trying to keep the allies united, especially amid public protest, would place the alliance under enormous strain.

Reaching the Dual-Track Decision

In 1979, Europe was transformed into a political battleground. It was not a battle between states with disparate interests, but between governments and domestic political groups opposed to NATO's nuclear weapons. A muddled mix of genuine concern and foreign encouragement motivated these advocacy groups. Across the alliance, NATO allies saw a Soviet propaganda campaign in "full swing." Soviet and Soviet-backed newspapers slammed the proposed deployment, while senior Soviet officials launched press campaigns and gave interviews arguing that Moscow was willing to negotiate and ultimately reduce its theater nuclear forces if only NATO would not deploy its LRTNF. Secretly, Soviet agents pressured Communist groups, like the Italian PCI, to protest modernization.[56] Soviet promises of unilateral arms reductions, often accompanied by darker threats about what would happen if NATO accepted LRTNF, revealed a clumsy Soviet effort to simultaneously lull and intimidate allied governments.[57]

The German government had already seen this play before over ERWs. Schmidt fought back with speeches of his own, emphasizing the importance of LRTNF as a bargaining chip. He managed to hold together his governing coalition, but the Germans worried that their stand in favor of LRTNF could not last forever. Schmidt worried about the political mood not only in Germany, but also in Belgium and the Netherlands. Socialist and Social Democratic parties in Western Europe had close ties, and Schmidt worried that if one ally, perhaps the Dutch, refused to accept the deployment, their "attitude might quickly spread to Belgium and then to Italy and the Scandinavian allies and even, possibly, to the Federal Republic."[58]

The allies hurried to reach agreement before opposition to the deployment could spread any further. The Germans and Americans pushed for a decision in 1979; both governments faced federal elections in 1980. The smaller allies, especially the Danes, the Dutch, and the Norwegians, wished to defer the decision to avoid difficult political problems at home. The larger powers in NATO leaned on their smaller allies to agree. They warned, pointedly, that if NATO's smaller members did not help carry NATO's burdens, they would be considered second-tier allies. As a carrot, the Americans also promised to announce a unilateral reduction of one thousand nuclear warheads in Europe. This would help the allies, especially the Dutch, argue that the alliance was reducing its reliance on nuclear weapons, even though the offer simply fulfilled an American plan to remove obsolete weaponry.[59]

On December 12, 1979, the NATO allies finally agreed to pursue the "two parallel and complementary approaches" of modernizing NATO's theater nuclear forces while also seeking arms-control negotiations with the Soviet Union. The decision was an impressive success for diplomatic coordination, but it worried some. NATO's new supreme allied commander, Bernard Rogers, warned that the dual track was a "folly." He worried that trading away nuclear weapons was a slippery slope for NATO and that the real beneficiary from any nuclear trade would be the USSR.[60]

The "Dual Track" helped paper over the gap in NATO states between those who believed that nuclear weapons remained essential to preserve peace in Europe and those who thought the only true means of achieving security was arms control and, ultimately, disarmament. Elected officials in the last decade of the Cold War understood there could be no modernization without a complementary commitment to arms control. When NATO announced that the allies had agreed to the Dual Track, the NATO communiqué emphasized that arms control was the solution to the security threat in Europe.[61]

The Politics of Disarmament

NATO's Dual-Track decision was the end of the beginning, not the beginning of the end, of NATO's nuclear crisis. Just months after the decision, officials worried that the "delicate package sewn together" in December by NATO foreign ministers was "beginning to unravel." The year 1980 saw a number of disagreements between the allies: the European allies thought American blood pressure ran too high over the Soviet invasion of Afghanistan, and allied consultations regarding the crisis were spotty and frustrating. The allies also disagreed over how to respond to turmoil in Poland. But these disagreements should not be overstated.[62] They paled in comparison to the threat to the alliance posed by a changing mood in European public opinion and changing policies in the United States.

In the year after he agreed to NATO's Dual-Track decision, Schmidt and his Social Democratic Party campaigned in the 1980 election as the "Party of Peace." Some of Schmidt's SPD colleagues, including the parliamentary chairman of the party, Herbert Wehner, gained attention and attracted public support by campaigning directly against LRTNF deployment. NATO diplomats understood that Schmidt was "seeking to have his cake and eat it," with the SPD gaining votes by championing disarmament, while Schmidt privately continued to support LRTNF deployment. But this seemed a dangerous line, and the allies worried Schmidt would be obligated by the SPD's campaign to turn against the Dual-Track decision. Indeed, in the middle of the election campaign, Schmidt called for a freeze on the proposed LRTNF deployment and was admonished by Carter in a letter American diplomats thought "brusque to the point of rude."[63]

German politicians, like the defense minister Hans Apel, believed that during the election something fundamental had changed in Germany. West Germans were, for the first time, engaging in "a radical debate" about the best way to maintain peace and security. Outside of Germany, some allied officials took this to an extreme: Alexander Haig thought Germany was finally at the point of "sliding away from their Atlantic connection" toward the East.[64] Haig's diagnosis went too far, and Schmidt held strong to his 1979 LRTNF position. After his reelection, Schmidt sent a message to Washington summing up prospects for German policy: while the peace movements had been stronger than he expected, the German government could manage to implement the agreed policy—as long the United States emphasized continuity of policy, too.[65]

While Schmidt was returned to office in 1980, Jimmy Carter was not so fortunate. Carter lost to Ronald Reagan, a former B-list film actor and governor of California who promised a muscular foreign policy. The allies, previously concerned that Carter would not fight for Europe if necessary, now faced an American president who gave the public impression of having an itchy trigger finger.

Reagan's policy pronouncements in 1981 focused on massive increases in American defense spending designed to ensure the containment of the USSR. London and Bonn fretted that if the Americans continued to dwell on the threat of Soviet strength, European publics would respond by pushing their governments for arms reductions, not increases. For many Europeans, the real threat to peace was not Soviet arms, but an arms race. Schmidt, in the cockpit of Europe's debate over NATO's defense policy, urged the Americans to refrain from "belligerent and bellicose" pronunciations, speeches, and interviews. This was the only way to prevent defense spending from becoming a highly visible political battle, and a battle the European allies felt sure they would lose. Reagan and his advisers, however, continued to speak about the need for defense spending and the Soviet threat, causing one British official to worry: "I think we have a very serious problem with the Americans."[66]

These worries seemed justified in early 1981 when Caspar Weinberger, Reagan's secretary of defense, shocked the allies by musing publicly that the US might reverse Carter's policy and deploy the neutron bomb. The ERW, the weapon that had soured relations in the 1970s and created such problems for NATO, was back in the news. Its reappearance, combined with still simmering emotions over the Dual-Track decision and broader worries about Reagan's bellicose policies, led to an outpouring of public protest. In the spring of 1981, major peace protests were held in European capitals, Japan, and in New York. American analysts noted that it was not just radicals, but "diverse, usually non-political people as well as activists" protesting the nuclear policy.[67]

Reagan blamed the public outcry squarely on Soviet propaganda. While some demonstrators may have been "sincere," others "were really carrying the propaganda ball for the Soviet Union." Opponents of nuclear deployment mocked the idea that they were the Kremlin's stooges. The British critic Christopher Hitchens labeled the notion "bullshit," for he himself had "written several pages against the weapon [ERW] for no extra pay."[68]

But there was more to Reagan's claim than a knee-jerk accusation. American diplomats and their allies at NATO met to share intelligence on "active measures" taken by both the KGB and other agencies to turn Europe against the LRTNF deployment. The Soviets and their Warsaw Pact allies provided leadership and money to antinuclear groups, both Communist and noncommunist. They distributed forged American diplomatic cables that ostensibly demonstrated American plans for the nuclearization of the Scandinavian countries. To try to develop links between the protests and government policy, Soviet diplomats made promises to European politicians, including more and cheaper oil to any ally that broke ranks on the LRTNF deployment. While the Kremlin might not have paid Hitchens, there is no doubt that the Soviet Union was waging what Brezhnev himself described as a "political propaganda" campaign against NATO's nuclear policy.[69]

Walter Laqueur, an American historian writing in the journal *Commentary*, sought to diagnose the new political atmosphere in Europe. He argued that a pacifist, neutralist attitude—"Hollanditis"—had emerged in the Netherlands that would sweep through Western Europe. Europeans would soon be clamoring, if they were not already, for neutrality in the Cold War and the abandonment of the US and NATO.[70] If Laqueur was correct—and his prognostications certainly matched some of the darker worries held by allies on both sides of the Atlantic in the preceding decade—then NATO might be lost.

The British FCO undertook a major study to find out. Logically, they began with Dr. Laqueur's patient zero. During the Vietnam years, the refrain at Dutch protests had been "Get the Netherlands out of NATO." In the early 1980s, however, British officials heard a subtle shift. It was now: "Get nuclear weapons out of NATO." What caught the attention and garnered the energies of Dutch citizens in the 1980s was not so much neutralism or pacifism, but the weapons themselves.[71]

As British embassies reported back, and officials in London compiled their study, a pattern emerged: in Belgium, there was no significant anti-NATO attitude, nor calls for neutralism, but there was strong antinuclear sentiment. In Italy, too, the LRTNF deployment was deeply unpopular, although NATO membership was popular. German public opinion, though it had always contained a strain of neutralist sentiment, did not see a rise in these feelings in 1981. The Foreign Office observed that the problem facing NATO was not an acute desire for neutralism nor pacifism. Instead, they were witnessing the breakdown of the domestic consensus in European states that NATO must rely on nuclear weapons for its defense.[72]

This breakdown led to another round of soul searching in NATO. For three decades, NATO's strategic logic had rested on the deployment of nuclear weapons to deter Soviet attack. Now, it seemed, citizens of NATO states had come to reject the weapons. The British officials decided to look more closely at the debate happening in Britain. One official attended a discussion of nuclear policy at a university. He was surprised by the high attendance and the deep passions of the audience, but astounded by their ignorance. He found problems with many of the arguments against nuclear weapons, but overall, and more "worryingly, many of the students seemed to have little idea even about such fundamental concepts as the NATO Alliance, its object and membership." The officials' anecdotal evidence matched with polling data from 1980: Whereas in 1961, 48 percent of British subjects had believed that "international affairs and defence" rated "as the most important problems facing the country," twenty years later, at the end of 1980, the number who felt the same way had fallen to a paltry 5 percent.[73]

NATO publics, the officials surmised, had not suddenly shifted their position on the alliance and nuclear weapons; instead, they simply thought less and less about them. When nuclear weapons and nuclear policy burst into the public consciousness because of the massive propaganda campaigns against the neutron bomb and theater nuclear forces, citizens in NATO countries had little context for understanding why NATO deployed such ferocious weapons.

Allied leaders, after all, shared their electorate's horror of nuclear weapons. Douglas Hurd, the British secretary of state in Margaret Thatcher's Conservative government that had replaced Callaghan's Labourites, believed that "concern about nuclear weapons is absolutely natural, and we should treat it as such."[74] The difference, however, was that allied leaders and their senior bureaucrats and military advisers assumed that the Soviet nuclear and conventional capacity made NATO's nuclear weapons indispensable. Where NATO governments believed nuclear weapons were a necessary evil, their citizens saw only evil.

Some politicians and officials chalked up antinuclear sentiment to the obtuseness of youth. For those thirty-four years old or younger, lamented one German politician, "war and post-war experience have no meaning," and "peace itself has largely lost its uniqueness." Whereas an older generation believed that peace could be achieved only with the right balance of diplomacy and military might, the younger generation had come to believe it could "be preserved without much effort." These were evergreen complaints; Nixon and Kissinger and their transatlantic colleagues had worried a decade before that a new, softer generation could not understand the basis of peace without having seen war. And back from the United States came the traditional American warning: If Europeans would not help do the hard work to ensure peace, then Americans might "forget the lessons of World War I and II and re-embrace isolationism—or general unilateralism."[75]

But there was another explanation for the generational gap and its effects for NATO and its nuclear policy. British officials, having carefully studied public opinion in Britain and Europe, placed the blame not on Soviet propaganda, nor on the ignorance of youth, although each played a role in developing the public opposition to the LRTNF deployment. Fundamentally, one FCO official wrote, Her Majesty's government was to blame—and, by extension, so too were other NATO governments. Since the 1960s, although both Labour and Conservative governments had supported NATO nuclear policy, neither had made either a strong or consistent case to maintain public support for NATO's deterrent. Labour had found the policy embarrassing for party reasons, and the Conservatives—according to the FCO—had been too complacent in assuming support for the policy.[76]

This pattern had echoed throughout NATO's history, as governments, knowing that the idea of war—let alone nuclear war—would have few proponents, sought to avoid public discussion of nuclear weapons and NATO's deterrent. For decades, the allies had described the alliance with emphasis on shared values and a common heritage, downplaying the enormously powerful military force at its core, trained and equipped to wage nuclear war.

By 1982, British officials worried they might "find that public opinion runs away from us" altogether, as the public and their parliamentarians turned fully against nuclear weapons. "If this happens," Margaret Thatcher's minister of defense, John Nott, warned, "we will lose our strategic deterrent—and much else besides."[77] For NATO allies to maintain their defense spending, their nuclear deterrent, and indeed the alliance itself, wrote another official, it was time to "take steps to explain the need for [nuclear weapons], which in turn involves explaining the whole basis of deterrence, how it relates to Alliance strategy, and so on."[78]

No such public education campaign was forthcoming from NATO or the allies. NATO governments, including even the bellicose Americans, continued to use the Dual-Track communiqué as their script. Indeed, even the Reagan administration reined in its rhetoric, trading bellicosity for the language of arms control. In November 1981, Reagan announced he would adhere to the Dual-Track agreement and cancel the deployment of LRTNF if only the Soviets would withdraw their weapons of the same range.[79] It is unlikely that Reagan or his advisers thought such a trade likely, but they were urged by European allies, like Schmidt, and Lord Carrington, now the secretary-general of NATO, to try to prove to European voters that the US was serious about arms control.[80]

Such an approach did nothing to alleviate the public insistence against nuclear weapons that concerned the allies. Demonstrations continued and intensified. At Greenham Common, the proposed deployment site in Britain for a complement of NATO's cruise missiles, a small group of female activists established a "peace camp" around the military base. In 1982, they called for the support of women across the United Kingdom. Thirty thousand arrived to partake in a candlelight vigil, and they decorated the base's fence with "children's pictures and other decorations—symbols of the life the nuclear missiles would destroy."[81] In Germany, the nascent Green Party opposed nuclear energy—civilian and military—as counter to its message of environmentalism, and gained support from many antinuclear activists. And everywhere, in the hands of both political activists and regular citizens alike, was the enormously popular, Pulitzer Prize–winning book by Jonathan Schell, *The Fate of the Earth*, with

FIGURE 10. An American flag is burned on the perimeter fence of the US Rhein-Main Air Base, near Frankfurt, Germany, by protesters demonstrating against NATO's decision to deploy Pershing II and cruise missiles in Western Europe, December 1982. National Archives Photo no. 330-CFD-DF-ST-83-09538.

its detailed, if not especially novel, message that a nuclear war would not only kill millions but remove the basic conditions required for human life on Earth. Intriguingly, Schell had come to a similar conclusion as British officials: "in spite of the immeasurable importance of nuclear weapons, the world has declined, on the whole, to think about them very much."[82] Now that NATO publics thought about them, they did not want them.

The NATO governments kept their heads down, working together to ensure that the LRTNF deployments of 1983 went ahead simultaneously, so as not to leave any single ally as the lone recipient of the new weapons. Negotiations with Moscow had begun in 1981, but Moscow remained unlikely to trade away its already-deployed weapons for weapons NATO had not put on station. There was no US-Soviet bargain, and by the end of 1983 NATO's theater nuclear forces were delivered to bases in Western Europe.

The Impact of Reykjavik and the INF Treaty

Antinuclear sentiment continued to grow in both the West and the East through-out the mid-1980s. Ironically, Soviet support for antinuclear protests in Europe helped create independent peace movements in East Germany that, in the end, contributed to the collapse of Soviet power and of the Iron Curtain.[83] But most surprising was a change in the attitudes of the American and Soviet leaders toward nuclear weapons.

Ronald Reagan, the man who dubbed the Soviet Union the "evil empire," and a new Soviet leader, Mikhail Gorbachev, both had come to believe it necessary to halt, and if possible reverse, the nuclear arms race. The most famous manifesta-tion of their shared concern came at a 1986 summit in Reykjavik when, for a fleeting moment, both men agreed to rid the world of nuclear weapons. When Margaret Thatcher learned that Reagan had almost bargained away the basis of NATO's security, she felt an "earthquake" beneath her feet. The Europeans, especially Thatcher and her German colleague, Helmut Kohl—Kohl's Christian Democratic Union (CDU) had replaced Schmidt in 1982 with the aid of Gen-scher's Free Democratic Party (FDP)—tried to explain to Reagan that if there were no nuclear weapons, there would be no European security to speak of.[84]

Reykjavik, perhaps, came the closest to fulfilling that nagging European fear that America might one day come to be ruled by a president who abandoned Europe's security for political rewards at home. Schmidt had worried that an extremist Goldwater or McGovern might become president; Reagan had man-aged to represent both extremes, taking what Europeans thought was too hard a tack in his first term and suddenly becoming too soft in his second. Had

Gorbachev and Reagan successfully struck their grand bargain, the world might have been transformed, but NATO would have withered.

Reagan and Gorbachev ultimately did not agree to eliminate all nuclear weapons, but they built on the momentum of Reykjavik to take a first step in reversing the nuclear arms race. In late 1987 Reagan agreed to eliminate all of the NATO ground-launched cruise missiles and Pershing II launchers NATO had deployed as a result of the Dual-Track decision. In exchange, the Soviet Union agreed to remove several types of launchers and their warheads, including the SS-20s. In effect, the two sides agreed to eliminate an entire class of weapons: those Intermediate Range Nuclear Forces (INF) that could strike targets at a distance of five hundred to fifty-five hundred kilometers.

For some, the INF Treaty was partway down the slippery slope predicted by Bernard Rogers. Rogers had been replaced as SACEUR by John Galvin by the time of the treaty, but he still blasted the treaty as "short-term political expediency." And while the Europeans had, since the 1970s, wanted to find a solution to the problem of the Soviet SS-20s, and indeed pushed Reagan on arms control, they feared a situation whereby NATO was stripped of any weapons with INF range. In the United States, Brent Scowcroft—Ford's national security adviser who would reprise the role under George H. W. Bush—thought the INF Treaty a mistake; NATO should be bargaining away its shorter-range weapons but keeping its intermediate weapons. Nonetheless, the Dual-Track decision had been premised on the idea of arms control, and the INF Treaty seemed to be the immaculate fulfillment of the NATO decision taken in 1979. No European leader interested in reelection was willing to speak publicly against the treaty, for their publics agreed with it wholeheartedly.[85]

After INF, each side retained its strategic nuclear capability (as governed by the SALT agreement) and its tactical nuclear weapons—what came to be called "short-range nuclear forces" (SNF). With INF gone, the importance of NATO's SNF increased dramatically as the "central political symbol in Europe" of the American commitment to NATO. The alliance's defense ministers, recognizing SNF's importance as early as 1983, agreed they would need to be modernized, and Supreme Headquarters had drawn up studies confirming the need for an update.[86]

In 1987, Reagan, meeting with other NATO heads of government, highlighted the fine distinction between the removal of INF and the need for NATO to maintain its nuclear capacity. While he told his fellow leaders that he would prefer to get rid of all nuclear weapons, the time was not right. NATO still required nuclear weapons to provide a viable deterrent to Soviet conventional military strength. What was more, the Soviets were still scheming to force NATO's "nuclear withdrawal" from Europe. Ultimately, Reagan said, there was a "priority higher than a nuclear-free alliance: that is a war-free alliance."[87]

The citizens of NATO countries, especially in Germany, did not make a fine distinction between a nuclear-free and war-free NATO. Instead, Reagan's secretary of state George Shultz reported that the INF Treaty had only whetted the European public's appetite for the elimination of more nuclear weapons. The problem became acute as German opponents of nuclear weapons raised the troubling notion that, by definition, NATO's SNF stationed in the FRG could be used only to strike targets in Germany—East or West—and thus to kill Germans. Kohl warned the allies that his citizens were "increasingly smitten with the notion of a central Europe devoid of nuclear weapons." The INF Treaty, hugely popular in Europe, seemed to offer the recipe for ridding the world of nuclear weapons: eliminating them class by class. Perhaps it was time to eliminate SNF.[88]

By coincidence, SNF were due for modernization. The Americans, supported by the British and French, began in earnest to press NATO to agree to a modernization plan to replace the nearly obsolescent weapons system. But Kohl's coalition partner, Genscher, not only wanted to avoid a modernization debate, but did not want to rule out a possible "zero" option for SNF. If NATO did not foreclose the "zero" option for SNF, the Americans worried, Moscow might push for the elimination of SNF in Europe. Such an offer would be "politically irresistible" to the governments of Europe; their citizens would stampede their leaders toward what NATO officials thought was the ultimate Soviet ambition: the "denuclearization" of Europe."[89] Kohl, under pressure due to a number of domestic political problems in addition to the nuclear issue, watched his political position deteriorate. In 1989 he shocked the allies by refusing to agree to the SNF upgrades, and announced that Germany would postpone any discussion of modernization until 1992.[90]

By 1989, denuclearization was no longer just a theoretical possibility. In Europe as a whole, and particularly in Germany, officials saw a shift in the "domestic security consensus" toward disarmament. The shift in public opinion against nuclear deterrence was not total, but it did not have to be. Coalition government meant that Genscher's small FDP held the balance of power. Genscher, sensing the shift in popular opinion, moved to a position on disarmament that held Kohl hostage. Either Kohl could acquiesce to Genscher's position, or the FDP might side with the now steadfastly antinuclear SPD. NATO diplomats watching Germany were not certain whether Kohl would trade the basis of Atlantic security for continued political power.[91]

In 1989, it was not at all obvious what could be done to ensure that NATO's nuclear weapons would be modernized, or, as important, not bargained away.

The new American president, George H. W. Bush, recognized that it was essential for NATO's survival not "to push Kohl to the political brink" on SNF modernization. Ultimately, the president's "key objective was to keep the Alliance together."[92] Bush's decision not to press Kohl on the issue prevented a sharp break within the alliance, but it did nothing to solve the impending obsolescence of NATO's SNF and its lack of INF in Europe.

Nor did it rule out SNF as a Soviet lever against NATO. In May 1989, Bush's secretary of state, James Baker, visited Moscow to meet with Gorbachev. In the press conference after their meeting, Gorbachev surprised Baker—and the world—by announcing that the Soviet Union would withdraw five hundred SNF weapons from Europe. Gorbachev said that such a withdrawal was possible because, presumably unlike the Americans, "we in Europe" think differently about nuclear weapons. What he did not mention was that the Soviets fielded approximately fourteen hundred such launchers, as compared to NATO's eighty-eight. Gorbachev would continue to offer SNF cuts if NATO would agree to negotiating with the ultimate goal of eliminating SNF from Europe—an offer "clearly designed to create mischief and to reopen wounds" in NATO.[93]

The forces pushing toward denuclearization—and by extension, the collapse of NATO—posed the most severe threat to NATO's endurance. Kohl, by declaring the postponement of a decision on modernization, had offered an unprecedented public repudiation of a decision the NATO allies had been working toward for years, and Gorbachev showed he would try to take advantage. Political shifts in Germany were drawing the FRG closer and closer toward a nuclear-free Germany. If the Germans would not permit nuclear weapons on German soil, the Americans assumed that other Europeans would follow suit; and if no nuclear weapons could be stationed in Europe, it was likely that the US Congress would push for the redeployment of American troops out of Europe. NATO's nuclear deterrent, and NATO itself, were imperiled not by disagreements about strategy or state interests, but by the political sentiments of citizens in democratic states, and especially the FRG.[94]

NATO governments had come up against domestic political opposition over ERWs, and failed to deploy the weapon. On LRTNF, they had succeeded, ultimately, but only after traveling a difficult road. But the LRTNF deployment, coupled with the promise of disarmament, had paved the way for public expectations that SNF could be dealt away, too. While the Dual-Track deployment was in itself a success, it was NATO's last gasp at nuclear modernization. As Baker traveled to meet allies in 1989, he heard the same message over and over: "NATO could not afford another crisis over deploying nuclear weapons."[95]

In 1989, all eyes were on Germany, both the great prize in the Cold War and the potential battleground in a hot war. In August, Scowcroft warned Bush that "managing our relations with Germany is likely to be the most serious geopolitical challenge our country faces over the next decade"—that is, he said, "unless we have to cope with a disintegrating Soviet Union."[96] In fact, as events in the coming months would show, these challenges were hardly distinct. What no one expected in 1989 was that the disintegration of the Soviet Union would save NATO from the challenges of nuclear disarmament that had pushed the alliance ever closer to the brink of collapse.

10

PROMISES ARE NEVER ENOUGH

December 20, 1991: The Soviet ambassador rose from his seat before the chairman could bang the gavel that would close the first meeting of the brand-new North Atlantic Co-operation Council (NACC). Ambassador Nikolai Afanassievsky had just received instructions from Moscow, and he had an announcement to make.

Throughout the day at NATO headquarters in Brussels, ambassadors and foreign ministers from the recently dissolved Warsaw Pact had met with their former enemies. Even before the dissolution of the Moscow-led alliance in July 1991, NATO had extended a "hand of friendship" to states of the pact in an effort to build "a new, lasting order of peace in Europe."[1] During the course of the first NACC, the representatives had agreed to a communiqué proclaiming their progress and plans for future meetings. But when Afanassievsky rose, he requested that any reference to the Soviet Union be removed from the meeting's communiqué. During the meeting, the Soviet Union had ceased to exist.

And yet the request of the ambassador of the now-former Soviet Union could not be met. The communiqué of the meeting had already been printed. NATO's secretary-general, Manfred Woerner, thinking quickly on his feet, offered to add a note to the communiqué reflecting Afanassievsky's statement. NATO, quite literally, had reduced the Soviet Union to a footnote in history.[2]

Why did NATO endure after Soviet power collapsed in Eastern Europe, and after the Soviet Union itself ceased to exist? Allied officials in the late 1980s and early 1990s would have found these questions odd. For even after the dramatic events of the fall of the Berlin Wall in 1989, the unification of Germany in 1990, and the failed coup in Moscow in 1991, the allies believed that NATO was the essential guarantor of security for Europe and the United States. NATO, said President George H. W. Bush in February 1990, months after the fall of the Berlin Wall, was now "more important than ever."[3]

Even before the fall of the Berlin Wall, Bush saw that NATO had a role to play even if the Cold War thawed. The alliance provided the stability and certainty necessary to manage changing relationships between East and West. Change was in the air in the spring of 1989. On May 12, Bush delivered the commencement address at Texas A&M University. His remarks were, in part, a response to Mikhail Gorbachev's dynamism. Earlier in the year, the lively Soviet leader had given a powerful speech at the United Nations, declaring that the world was changing, and that a new era of peaceful relations between NATO and the Warsaw Pact was at hand.

Bush, in his remarks to the graduates at College Station, acknowledged the tremendous changes taking place around the world and especially behind the Iron Curtain. The United States and NATO might be capable of beginning a new relationship with their Cold War enemies. But friendly relations, Bush said, could not simply be declared by Moscow. Time and again the leaders of the Soviet Union had used peaceful overtures to mask their true intentions. If Moscow wanted a new relationship, it would take time, and it would have to be earned: "promises are never enough."[4]

One month before Bush's speech, the North Atlantic Treaty celebrated its fortieth anniversary. During NATO's four decades, the allies had fretted over ebbs and flows of American leadership. They had chafed when Washington seemed domineering, when the Americans pushed for budget increases or diplomatic support the allies did not wish to extend. The darkest periods of the postwar transatlantic history, however, were not when American leadership was overbearing but when it appeared America might forget about the alliance. A lack of interest in NATO was decidedly not the case during the turmoil of the late 1980s and early 1990s.

From 1989 through the end of the George H. W. Bush administration, Washington took an assertive role in guaranteeing NATO's future. Some allies bristled at America's vision for a continued, even strengthened, NATO. But the Bush administration's dual insistence that a united Germany remain a member of NATO and that NATO must continue—even expand—as a bulwark against both a resurgent Russia and dangerous maneuvering between great powers in Europe ensured NATO survived the end of the Cold War.

By the end of the Bush administration, NATO had changed. There were fewer North American troops stationed in Europe, with fewer nuclear weapons. NATO adapted its war-fighting strategy to reflect that the countries on the alliance's eastern frontier no longer formed an anti-NATO alliance. Those former members of the Warsaw Pact on NATO's borders were beginning to develop relationships with NATO designed both to improve their security and to salt the earth against any return of Russian power in Eastern Europe.

Despite these changes—or in some cases because of them—NATO remained the preeminent security forum, organization, and command structure in Europe. No ally questioned the need to maintain the North Atlantic Treaty. American troops, armed with nuclear weapons, remained on the continent. An American supreme commander remained atop an integrated command structure that planned for war in Europe. In fact, NATO's military integration only deepened after collapse of the Warsaw Pact.

As in decades past, the arguments for maintaining this military alliance were unpopular and difficult to make in public. The Americans were guilty, like the other allies and NATO itself, of justifying the alliance's continuation by stressing adaptation to a new world. But despite the rhetoric and some real examples of NATO's "transformation" at the end of the Cold War, NATO remained in place, designed to preserve the postwar order: to keep the Russians out, the Americans in, and the Germans down.

Gorbachev Presents Challenges and Opportunity

The American conviction that NATO should manage any change in the Cold War status quo in Europe was based on a grim assessment of military might and the balance of state power in Europe. Indeed, in a sense, the end of the era known as the Cold War had little impact on the Bush administration's belief in the fundamental need for NATO; the argument for an American presence on the continent was rooted in the memory of the first half, not the second half, of the twentieth century. As Bush's national security adviser Brent Scowcroft wrote to Bush: "The basic lesson of the two world wars was that American power is essential to any stable equilibrium on the continent." Whether or not the Cold War ended, the Red Army would remain the "dominant military power on the Eurasian land mass." No matter what changed in Soviet rhetoric or in European politics, Scowcroft continued, "geopolitical realities will endure."[5]

The Bush administration entered office concerned that Ronald Reagan had been shortsighted in his dealings with Gorbachev. They were determined not to play into any Soviet traps in Europe. Scowcroft and his deputy, Robert Gates, both viewed Soviet policy in light of their understanding of Russian history. Moscow's policy had at is core, they believed, a long-standing concern with expanding Russian control and influence along its borders. Soviet policy was consistent with czarist policy, even if Communist ideology made Soviet efforts to expand more active and perhaps more dangerous than those of historic Russia. Gorbachev's speeches simply could not reverse decades, even centuries, of Moscow's habits and interests. Whoever was in charge in Moscow, the Americans expected, would be compelled to try to exert Russian influence beyond its borders, especially in Europe.[6]

When in March 1989 Gorbachev called for the end of Cold War structures—the NATO and Warsaw Pact alliances—Bush and Scowcroft both saw a Soviet effort to undermine American leadership in Europe.[7] When Gorbachev spoke of the states of the continent belonging to a "common European home," American officials heard the implication that America was a guest on the continent whose invitation might expire.[8] Like earlier Soviet peace offensives, such Soviet calls for reordering Europe were viewed by American officials as attempts to "seduce" the West, obscuring what was really an effort to gain influence and leadership in Europe.[9]

The seduction seemed to be working. In June 1989, Gorbachev's speeches captured public attention in Western Europe. American officials watched with concern as the Soviet leader visited the FRG and was "mobbed by Germans" who cheered his calls for disarmament, the removal of short-range nuclear forces (SNF) from Europe, and a new conception of politics in Europe that did away with the Cold War alliances.[10] Here, perhaps, was the younger, more sophisticated Soviet leader the allies had worried the Soviet Union might one day produce.

As the Americans eyed Gorbachev warily, they worried about West Germany's future orientation. State Department officials were fond of Churchill's quip: the "Germans are either at your throat or at your feet." Clearly, as one American diplomat put it, "We liked them at our feet."[11] By the end of the 1980s, American diplomats feared that antinuclear sentiment among younger German voters might grow into an active effort to reject alliance with the United States.[12] The generational split in German public opinion that German politicians had warned of earlier was real and measurable in the 1980s: Germans who were sixty years old or more told pollsters that NATO was an "appealing" term, while nearly half (47 percent) of Germans under the age of thirty found it "unappealing." And while few Germans favored the immediate withdrawal of the FRG from NATO, ambivalent and negative attitudes were gaining ground. More and more Germans believed that it would not matter if the FRG withdrew from NATO.[13] While Germans were not hankering to leave the alliance, there was a growing sense that NATO was expendable. The possibility loomed that if the Germans had a choice, they might conceivably trade membership in NATO for something they did desire: the reunification of East and West Germany.

In the 1980s, few would have given German unification betting odds. American officials, let alone their European allies, could imagine no situation whereby "reunification would be possible or even desirable."[14] Nor did they believe that the West Germans thought unification likely in the twentieth century.[15] But the politics of reunification were ever present in Germany, and it worried the Americans that Gorbachev might win German hearts and minds.

Scowcroft advised Bush in March to "send a clear signal to the Germans" that the US was "ready to do more" on unification.[16] This would steal some of Gorbachev's appeal and reassure the Germans that their best chance for reunification was as a NATO ally. Bush delivered an important speech in Mainz, in May 1989. In what was essentially a pledge of the right of Germans to unify, he called for the "self-determination of all Germany."[17]

Bush's nod to what was at that time only a hypothetical possibility of German unification was important. But alone it was not sufficient to combat Gorbachev's public approval. At the end of March 1989, Bush worried that the Soviet leader had "eroded U.S. leadership in Europe." If the United States did not regain that leadership, he warned his senior advisers, "things are going to fall apart."[18]

The Bush administration could not match Gorbachev's rhetoric and promises of nuclear withdrawals in Europe, for NATO strategy required the deployment of SNF. Already in 1989, as discussed in the previous chapter, it was uncertain whether NATO's SNF would be modernized or even allowed to remain in Germany. But if there was a change in the balance of conventional forces in Europe, the need for SNF modernization would become considerably less acute.

Bush seized on the issue of conventional force reductions as both a public example of American leadership and a shrewd strategic move. American officials drew up a proposal calling for an agreed ceiling of American and Soviet troops in Europe—each state would be allowed to deploy a maximum of 275,000 troops outside its national borders. Because the United States deployed fewer troops in NATO Europe than the USSR did in Warsaw Pact states, the effects would be disproportionate: the USSR would have to cut 325,000 troops and the US only 30,000.[19]

Bush wrote to his NATO colleagues to convince them that his proposal should be the allies' bargaining position in negotiations for a possible Treaty on Conventional Armed Forces in Europe (CFE). The CFE plan was about far more than seizing the spotlight; it was about using Gorbachev's rhetoric against him. Bush explained that political problems in the Warsaw Pact would likely result in the reallocation of resources away from military spending. Now was the time when the pact would be most willing to make deep cuts. In Bush's view, 1989 offered an "unprecedented opportunity to begin lifting the West of the shadows cast by the overwhelming conventional forces which the Soviet Union and its allies have

FIGURE 11.   Children in Gerolzhofen, West Germany, wave and give the peace sign to a Canadian armored vehicle during NATO maneuvers in September 1982. The Canadian soldier, top right, returns the peace sign. © Government of Canada, reproduced with the permission of Library and Archives Canada (2017). Library and Archives Canada / Department of National Defence fonds/ e011171110.

amassed against us since 1945." Ultimately, Bush's plan was to create conditions "difficult to reverse by any future Soviet leader or set of leaders."[20]

The allies—especially Margaret Thatcher—took some convincing. They remained, as always, sensitive to any talk of withdrawal of American troops from Europe. But Bush ameliorated their concerns with a commitment to maintain US troops and a nuclear deterrent in Europe. The allies agreed in May to champion the American CFE proposal.[21] Even before the fall of the Berlin Wall, the Americans were trying to seize on the disarray behind the Iron Curtain to push Soviet military might out of Eastern Europe.

In May 1989, the NATO leaders met to celebrate the alliance's fortieth birthday and trumpet the CFE proposal. Publicly, they pointed to the political changes occurring in the Soviet Union and Eastern Europe as hopeful signs that East and West might transform their relationship from one of "military antagonism" to "peaceful competition."[22] They did not point out that political shifts in Eastern Europe since 1945 had only brought crisis—in East Berlin in 1953, Hungary in 1956, Czechoslovakia and elsewhere in 1968, and Poland in 1980–1981. Given the results of these earlier efforts to change political systems in the Warsaw Pact, NATO officials agreed with a British diplomat's sentiment that there "could hardly be a worse time to loosen the stability of NATO."[23]

As spring turned to summer, and summer to fall, the NATO allies watched and worried over the changes in Eastern Europe. Throughout 1989, the Warsaw Pact states had gradually decreased their cooperation on border security, and some loosened the rules for crossing borders. East Germans numbering in the hundreds of thousands traveled to neighboring countries in the hopes they might find a way to West Germany. Some managed to flee, but many who did not took refuge in the FRG's embassies in Budapest, Prague, and Warsaw, overcrowding them and creating an embarrassing spectacle. In October, the East German regime sealed its borders to stanch the outflow. East German citizens protested the border closings in increasingly violent demonstrations. A few months before, at Tiananmen Square, the Chinese government had massacred protesters. It was unclear whether the East Germans might crack down too, and what role the Soviets would play.

NATO and Live Oak, the tripartite military structure set up during the Berlin crisis, had plans in case conflict broke out in the satellite states. Any crisis might result in fighters, refugees, or both spilling into NATO territory. But NATO or Live Oak action was considered by the allies to be a last resort. As one American official put it, any military maneuvers or actions by the West would "needlessly escalate matters to the level of East-West confrontation," perhaps causing the satellite governments to rally around Moscow's flag. NATO's guiding policy was to remain vigilant but avoid treating any crisis as an East-West confrontation. But in case of Soviet military intervention into the GDR—the worst-case scenario— NATO forces would be put on alert, as would be strategic nuclear forces. There would be little margin for error, for this was "among the World War III scenarios" for which NATO planners had prepared for decades.[24]

After the Fall of the Berlin Wall

But World War III did not come about in 1989. Instead, on a surprisingly peaceful evening in November, protesters tore down the Berlin Wall and reduced to rubble the great symbol of a divided Germany and a divided Europe. In retrospect, some—like the British foreign secretary Douglas Hurd—have argued that the fall of the Berlin Wall might have offered an opportunity for great creativity in diplomacy. Bush might have sought "to remake the world," as Roosevelt had wished to do after the Second World War.[25]

Brent Scowcroft recognized that after the fall of the wall America was at "a strategic crossroads in Europe." But the intersecting paths, in his view, were not between remaking the world or standing pat. In his view, the choice was between America retaining its role on the continent or a retreat into isolationism. Neither Bush nor Scowcroft seriously considered the latter choice. They believed America was, and must remain, a "European power," and that NATO was the vehicle for maintaining that position.[26]

Even before the fall of the wall, Bush had warned that NATO must not "disperse out of euphoria."[27] After November 1989, the Americans worried that allied publics might think all security concerns in Europe had evaporated. Such an attitude could be even more dangerous than the Cold War. By December 1989, Scowcroft was advising the president that if the allied states were to simply "declare victory and shed their share of the common burdens," NATO would be left hollow. The result would be "instability on a scale not seen since the aftermath of World War II."[28]

Instability would have three specific manifestations. In the short term, the allies feared the Soviets would play on the NATO allies' fears of the FRG and press London, Paris, and The Hague to accept a greater role for Moscow in European diplomacy. If the Soviets called a "German peace conference" and pushed for a demilitarized or neutral Germany, an NSC staffer speculated, "many if not most European leaders would be attracted by the idea of bringing some order and predictability to German reunification." This was no idle hypothesis. Only a few months later Margaret Thatcher would tell the French president, François Mitterrand, "We might one day need the Soviet Union as a counter-balance to a united Germany."[29]

The Americans also saw a threat to America's role and Europe's stability in the European Community's moves toward greater integration. In the late 1980s, the European Community had begun greater economic and fiscal integration, and Paris was pushing for greater defense cooperation. Scowcroft warned Bush that as the EC developed, the United States would have to work to maintain its relevance in European politics. Otherwise, American citizens and politicians might become alienated from Europe, generating the "new form of isolationism" in the United States that had so worried Nixon and Kissinger.[30]

The Americans worried that if the Warsaw Pact were to fully collapse, the result would be an "enormous vacuum of power and influence in Eastern Europe."

The Germans and the Soviets would both vie for influence in the region, forcing Europe back into the "cyclical pattern or Russo-German conflict and condominium that bedeviled Europe from 1870 to 1945." America must "stand between Germany and Russia in Central Europe," one staffer put it, to prevent Germany asserting its power in the East and clashing with the USSR.[31]

NATO could solve all these problems. Keeping the FRG tied to the alliance would calm fears in Western Europe and remove any German need to provide, independently, for its own security; the fear for decades was that this would require a German nuclear weapon. Maintaining the alliance would ensure the United States played a key role in shaping European defense policies and prevent the EC from developing as an alternative to NATO, with the attendant isolationist implications for American politics. NATO, too, would help prevent any need for Germany to seek security arrangements with the states of Eastern Europe, and would prevent German-Soviet competition. In this argument lay the logic that would propel NATO's expansion east of Germany in the years to come.

When American officials considered their response to changes in Europe, they looked to Europe's past. And the past was not promising. Scowcroft saw no reason to believe that Europeans could avoid war on their continent without an American presence. NSC staffers agreed with the columnist Steve Rosenfeld's December 1989 piece in the *Washington Post* contrasting 1930s Europe with that of the 1990s: the only difference, but all the difference, was that "the United States is in, not out."[32]

The other allies wanted the Americans "in," too. Mitterrand and the French wanted the United States to maintain its commitment to the continent, even if the French had hopes for a future European-only security and defense policy.[33] For the British, keeping American troops in Europe was their "first aim," both to "deter the Soviet Union" and limit the chance "Germany might again fall under dangerous leadership at some future time."[34] The real question, however, was whether the Germans wanted the Americans to stay in—in Germany, and in Europe.

Chancellor Helmut Kohl told Secretary of State James Baker and Douglas Hurd in January 1990 that NATO "need not worry," for Germany's "home is in the West."[35] And yet Kohl's public remarks on the future of the FRG and NATO were ambiguous. Kohl was trying to manage relations with his NATO allies, a Soviet Union perennially frightened about German revanchism, and the citizens of East and West Germany. He had no incentive to put a fine point on the matter of Germany's future in NATO.[36] But Washington worried that Kohl's tactical ambiguity left open the door for a Soviet maneuver: Gorbachev might appeal to an "emotional German electorate" and force Germany to redefine its relationship with NATO as the price for Soviet acceptance of German unification. The allies had little faith that if Moscow offered such a trade, even the pro-NATO Kohl would reject the alliance to "do what he must—even at the expense of NATO and the U.S. link—to become the Chancellor who united Germany."[37]

In the first months of 1990 the Americans remained wary of Soviet schemes to weaken NATO and kindle political pressure in Germany for the withdrawal of American troops.[38] But the Soviets did not offer the blockbuster deal that worried Washington. As Germans began to focus more and more on the prospects and possibilities of unification, officials in NATO countries began to think about what relationship East German territory would have to NATO.

The simple assumption in Germany in February was that Gorbachev "could not possibly agree" to the GDR becoming a part of NATO's military structure.[39] Genscher, Kohl's FDP coalition partner and the FRG foreign minister, wanted to offer the Soviets strict assurances that NATO would not move eastward. Genscher believed such a promise was essential to help preserve Gorbachev's political position in Moscow. And Gorbachev's preservation was essential, for another Soviet leader might be more opposed to unification.[40] On January 31, at Tutzing, in Bavaria, Genscher declared that "an expansion of NATO territory to the East, in other words, closer to the borders of the Soviet Union, will not happen."[41] His willingness to make such concessions was based on a nuanced understanding of Gorbachev's sensitive political position in Moscow. But they also appeared to US officials to sum up the weak political will of German leaders that threatened NATO.[42]

James Baker, however, was willing to work with Genscher's announcement—what became known as the "Tutzing formula"—when Baker met with Gorbachev. In Moscow, on February 9, 1990, Baker told the Soviet leader that NATO's "jurisdiction" would not extend "one inch eastward."[43] Baker's comments were a variation on Genscher's formula, but like Genscher's comments about "expansion of NATO territory," it was ambiguous language that had no clear relationship to the North Atlantic Treaty; NATO had no "jurisdiction." Gorbachev responded to Baker by saying that "any extension of the zone of NATO would be unacceptable," but he left the meeting without making any sort of clarifying statement or gaining any written agreement from Baker.[44]

While Baker was in Moscow, NSC officials in Washington determined that the Genscher formula was impracticable. How could a unified Germany be a member of a defensive alliance while part of its territory was not subject to the treaty? The NSC staff preferred to describe East German territory in a unified FRG as having a "special military status." Baker, apprised of the significance of the matter, began walking back his comments to Gorbachev before he even left Moscow. He told reporters that his comments had not been about whether or not East German territory would be in NATO, but only whether NATO forces would deploy there.[45]

The next day, however, Kohl arrived in Moscow to meet with Gorbachev. Before meeting his Soviet hosts, Kohl had two updates from the Americans. First was a note from Baker describing his meeting with Gorbachev, still with reference to Baker's "not one inch eastward" statement. Second was a more recent letter from Bush indicating that the American position was that East Germany territory might have a "special military status" but that the defense obligations of the alliance would cover all of a unified Germany. Kohl's meeting with Gorbachev was significant because Gorbachev agreed to the prospect of unification. But as the conversation turned to NATO's future, Kohl took a line closer to the Tutzing formula, seeming to draw on Baker's, not Bush's, note. He told Gorbachev he could accept a plan restricting NATO forces to West German territory and converting the East German army into a border police–type force. Gorbachev surprised the Germans by seeming to care little about the issue and by not linking NATO's status directly with German unification. Kohl's adviser recorded: "No demand for a price and no pressure. What a meeting!"[46] There was, again, no clarification or commitment linking unification and the alliance.

Clearly the issue of NATO's status had been muddled by the meetings. Both Baker and Kohl had provided unclear or incomplete explanations to Gorbachev, and the Soviets were too disorganized, and Gorbachev too distracted, to seize on Baker's comments as an American commitment on NATO's future.[47] The issue would take on an outsize significance later in the 1990s.[48] But the events of the spring and summer of 1990, after Gorbachev's meetings with Baker and Kohl, make clear that the February confusion was only a small element in the larger story of Germany's role in NATO and, ultimately, NATO's expansion.

What was clear, immediately following Kohl's meeting with Gorbachev, was that Kohl and Genscher had begun to bargain with Moscow on NATO's future against Bush's line, and without the involvement of any other allies bound to the treaty.[49] The Americans believed it essential that Kohl commit himself firmly to NATO, or the issue would become a political football. In the constellation of German political parties, both the opposition SPD and Genscher's FDP were willing to reconsider Germany's ties with NATO. If NATO's future were to become a key point of the domestic political debate in Germany, the Americans expected German opinion would be pulled toward the left. Kohl could either lose his government or be drawn leftward, too; either way, the move would be "toward a Germany completely out of NATO."[50]

German Unification and NATO Membership

The chancellor's remarks about NATO and East Germany convinced the Americans that it was time for an "honest and unadorned talk with Kohl about his bottom-line on security issues."[51] In the diplomacy of German unification, the "principal objective" of the United States was to get Kohl to agree "not to alter Germany's full security commitment to NATO," including the presence of US forces and nuclear weapons in Germany and the FRG's participation in NATO's integrated military command.[52] Without Germany in NATO, the Americans thought, the alliance would fall apart. But they worried that even if Germany opted for some sort of weaker association with the alliance, or withdrawal from the integrated command like France had done under de Gaulle, "NATO will be finished as a viable security institution."[53]

The Americans wanted NATO to survive, and the Germans wanted to unify. This was the basis for a quid pro quo.[54] Bush invited Kohl to Camp David in late February 1990 to "cement a historic bargain"—Germany would not alter its relationship to NATO, and the United States would guide a great power diplomatic solution that would not interfere with the achievement of German unity.[55]

At Camp David, Bush maintained his support for unification and underscored the importance of Germany remaining a full member of NATO; Kohl agreed.[56] At a press conference afterward, Bush described the understanding he had reached with Kohl: that a unified Germany would "remain a full member of the North Atlantic Treaty organization, including participation in its military structure," that US troops would remain stationed in a united Germany, and that the GDR "should have a special military status."[57] Three days later Bush called Gorbachev to convey what he and Kohl had agreed. Gorbachev did not agree to this plan, nor did he rule it out. But the suggestion that East Germany would not be included in NATO—that NATO was not going to "move" eastward—was clearly dispelled by the end of February.[58] It was after the Camp David meeting that Bush, working to convince Margaret Thatcher of the need to move quickly on German unification, told the prime minister that NATO was "fundamental, indeed more important than ever."[59]

With Kohl and Bush on the same page, the Americans sought to establish a pattern of diplomatic negotiations that would result in Soviet acquiescence to NATO membership for a united Germany.[60] The Americans decided on a formalized series of talks that included the German states and the four former occupying powers (Britain, France, the US, and the USSR)—what came to be known as the "2+4." These talks were the best means for ensuring German politics did not interfere with the matter of NATO membership. They were also a means of insulating German decisions on defense policy from Moscow, and, as Baker put it, preventing the Germans and Soviets from "going off alone and cutting a private deal." He was thinking of those earlier deals: of Brest-Litovsk in 1918, at Rapallo in 1922, and the Molotov-Ribbentrop Pact of 1939.[61]

The Americans deftly ensured that the talks would focus on a unified Germany's external relations, including the still unsettled German-Polish border and the rights of the former occupying powers in Berlin. But, critically, the Americans argued that NATO's obligations in East Germany, Germany's decision to remain a party to the alliance, the size of the German army, and the deployment of nuclear weapons in the FRG were all sovereign German decisions and not eligible for discussion in the 2+4 setting.[62] Although the West Germans, British, and French each had their quibbles, the Americans convinced them to play by the game plan.

The other NATO allies, however, remained on the periphery of these talks. A number of the other NATO foreign ministers made known their worry that they, and NATO itself, were being left out of discussions and diplomacy that would shape the alliance's future. When the other allied foreign ministers learned about the 2+4 formula at a conference in Ottawa, Genscher told them: "You are not part of the game."[63] The stinging comment was accurate. NATO's future at the end of the Cold War was shaped largely by the United States and the other largest allies. But few comments could have been better calculated to warm the bitter memories and fears many Western Europeans harbored of their German allies.

The setup of the 2+4 was transparently in the American interest and provided no formal opportunity for Moscow to weigh in on the German-NATO relationship. But the Soviets still had not conceded the acceptability of a unified Germany's membership in NATO. They did not need a formal invitation to discuss their views, and if Moscow had truly wished to stand in the way of the American plan, they might have done so by any number of means. Throughout the 2+4 talks that continued from February through September, American officials could never be sure that a Soviet diplomat, or perhaps the Soviet minister of foreign affairs Eduard Shevardnadze himself, might not simply announce at a press conference the offer Washington feared so deeply: German neutrality for German unification.[64]

The Soviets never made such a move against NATO. The great irony was that NATO worked in the Soviet interest, too. NATO had managed to do what Imperial Russia and Stalin's Soviet Union could not: limit the possibility—and the historical reality—of Germany striking a militarist and revanchist policy in Europe. Kohl himself believed that "in the end the Russians would want Germany in NATO—albeit for not very friendly reasons."[65] The Americans, though wary of Soviet intrigues, did come to realize that the Soviet Union wanted Germany in NATO, and the United States in Europe.[66] As during the MLF talks twenty-five years earlier, Germany's allies sold Moscow on NATO's role as a means of keeping Germany down.[67]

At the end of May, during a visit to Washington, Gorbachev acquiesced in principle to the Germans' right to join whatever alliance the Federal Republic wished—that is, to stay in NATO.[68] Gorbachev might not have liked this option—surely he did not. And yet, as on the matter of unification itself, he had few tools to prevent it. He had no money to spend, had renounced intervention, and his rhetoric had bound him to supporting freedom of determination—including the FRG's freedom to choose to join NATO.[69]

Yet Gorbachev and Shevardnadze were under attack in Moscow for allowing Germany to move toward unification. Their acceptance of a unified Germany in NATO would bring them under even more pressure at home.[70] Already, in April, Shevardnadze hinted that he and Gorbachev required some concessions to accept a unified Germany's membership in NATO. He suggested that NATO adopt a "no first use" policy for its nuclear weapons, and a public statement by the alliance that the USSR was no longer an enemy.[71] Robert Zoellick, counselor at the State Department, created a package of "incentives" for Moscow: the allies would commit not to station NATO forces in the GDR during a transition period, and NATO would reevaluate its war-fighting strategy, among other things. In addition to these policy promises, the Americans and Germans prepared to provide the financial credit Gorbachev desperately needed in exchange for his quick removal of Red Army troops from East Germany.[72]

The Rhetorical Transformation of the Alliance

Partly to convince Moscow of NATO's good intention, the United States and the other NATO allies prepared to give the alliance a face-lift at a summit meeting in London in July. In London, they published a communiqué outlining the policies designed to "sweeten the pill" for Moscow and help Gorbachev accept a unified Germany's membership in NATO.[73]

The Soviet Union was not the only audience for the NATO communiqué. As he surveyed the international landscape in 1990, Bush remained worried that the "real danger came from a general sense of euphoria that everything was going swimmingly."[74] Other allies observed "high public expectations that NATO will quickly adapt its strategies and approach to security."[75] David Abshire, a former American ambassador to NATO, warned Scowcroft that NATO appeared to its public more and more as "an anachronism," and that soon, "budget cutters on Capitol Hill" would eye it greedily.[76]

Bush and his advisers continued to worry that public opinion in the US might grow isolationist; they also always had in the back of their minds worry that protectionist European Community policies might lead to economic conflict that would undermine the alliance. Now the changes in the East raised questions about NATO's relevance.[77] The Americans saw the London Summit as an important moment to "fix the Alliance's image for Europeans publics," and especially to ensure that antinuclear advocates did not transform the momentum from unification to push for denuclearization in Germany or Europe.[78]

At London, the NATO allies declared that Central and Eastern Europe "is liberating itself," while the USSR was "embarking on the long journey toward a free society." Because of these changes, "this Alliance must and will adapt." After the end of the Cold War, Scowcroft would write that NATO had been transformed into "a political instrument of European stabilization rather than one of military confrontation."[79]

The most significant elements of NATO's transformation after London were changes to its nuclear strategy and a new diplomatic relationship with the states of the former Warsaw Pact. Bush declared that NATO would use nuclear weapons only as a "last resort," and would also reduce the alliance's reliance on the weapons.[80] The "last resort" formulation did not go as far as the Soviets wanted—it was not a pledge of "no first use," as Shevardnadze had suggested. At the same time, the strategy went further than either Thatcher or Mitterrand wished; it rekindled traditional European fear that the United States would plan to fight a prolonged conventional conflict on the continent.[81] Nonetheless, the policy change helped NATO advertise itself as stepping back from the nuclear brink. The allies agreed, also, to launch a much more sweeping review of alliance military doctrine, given the enormous changes to their former enemies' structure in Europe.

The second major innovation was NATO's invitation to the states of Central and Eastern Europe, including the Soviet Union, to send representatives to NATO to establish a standing diplomatic relationship. The public offer allowed the Soviet leadership to argue to its hard-liners at home that a NATO willing to establish liaison with former enemies was no longer a threat. The Soviets seized on this both as a tangible symbol of NATO's transformation and in hopes of using liaison to push for further transformation of the alliance.[82] But, left unsaid, the Americans' "original concept" for liaison "anticipated" requests of former Warsaw Pact states to join NATO.[83] Before the end of the Bush administration, the liaison program would develop into something far more profound than advertised.

The London Summit was convincing—at least to the Soviet audience. Less than two weeks after London, Kohl met with Gorbachev at Stavropol from July 14 to 16. Kohl told Gorbachev that after unification, there would be "no NATO 'structures' in GDR" while Soviet forces remained there. After the Soviet withdrawal, there would be no foreign troops or nuclear weapons stationed in East German territory, but the alliance could pre-position equipment and have airfields there. Article 5, the critical element of the North Atlantic Treaty, would apply to all German territory immediately after unification.[84] On July 16, 1990, a Reuters cable traveled around the world: Gorbachev had said on Soviet television that the USSR would accept the NATO membership of a united Germany.

The credit for Soviet acceptance of unified Germany's membership in NATO was due both to the policies and the rhetoric of NATO's London Declaration.[85]

Overall, however the transformation of NATO was far less total than the London communiqué advertised.[86] As Peter Rodman, an NSC staff member, put it, NATO's transformation from a military organization to a "political" organization was "a cliché of the current period." NATO had always had a political function, so in a sense, the cliché was a truism. For anyone who believed NATO no longer had a military role, the contemporary advertisement was "escapism." NATO remained a tool for ensuring security, and it did this by organizing and commanding military forces in Europe.

In the late 1960s, when hopes for détente had raised doubts about the need for NATO, the British minister of defense Denis Healey had quoted Hilaire Belloc's poem "Jim": Surely it was better to "keep a-hold of nurse / For fear of finding something worse." Over twenty years later, British officials, along with their American allies, maintained this attitude. In 1990 Thatcher hosted a seminar at Chequers to discuss Germany and future policy. Her private secretary Charles Powell's account of the meeting notes just how important it was to hang on to NATO, for "the fact that things had gone the West's way for the last year or so did not save us from continuing to guard against something worse."[87]

And something worse was not an abstract worry—in 1990, it meant to American officials a "renewed Russian threat."[88] The Soviet Union's military forces had not evaporated. The USSR remained a nuclear superpower, and even with negotiated troop reductions, Moscow was expected to command somewhere between fifty and sixty-five divisions west of the Urals, with the possibility of reinforcing those troops from east of the mountain range.[89]

A crisis in Lithuania, one of the Soviet republics, was an example of how change in the East might swiftly turn into conflict. In March 1990, the Lithuanians declared independence, but Moscow rejected the idea. Moscow was not about to let Lithuania go: it was the home of the Soviet Baltic Fleet's headquarters, hosted air defense sites and radars, and played a nuclear role in the defense of the Soviet Union. The Soviets put pressure on the Lithuanians by cutting off energy, and established an economic blockade. The allies worried the Soviet military might maneuver Gorbachev into using force, or even to replace him with someone less moderate.[90] It was not difficult to imagine similar scenarios breaking out in other Soviet republics. Such crises might spill out into the Soviet borderlands, leading even to the return of Soviet troops to Eastern Europe.[91] NATO would not stand idly by, and if Lithuania erupted, for instance, Bush expected to face significant domestic pressure from Baltic-Americans to act.

Lithuania put an exclamation point on American thinking about the continued security situation in Europe. Despite the changes to how NATO was described, and indeed, some changes to the alliance's strategy and the innovation of liaison with nonmember states, the NSC staff was convinced that "NATO's traditional mission—containing Soviet power—will not disappear."[92]

Security Concerns in the Early 1990s

At the end of the Cold War, journalists posed a "trick question" to Bush: "Who is the enemy now?" He would reply that the enemy was "apathy and unpredictability."[93] Bush's answer was a good one; it made sense in terms of the great changes sweeping through international relations at the beginning of the 1990s. But like so much rhetoric employed in the defense of NATO since 1949, Bush's line obscured two serious and interrelated security concerns that made apathy and unpredictability real threats in American eyes: uncertain strategic alignments in Central and Eastern Europe, and pressure in Western Europe for an integrated and expanded European Community with its own security and defense policy.

After the London Summit the attention of President Bush and his cabinet, along with the senior leadership of other NATO allies, turned toward the Persian Gulf. The US would press for NATO's involvement in the Gulf War, and NATO would monitor the crisis with AWACS aircraft and send forces, including air defense forces, to protect Turkey in case Saddam Hussein tried to widen the war. Other allies understood the American pressure as an effort to give NATO "potential long term advantages," perhaps by offering more public justifications for its continuation.[94] Throughout the rest of the Bush administration, American officials in the NSC and elsewhere worked quietly toward the "overall goal" of keeping "NATO strong and viable for the foreseeable future."[95]

No matter the bleak prospects of the USSR in 1990, Rodman argued in another memorandum to Scowcroft, the future would ultimately hold "a Soviet Union or Russia that would recover its strength."[96] Some officials, even before the formal offer of liaison made at London, argued that the alliance must not only retain its role of continuing to serve as a check on Soviet power, but also "ensure that the decline of the threat is irreversible."[97]

By reaching out to the states of Eastern Europe, NATO might help institutionalize their new political and economic reforms. These changes were the "surest way to contain and deter the military threat."[98] At the same time, Washington began developing bilateral military-to-military exchange with Eastern Europeans. The "unspoken end" of this American policy was to ensure that "in the event of armed conflict in Europe, the East Europeans would support U.S. Objectives—either through active cooperation or friendly neutrality."[99] American policy toward Eastern Europe, of which NATO was a part, focused on preventing any future reconstitution of Soviet or Russian influence in Eastern Europe.

Did this mean expanding NATO's membership? In August 1990 the Czechoslovak leader Václav Havel asked how NATO would respond if Prague requested membership in the alliance.[100] By October 1990, "all agencies" in the United States government were agreed that "East European governments should not be invited to join NATO anytime in the immediate future." Nonetheless, officials in the Office of the Secretary of Defense and the State Department Policy Planning Staff preferred to "keep the door ajar and not give the East Europeans the impression that NATO [is] forever a closed club."[101]

In 1990, the issue was simply too explosive to be formally considered in a policy review. Instead, the American policy was to avoid ambiguous answers on membership, not to speculate on extending NATO membership to the Soviets' former allies, and to avoid a formal study of the topic. Nonetheless, NSC officials believed "NATO must recognize the relationship between its vital interests and any Soviet effort to reassert hegemony over Central and Eastern Europe."[102]

Setting the conditions to prevent a return of Soviet influence to Eastern Europe required careful timing. In March 1991, for instance, the European Strategy Steering Group (ESSG), a small group of senior interagency officials chaired by Robert Gates, had sought to define precisely why NATO was essential to American policy. They identified three specific reasons: First, NATO would deter and defend against any reconstituted Soviet threat. Second, it would defend against non-Soviet threats, perhaps arising from North Africa or the Middle East. Third, it was expected NATO would "help provide a security environment which dissuades any Soviet reentry into Central and Eastern Europe or coercion or intimidation of that region"[103]

But before the United States could achieve the third goal—prevention of Soviet reentry—the Red Army first had to exit. The most important priority for the US in the region was "the complete end of Soviet hegemony and withdrawal of Soviet forces," along with the consolidation of the largely pro-American political and economic reforms in the region.[104]

The United States, concluded the ESSG in March 1991, did "wish to establish that Eastern Europe falls within the core security concerns of NATO," although it separated this from a suggestion of expanded membership—that was "premature." The ESSG refused to "discuss hypotheticals about the future," not because they were unthinkable, but because it was important to keep the Soviets rolling east.[105] It is not difficult to imagine how loose talk of NATO expansion would have dramatically slowed the Red Army's exodus from bases in its former satellites.

But just because membership was not yet up for discussion did not mean there was no room for security cooperation between the former states of the

Warsaw Pact and NATO. In February 1991, three Eastern European countries sought early talks with NATO on security arrangements. While the details remain classified, the United States agreed to the idea as long as it was ad hoc, informal, low key, and confidential. As NSC staff recognized, discussion of security arrangements between these states and NATO was the "logical dev[elopment] of [the] liaison function."[106] In an effort to avoid alarming the Soviets, the NATO allies used creative euphemisms: training in "airspace management," for instance, offered a "euphemism" for programs to help former Warsaw Pact states improve their air defense systems.[107]

Just as American officials considered how to strengthen NATO as a bulwark against a regrouped USSR, they came to see Western European efforts toward greater integration as a possible threat to NATO. Throughout 1990, the European Community had deepened its plans for fiscal and economic integration, and its members spoke of increasing cooperation in security and defense policy, too. Part of this push grew out of a long-term French vision for Europe, but it was accentuated by Paris's worries about the reliability of the American commitment to Europe after the 1987 Reykjavik summit. German unification made the European Community even more important to France, for in an unfederated Europe a unified Germany would dominate others economically.[108] After the fall of the Berlin Wall, Washington recognized that to stand in the way of European demands would strain the alliance.[109]

Nonetheless, the Americans worried that if the Europeans organized their own defenses, separate from NATO, it would undermine domestic support for NATO in the United States. Furthermore, it was unclear from Washington's vantage point whether Europeans "can or truly wish to realize the integration of foreign, security and defense policy." The French and Germans, for example, had plans to create an integrated army brigade outside of NATO, but the CIA dismissed the plan as militarily useless.[110]

The Americans determined that they could not "quash" the impulse in European capitals for European security cooperation, but they could seek to prevent any European development that might harm NATO. Washington indicated to its allies that the United States would be pleased if the Europeans were to cooperate on a foreign and defense policy for issues outside Europe.[111] If new European plans would compete with NATO or create redundant common structures, however, the American government would oppose them.

The American premise in 1989 had been that the Europeans could not keep peace in Europe by themselves. Nothing had changed by 1990 or 1991. There was no confidence in the United States government, or in NATO's higher echelons, that Europeans, the European Community, or the Conference on Security and Cooperation in Europe could serve as a substitute for NATO if Moscow one day "contemplates another westward push."[112] Early postwar American hopes that Europeans could and would be capable of building up their own effective defenses were long gone.

The immediate stake, however, was in American domestic support for NATO.[113] The Bush administration knew that many in Washington expected the financial benefits of a "peace dividend." If the Europeans looked like they were creating "an alternative to NATO," the calls for the return of American troops from Europe might become unmanageable.[114]

In 1991, American efforts and European political developments served to put a brake on any European development that would challenge NATO. John Major replaced Margaret Thatcher as prime minister of the UK. Where Thatcher's dislike of the EC had made it easier for the Western Europeans to cooperate without London, Major's interest in Europe but preference for sovereign defenses—a position shared by the Dutch—complicated the matter. American officials launched what Mitterrand called "a major American offensive" against a European common defense. Ultimately, the Americans were able to drive a wedge between the Germans and French, whose agreement would have been essential for any major step toward a European defense identity. Genscher and Baker signed a joint declaration stating that NATO was "the principal venue for consultation and the forum for agreement on all policies bearing on the security and defense commitment of its members."[115] The Europeans would continue inching toward greater defense cooperation, but there was no question that a common European defense could substitute for NATO and the American commitment.

Toward the end of 1991, the Americans pressed the allies to use the December summit in Rome to "reaffirm" that NATO was the "essential foundation for European stability and security."[116] But the Americans understood that after the dramatic changes in Europe, the alliance's "East-West mission" was all but "accomplished in the minds of allied publics."[117] As Woerner told Bush, it was essential to describe NATO as a tool for "confronting instability and uncertainty" rather than confronting the East.[118]

There were real and significant changes announced at Rome: The allies unveiled NATO's new military strategy, and also promised to cut its sub-strategic nuclear weapons inventory by a whopping 80 percent. The United States also agreed that NATO should publicly acknowledge developments in European integration. The Rome communiqué acknowledged the importance of a "European pillar" in the alliance, but expressed the American preference that the European pillar be developed within the framework of the Western European Union, an organization closely linked with NATO.

But all the changes were not advertised publicly. The Americans had used the acknowledgment of the European pillar as a bargaining chip to get allied agreement to plans for closer liaison with the East. In 1990, at London, all the allies had agreed to extend an olive branch to the Warsaw Pact, but they had done so for a variety of reasons. The Canadians, for instance, believed dialogue would be the first step not to build up NATO, but to "build down NATO" into a forum for consultations rather than security cooperation.[119]

Building down NATO was not what the former satellites wanted, nor was it the American goal.[120] American officials believed that if NATO did not take account of the changed security interests of the former Warsaw Pact states, it would lose an opportunity to extend its influence in Eastern Europe. As a result, NATO would be less effective in "enveloping German power" as Germany looked east, and, ultimately, would lose its ability to respond to a future Russian threat.[121]

In the lead-up to Rome, the US delegation to NATO recommended that the summit be used to take Eastern European liaison with the alliance to a "qualitatively new level," beyond information sharing to consultation and technical assistance. This "would, at least implicitly, open the door to possible full or associate NATO membership in the future."[122]

Washington was not yet prepared to open this door, but it did press an institutional innovation on NATO that would keep the proverbial door ajar. The US proposed a new North Atlantic Cooperation Council (NACC) at NATO to build on the liaison relationship and create a more formal forum for security cooperation with the East. In the words of the US delegation, the NACC offered "unprecedented opportunities to assist the transformation of the security policies of the [Central and Eastern European] countries, and thereby maintain the Alliance's position at the center of building a new Europe."[123] The NACC was meant to focus on defense cooperation: converting the former armies of the Warsaw Pact to systems of civil-military relations, to transform offensive doctrine into defensive.[124] These new policies and doctrine would help insulate the Eastern European militaries from resurgent nationalism and dampen the possibility of East-East conflict.[125] But these changes would also begin to slowly erode and reverse decades of Soviet influence in Eastern Europe. The French begrudgingly accepted the NACC in exchange for acknowledgment of a European pillar. The Eastern Europeans, who the Americans believed were now the "biggest supporters" of NATO, welcomed it.[126]

The Bush administration was committed to maintaining NATO as an instrument for exercising power in Europe, as a check on German power, and to preserve the capability to defend against a renewed Soviet threat. But this calculation appears in no NATO communiqué. Instead, the NSC staff—despite their private hard-nosed assessments of NATO's necessity—recommended advertising NATO publicly as "an alliance of shared values."

The description was political pablum, easily digestible by the allied governments and their voters at a time when few were thinking about the need to preserve the military organization as a bulwark against future aggression. But there was a catch. As the NSC staff noted, if NATO was an alliance of values, as it proclaimed, the newly democratic "Havels of the East" will ask why they cannot join. But in this new formula, the answer was that they could: NATO, as an alliance of values, was expandable, and it could establish liaison with other states, perhaps even offer membership, as necessary to help meeting strategic needs in Europe. "Indeed," wrote one NSC staffer on the eve of the Rome summit, "we would make the expansion of NATO a goal."[127]

A month after the Rome Summit and allied agreement to establish the NACC, the states of East and West met in Brussels for the fateful meeting during which the Soviet Union expired. The NACC would hold more meetings but ultimately fizzle. Although it was meant to be a forum for organizing security cooperation with former Warsaw Pact states, it was politically impossible to develop such a forum in 1991 and exclude the Soviet Union. The United States was always careful to include the Soviet Union, and later Russia, in NATO's liaison programs to prevent Moscow from feeling isolated.[128] But, after the dissolution of the Soviet Union, when the NACC grew to include all former Warsaw Pact allies and former Soviet republics, it had ballooned to unmanageable proportions.[129]

At the same time, the collapse of the USSR changed calculations in Washington. There was no longer a need to be so careful in considering expanding NATO's membership. In fact, there were other factors necessitating that expansion begin in earnest.

The Imperative to Expand

"Despite the communiqué rhetoric," Stephen Flanagan, a member of the Policy Planning Staff, wrote to his colleagues in the State Department, "we know that NATO's continuing solidarity is not primarily a consequence of our common values." It was the mistrust European states held for each other, fear of "Russian backsliding," and the possibility of instability in Eastern Europe that held the alliance together. But now, with the collapse of the Soviet Union, the "old superglue of a common, looming threat, is gone."[130] The Soviet Union had made it easier to keep the allied states bound together, but its disappearance hardly meant that NATO was no longer necessary.

In 1997, during the presidency of Bill Clinton, NATO invited the Czech Republic, Hungary, and Poland to join NATO; the three states acceded to the

North Atlantic Treaty in 1999. This was not a new idea. In fact, by 1999, the notion that NATO could, and possibly should, expand if the Soviet Union collapsed was more than three decades old. During the Johnson administration, Zbigniew Brzezinski, then a policy planner, had argued that NATO might one day serve as an instrument for winning the peace after the Cold War. The partnership between the United States and Europe embodied in NATO, he wrote, was the essential precondition for "building world order on the basis of collaboration among the more developed nations, perhaps including eventually some of the Communist states."[131]

But the logic for NATO expansion had been laid out most clearly in American thinking during the Bush administration. In fact, the Bush administration's efforts to present NATO to Moscow as a changed institution, especially the development of liaison relationships, had been the necessary first steps for NATO enlargement. By the time of Flanagan's memo in May 1992, American officials were considering the "initial entry of some C[entral and] E[astern] E[uropean] states into NATO in the mid-1990s."[132]

Although NATO expansion was not yet official or public US policy, memorandums of conversation and letters between Bush-era officials make a clear case for NATO expansion. NATO needed to expand to the states of the former satellites, they argued, to maintain peace in Europe and to maintain American power on the continent. And specific developments in both Western and Eastern Europe convinced them this expansion was necessary.

First, although the Americans had poured cold water on French hopes for European defense plans, the growth and integration of the European Community in the early 1990s continued to worry the Americans. Washington expected that as the European Community expanded eastward in search of markets, former Soviet satellites would join the EC. As they joined the EC, they would join the Western European Union (WEU)—the organization formed as the European impetus for NATO in 1948 and expanded to include the FRG in 1954. Even if these new states were not members of NATO, the overlap between memberships and responsibilities in NATO and the WEU would force American "collective security responsibilities [to] expand on a de facto basis as the WEU expands." Even without a formal treaty commitment, the Americans believed that they would be responsible for protecting all members of the EC. While American officials thought such expansion was "not a bad thing per se," they saw a problem in their lack of control over the expansion. Washington was not interested in ceding the de facto decision making on NATO membership to the European Community, and it was unacceptable to Washington that Brussels would set the standard for admission to security commitments.[133] British officials agreed with the Americans that it was essential to avoid a divergence between memberships.

"To prevent this," wrote Barry Lowenkron of the NSC staff in March 1992, "we favor opening up the Alliance to new members."[134] The expansion of the European Community—and later the European Union—and that of NATO were critically, if informally, linked.

Just as the Americans were thinking about European expansion, they were worried about the North Atlantic Cooperation Council's future. The new council was not living up to the expectation of its Central and Eastern European members. The former Soviet allies wanted closer security cooperation with NATO than was being offered. Washington worried that if the former countries of Eastern Europe became convinced that the NACC was "a permanent second class waiting room, they will be driven to seek the options to fill their security vacuum." What if the French or the Germans offered, by themselves, limited security guarantees to Poland or Hungary? Over Europe hung the specter of the rickety alliances and political maneuvering among European states that had twice contributed to the outbreak of global war.[135] Even after the end of the Cold War, the legacy of the First and Second World War shaped American thinking about NATO.

NATO expansion would help the Americans control the shape of European security in the era of the expanding European Community, and it would also prevent the states of Eastern Europe from seeking other, possibly destabilizing, security guarantees. But Washington also saw NATO expansion as the answer to NATO's perennial problem: the apathy toward, if not quite the rejection of, the alliance felt by so many traditional allies' publics. The Americans had not forgotten the antinuclear protests in Germany of the 1980s, and they remained concerned that German unification might encourage a public push to move American weapons and troops out of the FRG. The Americans deemed it "unlikely" that the FRG would "host 95% of our military presence in Europe for much longer." Citizens in the traditional allied states simply did not feel threatened enough to host large American bases. And if the Americans were forced out of Germany, they would have nowhere to go. And yet here were Eastern European countries requesting an opportunity to play a role in NATO. If anyone were to bet, Tom Niles of the State Department wrote in 1992, "whether a given U.S. Army brigade would be more welcome in Germany or Poland in 1995, we'd put money on the latter." Better yet, the old "Soviet caserns" in Poland could be snatched up for "a bargain," and American troops "would be local heroes."[136] If NATO was going to continue, wrote Niles, "we need more real estate."

Ultimately, American officials believed that whether the countries of Eastern Europe joined NATO or not, the alliance would be under pressure to "ensure stability of Western interests in the East"—that is, to protect the satellites of the former Warsaw Pact. This pressure would only grow as those states became more closely integrated with Western Europe. Admittedly, Niles wrote, the policy of expansion looked like "all risk and no gain," by taking on security responsibilities for new states.[137] But in 1992 it looked like failure to expand would cause NATO to deteriorate and risk the instability in Europe that they knew was far riskier: two World Wars had proved it.

LOOKING FORWARD, LOOKING BACK

It is too much to argue that allied leaders created and maintained NATO as an institution to guarantee peace in Europe even if the Soviet Union collapsed. Estimates of the Cold War's projected life span varied wildly but were, for the most part, pessimistic and assumed the conflict would last much longer than it did. Zbigniew Brzezinski, in the 1960s, could write of future collaboration with Warsaw Pact states. Even as early as 1948 George Kennan had suggested that security arrangements should be drafted "so as to make it not too difficult for people like Czechs to join later if they get some sort of chance."[1] A few officials guessed correctly, many did not.

What is clear, however, is that the logic that led to both the signing of the North Atlantic Treaty and the continued maintenance of NATO was not dependent on an ideological cold war for sustenance. As long as there was a state with enough military power—be it the Soviet Union, later Russia, or potentially Germany—to challenge other governments, it was essential to have a system of defense in place that would not only minimize exposure to blackmail but persuade the potential blackmailer to make no demands in the first place. Although the creative diplomacy that led to NATO required both the recent memory of the Second World War and the fear of Soviet-Communist domination, the argument for protection against blackmail was timeless. So timeless, in fact, that it led Bush administration officials to identify numerous benefits in NATO's expansion to the east even after the fall of the Berlin Wall. But the Bush administration was extremely careful in its consideration of NATO expansion. That officials identi-fied possible benefits of NATO expansion hardly means that those same officials would have seen strategic wisdom in expanding NATO membership had Bush defeated Clinton in 1992. That time for expansion had not come by the end of the Bush administration.

But the time did come, for a different group of officials, in the 1990s. The first round of post–Cold War NATO enlargement occurred when the Czech Republic, Hungary, and Poland joined the alliance in 1999. In 2004 and 2009, nine more former members of the Warsaw Pact, including several former Soviet republics, acceded to the treaty. According to available accounts, NATO expansion began when it did because of the idealistic policy preference of President Bill Clinton's national security adviser Anthony Lake combined with forceful arguments for accession made by the former Warsaw Pact states.[2] What we do not know, and what historians will need to determine, is what these general arguments meant in terms of specific hopes and fears. Historians will need to consult the policy mem-orandums, the cable traffic, and the intelligence analysis to determine whether the allies and soon-to-be allies saw an acute security concern. Up until 1991, thinking about NATO expansion had been predicated on hard-nosed assess-ments of the balance of power. Was 1999 a time of change or continuity? Did the Clinton administration, like the Bush administration before it, believe that it was essential to salt the earth against future Russian resurgence in the region, or had this concern evaporated? Did the Eastern Europeans imply, as had Turkish diplomats before them, that they would seek other security arrangements if not invited into NATO? Only after historians answer these questions will we know whether the allies chose to enlarge NATO on the basis of calculated geopolitical assessments or in a fit of absence of mind.

Even before NATO enlargement began in earnest, NATO had already expanded its functional responsibilities. The alliance took on a role as convener of mili-tary interventions outside the treaty area, with major interventions in the former Yugoslavia in the 1990s. George H. W. Bush and his secretary of state, James Baker, had not wanted NATO or the United States to deploy troops there. "We don't have a dog in that fight," as Baker put it.[3]

Just as NATO's peace offering of liaison relationships with the Warsaw Pact ultimately led to security relationships with some of them, the broad language the Americans used to sell the alliance at the end of the Cold War had con-sequences. By arguing that NATO could prevent instability, but not explain-ing that it had unspoken ends in mind, the alliance presented itself as if it had a dog in every fight. NSC staffers considering possible NATO involvement in the conflict in Bosnia recognized the rhetorical trap. They thought military involvement was dangerous and unwise, but that it would be difficult for NATO to avoid. The issue was "not just one of NATO failing to act," but of individual states, or perhaps another institution, bypassing NATO and making it look irrelevant. Allied publics would see NATO standing on the sidelines. This might have led to greater skepticism about the value of maintaining NATO, further reducing public and political willingness to support the alliance.[4] Although NATO did not directly intervene in the former Yugoslavia in the Bush years, it would conduct military operations in Bosnia in 1995 and Kosovo in 1999.

NATO's "out-of-area" role expanded geographically after the September 11, 2001, terror attacks on the United States. For the first and only time in its history—so far—the NATO allies activated article 5 of the North Atlantic Treaty. Quickly, however, the other allies grew embittered when the United States created its own coalitions to fight the Taliban and al-Qaeda. Washington's policy, according to the assistant secretary-general for defense planning and operations, Edgar Buckley, "devalued the importance of strategic solidarity." Although the initial combat phases of Operation Enduring Freedom in Afghanistan were not NATO operations, NATO would go on to take an enormous role in security and reconstruction efforts in Afghanistan.[5] This involvement would breed problems in the alliance, as strict rules of engagement for some European troops raised old questions about a European "will to fight." When the war on terror expanded to Iraq, it caused another rift, this one like the Suez crisis over four decades before. In 2003 the United States, the United Kingdom, and other NATO allies invaded Iraq, while others, including France, Germany, and Canada, abstained or even argued against American policy.[6] Later out-of-area operations in Libya created more friction between the allies.[7]

Policy makers on both sides of the Atlantic seem to have succumbed, sooner or later, to the temptation to use NATO because it was there. This temptation had long existed. Individual allies had always dreamed of harnessing NATO to their own imperial gambits. Even Eisenhower initially thought NATO the right instrument if military action over Suez became necessary. And Americans deeply resented criticism by NATO allies over US actions in Vietnam, wishing instead the alliance would provide some political, if not military, support for their war. For decades, however, the allies had managed to restrict NATO's out-of-area operations because the costs outweighed the benefits. Out-of-area operations might have drummed up public support for the alliance in the short term, but what if NATO went on a failed adventure? What would be the longer-term effect of support for the alliance? And what about the rest of the world? John Foster

Dulles, in particular, had always understood that if NATO intervened abroad, it might make friends, but more likely it would make enemies.

Both the limited European appetite for defense spending and the uncertain, often frictional NATO out-of-area operations reinforced Cold War views of pusillanimous Europeans and unilateralist Americans. But had NATO created this problem for itself—had it been *too* successful? Was the public rejection of power politics NATO's fault?

It is a crucial question for understanding NATO's past and its future. American support for a treaty and the military components that followed were based, at the dawn of the alliance, on the assumption European publics would regain their "will to fight." In this formulation, Europe would, someday, accept full responsibility for defense establishments that could hold their own in a world of other armed states. But US officials very quickly came to doubt that Europe could ever be self-sufficient. They became so concerned that a purely European system of defense cooperation would fail that they took extraordinary measures to hinder European integration. The inability of Europe to defend itself, in the eyes of officials on both sides of the Atlantic, was endemic to the continent: it lay in Europe's geography, its history, and its politics.

But if allied leaders had thought more deeply about the root of European citizens' views on NATO—and especially on defense spending, military establishments, and nuclear armaments that made NATO what it was—they might have come to a different conclusion. Perhaps it was not that the people of Europe had forgotten the lessons of the World Wars that NATO leaders remembered, but that they had learned a different lesson. They would quote Isaiah before Vegetius, and argue that peace lay in the rendering of swords into plowshares. Partway through the Cold War, at least, European publics came to see arms—especially nuclear weapons—as the problem, not the solution. And they had their historical analogy, too. Where the allied leaders focused on the appeasement that preceded the Second World War, the peace movement focused on the arms race that preceded the First.

NATO officials simply never found an effective means to explain why, if the people of Europe were from Venus, they were from Mars.[8] Even today, allied leaders struggle to explain the need for NATO to their voters. Patrick Stephenson, a former NATO speechwriter, put it bluntly: "NATO has a hard time contributing to [the] conversation" about transatlantic security. Repeating arguments made regularly over more than sixty years, he argues that the "downward trend" in support for the alliance, "more than any massed army—is NATO's existential threat."[9] And yet the same logic that propelled leaders to continue the alliance past the end of the Cold War also precludes them from making an unadorned and direct case for NATO. Indeed, if the leaders of the alliance ever actually believed that their citizens could show the "spine" that George Kennan thought they had, they might have let NATO gradually fade into the history books.

NATO's prospects, figured one external observer after a visit to the alliance's headquarters, were bleak. Throughout NATO Europe there was a "growing view of the public everywhere . . . that the older forms of force are out of date, and irrelevant to real defence problems." There was a sense that "the danger is diminishing and that defence expenditure is becoming unnecessary." If NATO does not check this decline, it is "all too likely that it will collapse like a sand castle."[10]

Was this a quote from 2005? From 1995? Or 1975 or 1965? Perhaps only the syntax gives away the game, for this was the view of the British military thinker Basil Liddell Hart in 1955. And yet his observations were echoed time and again over the seventy years—and still counting—of NATO's existence. NATO continued, and so did the doubts.

It is a challenge to bring the history of NATO any closer to the present than 1991. One of the arguments that drives this book—that the decisions and policies allied leaders took to maintain NATO were made in secret and differed from their public rhetoric—warns against any assumption that we can truly know the sources of contemporary policy. And yet it is an even greater challenge not to consider the connections between NATO's Cold War and what came after. If history is not repeating itself, do the policy papers and memorandums of conversation of post–Cold War NATO officials at least rhyme with the archival record?

In the second decade of the twenty-first century, Russia is flexing its military muscles in Europe. Russia's strike aircraft carry out simulated nuclear attacks against its neighbors, bomber patrols probe the air defenses of European and North American allies, and Russian submarines play cat-and-mouse games off European shores. While "we had thought that peace had returned to Europe for good," lamented the German foreign minister in 2016, "the question of war and peace has returned to the continent."[11]

In 2014, military units of the Russian Federation invaded the territory of its sovereign neighbor, Ukraine. Although Moscow initially denied sending troops, Russia later annexed a strategic portion of Ukraine—Crimea—in March of that year. The Russian takeover of Crimea echoed Georges Pompidou's warning of a Soviet "camouflage advance," whereby Moscow, using measures short of war and relying on ambiguous invitations extended by parts of a population, might conquer new territory. During the 1970s and 1980s, the allies believed that NATO and the states on NATO's periphery were so weak that only the geriatric timidity of the Kremlin's leadership prevented a Soviet bid for expansion. More than forty-five years ago, Kissinger warned the allies that if NATO was not prepared, "some younger, more ruthless Soviet leader would test us, and the alliance would fall apart."[12] Some Americans wondered if Gorbachev posed this threat; now some wonder if Vladimir Putin is the embodiment of this menace.

But Russia, in many ways—and especially in terms of power—is not the Soviet Union. Nor did NATO fall apart after the Crimea operation; in fact, Russian operations led to the forward deployment of NATO troops in the Baltic states. As one official remarked in 1976, "As has been the case in the past when NATO has been in the doldrums," Moscow "does us the great service of waking us up."[13]

NATO-Moscow antagonism is not the only contemporary issue reminiscent of NATO's earlier life. The fears of allied leaders on both sides of the Atlantic, that Europeans would come to reject defense spending and the utility of military force, largely came true. In the late 1970s, the Carter administration urged each ally to spend 3 percent of its national GDP on defense; now, only a handful of NATO states spend over 2 percent.

European citizens say they will be unwilling to use their limited military force to defend their allies, perhaps even themselves. In 2015, polling done by the Pew Research center revealed that only 38 percent of Germans would use force to defend an ally in accordance with article 5 of the North Atlantic Treaty.[14] But Europeans had said the same thing during the Cold War, too. In 1980, the British Foreign Office reported a French public opinion poll on the use of force. Reportedly, two-thirds of respondents "thought that if the Russians invaded France the appropriate response would be to negotiate."[15]

Concerns about the lack of European defense spending and the public rejection of war as an option receive lots of media attention, given Russian chest-thumping. Analysts at think tanks like RAND publish pieces analyzing the military outcome of a Russian invasion of exposed bits of NATO territory like the Baltics.[16] But the exposed Baltics stand in as today's Berlin; NATO has always had exposed salients. The real fear of allied leaders is likely the same as it was for decades past: that their ability to counter claims and demands made by Moscow will be hamstrung by a mutual knowledge that the people of Europe would give away much in exchange to keep war off the continent. NATO, according to this logic, is necessary because the people of Europe are not interested in going to war.

As American officials pillory the European governments for their unwillingness to spend more on defense, the Europeans look back at the American domestic political scene with trepidation.[17] For so much of the Cold War, European officials worried that the American electorate would choose a president who would not or could not lead NATO. In 2016, the Republican nominee for president campaigned against NATO—and Donald J. Trump does not have the intellectual chops of, says, Robert Taft, to offer another vision of world affairs. Trump told reporters that NATO was "obsolete and expensive." He personifies the possible rise to power of the next generation of Americans that NATO officials had so feared, a generation that Lord Cromer thought celebrated the "rejection of history and its lessons for mankind."[18] As candidate Trump explained his views on NATO: "So, uh, I look at, I look at the fact that it was a long time ago."[19]

Trump has continued to sound an uncertain trumpet since his inauguration as president. In May 2017, Trump addressed the allies at NATO's newest headquarters in Brussels. The secretary of state, secretary of defense, and national security adviser had all made sure the speech would contain an endorsement of the orthodox interpretation of article 5—to help calm European fears that America was ceding its role as a European power. Not until the president was speaking did his advisers realize he had changed the speech to omit any mention of the critical piece of the treaty.[20] The current threat posed to NATO is, as the alliance leaders feared in the past, a problem of democracy. Counterintuitively, Donald Trump's election does not signal an American public that has soured on the alliance. It seems the opposite is true. One 2017 Gallup poll show more Americans think NATO should be maintained—80 percent—than at any time since 1989.[21]

What would happen if NATO were to collapse? Would the people of Germany press their governments to build a capability for independent defense, including nuclear weapons? How would the other states of Europe react? Would Britain try to balance the continent from offshore, and would France seek to make alliances with states that lay between Germany and Russia? Would Russia, free from fears of further NATO encroachment, turn inward to focus on national improvement, or seek to expand its influence, even territory?[22] And if the balance of power in Europe faltered—if one state became so dominant that others thought it necessary to wage war, would the United States once again put its thumb on the scales, or sit out the war? If the US were to arrive late once more, there might be nothing left. Or if the Europeans acquiesced to the rise of a new overwhelming power on the continent, would the Americans take it in stride or fight to regain influence on a continent considered so important for so long? The problem is not that there is a right or wrong answer to the above. The problem is that it is possible to conceive of scenarios where citizens supported governments that followed any one of these policies. They have tried them all before.

But where NATO leaders used to worry that voters too distant from the Second World War would not understand NATO, they now argue that a misunderstanding of the Cold War will imperil the alliance.[23] This argument has even more validity than claims about international politics based on the Second World War. Too often, NATO has been explained as part of an American Cold War policy, dominated by ideological fervor and unthinking anticommunism; as an overcharged response to a nonthreat. But the alliance, of which the United States was a crucial but hardly the sole champion, did not endure because of inertia, sloth, or without consideration of a host of other options. Many of the allies would have readily paraphrased Churchill's aphorism that the "only thing worse than fighting with allies is fighting without them!"[24] The allies decided, again and again, that NATO was the best means for not needing to fight at all.

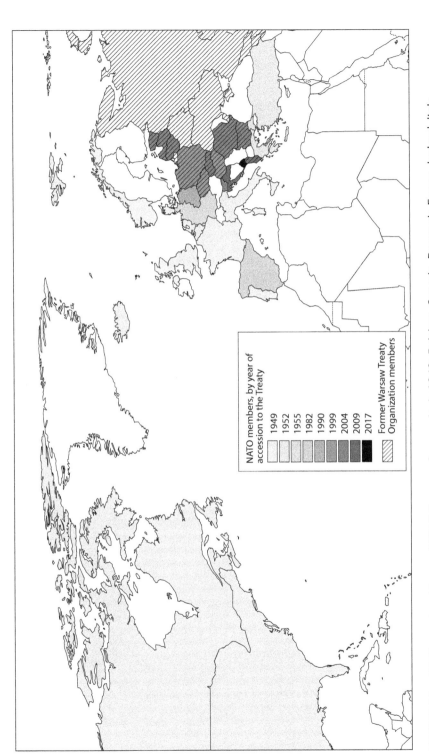

FIGURE 12. NATO membership as of 2018 (by year of accession): 1949: Belgium, Canada, Denmark, France, Iceland, Italy, Luxembourg, the Netherlands, Norway, Portugal, United Kingdom, United States. 1952: Greece, Turkey. 1955: Federal Republic of Germany. 1982: Spain. 1999: Czech Republic, Hungary, Poland. 2004: Bulgaria, Estonia, Latvia, Lithuania, Romania, Slovakia, Slovenia. 2009: Albania, Croatia. 2017: Montenegro.

Acknowledgments

I owe so much to so many for all the support necessary for this project. Teachers, especially Robert Bothwell and Adam Chapnick at the University of Toronto, kindled my interest in international affairs and diplomatic history. My teachers at Temple University, especially Richard H. Immerman, William I. Hitchcock, Ronald J. Granieri, Vladislav Zubok, and Jay Lockenour, taught me, each in his own way, what it means to be a historian. Lawrence S. Kaplan offered helpful advice. At Southern Methodist University's Center for Presidential History, I learned more from Jeffrey A. Engel and Tom Knock, and had the pleasure to work with Brian Franklin, Aaron Crawford, Ronna Spitz, and Evan McCormick. A return "home" to the University of Toronto has offered the funds and fellowship essential for finishing this study.

The research for this project was made possible by financial support from a number of institutions. Temple University's CENFAD, College of Liberal Arts, and the Graduate School all provided funds. A Doctoral Award from the Social Sciences and Humanities Research Council of Canada helped immeasurably. Fellowships and awards from the German Historical Institute in Washington, DC, the Society for Historians of American Foreign Relations, the Eisenhower Foundation, and the John F. Kennedy Library Foundation, plus a Moody Grant from the Lyndon Baines Johnson Foundation and a travel grant from the Gerald R. Ford Presidential Foundation, funded research in the US, the UK, and Brussels.

I have benefited from the expertise of archivists and declassification staffs at a range of archives: the NATO Archives in Brussels, the National Archives at College Park, the National Archives of the United Kingdom, Library and Archives Canada, the Bodleian Library, the Liddell Hart Center for Military Archives, the Cadbury Special Collections at the University of Birmingham, the Churchill Archives Centre, Cambridge University, and the Eisenhower, Kennedy, Johnson, Nixon, Ford, Carter, and George H. W. Bush presidential libraries.

I would like to acknowledge the Trustees of the Liddell Hart Centre for Military Archives, King's College London, for permission to quote from the papers of General Hastings Lionel Ismay, First Baron of Wormington, and of Captain Sir Basil Henry Liddell Hart. Permission was granted on behalf of the Cadbury Research Library (as owners of the physical diaries) to publish brief quotations from the diary of Sir Evelyn Shuckburgh.

I owe great thanks to Cornell University Press. Michael J. McGandy helped shape this project and provided crucial guidance. Sara R. Ferguson, along with Martin Beeny, Meagan Dermody, Carmen Adriana Torrado Gonzalez, Richanna Patrick, Scott Levine, and William O'Dell Wehling transformed a manuscript into this book. I'm grateful for copy editor Glenn Novak's careful attention to detail and for Bill Nelson's mapmaking skills. Thanks, too, to Stephanie Orfano of UofT's Scholarly Communications and Copyright Office and the assistance of Elisabetta Kerr. Two anonymous reviewers, along with Frank Gavin, offered helpful advice on the manuscript. Any errors that remain despite the efforts of this legion of editors and reviewers remain mine alone.

My parents, Eric and Cathy, did so much to support this project. Thanks to my Mom and Dad, and my sister Hilary, for all their encouragement. Brian and Jo provided good cheer. This book is dedicated to Nicole and our boys Henry and Charles, who mean the world to me.

A Note on Sources

Given the argument of this book—that NATO should not be considered only as an international organization but as an instrument of great-power politics and the basis for a Pax Atlantica—the background literature includes histories of the foreign policies of several allied states, as well histories of the great crises and events of the Cold War era. Because a bibliography covering great-power politics from the 1940s to the early 1990s would be lengthy to the point of unhelpful, and exceptional only in any minor omission, I have refrained from making a separate list here. One list that will be more helpful is a catalog of the primary sources I consulted for this book. The list at the end of this section also includes abbreviations and acronyms used in the notes.

Library stacks creak under piles of books with "NATO" in the title. It has been political scientists and practitioners, not journalists, who have written the first drafts of NATO history. Historians have been somewhat curious in their approach to NATO. The great majority of work on the alliance and the institution has been parceled out in journal articles and edited collections, many of which are cited below. Few historians have turned to NATO itself as the subject of monographs, especially when compared to other major topics in international affairs or US foreign relations. The one outstanding exception, of course, is Lawrence S. Kaplan, who pointed out the relative lack of work on NATO while undertaking Herculean efforts to fill the gaps with general and more specific books of his own. Another is John Milloy, whose excellent *The North Atlantic Treaty Organization, 1948–1957* (McGill–Queen's University Press, 2006) explores the nonmilitary aspects of NATO and disagreements in the alliance about just what else the organization should be doing. For a thorough exploration of the Atlanticist notion in the US diplomatic corps, readers can do little better than to read Kenneth Weisbrode's *The Atlanticists: A Story of American Diplomacy* (Santa Ana, CA: Nortia Press, 2015).

My thinking about NATO's place in international relations has been deeply influenced by four books in particular. In the first place, Marc Trachtenberg's *A Constructed Peace* (Princeton University Press, 1999) identifies a "NATO system" and places that system at the heart of postwar transatlantic and European international relations. John Lewis Gaddis, in his *Strategies of Containment* (Oxford University Press, 1982; 2005), explains how George F. Kennan had identified and grappled with the very same fears that so many officials, on both sides of the Atlantic, would wrestle with for decades: propaganda, psychological malaise, and the nonmilitary threat the Soviet Union posed to the balance of power. It is one of the fascinating aspects of NATO's history that Kennan identified the problem NATO was trying to solve, but seems never to have been convinced that NATO offered the correct solution. Gaddis's book also references Hilaire Belloc's "Jim, Who Ran Away from His Nurse, and Was Eaten by a Lion," although I found a different reference to the poem (and a NATO connection) in the National Archives of the United Kingdom. Melvyn P. Leffler's *Preponderance of Power: National Security, the Truman Administration, and the Cold War* (Stanford University Press, 1992) encouraged me to think about how US geopolitical thinking straddled the year 1945, and led me to look for similar connections in other states. In the midst of my project, Francis J. Gavin published *Nuclear Statecraft: History and Strategy in America's Atomic Age* (Cornell University Press, 2012), which pushed me to see important connections between the nuclear and nonnuclear side of NATO's history.

Other studies have connected the history of national foreign policies with NATO. For France, key works include William Hitchcock's *France Restored: Cold War Diplomacy and the Quest for Leadership in Europe, 1944–1954* (University of North Carolina Press, 1998) and Frédéric Bozo's *Two Strategies for Europe: De Gaulle, the United States, and the Atlantic Alliance* (Rowman & Littlefield, 2000). Irwin Wall's works, and especially *France, the United States, and the Algerian War* (University of California Press, 2001), illuminate the connection between Algeria and NATO. Thomas Schwartz's *America's Germany: John J. McCloy and the Federal Republic of Germany* (Harvard University Press, 1991) and *Lyndon Johnson and Europe: In the Shadow of Vietnam* (Harvard University Press, 2003) both provide important evidence and analysis for understanding the origins and shape of the alliance. Jeffrey A. Engel's *When the World Seemed New: George H. W. Bush and the End of the Cold War* (Houghton Mifflin Harcourt, 2017) connects NATO's history to the history of the end of the Cold War, and Engel's research helped unlock important records for my study. A large number of other important histories of national foreign policies, specific crises and events, and personalities were all essential to this study and appear in the notes.

The most important published primary collections for the study of NATO include volumes of *Aktzen zur Auswärtigen Politik der Bundesrepublik Deutschland* [AAPD]; *Documents on Canadian External Relations* [DCER]; *Documents Diplomatiques Français* [DDF]; *Documents on British Policy Overseas* [DBPO]; *Foreign Relations of the United States* [FRUS]; and online databases like the Declassified Document Reference System [DDRS], the Digital National Security Archive [DNSA], and the Cold War International History Project's document readers, *The Euromissiles Crisis and the End of the Cold War: 1977–1987* [*Euromissiles*]. More and more primary-source collections are available online. Especially useful are the President's Office Files [POF] available from the John F. Kennedy Library Digital Collections [JFKLDC], and important memoranda of conversations at the Gerald Ford Library Virtual Library [GFL/VL].

During my work on this book, the NATO Archives digitized and made available online a large swath of documents, including the early official histories of SHAPE. These records complement the NATO Archive's more carefully curated online collections, especially the "Military Planning for Berlin Emergency" [MPBE], and "Future Tasks of the Alliance—'Harmel Report'" [Harmel]. The newly digitized collections, as well as the records available for viewing at NATO Headquarters, will be important for future studies of the alliance.

Until NATO releases more records—especially the Private Office files—the lion's share of research must still be done in national archives. This is true for two reasons. First, NATO records bear the hallmarks of a committee product: they have been agreed upon and smoothed over, and they often leave out the messy bit. National archives, however, particularly the reporting telegrams and letters from national delegations, reveal how the sausage was made: in the corridors of the headquarters, in private lunches, in carefully selected and confidential meetings. It is not uncommon, in the study of a particular day of meetings at NATO, to refer, for instance, to a council record and Military Committee document from the NATO Archives, a personal letter from the British permanent representative, and two similar but differing summary reports from, say, the Canadian and American delegations to Ottawa and Washington, respectively. This is a function of the different declassification regimes in NATO states, but also represents just how the alliance worked. Second, NATO was both the design and instrument of allied states; to fully grasp both the function and importance of NATO, it must be understood within the machinery of government that directed the international affairs of the major allies.

TABLE 1   List of abbreviations and acronyms

Bibliographical Abbreviations and Acronyms	
Official Archives	
NATO	**Archives of the North Atlantic Treaty Organization, Brussels, Belgium**
DDEL	**Dwight D. Eisenhower Presidential Library, Abilene, KS**
AWF	Papers as President of the United States, 1953–1961 (Ann Whitman File)
	Administration Series
Whitman	Ann Whitman Diary Series
	Cabinet Series
	DDE Diary Series

(Continued)

TABLE 1 (Continued)

Bibliographical Abbreviations and Acronyms

	International Series
	Name Series
	NSC Series
	White House Central File
WHO	White House Office
NSC	National Security Council Staff Papers
OSS	Office of the Staff Secretary
	Subject Series
INTL	International Series
State	State Department
DOD	Department of Defense
SANSA	Special Assistant for National Security Affairs
SAS	Special Assistant Series
	Alfred M. Gruenther Papers
Jackson	C.D. Jackson Papers
	Christian A. Herter Papers
Smith	Gerard C. Smith Papers
Dulles	John Foster Dulles Papers
WHM	White House Meeting File
Chron	Chronological File
NP	Lauris Norstad Papers
	Robert J. Schaetzel Papers
BPL	**George H. W. Bush Presidential Library, College Station, TX**
NSC	National Security Council
APNSA	APNSA (Office of the Assistant to the President for National Security Affairs) Files
Blackwill	Blackwill, Robert D. [NSC European and Soviet Affairs]
Chellis	Chellis, Craig
Gompert	Gompert, David C.
Holl	Holl, Jane
Kanter	Kanter, Arnold [NSC Defense Policy / Arms Control]
Koch	Koch, Susan
Lowenkron	Lowenkron, Barry
PA	PA Files
Rice	Rice, Condoleezza [NSC European and Soviet Affairs]
Rostow	Rostow, Nicholas [NSC legal adviser]
Wayne	Wayne, Earle Anthony
Wilson	Wilson, Heather [NSC Defense Policy / Arms Control]
Zelikow	Zelikow, Philip [NSC European and Soviet Affairs]
Scowcroft	Scowcroft, Brent, Collection; German Unification Files
GFL	**Gerald Ford Presidential Library, Ann Arbor, MI**
Laird	Melvin R. Laird Papers
Burns	Arthur F. Burns Papers

Bibliographical Abbreviations and Acronyms

JCL	**Jimmy Carter Presidential Library, Atlanta**
NSC	National Security Council Institutional Files
JFKL	**John F. Kennedy Presidential Library, Boston**
NSF	National Security File
Bundy	McGeorge Bundy Papers
Neustadt	Richard E. Neustadt Papers
Nunnerley	David Nunnerley Papers
Schlesinger	Arthur M. Schlesinger Jr. Papers
Yarmolinsky	Adam Yarmolinsky Papers
LAC	**Library and Archives Canada, Ottawa**
RG24	Record Group 24—National Defence
RG25	Record Group 25—External Affairs
LBJL	**Lyndon B. Johnson Presidential Library, Austin, TX**
NSF	National Security File
AF	Agency File
CF	Country File
Komer	Robert Komer File
Name	Name File
	Cabinet Papers
Aides	Office Files of the White House Aides
Bellinger	Cecil Bellinger
	White House Central File Subject Files, 1963–1969
Bator	Personal Papers of Francis M. Bator
NARA	**National Archives and Records Administration, College Park, MD**
RG59	Record Group 59: General Records of the Department of State
BAA	Bureau of African Affairs
OIAA	Office of Inter-African Affairs
RPM	Records of the Political-Military Adviser
EUR	Bureau of European Affairs
DAS	Deputy Assistant Secretary
Schaetzel	Subject Files (J. Robert Schaetzel), 1961–1966
GER	Country Director for Germany
FRG	Records Relating to the Federal Republic of Germany, 1954–1967
APMA	[Office of] NATO and Atlantic Political-Military Affairs
NATO Affairs	Records Relating to NATO Affairs, 1959–1966
Trilateral	Records Relating to NATO Trilateral Discussions, 1965–1968
	Office of Atlantic Political and Military Affairs
	Records Relating to NATO, 1957–1964
	Subject Files, 1953–1962
	Office of Regional Planning & UN Adviser
	Records Relating to Planning and United Nations Matters, 1959–1967
	Records of the Office of European Regional Affairs

(Continued)

TABLE 1   (Continued)

Bibliographical Abbreviations and Acronyms

	Records of the Director, 1955–1960
	Records of the NATO Adviser, 1957–1961
	Subject Files, 1945–1958
	Central Decimal Files
	Central Foreign Policy Series
Misc.Lot	Miscellaneous Lot Files
Misc.Office	Miscellaneous Office Files of the Assistant Secretaries of State for European Affairs, 1943–1957
	Office of the Executive Secretariat
	Multilateral Force Documents, 1960–1965
Bohlen	Records of Ambassador Charles E. Bohlen, 1942–1971
	Records of Robert W. Komer, 1948–1968
	Records Relating to the Acheson–NATO Exercise, 1966
PPC	Policy Planning Council
WE	Records of the Office of Western European Affairs
France	Subject File Relating to France, 1944–1960
Ball	Records of Under Secretary of State George W. Ball, 1961–1966
RG84	Record Group 84: Records of the Foreign Service Posts of the Department of State
	Belgium, U.S. Mission to NATO, Brussels
	Classified Central Subject Files, 1965–1970
RG469	Record Group 469: Records of the US Foreign Assistance Agencies, 1948–1961
OAEO	Office of African and European Operations
	Subject Files, 1955–1959
TNA	**The National Archives of the United Kingdom, Kew**
CAB	Records of the Cabinet Office
	CAB 128: Minutes (CM and CC Series)
	CAB 134: Miscellaneous Committees: Minutes and Papers
DEFE	Records of the Ministry of Defence
	DEFE 7: Ministry of Defence prior to 1964
FO or FCO	Records of the Foreign Office and Commonwealth Office and predecessors
	FCO 28: Northern Department and East European and Soviet Department
	FCO 41: Western Organisations and Co-ordination Department
	FCO 49: Planning Staff and Commonwealth Policy and Planning Department
	FO 115: Embassy and Consulates, United States of America: General Correspondence 1791–1967
	FO 146: Embassy and Consulates, France: General Correspondence
	FO 371: Political Departments: General Correspondence, 1906–1966
	FO 462: Correspondence Respecting the United States of America
	FO 800: Private Offices: Various Ministers' and Officials' Papers

Bibliographical Abbreviations and Acronyms

	FO 953: Information Policy Department and Regional Information Departments
	FO 1042: Embassy, Bonn, West Germany, General Correspondence
	FO 1116: UK Delegation to NATO: Registered Files
PREM	Records of the Prime Minister's Office
	PREM 11: Correspondence and Papers, 1951–1964
	PREM 13: Correspondence and Papers, 1964–1970
	PREM 15: 1970–1974
	PREM 16: 1974–1979
	PREM 19: 1979 onwards
RNL	**Richard Nixon Presidential Library and Museum, Yorba Linda, CA**
NSC	National Security Council Files
Inst	Institutional Files Collection
HAK	Henry A. Kissinger Office Files Collection

Personal Papers and Manuscript Collections

	Bodleian Library, Oxford University, Oxford, UK
	Modern Political MSS
	Harold Macmillan, Earl of Stockton
	Harold Wilson, Lord Wilson of Rievaulx
	Sir (D'Arcy) Patrick Reilly
	Churchill Archives Centre, Churchill College, Cambridge, UK
	Papers of Lord Gladwyn
	Papers of Sir Frank Roberts
LHCMA	**Liddell Hart Centre for Military Archives, King's College London**
Ismay	Ismay, Gen. Hastings Lionel, 1st Baron Ismay of Wormington
Hart	Liddell Hart, Capt. Sir Basil Henry (1895–1970)
CRL	**Special Collections, Cadbury Research Library, University of Birmingham**
	Papers of Sir Evelyn Shuckburgh

Notes

INTRODUCTION

1. "Notes on visit to Fontainebleau and SHAPE (Sept.–Oct. 1955)," LH11/1955/6, LHCMA.

2. See E. Timothy Smith, "Beyond the Water's Edge: Liberal Internationalist and Pacifists Opposition to NATO," in *The Romance of History: Essays in Honor of Lawrence Kaplan*, ed. Scott L. Bills and E. Timothy Smith (Kent, OH: Kent State University Press, 1997), 40ff.; Lord Carver quoted in Michael Klare, "The Inescapable Links: Interventionism and Nuclear War," in *Search for Sanity: The Politics of Nuclear Weapons and Disarmament*, ed. Paul Joseph and Simon Rosenblum (Boston: South End, 1984); Lawrence S. Kaplan, "Strategic Problems and the Central Sector," in *Blueprints for Battle: Planning for War in Central Europe, 1948–1968*, ed. Jan Hoffenaar and Dieter Krüger (Lexington: University Press of Kentucky, 2012), 13; "The Basic Problem in Defence Planning," February 25, 1957, LHCMA/LH/11/1957/7.

3. "The Political Aspects of NATO," speech by Lord Ismay to NATO Defense College, September 9, 1955, LHCMA/Ismay/3/17/1/1/b.

4. For a consideration of Warsaw Pact views of NATO and questions about what NATO achieved see Vojtech Mastny, "NATO at Fifty: Did NATO Win the Cold War? Looking over the Wall," *Foreign Affairs* 78, no. 3 (May/June 1999): 176–89.

5. Quoted in Charles Ruud, *The Constant Diplomat: Robert Ford in Moscow* (Montreal: McGill–Queen's University Press, 2009), 39.

6. Theodore Achilles, oral history interview by Robert D. McKinzie, November 13 and December 18, 1972, Harry S. Truman Presidential Library and Museum.

7. "Alternatives for Future European Developments and Implications for US policy—short, medium, and long run," March 7, 1966, Bator/27/NATO Crisis 1966/LBJL.

8. Lord Ismay, "Pax Atlantica," *Unilever Magazine*, Winter 1954; also available in the NATO online library, www.nato.int/docu/articles/1954/a54000a.htm. For the idea of a "NATO system" see Marc Trachtenberg, *A Constructed Peace: The Making of the European Settlement, 1945–1963* (Princeton, NJ: Princeton University Press, 1999), 95–145.

9. "Alternatives for Future European Developments and Implications for US policy—short, medium, and long run," March 7, 1966.

10. "The Rome Summit and NATO's mission," undated, Holl/CF01937/BPL.

11. Lester Bowles Pearson's acceptance speech, on the occasion of the award of the Nobel Peace Prize in Oslo, December 10, 1957, at www.nobelprize.org, http://www.nobelprize.org/nobel_prizes/peace/laureates/1957/pearson-acceptance.html. See also Kathleen Burk, "The Anglo-American 'Special Relationship' in the Atlantic Context during the Late 1940s and 1950s," in *Defining the Atlantic Community: Culture, Intellectuals, and Policies in the Mid-Twentieth Century*, ed. Marco Mariano (New York: Routledge, 2010), 149.

12. Wallace J. Thies, *Why NATO Endures* (New York: Cambridge University Press, 2009); Thomas Risse-Kappen, *Cooperation among Democracies: The European Influence on U.S. Foreign Policy* (Princeton, NJ: Princeton University Press, 1995); Andrew Preston, "The Spirit of Democracy," in *Uncertain Empire: American History and the Idea of the Cold War*, ed. Joel Isaac and Duncan Bell (Oxford: Oxford University Press, 2012), 143.

13. Dirk U. Stikker, *Men of Responsibility: A Memoir* (New York: Harper & Row, 1966), 363. See also Lauris Norstad Oral History, p. 164, DDEL.

14. Robert Cutler to Christian Herter, March 13, 1958, WHO/SANSA/NSC/Briefing Notes/16/Spain, US Policy toward/DDEL.

15. Memorandum by Third Secretary, Embassy in the United States, March 23, 1948, DCER:14, d315.

16. Dean Acheson to Donnelly, July 6, 1965. *Dean Acheson Papers* (Wilmington, DE: Scholarly Resources Inc., 2004), microfilm, General Correspondence, Box 29, Folder 375. Contrast with Thies, *Why NATO Endures*, 297.

17. Charles S. Maier, "The Making of 'Pax Americana': Formative Moments of United States Ascendancy," in *The Quest for Stability: Problems of West European Security, 1918–1957*, ed. R. Ahmann, Michael Howard, and Adolf M. Birke (Oxford: Oxford University Press, 1993), 391; Thomas W. Gijswijt, "Beyond NATO: Transnational Elite Networks and the Atlantic Alliance," in *Transforming NATO in the Cold War: Challenges beyond Deterrence in the 1960s*, ed. Andreas Wenger, Christian Nuenlist, and Anna Locher (London: Routledge, 2007), 60.

18. Gijswijt, "Beyond NATO," 60. See also Valerie Aubourg, "Organizing Atlanticism: The Bilderberg Group and the Atlantic Institute, 1952–1963," in *The Cultural Cold War in Western Europe, 1945–1960*, ed. Giles Scott-Smith and Hans Krabbendam (Portland, OR: Frank Cass, 2003).

19. Handwritten notes by McGeorge Bundy, March 21, 1964, LBJL.

20. Memorandum for Bundy, "Presidential Meeting with de Gaulle," May 26, 1961, NSF/70A/France-General/JFKL; Schaetzel to Rostow, February 19, 1963, and Butterworth to Achilles, February 13, 1963, both in RG59/EUR/DAS/Schaetzel/1/Canadians/NARA.

21. Quoted in Nigel Hamilton, *Monty: The Battles of Field Marshal Bernard Law Montgomery* (London: Hodder & Stoughton, 1994), 801.

22. Letter from Sir C. Mallaby (Bonn) to Sir J. Fretwell, November 8, 1989, in *Documents on British Policy Overseas, Series III, Vol. VII, German Unification*, ed. P. Salmon, K. A. Hamilton, and S. R. Twigge [hereafter *DBPO*:3:7], 95; Alistair Horne, *Harold Macmillan*, vol. 2, *1957–1986* (New York: Viking, 1989), 135.

23. Lord Carrington, *Reflect on Things Past: The Memoirs of Lord Carrington* (London: Collins, 1988), 322–23.

24. See D. R. Thorpe, *Supermac: The Life of Harold Macmillan* (London: Chatto & Windus, 2010), 69; Piers Brendon, *The Decline and Fall of the British Empire, 1781–1997* (New York: Alfred A. Knopf, 2008), 498.

25. For consideration of how the lessons of the World Wars combined with a pre–Cold War theory of geopolitics to shape postwar American national security policy see Melvyn P. Leffler, *A Preponderance of Power: National Security, the Truman Administration, and the Cold War* (Stanford, CA: Stanford University Press, 1992).

26. Ismay, "Pax Atlantica."

27. Bernard Law Montgomery, *Memoirs* (London: Collins, 1976), 509.

28. Participant memoirs include Escott Reid, *Time of Fear and Hope: The Making of the North Atlantic Treaty, 1947–1949* (Toronto: McClelland & Stewart, 1977); Nicholas Henderson, *The Birth of NATO* (Boulder, CO: Westview, 1983). On the origins of NATO see Lawrence S. Kaplan, *NATO 1948: The Birth of the Transatlantic Alliance* (Lanham, MD: Rowman & Littlefield, 2007); *NATO before the Korean War: April 1949–June 1950* (Kent, OH: Kent State University Press, 2013).

1. THE SPECTRE OF APPEASEMENT

1. Memorandum by Mr Bevin for the Cabinet, Review of Soviet Policy, January 5, 1948, *DBPO*:1:10, d9. Bevin's analysis of the Soviet threat is similar to the assessment made by George Kennan in 1946.

2. Meeting between Mr Bevin and Mr Marshall, December 19, 1946, *DBPO*:1:10, d9.

3. "Summary of a Memorandum Representing Mr. Bevin's Views on the Formation of a Western Union," enclosure to British Ambassador (Inverchapel) to the Secretary of State, January 13, 1948, *Foreign Relations of the United States, 1948*, vol. III *(hereafter FRUS:1948*:III), d3. Bevin had previewed this thinking with Marshall, as well as with French and Canadian statesmen, in December. Chargé in London (Gallman) to the Secretary of State, December 22, 1947, *FRUS:1948*:III, d1. See also Alan Bullock, *Ernest Bevin, Foreign Secretary, 1945–1951* (New York: Oxford University Press, 1985), 517.

4. For quotation and Kennan's thinking in this period, see John Lewis Gaddis, *Strategies of Containment: A Critical Appraisal of Postwar American National Security Policy during the Cold War* (New York: Oxford University Press, 2005), 33–34. For the full quotation regarding "Kremlin towers" see *Measures Short of War: The George F. Kennan Lectures at the National War College, 1946–47*, ed. Giles D. Harlow and George C. Maerz (Washington, DC: National Defense University Press, 1991), 314.

5. "Summary of a Memorandum Representing Mr. Bevin's Views on the Formation of a Western Union," January 13, 1948.

6. Memorandum of Conversation, by the Under Secretary of State (Lovett), *FRUS:1948*:III, d9. See also Record of a Conversation between Mr. Bevin and M. Bidault, December 19, 1947, *DBPO*:1:10, d1.

7. "Summary of a Memorandum Representing Mr. Bevin's Views on the Formation of a Western Union," January 13, 1948.

8. Secretary of State to the Embassy in France, February 24, 1948, *FRUS:1948*:IV, d473.

9. John Lewis Gaddis, *The Long Peace: Inquiries into the History of the Cold War* (New York: Oxford University Press, 1987), 35–36.

10. Kurt Schumacher quoted in Thomas Alan Schwartz, *America's Germany: John J. McCloy and the Federal Republic of Germany* (Cambridge, MA: Harvard University Press, 1991), 54; William I. Hitchcock, *France Restored: Cold War Diplomacy and the Quest for Leadership in Europe, 1944–1954* (Chapel Hill: University of North Carolina Press, 1998), 93.

11. Memorandum from USSEA to Prime Minister, March 14, 1948, *Documents on Canadian External Relations* (hereafter *DCER*), 14, d430.

12. The British Embassy to the Department of State, March 11, 1948, *FRUS:1948*:III, d37.

13. Secretary of State for Commonwealth Relations to High Commissioner for the United Kingdom, March 10, 1948; Ambassador in United States to USSEA, March 11, 1948, both in *DCER*:14, d296 and d299, respectively.

14. Memorandum by the Director of the Office of European Affairs (Hickerson) to the Secretary of State, March 8, 1948, *FRUS:1948*:III, d31.

15. Memorandum by the Director of the Office of European Affairs (Hickerson) to the Secretary of State, March 8, 1948.

16. Memorandum by the Secretary of State to President Truman, March 12, 1948, *FRUS:1948*:III, d40.

17. For the domestic political background of the resolution see Lawrence S. Kaplan, *NATO and the United States: The Enduring Alliance* (Boston: Twayne, 1988), 34.

18. Secretary of State to the British Ambassador (Inverchapel), March 12, 1948, *FRUS:1948*:III, d38.

19. Minutes of the Third Meeting of the United States–United Kingdom–Canada Security Conversations, Held at Washington, March 24, 1948, *FRUS:1948*:III, d57.

20. Minutes of the First Meeting of the United States–United Kingdom–Canada Security Conversations, Held at Washington, March 22, 1948, *FRUS:1948*:III, d54.

21. Minutes of the Fourth Meeting of the United States–United Kingdom–Canada Security Conversations, Held at Washington, March 29, 1948, *FRUS:1948*:III, d61.

22. British Embassy to the Department of State, undated, *FRUS:1948*:III, d96.

23. On British delays because of American politics see Bullock, *Ernest Bevin*, 569. The exploratory talks were to be kept secret because of the "political campaign" in the US. Minutes of the First Meeting of the Washington Exploratory Talks on Security, July 6, 1948, 11:30 a.m., *FRUS:1948*:III, d112.

24. Memorandum by the Chief of the Division of Western European Affairs (Achilles) to the Director of the Office of European Affairs (Hickerson), *FRUS:1948*:III, d99. The British interlocutor was Donald Maclean.

25. Ambassador in United States to Under-Secretary of State for External Affairs, May 8, 1948, *DCER*:14, d341.

26. Ambassador in United States to Under-Secretary of State for External Affairs, May 8, 1948.

27. Memorandum by the Participants in the Washington Security Talks, July 6 to September 9, Submitted to Their Respective Governments for Study and Comment, September 9, 1948, *FRUS:1948*:III, d150.

28. Record of a conversation between Mr Bevin and M. Schuman, held at the Foreign Office on 13 January, *DBPO*:1:10, d210.

29. James George Eayrs, *In Defense of Canada: Growing Up Allied* (Toronto: University of Toronto Press, 1980), 105.

30. Minutes of the Seventh Meeting of the Washington Exploratory Talks on Security, September 10, 1948, 4 p.m., *FRUS:1948*:III, d151.

31. Memorandum by the Director of the Policy Planning Staff (Kennan), November 24, 1948, *FRUS:1948*:III, d182; Bullock, *Ernest Bevin*, 644–45.

32. Reid, *Time of Fear and Hope*, 158.

33. "Effects of Communist control in an NAT country," undated draft from Franklin to Fessenden, EUR/Records Relating to the North Atlantic Treaty Organization, 1947–1953/ 7/Communist Control in NAT Country/NARA.

34. Henderson, *Birth of NATO*, 67, 74, 89–93; quote at 89–90 and 93. Emphasis in original.

35. Quoted in Robert H. Ferrell, "The Formation of the Alliance, 1948–1949," in *American Historians and the Atlantic Alliance*, ed. Lawrence S. Kaplan (Kent, OH: Kent State University Press, 1991), 19.

36. "The Political Aspects of NATO," Speech by Lord Ismay to NATO Defense College, September 9, 1955, LHCMA/Ismay/3/17/1/1/b.

37. On the early defense plans, especially the Medium Term Defense Plan, see Ferrell, "Formation of the Alliance," 27. For earlier plans see Robert Allen Wampler, "Ambiguous Legacy: The United States, Great Britain and the Foundations of NATO Strategy, 1948–1957" (PhD diss., Harvard University, 1991), 2–5. See also Gregory Pedlow, "The Evolution of NATO Strategy, 1949–1969," in *NATO Strategy Documents, 1949–1969*, ed. Gregory W. Pedlow (Brussels: North Atlantic Treaty Organization, 1999), https://www. nato.int/archives/strategy.htm (electronic publication).

38. Ambassador in United States to SSEA, April 29, 1949, *DCER*:15, d351.

39. Directive from the Defense Committee to the North Atlantic Military Committee, M.C.-1, October 6, 1949, established the Military Committee, the Standing Group (which lasted until 1966), and the short-lived regional planning groups. NATO Online.

40. Memorandum from Secretary of Chiefs of Staff Committee to Secretary to the Cabinet and USSEA, June 30, 1949, and "A concept of North Atlantic Defence Organization" (June 1940), both in *DCER*:15, d362.

41. Ambassador in the United States to SSEA, December 19, 1950, *DCER*:16, d632.

42. Quoted in Supreme Headquarters Allied Powers Europe, *SHAPE History: The New Approach, 1953–1956*, vol. 3 (1976), 18. NATO Online.

43. Robert Endicott Osgood, *NATO, the Entangling Alliance* (Chicago: University of Chicago Press, 1962), 74; Kaplan, *NATO before the Korean War*.

44. Memorandum by the Secretary of State on a Meeting with the President, July 31, 1950, *FRUS:1950*:III, d106.

45. United States High Commissioner for Germany (McCloy) to the Secretary of State, August 3, 1950, *FRUS:1950*:III, d116.

46. Ambassador in the United Kingdom (Douglas) to the Secretary of State, August 8, 1950, *FRUS:1950*:III, d124.

47. Ambassador in the United Kingdom (Douglas) to the Secretary of State, August 8, 1950.

48. Ambassador in the Netherlands (Chapin) to the Secretary of State, January 11, 1951, *FRUS:1951*:III, Part 1 (hereafter *FRUS:1951*:III:1), d222.

49. For "model" see Memorandum of the North Atlantic Council, New York, September 15, 16, 18, and 26, and October 2, 1950, attached to *DCER*:16, d570. See also Supreme Headquarters Allied Powers Europe, *SHAPE History: Origin and Develoment of SHAPE*, vol. 1 (1953), 358–60; *SHAPE History: The New Approach*, 340. On German integration see Secretary of State and the Secretary of Defense (Johnson) to the President, September 8, 1950, *FRUS:1950*:III, d172.

50. For a full list of SACEUR's responsibilities see *SHAPE History: Origin and Development of SHAPE*, 21.

51. Secretary of State and the Secretary of Defense (Johnson) to the President, September 8, 1950.

52. Norstad Oral History, OH-558, DDEL, p. 41. See also Stephen E. Ambrose and Morris Honick, "Eisenhower: Rekindling the Spirit of the West," in *Generals in International Politics: NATO's Supreme Allied Commander, Europe*, ed. Robert S. Jordan (Lexington: University Press of Kentucky, 1987).

53. Michael Hogan, *A Cross of Iron: Harry S. Truman and the Origins of the National Security State, 1945–1954* (New York: Cambridge University Press, 1998), 235–36.

54. "Excerpt from General Gruenther's testimony before the Committee on Foreign Relations and the Committee on Armed Services in connection with the Mutual Security Act of 1951," Misc.Lot/Misc.Office/22/Memorandums—George W. Perkins/NARA. Note that the reference was to the removal of ground troops, not American air forces.

55. Eisenhower Statement on Withdrawing Troops from Europe, Perkins to Parsons, October 18, 1951, Misc.Lot/Misc.Office/22/Memorandums—George W. Perkins/NARA.

56. Notes on a Meeting at the White House, January 31, 1951, *FRUS:1951*:III:1, d248.

57. Conversation between the Secretary of State and General Eisenhower, July 3, 1951, FO 800/652.

58. United States Special Representative in Europe (Katz) to the Administrator for Economic Cooperation (Foster), July 16, 1951, *FRUS:1951*:III:1, d124. See Wampler, "Ambiguous Legacy," 146–52, for context.

59. Notes on a Meeting at the White House, January 31, 1951, *FRUS:1951*:III:1, d248.

60. Dean Acheson, *Present at the Creation: My Years in the State Department* (New York: W. W. Norton, 1969), 730.

61. Circular Despatch on the Rome Meeting, December 8, 1951, *DCER*:17, d512; Report on the Ministerial Meeting of the North Atlantic Council, Paris, December 15–18, 1952, December 29, 1952, *DCER*:18, d501; for "Whither NATO?" see Memorandum from Head, Economic Division to USSEA, February 10, 1953, *DCER*:19, d477.

62. For the origins of the organization's staff see Robert Jordan, *The NATO International Staff/Secretariat, 1952–1957* (Oxford: Oxford University Press, 1967).

63. Baron Ismay, Hastings Lionel Ismay, *The Memoirs of General the Lord Ismay, K.G., P.C., G.C.B., C.H., D.S.O* (Toronto: Heinemann, 1960), 460–61. Ismay was widely admired, but expectations were set too high for his secretary-generalship; he was

"unreasonably expected . . . to be a superman—a 'civilian Eisenhower.'" Report on the Ministerial Meeting of the North Atlantic Council, Paris, December 15–18, 1952.

64. Conversation between the Secretary of State and the Turkish Ambassador, September 5, 1951; and Secretary of State's Conversation with the Norwegian Prime Minister and Minister of Defence, September 6, 1951, both in FO 800/652.

65. *SHAPE History: Origin and Development of SHAPE*, 399.

66. *SHAPE History: The New Approach*, 15.

67. *SHAPE History: The New Approach*, vii; Ismay quoted in Delegation to North Atlantic Council to USSEA, June 18, 1953, *DCER*:19, d483.

68. This is the thrust of Wampler, "Ambiguous Legacy"; Lincoln Gordon quoted at 598.

69. Montgomery, *Memoirs*, 517.

70. Montgomery, 516–17.

71. Marc Trachtenberg, "A 'Wasting Asset': American Strategy and the Shifting Nuclear Balance, 1949–1954," *International Security* 13, no. 3 (Winter 1998–1989): 5–49.

72. See the chapter titled "The Nuclearization of NATO and U.S.–West European Relations" in Marc Trachtenberg, *History and Strategy*, Princeton Studies in International History and Politics (Princeton, NJ: Princeton University Press, 1991). For another take on NATO and atomic strategy see Andrew Johnson, *Hegemony and Culture in the Origins of NATO Nuclear Strategy, 1945–1954*. On MC48 see Pedlow, *NATO Strategy Documents*; Marc Trachtenberg, *The Cold War and After: History, Theory, and the Logic of International Politics* (Princeton, NJ: Princeton University Press, 2012), 142–53; and *Constructed Peace*, 156–78. On Eisenhower's "new look" policy see Robert R. Bowie and Richard H. Immerman, *Waging Peace: How Eisenhower Shaped an Enduring Cold War Strategy* (New York: Oxford University Press, 1998), 178–201; and Gaddis, *Strategies of Containment*, 128–98.

73. Report on the Ministerial Meeting of the North Atlantic Council on April 23, 1954, *DCER*:20, d281.

74. Quoted in Wampler, "Ambiguous Legacy," 643. See also cabinet records C.81(54), December 2, 1954, CAB 195/13.

75. Saki Dockrill, *Britain's Policy for West German Rearmament, 1950–1955* (Cambridge: Cambridge University Press, 1991), 42, 48–49.

76. Extract from Letter from Delegation to North Atlantic Council to USSEA, December 23, 1953, *DCER*:19, d546; Telegraphic Summary, by the United States Delegation, December 6, 1953, *FRUS:1952–1954*:II, d349.

77. See especially "Protocol III on the Control of Armaments, October 23, 1954," one of the protocols of 1954 modifying the Brussels Treaty, online at Avalon Project of the Yale Law School, Lillian Goldman Law Library, http://avalon.law.yale.edu/20th_century/we005.asp.

2. THE APPLE CART

1. Memorandum of a Telephone Conversation between the President in Augusta, Georgia, and the Secretary of State in Key West, Florida, November 27, 1956, 9:25 a.m., *FRUS:1955–1957*:XVI, d618.

2. Memoranda of Discussion at the 375th Meeting of the National Security Council, August 7, 1958, *FRUS:1958–1960*:XIV, d6.

3. William Stevenson, *A Man Called Intrepid: The Secret War* (London: Macmillan, 1976), 155.

4. Untitled minute by [Lord] Reading, June 14, 1956, FO 371/124805. See also Ismay to Winston Churchill, March 20, 1954, Ismay/3/12/27/LHCMA, and Eden in "Four-Power Talks," C.P.(55)99, July 27, 1955, CAB 129/76, and General Alfred Gruenther's late-1954 remarks in Trachtenberg, *Constructed Peace*, 180.

5. National Intelligence Estimate, November 1, 1955, *FRUS:1955–1957*:XIX, d39.

6. "Daily Intelligence Abstracts of Interest to Working Groups—No. 581," March 16, 1956, DDRS/CK3100329121.

7. "Trends and Implications of Soviet Policy," Report by the Chairman of the Working Group on Trends of Soviet Policy, December 3, 1955, C-M(55)121, NATO.

8. Telegram from the Secretary of State to the Department of State, December 17, 1955, *FRUS:1955–1957*:IV, d13; "Outline for a Speech by the Secretary of State," May 19, 1955. *FRUS:1955–1957*:XIX, d23.

9. Cabinet Secretary's Notebook entry C.M.21(55), July 7, 1955, CAB 195/14.

10. Letter from Nelson Rockefeller to Eisenhower, September 26, 1955, DDRS/CK3100218974. See also Memorandum of Discussion at the 262d Meeting of the National Security Council, October 20, 1955, *FRUS:1955–1957*:IV, d9.

11. Paper Prepared in the Department of State, October 3, 1955, *FRUS:1955–1957*:XIX, d36; Daily Intelligence Abstracts No. 549, January 31, 1956, DDRS/CK3100040602.

12. National Intelligence Estimate 100-7-55, "World Situation and Trends," *FRUS:1955–1957*:XIX, d39.

13. Greunther to Rockefeller. October 8, 1955, DDRS/CK3100273471.

14. Draft of message for General Gruenther from Col. Goodpaster, October 22, 1955, DDRS/CK3100241767.

15. The Future of the North Atlantic Treaty Organisation, C.P.(56)112, May 2, 1956, CAB 129/81.

16. See John Milloy, *The North Atlantic Treaty Organization, 1948–1957: Community or Alliance?* (Montreal: McGill–Queen's University Press, 2006), Pearson's views at 164.

17. Dana Wilgress to Lord Ismay, March 19, 1956, Ismay/3/12/32a/LHCMA; Harold Macmillan to Crawford, October 26, 1955; J. C. W. Bushell to D. A. Greenhill, October 31, 1955, both in FO 371/118546.

18. Telegram from the United States Delegation at the North Atlantic Ministerial Meeting to the Department of State, December 16, 1955, *FRUS:1955–1957*:IV, d11; Telegram from the Secretary of State to the Department of State, December 17, 1955. *FRUS:1955–1957*:IV, d13.

19. Telegram from the United States Delegation at the North Atlantic Ministerial Meeting to the Department of State, December 16, 1955.

20. Telegram from the United States Delegation at the North Atlantic Council Ministerial Meeting to the Department of State, December 17, 1955, *FRUS:1955–1957*:IV, d14; Memorandum of Discussion at the 271st Meeting of the National Security Council, Washington, December 22, 1955, *FRUS:1955–1957*:IV, d17.

21. Telegram from the United States Delegation at the North Atlantic Ministerial Meeting to the Department of State, December 16, 1955.

22. Telegram from the Embassy in the United Kingdom to the Department of State, July 27, 1956, *FRUS:1955–1957*:XVI, d7.

23. Telegram from the Department of State to the Secretary of State, at Lima, July 28, 1956, *FRUS:1955–1957*:XVI, d14. Eisenhower's views in Memorandum of a Conversation with the President, White House, Washington, July 28, 1956, 10 a.m., *FRUS:1955–1957*:XVI, d16. See also Telegram from the Embassy in the United Kingdom to the Department of State, July 29, 1956, 6 p.m., *FRUS:1955–1957*:XVI, d21; Memorandum of a Conference with the President, White House, Washington, July 27, 1956, 8:30 a.m., *FRUS:1955–1957*:VI, d3. See also "M. Couve de Murville, Ambassadeur de France à Washington, à M. Pineau, Ministère des Affaires Étrangères," no. 4618–4629, *DDF*:1956:2, d91.

24. Prime Minister's Personal Minute M.191/56 to Foreign Secretary, August 26, 1956, FO 371/119174; FO 1495 to Paris, August 28, 1956, FO 371/119174. On Canadian support for discussions at NATO see Secretary's Notebook for August 28, 1956, C.M.62(56).

25. Washington 1758 to FO, August 29, 1956, FO 371/119174.

26. For the council proceedings see UKDel635 Saving to FO, September 6, 1956, FO 371/119175. Terence Robertson argues "Pineau was always of the opinion that the crisis was more of a NATO affair than one for the United Nations." Terence Robertson, *Crisis: The Inside Story of the Suez Conspiracy* (Toronto: McClelland & Stewart, 1964), 100; "Summary Record of a meeting of the Council held at the Palais de Chaillot, Paris, XVIᵉ, on Wednesday, 5th September at 3:30 pm," September 8, 1956, C-R(56)48, NATO.

27. Memorandum of Discussion at a Department of State–Joint Chiefs of Staff Meeting, Pentagon, Washington, August 31, 1956, 11:30 a.m., *FRUS:1955–1957*:XVI, d156.

28. Telegram from the Department of State to the Embassy of the United Kingdom, August 30, 1956, *FRUS:1955–1957*:XVI, d154; Memorandum of a Conversation, Secretary Dulles' Suite, Waldorf Astoria, New York, October 5, 1956, 10:15 am, *FRUS:1955–1957*:XVI, d300.

29. Memorandum of Conference with the President, White House, Washington, October 27, 1956, 11 a.m., *FRUS:1955–1957*:XVI, d387.

30. Memorandum of Conversation, Department of State, Washington, October 30, 1956, 3:28 p.m., *FRUS:1955–1957*:XVI, d431.

31. UKDel182 to FO, October 31, 1956, FO 371/121783.

32. Memorandum of Discussion at the 302d Meeting of the National Security Council, Washington, November 1, 1956, 9 a.m., *FRUS:1955–1957*:XVI, d455.

33. Memorandum of Discussion at the 302d Meeting of the National Security Council, Washington, November 1, 1956.

34. Diane B. Kunz, "The Importance of Having Money: The Economic Diplomacy of the Suez Crisis," in *Suez 1956: The Crisis and Its Consequences,* ed. William Roger Louis and Edward Roger John Owen (Oxford: Clarendon, 1991), 215; and *The Economic Diplomacy of the Suez Crisis* (Chapel Hill: University of North Carolina Press, 1991); Richard E. Neustadt, *Alliance Politics* (New York: Columbia University Press, 1970), 26–29.

35. Memorandum of Conversation, November 12, 1956, DDRS/CK3100237673; "M. Couve de Murville, Ambassadeur de France à Bonn, à M. Pineau, Ministère des Affaires Étrangères," no. 3607–3610, *DDF*:1956:3, d275.

36. "M. Couve de Murville, Ambassadeur de France à Bonn, à M. Pineau, Ministère des Affaires Étrangères," no. 3607–3610.

37. Western European Chiefs of Mission Conference, Paris, May 6–8, 1957: Summary Conclusions and Recommendations. May 8, 1957, *FRUS:1955–1957*:IV, d251. On Hungary see Untitled Draft Statement by the Secretary of State, December 3, 1956, 4/Meetings with the President Aug. thru Dec. 1956 (2), in *The Papers of John Foster Dulles and of Christian A. Herter, 1953–1961: The White House Correspondence and Memoranda Series* (Frederick, MD: University Publications of America, 1986).

38. Telegram from the Mission at the United Nations to the Department of State, December 6, 1956, *FRUS:1955–1957*:XVI, d638.

39. Paul-Henri Charles Spaak, *The Continuing Battle: Memoirs of a European, 1936–1966,* trans. Henry Fox (London: Weidenfeld & Nicolson, 1971), 259.

40. Telegram from the Delegation at the North Atlantic Ministerial Meeting to the Department of State, December 11, 1956, *FRUS:1955–1957*:XVI, d647.

41. Message from the Secretary of State to the President, December 11, 1956, *FRUS:1955–1957*:IV, d45.

42. Memorandum for various State Department officials from John W. Hanes Jr., December 5, 1956, Dulles/WHM/4/Meeting with the President January 1956 through July 1956 (1)/DDEL.

43. Paris 6080 (DULTE 7) to Secretary of State, December 10, 1956, DDRS/CK3100231439. Eisenhower's relief in Col. Goodpaster to Minnich [Eisenhower to Dulles], December 12, 1956, WHO/OSS/Subject/State/1/State Department/DDEL.

44. Paris POLTO 1393 to Secretary of State, December 12, 1956, RG84/OAEO/Subject Files, 1955–59/41/NATO/NARA. (POLTO is a telegram series indicator.)

45. Luxembourg126 to Secretary of State, December 18, 1956, RG84/OAEO/41/Subject Files, 1955–59/NARA.

46. On disagreement between NATO allies at the UN see Keith Kyle, *Suez* (London: Weidenfeld & Nicolson, 1991), 13. See also Lawrence S. Kaplan, *NATO and the UN: A Peculiar Relationship* (Columbia: University of Missouri Press, 2010), 1, 27.

47. Message from the Secretary of State to the President, December 11, 1956, *FRUS:1955–1957*:IV, d45.

48. "Summary Record of a Meeting of the Council held at the Palais de Chaillot, Paris, XVIe, on Tuesday, 11th December, 1956 at 3.30 p.m.," December 11, 1956, C-R(56)70, NATO.

49. Butler's threat was in case the Suez Canal was not quickly cleared of scuttled ships. Telegram from the Embassy in the United Kingdom to the Department of State, November 26, 1956, *FRUS:1955–1957*:XVI, d614; Secretary's Notebook for November 29, 1956, C.M.92(56)/205. Eisenhower was not worried Britain would leave NATO over Suez but thought there was a greater possibility Britain might leave the UN. Memorandum of a Telephone Conversation between the President in Augusta, Georgia, and the Secretary of State in Key West, Florida, November 27, 1956, 9:25 a.m., *FRUS:1955–1957*:XVI, d618.

50. Salisbury's concern was that Britain would alienate NATO, or the US over NATO, by withdrawing troops from Germany for financial reasons. Secretary's Notebook for December 7, 1956, C.M.97(56).

51. Verbatim Record of the Seventy First Meeting of the Council held on Wednesday, 12th December, 1956, at 10.30 a.m. at the Palais de Chaillot, Paris, XVIe, December 12, 1956, C-R(56)71, NATO.

52. Verbatim Record of the Sixty Ninth Meeting of the Council held on Tuesday, 11th December, 1956, at 10.30 a.m. at the Palais de Chaillot, Paris XVIe," December 11, 1956, C-VR(56)69(Final), NATO.

53. Memorandum of Conference with the President, Washington, December 15, 1956, 2:30 p.m., *FRUS:1955–1957*:IV, d54.

54. For the Italians see Verbatim Record of the Sixty Ninth Meeting of the Council held on Tuesday, 11th December, 1956, at 10.30 a.m. at the Palais de Chaillot, Paris XVIe, December 11, 1956. For the Belgians see Telegram from the United States Delegation at the NAC Ministerial Meeting to Department of State, December 12, 1956; Message from the Secretary of State to the President, December 11, 1956, *FRUS:1955–1957*:IV, d43. For the British see Telegram from the United States Delegation at the North Atlantic Ministerial Meeting to Department of State, December 11, 1956, *FRUS:1955–1957*:IV, d41.

55. Thomas Risse-Kappen, *Cooperation among Democracies: The European Influence on U.S. Foreign Policy* (Princeton, NJ: Princeton University Press, 1995), 104; Maurice Vaisse, "Post-Suez France," in *Suez 1956: The Crisis and Its Consequences*, ed. William Roger Louis and Edward Roger John Owen (Oxford: Oxford University Press, 1989).

56. Richard E. Neustadt, *Alliance Politics* (New York: Columbia University Press, 1970), 28; Victor H. Feske, "The Road to Suez: The British Foreign Office and the Quai d'Orsay, 1951–1957," in *The Diplomats, 1939–1979*, ed. Gordon Alexander Craig and Francis L. Loewenheim (Princeton, NJ: Princeton University Press, 1994), 193; George Armstrong Kelly, *Lost Soldiers: The French Army and Empire in Crisis, 1947–1962* (Cambridge, MA: MIT Press, 1965), 192–93.

57. Telegram from the Delegation at the North Atlantic Ministerial Meeting to the Department of State, December 11, 1956, *FRUS:1955–1957*:XVI, d647.

58. Telegram from the United States Delegation at the North Atlantic Ministerial Meeting to Department of State, December 11, 1956, *FRUS:1955–1957*:IV, d41.

59. Northern European Chiefs of Mission Conference, London, September 19–21, 1957: Summary of Proceedings, *FRUS:1955–1957*:IV, d252.

60. Thomas M. Campbell Jr., "NATO and the United Nations in American Foreign Policy: Building a Framework for Power," in *NATO after Thirty Years*, ed. Robert Clawson (Wilmington, DE: Scholarly Resources, 1981), 133.

61. Quoted in Dwight D. Eisenhower, *Waging Peace, 1956–1961: The White House Years* (Garden City, NY: Doubleday, 1965), 99.

62. Memorandum of Conference with the President November 20, 1956, 5:30 p.m., dated November 21, 1956, 4/Meetings with the President Aug. thru Dec. 1956 (2)/*Papers of John Foster Dulles and of Christian A. Herter, 1953–1961: White House Correspondence and Memoranda Series*.

63. John Dickie, *"Special" No More: Anglo-American Relations, Rhetoric and Reality* (London: Weidenfeld & Nicolson, 1994), 98.

64. Alistair Horne, *Harold Macmillan*, vol. 2, *1957–1986* (New York: Viking, 1989), 25.

65. Cf. Harold Macmillan, *Riding the Storm, 1956–1959* (London: Macmillan, 1971), 240. "Junior partner" in Memorandum of a Conversation, Mid-Ocean Club, Bermuda, March 21, 1957, 10:30 a.m., *FRUS:1955–1957*:XXVII, d268.

66. Matthew Jones, *The Official History of the UK Strategic Nuclear Deterrent*, vol. 1 (London: Routledge, 2017), 98–99.

67. Diary Entry by the President, March 21, 1957, *FRUS:1955–1957*:XXVII, d271; Eisenhower, *Waging Peace*, 124; Washington92 to FO, March 25, 1956, PREM 11/1836.

68. Eisenhower, *Waging Peace*, 125.

69. Northern European Chiefs of Mission Conference, London, September 19–21, 1957: Summary of Proceedings, *FRUS:1955–1957*:IV, d252.

70. Robert A. Divine, *The Sputnik Challenge* (New York: Oxford University Press, 1993), 17, 34; W. W. Rostow, *The Diffusion of Power: An Essay in Recent History* (New York: Macmillan, 1972), 74–85.

71. Letter from Prime Minister Macmillan to President Eisenhower, October 10, 1957, *FRUS:1955–1957*:XXVII, d304.

72. Harold Caccia to Philip de Zulueta, September 18, 1957, PREM 11/2329.

73. Letter from President Eisenhower to Prime Minister Macmillan, October 11, 1957, *FRUS:1955–1957*:XXVII, d305.

74. Memorandum of Conversation with the President, October 15, 1957, Dulles/WHM/5/Meetings with the President—1957 (2)/DDEL.

75. Letter from Macmillan to Eisenhower, transmitted on October 16, 1957, *FRUS:1955–1957*:XXVII, d306.

76. Letter from Macmillan to Eisenhower, transmitted on October 16, 1957.

77. Washington 2088 to FO, October 15, 1957, PREM 11/2329.

78. Secretary's Notebook for October 21, 1957, C.C.74 (57).

79. "Washington Talks—Outline of British Approach," October 20, 1957, PREM 11/2329.

80. Memorandum of Conference with the President, October 22, 1957, dated October 31, 1957, WHO/OSS/Subject/State/2/State Department/DDEL; "An Appraisal of NATO," undated brief for Macmillan Talks, October 23–25, 1957, DDRS/CK3100229038.

81. Record of a Meeting, Secretary of State Dulles' Office, Department of State, Washington, October 17, 1957, 5 p.m., *FRUS:1955–1957*:XXVII, d307.

82. Memorandum of a Conversation, Department of State, Washington, October 18, 1957, *FRUS:1955–1957*:XXVII, d308.

83. Memorandum of Conference with the President, October 22, 1957, dated October 31, 1957, WHO/OSS/Subject/State/2/State Department/DDEL. See also Record of a Meeting, Secretary of State Dulles' Office, Department of State, Washington, October 17,

1957; Memorandum of a Conversation, Department of State, Washington, October 18, 1957.

84. Memorandum from the Ambassador to Canada (Merchant) to the Secretary of State, October 19, 1957, *FRUS:1955–1957*:XXVII, d309.

85. As Dulles later put it to Lloyd: "Just as our bilateral Declaration of Common Purpose was designed to express ideas which could be projected into NATO, so NATO in turn should express ideas which could equally apply to and be received by all the free world." Dulles to Selwyn Lloyd, December 4, 1957, Dulles/Chron/15/December 1957 (3)/DDEL.

86. Memorandum from the Secretary of State to the President [with enclosures], October 21, 1957, *FRUS:1955–1957*:XXVII, d310.

87. Desmond Donnelly to Acheson, September 28, 1960, AP/Gen. Corr./8/105.

88. Memorandum of a Conversation, British Embassy, October 23, 1957, 3 p.m., *FRUS:1955–1957*:XXVII, d316.

89. Secretary's Notebook for December 31, 1957, C.C.86(57).

90. Harold Macmillan, *The Macmillan Diaries: Prime Minister and After, 1957–1966*, ed. Peter Catterall (London: Macmillan, 2011), 67.

91. Macmillan, *The Macmillan Diaries,* 67.

92. The Present Political Situation, October 23, 1957, DDRS/CK3100243120; Closer US-UK Relations and Free World Cooperation, October 23, 1957, DDRS/CK3100322048; Free World Cooperation; Meeting Presided over by the President and Prime Minister Macmillan, October 24, 1957, 10:30 a.m., DDRS/CK3100075459; "An Appraisal of NATO."

93. Free World Cooperation; Meeting Presided over by the President and Prime Minister Macmillan, October 24, 1957.

94. Free World Cooperation; Meeting Presided over by the President and Prime Minister Macmillan, October 24, 1957. After the Washington talks, officials from London and Washington formed secret working groups to coordinate policy and operations. Matthew Jones, "Anglo-American Relations after Suez, the Rise and Decline of the Working Group Experiment and the French Challenge to NATO, 1957–1959," *Diplomacy & Statecraft* 14, no. 1 (March 2003): 49–79.

95. Memorandum of a Conversation, White House, Washington, October 24, 1957, 10:30 a.m., *FRUS:1955–1957*:XXVII, d320.

96. Timmons to Wolf, October 30, 1957, RG59/EUR/Records of the Director, 1955–60/Correspondence Files, 1955–1959/1/RA Correspondence, 1957/NARA.

97. Burgess to Elbrick, October 17, 1957, RG59/EUR/Records of the Director, 1955–60/Correspondence Files, 1955–1959/1/RA Correspondence, 1957/NARA.

98. Macmillan, *Riding the Storm,* 313.

99. "Memorandum of a Conversation, Department of State, Washington, October 25, 1957, *FRUS:1955–1957*:IV, d59. Eisenhower had been warned before the meeting that the Macmillan talks "may be interpreted in some NATO quarters as indicating that the Anglo-American Alliance will henceforth be the forum in which the basic Western decisions will be taken." Memorandum for the President, October 23, 1957, DDRS/CK3100238980.

100. Memorandum of a Conversation, White House, Washington, October 25, 1957, 2:05–2:32 p.m., *FRUS:1955–1957*:XXVII, d332; Memorandum of a Conversation, Washington, October 23, 1957, *FRUS:1955–1957*:XXVII, d317.

101. Quoted in Eisenhower, *Waging Peace,* 214.

102. Memorandum of a Conversation, White House, Washington, October 23, 1957.

103. Dulles to Selwyn Lloyd, November 2, 1957, 15/November 2, 1957/*The Papers of John Foster Dulles and Christian A. Herter, 1953–1961, Chronological Correspondence Series* (Frederick, MD: University Publications of America, 1986).

104. Dulles to Nitze, November 3, 1957, 15/1957 (3)/DHCC.

105. On the close relationship between the Macmillan talks and NATO meeting see Fisher Howe to the Under Secretary, "NATO Heads of Government Meeting," November 4, 1957, WHO/SANSA/SAS/Subject/6/NATO Meeting—December 1957 (1)/DDEL.

106. Dulles to Stevenson, November 5, 1957, 15/November 1957 (3)/*DHCC.*

107. Preliminary Memorandum RE: U.S. Position at North Atlantic Treaty Council December 1957, Adlai E. Stevenson, November 4, 1957, DDRS/CK3100210807.

108. "NATO Heads of Government Meeting," Stevenson to the Secretary, November 29, 1957, and "Economic Defense Coordination," Stevenson to the Secretary, December 5, 1957, both in PPC/Subject Files, 1954–1962/151/Europe, 1957/NARA.

109. For the international confusion caused by Stevenson's appointment and then failure to attend the meeting see "Relations with the Soviet Union," Cabinet Memorandum, January 21, 1958, C.(58)9.

110. Untitled memorandum, November 7, 1957, WHO/SANSA/SAS/Subject/6/ NATO Meeting—December 1957 (1)/DDEL.

111. "December NATO Meeting of Heads of Government: Scope and U.S. Objectives," November 7, 1957, WHO/SANSA/SAS/Subject/6/NATO Meeting—December 1957 (1)/DDEL.

112. Harmonization of NATO Policies through Political Consultation (Background Paper), NATO Heads of Government Meeting, Paris, December 16–18, 1957, December 4, 1957, DDRS/CK3100241796.

113. Telegram from the Ambassador in Germany (Bruce) to the Department of State, November 19, 1957, *FRUS:1955–1957*:IV, d61.

114. Hans-Peter Schwarz, *Konrad Adenauer: A German Politician and Statesman in a Period of War, Revolution and Reconstruction*, vol. 2, *The Statesman: 1952–1957*, trans. Geoffrey Penny (Providence: Berghahn Books, 1997), 311–24.

115. Letter from Chancellor Adenauer to the Secretary of State, November 19, 1957, *FRUS:1955–1957*:IV, d62.

116. Telegram from the ambassador in Germany (Bruce) to the Department of State, November 19, 1957.

117. Memorandum of a Conversation, British Embassy, Paris, December 14, 1957, 11:30 a.m., *FRUS:1955–1957*:IV, d72.

118. Paris1993 to Secretary of State, October 21, 1957, DDRS/CK3100116246; Norstad to Eisenhower, November 7, 1957, DDRS/CK3100662590. On the stockpile and its place in the broader policy of nuclear sharing in the Eisenhower era see Trachtenberg, *Constructed Peace*, esp. 193–207.

119. Memorandum of Conference with the President, October 22, 1957, dated October 31, 1957. WHO/OSS/Subject/State/2/State Department/DDEL. See also "Memorandum of Discussion, Wednesday, November 6, 1957, at the State Department," undated, DDRS/CK3100307791.

120. Memorandum of Discussion at the 348th Meeting of the National Security Council, Washington, December 12, 1957, *FRUS:1955–1957*:IV, d69; "Comments by Robert Cutler on Draft #3—December 9, 1957," WHO/SANSA/SAS/Subject/6/NATO Meeting—December 1957 (2)/DDEL.

121. Memorandum of Conference with the President, December 11, 1957–10:00 a.m., December 12, 1957, WHO/OSS/ITM/3/NATO Meeting, December 1957/DDEL; Memorandum to the President from Cutler, "NATO Meeting," November 26, 1957, WHO/ SANSA/SAS/Subject/6/NATO Meeting—December 1957 (2)/DDEL.

122. General Norstad, SHAPE, from General Goodpaster, November 26, 1957, WHO/ OSS/ITM/3/NATO Meeting, December 1957/DDEL; Eisenhower, *Waging Peace*, 230; Memorandum of Conference with the President, December 11, 1957—10:00 a.m.

123. White House communication from Goodpaster to Adams, December 17, 1957, DDRS/CK3100268729; John S. D. Eisenhower, *Strictly Personal* (Garden City, NY: Doubleday, 1974), 197.

124. Macmillan diary entry for December 16, 1957, Macmillan, *The Macmillan Diaries*, 77.

125. For a less generous observation by Macmillan see Record of Prime Minister's Meeting with President Eisenhower, December 16, 1957, PREM 11/1845.

126. Department of State 4558 to London (Eisenhower to Macmillan), December 26, 1957, DDRS/CK3100216007.

127. Trachtenberg, *Constructed Peace*, 194.

128. Secretary's Notebook for December 20, 1957, CC(57)84, CAB 195/17/4; "Staff Notes No. 290," January 29, 1958, DDRS/CK3100256067.

129. Macmillan, Spaak, and the Turks pushed this idea; most countries were noncommittal, and the Scandinavians and Canadians were especially opposed. Note by the Canadian Delegation, Committee of Political Advisers, April 24, 1958, AC/119-WP(58)341, NATO. See also "Relations Between NATO and the Baghdad Pact," February 15, 1957, CM(57)20, NATO.

130. C. D. Jackson to J. W. Jessup, December 26, 1957, Jackson/69/Log-1957 (4)/DDEL.

131. Entry for December 14, 1957, Macmillan, *The Macmillan Diaries*, 76; Secretary's Notebook for December 31, 1957, C.C.86(57).

132. Secretary's Notebook for December 31, 1957, C.C.86(57).

133. "Comments on the Record of the Washington Conference," Jebb to Lloyd, January 15, 1958, PREM 11/2329.

134. Irwin M. Wall, *France, the United States, and the Algerian War* (Berkeley: University of California Press, 2001), xi.

135. Memorandum of Conversation, May 21, 1958, *FRUS:1958–1960*:VII:2, d8; Telegram from the Embassy in France to the Department of State, June 10, 1958, *FRUS:1958–1960*:VII:2, d19; Telegrams from the Embassy in France to the Department of State, May 21 and June 10, 14, 19, 30, 1958, *FRUS:1958–1960*:VII:2, docs. 9, 19, 21, 22, 29.

136. This part redacted from *FRUS:1958–1960*:VII:2, d344, but available in "Anglo-American Relations with General de Gaulle's Government," Memorandum of Conversation, June 9, 1958, DDRS/CK3100050804.

137. Memorandum from the Assistant Secretary of State for European Affairs (Elbrick) to Acting Secretary of State Herter, May 27, 1958, *FRUS:1958–1960*:VII:2, d12.

138. This is what de Gaulle told Jebb. Paris331 to Foreign Office, June 25, 1958, PREM 11/2326.

139. "Brief No. III (b) 'N.A.T.O: Military Strategy,'" for Prime Minister's Visit to Paris, June 29–30, PREM 11/2326; Record of Conversation with M. Spaak at her Majesty's Embassy, Paris, on June 30, 1958, PREM 11/2326.

140. Paris331 to Foreign Office, June 25, 1958.

141. Record of Conversation with M. Spaak at her Majesty's Embassy, Paris, on June 30, 1958, PREM 11/2326.

142. Paraphrased in Minute by A. D. F. Pemberton-Pigott, July 6, 1956, FO 371/137819. Difficulties posed by changing the treaty in UKDel141 Saving to FO, July 3, 1958, FO 371/137819.

143. Record of Conversation with M. Spaak at her Majesty's Embassy, Paris, on June 30, 1958, PREM 11/2326.

144. Record of Conversation with M. Spaak at her Majesty's Embassy, Paris, on June 30, 1958.

145. Memorandum of Conversation, Dulles and de Gaulle July 5, 1958, at the Hotel Matignon, RG59/Bohlen/12/361.1 De Gaulle 1958/NARA.

146. Memorandum of Conversation, Dulles and de Gaulle July 5, 1958, at the Hotel Matignon.

147. Memorandum of Conversation, July 5, 1958, *FRUS:1958–1960*:VII:2, d355; Memorandum of Conversation, July 9, 1958, *FRUS:1958–1960*:VII:2, d39.

148. Memorandum of Conversation, July 9, 1958.

149. Memorandum of Conversation, July 10, 1958, DDRS/CK3100297901.

150. Hervé Alphand, *L'Étonnement d'être*, journal 1939–1973 (Paris: Fayard, 1977), 290.

151. Wall, *France, the United States, and the Algerian War.*

3. TIED TOGETHER BY HISTORY

1. Letter from President de Gaulle to President Eisenhower, September 17, 1958, *FRUS:1958–1960*:VII:2, d45. Text of the letters and accompanying memorandum to Eisenhower and Macmillan are in *DDF*:1958:2, docs. 170 and 165 respectively.

2. Roberts to Hoyer Millar, December 8, 1958, FO 371/137826. For de Gaulle's ignorance on NATO see "De Gaulle Letter," Memorandum of Conversation, October 20, 1958, DNSA/BC00222; Telegram from the Embassy in France to the Department of State, June 1, 1958, *FRUS:1958–1960*:VII:2, d16; UKDel254 to FO, October 7, 1960, FO 371/154576. On efforts by French officials to explain NATO to de Gaulle see "Memorandum of Conversation, Paris, October 31, 1958," RG59/WE/France/4/Memos of Conversation 1958 (folder 2)/NARA; UKDel359 to FO, November 4, 1958, FO 371/137824. Regarding problems of interpretation related to de Gaulle's discussion of NATO see Frédéric Bozo, *Deux stratégies pour l'Europe: De Gaulle, les États-Unis et l'Alliance atlantique: 1958–1969*, Espoir (Paris: Plon, Fondation Charles de Gaulle, 1996), 38.

3. UKDel287 to FO, October 7, 1958. See also UKDel275 to FO, October 3, 1958, FO 371/137820; UKDel359 to FO, November 4, 1958, FO 371/137824.

4. London to Department of State, March 11, 1959, DDRS/CK3100093498. State Department intelligence officials thought de Gaulle's worldview "essentially an 18th-century one." "Problems and Prospects of the fight Republic," INR Intelligence Report no. 8374, December 6, 1960, *FRUS:1958–1960*:VII:2, d424.

5. John Leddy Oral History, LBJL.

6. "De Gaulle Assails U.S. Policy on Ruhr: Also Condemns Western Union Defense Plan, Paris Regime—Cool on Marshall Aid," Harold Callender, *New York Times*, November 18, 1948, 1.

7. Memorandum of Conversation, December 21, 1959, *FRUS:1958–1960*:VII:1, d559. For French officers' take on de Gaulle's refusal to understand NATO see Frank Roberts to Rumbold, November 11, 1959, FO 371/146310, and Roberts to Rumbold, January 23, 1959, FO 371/146305.

8. Serge Berstein, *The Republic of de Gaulle, 1958–1969*, trans. by Peter Morris (New York: Cambridge University Press, 1993), 92. See also Memorandum of Conversation, April 26, 1962, NSF/226/NATO, Weapons, Cables, France/JFKL.

9. UKDel359 to FO, November 4, 1958, FO 371/137824.

10. "CPX 7: Final Address by D/SACEUR," April 19, 1957, AWF/Name/21/Montgomery, F/M 1957 thru 1959 (2)/DDEL.

11. M. Chauvel, Ambassadeur de France à Londres, à M. Couve de Murville, Ministère des Affaires Étrangères, October 25, 1958, *DDF*:1958:2, d283.

12. Roberts to Rumbold, October 2, 1958, FO 371/137820. British officials told their European colleagues that Montgomery was the "stupidest man in the United Kingdom on political subjects." Bonn798 to the Secretary of State, October 31, 1958, DNSA/BC00226. See also UKDel214 to FO, June 19, 1959, PREM 11/3002.

13. For similar thinking by Macmillan and Eisenhower see "The Present Political Situation," October 23, 1957, DDRS/CK3100243120; Memorandum of Conversation at the White House, June 11, 1958 2:30 p.m., Dulles/Chron/16/ June 1958 (3)/DDEL. See also

M. Alphand, Ambassadeur de France à Washington, à M. Louis Joxe, Secrétaire Général du Département," October 2, 1958, *DDF*:1958:2, d221.

14. Translation of untitled and undated memorandum by Spaak, October 15, 1958, NP/90/NATO General (6)/DDEL.

15. FO7124 to Washington, October 9, 1958, PREM 11/2328.

16. Memorandum of Conversation, October 6, 1958, *FRUS:1958–1960*:VII:2, d50.

17. Memorandum of Conversation, "de Gaulle's Proposals on NATO," November 3, 1958; Diary entry for October 8, 1958, *MD:PM*, 163. Norstad also received a copy of the memorandum from one of de Gaulle's lieutenants: UKDel345 Saving to FO, October 15, 1958, FO 371/137821.

18. "Note du Département," September 25, 1958, *DDF*:1958:2, d200.

19. For "nearly hysterical" see "De Gaulle Letter," Memorandum of Conversation, October 20, 1958, DNSA/BC00222; Memorandum of Conversation, October 6, 1958; *FRUS:1958–1960*:VII:2, d50; Telegram from the Embassy in Italy to the Department of State, October 18, 1958, 11 p.m., *FRUS:1958–1960*:VII:2, d61.

20. Bozo, *Deux stratégies pour l'Europe*, 37; FO7124 to Washington, October 9, 1958, PREM 11/2328; UKDel269 to FO, October 1, 1958; Paris451 to FO, October 2, 1958, FO 371/137820; Seydoux to Couve de Murville, October 28, 1958, *DDF*:1958:2, d293. Blankenhorn, the German ambassador, found the note "even worse than he had supposed": UKDel277 to FO, October 3, 1958, FO 371/137820.

21. Bruce in Telegram from the Embassy in Germany to the Department of State, October 9, 1958, *FRUS:1958–1960*:VII:2, d159; Bonn815 to the Secretary of State, October 15, 1958, DNSA/BC00218. On German insistence that there were only two superpowers see Seydoux to Couve, October 26, 1958, *DDF*:1958:2, d286.

22. Letter from President Eisenhower to President de Gaulle, October 20, 1958, *FRUS:1958–1960*:VII:2, d63. On de Gaulle's frustration see Paris485 to FO, October 21, 1958, PREM 11/3002; Note Pour le Cabinet du Ministère, October 22, 1958, *DDF*:1958:2, d276. Alphand quoted in Washington2833 to FO, October 20, 1958, FO 371/137822.

23. M. Chauvel, Ambassadeur de France à Londres, à M. Couve de Murville, Ministère des Affaires Étrangères, October 25, 1958, *DDF*:1958:2, d283.

24. Memorandum on "The de Gaulle Proposals," attached to letter from Elbrick to the Secretary, "Your Meeting Today with General Gruenther and Mr. McCloy," October 16, 1958, RG59/WE/France/2/De Gaulle Government, 1958/NARA. Caccia passed on Lloyd's caution to Dulles: see Memorandum of Conversation, October 17, 1958. *FRUS:1958–1960*:VII:2, d59. For British concerns about trade see Telegram from the Department of State to the Embassy in the United Kingdom, October 8, 1958, *FRUS:1958–1960*:VII:2, d51; FO 2308 to Paris, October 20, 1958, FO 371/137822.

25. Scribbled on Paris483 to FO, October 21, 1958, PREM 11/3002.

26. FO7124 to Washington, October 9, 1958. PREM 11/2328.

27. "De Gaulle Letter," Memorandum of Conversation, October 20, 1958, DNSA/BC00222; Memorandum of Conversation, October 27, 1958, *FRUS:1958–1960*:VII:2, d65; Washington2900 to FO, October 27, 1958; and FO7587 to Washington, October 28, 1958, both in FO 371/137823.

28. Bruce recommended tripartite talks as a "means [of] opening de Gaulle's eyes [to the] major problems and dangers inherent in his proposal": Telegram from the Embassy in Germany to the Department of State, October 9, 1958, *FRUS:1958–1960*:VII:2, d159.

29. Telegram from the Department of State to the Embassy in France, October 31, 1958, 8:52 p.m., *FRUS:1958–1960*:VII:2, d67; Letter from the British Ambassador (Caccia) to Secretary of State Dulles, November 7, 1958, *FRUS:1958–1960*:VII:2, d68.

30. Telegram from the Embassy in France to the Department of State, November 29, 1958, *FRUS:1958–1960*:VII:2, d75.

31. Alphand to Couve, December 4, 1958, *DDF*:1958:2, d390.

32. Memorandum of Conversation, December 4, 1958, *FRUS:1958–1960*:VII:2, d136.

33. Alphand to Couve, December 4, 1958.

34. Alphand, *L'Étonnement d'être*, 292.

35. Memorandum of Conversation, December 10, 1958. *FRUS:1958–1960*:VII:2, d78.

36. Memorandum of Discussion at the 390th Meeting of the National Security Council, December 11, 1958, *FRUS:1958–1960*:VII:1, d163.

37. Telegram from Secretary of State Dulles to the Department of State, December 15, 1958, *FRUS:1958–1960*:VII:2, d82.

38. London3311 to SecState, December 22, 1958, NP/99/DeGAULLE, Charles (2)/ DDEL.

39. Note du Département, December 17, 1958, *DDF*:1958:2, d427; London to Secretary of State, 3311, Section 2 of 2, December 22, 1958, NP/99/DeGAULLE, Charles (2)/ DDEL.

40. "Secretary agreed to ——," December 16, 1958, RG59/Bohlen/12/361.1 De Gaulle 1958/NARA; "U.S.-UK-French Talks on the Far East," January 15, 1959, RG59/BAA/ OIAA/RPM, 1951–1963/4/Tripartite I/NARA.

41. General de Gaulle's Plan: Record of Tripartite Meeting Held in State Department on February 3, 1959, FO 371/146306. See Couve to Alphand, January 18, 1959, *DDF*:1959:1, d33.

42. Memorandum of Conversation, January 9, 1959, *FRUS:1958–1960*:VII:2, d87. See also Alphand, *L'Étonnement d'être*, 300; Washington78 to FO, January 10, 1959, FO 371/146303; "De Gaulle's Views on Tripartite Consultations," Memorandum of Conversation, January 22, 1959, RG59/WE/France/3/Memos of Conversation 1959 (folder 2)/ NARA; "Secretary's Conversation with General Norstad," Memorandum, February 12, 1959, DNSA/BC00762.

43. Memorandum of Conference with the President, February 9, 1959–10:30 a.m., February 10, 1959, WHO/OSS/Subject/DOD/4/Joint Chiefs of Staff (6)/DDEL.

44. Memorandum for the Record by the President's Assistant Staff Secretary (Eisenhower), March 3, 1959, *FRUS:1958–1960*:VII:1, d192.

45. Synopsis of State and Intelligence material reported to the President, February 28, 1959, DDRS/CK3100105145; Paris POLTO 2446 to Secretary of State, February 28, 1959, DDRS/CK3100226231.

46. Memorandum of Conversation, March 3, 1959, *FRUS:1958–1960*:VII:1, d194; this was Frank Roberts's paraphrase of information given to him by the French. UKDel145 to FO, March 2, 1959, FO 371/146394; Memorandum of Conversation, January 27, 1959, *FRUS:1958–1960*:VII:2, d90.

47. Norstad quoted by Roberts, UKDel145 to FO, March 2, 1959, FO 371/146394.

48. Memorandum of Conversation, March 3, 1959, *FRUS:1958–1960*:VII:1, d194.

49. The Berlin crisis is the subject of chapter 4.

50. UKDel122 to FO, March 4, 1959, FO 371/146394.

51. The text of the French text presented to the council, in English translation, is in UKDel129 to FO, March 6, 1959, FO 371/146394.

52. UKDel114 to FO, February 28, 1959; UKDel148 Saving to FO, March 3, 1959; UKDel122 to FO, March 4, 1959, all in FO 371/146394.

53. Memorandum of Conversation, March 3, 1959, *FRUS:1958–1960*:VII:1, d194; Memorandum from Herter to Eisenhower, March 4, 1959, *FRUS:1958–1960*:VII:1, d195.

54. Memorandum of Conversation, March 4, 1959, *FRUS:1958–1960*:VII:2, d97.

55. Memorandum of Conversation, March 11, 1959, *FRUS:1958–1960*:VII:1, d201; Alphand to Couve, March 11, 1959, *DDF*:1959:1, d148.

56. Telegram from the Department of State to the Embassy in France, March 22, 1959, *FRUS:1958–1960*:VII:1, d206.

57. "General Problems, including Far East, Near East and World Wide Strategy," March 22, 1959, DDRS/CK3100493552.

58. "General Problems, including Far East, Near East and World Wide Strategy," March 22, 1959; Memorandum of Conference with the President, March 22, 1959, 9 a.m. (DDRS—1958–1960).

59. Telegram from the Department of State to the Embassy in France, March 22, 1959.

60. Memorandum of Conversation, January 9, 1959, *FRUS:1958–1960*:VII:2, d87.

61. "Tripartite Talks on Africa," Draft Memorandum for the President, under cover of memo from Murphy to the Secretary, April 22, 1959, RG59/BAA/OIAA/RPM/4/Tripartite 1/NARA.

62. "Fourth Tripartite Talks on Africa," April 21, 1959, RG59/PPC/Subject Files, 1954–1962/148/Africa, 1959–60/NARA.

63. "Fifth Tripartite Talk on Africa," April 21, 1959, RG59/PPC/Subject Files, 1954–1962/148/Africa, 1959–60/NARA.

64. "Fifth Tripartite Talk on Africa," April 21, 1959.

65. Memorandum from the Assistant Secretary of State for European Affairs (Merchant) to Secretary of State Herter, May 5, 1959, *FRUS:1958–1960*:VII:2, d111.

66. Memorandum of Conversation, May 1, 1959, 3:30 p.m., *FRUS:1958–1960*:VII:2, d109.

67. UKDel345 Saving to FO, October 14, 1958, FO 371/137821.

68. Letter from President de Gaulle to President Eisenhower, May 25, 1959, *FRUS:1958–1960*:VII:2, d117. The atomic issue, according to Couve, was "linked" with the other issues of tripartite talks: global strategy, military planning, and decisions on the use of atomic weapons. Memorandum of Conversation, May 24, 1959, *FRUS:1958–1960*:VII:2, d116.

69. Record of Conversation between the Secretary of State and General Norstad at Chequers on June 29, 1959, FO 371/146404; UKDel209 Saving to FO, July 2, 1959, FO 371/146403.

70. Mollet in Roberts to Hoyer Millar, June 24, 1959, FO 371/146309. See also Minute by Jebb to the Secretary of State, July 22, 1959, FO 371/146310; BJSM Washington MD 380 to Ministry of Defence, London, June 13, 1959, FO 371/146308.

71. Memorandum from the Assistant Secretary of State for European Affairs (Merchant) to the Secretary of State, July 10, 1959, *FRUS:1958–1960*: XIII, d294.

72. Alphand, *L'Étonnement d'être*, 303–4.

73. Roberts to the Secretary of State, July 17, 1959, FO 371/146405.

74. Diary entry for August 15, 1959, Shuckburgh Diary, MS191/1/2/7, CRL.

75. Diary entry for August 15, 1959, Shuckburgh Diary.

76. "Memorandum" [translation of Spaak's July 1959 memorandum], NP/107/Gen. Norstad-Miscellaneous (2)/DDEL.

77. Roberts to the Secretary of State (Lloyd), July 21, 1959, FO 371/146405.

78. Washington TOPOL 141 to USRO Paris, July 18, 1959, NP/47/France 1955–1959/DDEL; Roberts to Secretary of State, July 22, 1959, FO 371/146405.

79. Roberts to the Secretary of State, July 21, 1959, FO 371/146405; Washington TOPOL 141 to USRO Paris, July 18, 1959.

80. "Some Possible Topics for Western Heads of Government Discussions," August 20, 1959, RG59/PPC, Subject Files, 1954–1962/151/Europe 1959/NARA.

81. Memorandum of Conference with the President, August 21, 1959, WHO/OSS/Subject/State/3/State Department/DDEL.

82. Memorandum of Conversation, September 2, 1959, noon, *FRUS:1958–1960*:VII:2, d130. See also Memorandum of Conversation, September 2, 1959, 4 p.m., *FRUS:1958–1960*:VII:2, d131; Vernon A. Walters, *Silent Missions* (Garden City, NY: Doubleday, 1978), 489.

83. On Laos see Memorandum of Conversation, September 15, 1959, RG59/WE/France/3/Memos of Conversation 1959 (folder 2)/NARA. On arms see Hood to Rumbold, September 11, 1959, FO 371/146310. On both see Memorandum for the President, "Status of the Matters Discussed with You during Your Recent Trip to Europe," WHO/OSS/Subject/State/3/State Department/DDEL. State Department officials told the British that Eisenhower had agreed to establish "tripartite *ad hoc* 'staff groups'" that would include both military and political groups, since "that was what the French wanted." Hood to Rumbold, September 11, 1959, FO 371/146310; "N.A.T.O. Matters," by A. D. F. Pemberton-Pigott, October 5, 1959, FO 371/146345; Telegram from the Embassy in France to the Department of State, September 15, 1959, 5 p.m., *FRUS:1958–1960*:VII:2, d137; Memorandum of Conference with President Eisenhower, November 4, 1959, *FRUS:1958–1960*:VII:1, d226.

84. "Status of the Matters Discussed with You during Your Recent Trip to Europe"; Memorandum of Conference with President Eisenhower, November 4, 1959.

85. "General NATO Cooperation," October 6, 1959, RG59/APMA, Subject Files, 1953–1962/17/France, vol. 1/NARA.

86. Memorandum of Conversation, Paris, September 30, 1959, RG59/WE/France/3/Memos of Conversation 1959 (folder 2)/NARA.

87. Roberts to Hoyer Millar, October 8, 1959, FO 371/146344.

88. Diary entry for October 6, 1959, Shuckburgh Diary, MS191/1/2/8, CRL.

89. Caccia to Rumbold, October 13, 1959, FO 371/146344.

90. Rumbold to the Secretary of State, December 16, 1959, FO 371/146406.

91. Roberts to Hoyer Millar, December 4, 1959. Christopher Steel heard the same in Germany. See Steel to Hoyer Millar, December 8, 1959, FO 371/146406.

92. Jebb to Rumbold, December 2, 1959, FO 371/146310.

93. The American record is Record of Meeting, December 20, 1959, *FRUS:1958–1960*:VII:2, d151. For the British record see Extract from Record of a Tripartite Meeting at Rambouillet at 10.15 a.m. on December 20, 1959, FO 371/152095.

94. Minute for Sir F. Hoyer-Millar, "Proposed Tripartite Discussions," from P. Dean, December 21, 1959, FO/371/152095. See also Minute by Hoyer Millar, February 26, 1960, and initialed by Lloyd, on back of buck slip for "The Prime Minister's visit to General de Gaulle," February 26, 1960, FO 371/152096.

95. To make matters worse, Germany would likely come to lead the EEC. Chronological Minute of 3 p.m. meeting, November 29, 1959, PREM 11/2679.

96. Prime Minister's Personal Minute to the Foreign Secretary, M506/59, December 22, 1959, PREM 11/3002.

97. "Extract from Record of Conversation between the Secretary of State and Mr. Herter at the American Embassy in Paris on December 21, 1959," FO 371/152095.

98. Hoyer-Millar to Secretary of State, January 13, 1960, FO 371/152095; De Zulueta to A. C. I. Samuel, February 1, 1960, FO 371/152095.

99. PM's Personal Minute to Foreign Secretary, M. 522/59, December 24, 1959, FO 371/152095.

100. Letter from Secretary of State Herter to Foreign Minister Couve de Murville, December 30, 1959, *FRUS:1958–1960*:VII:2, d153. See also Minute by Hoyer-Millar to Dean, Rumbold, and Private Secretaries, January 11, 1960, FO 371/152095.

101. "Annex A: History of the Proposals for 'Tripartite Consultations,'" undated, FO 371/152098.

102. Paris187 to FO, May 19, 1960, PREM 11/3005.

103. "Extract from the Prime Minister's Conversation with President Eisenhower at 4 p.m. on Wednesday, May 18[, 1960]," undated, FO 371/152098. See also the entry for May 21, 1960, *MD:PM*, 301.

104. Washington1064 to FO, May 25, 1960, FO 371/152098.

105. In the margins an updated translation reads: "i.e. the power to decide the course of affairs." "Memorandum of Conversation," May 18, 1960, 5–6:20 p.m., May 18, 1960, AWF/INTL/44/Paris Meetings May 1960 (1)/DDEL. The British record is "Record of Meeting at the Elysée Palace at 5 o'clock on Wednesday, May 18," May 19, 1960, PREM 11/3005.

106. Memorandum of Conversation, May 18, 1960, *FRUS:1958–1960*:VII:2, d173.

107. "Tri-Partite Consultations," Minutes, May 21–23, 1960, FO 371/152097; Message from Prime Minister Macmillan to President Eisenhower, May 25, 1960, *FRUS:1958–1960*:VII:2, d177; "Tripartite Consultations," by Peter Ramsbotham, June 14, 1960, FO 371/152100; Department of State TODEL 7 to Amembassy, Manila (Calhoun), June 15, 1960, WHO/OSS/INTL/5/France—vol. 3 of 3 (3)/DDEL.

108. "Text of Statement to N.A.T.O. Council on Tripartite Talks," attached to CRO50 to various posts, June 15, 1960, FO 371/152099.

109. "Tripartite Talks" North Atlantic Council, June 8, 1960, Prepared by UKDel, June 9, 1960, FO 371/152099.

110. UKDel269 to FO, October 1, 1958, FO 371/137820.

111. Roberts to Tompkins, July 1, 1960, FO 371/152100. Spaak expressed similar thoughts; see UKDel191 to FO, June 11, 1960, FO 371/152099; Telegram from the Department of State to the Embassy in France, June 17, 1960, 11:06 a.m., *FRUS:1958–1960*:VII:2, d183.

112. Roberts to Tompkins, July 1, 1960.

113. Memorandum of Conversation, June 20, 1960, *FRUS:1958–1960*:VII:2, d184.

114. Memorandum of Telephone Conversation between President Eisenhower and Secretary of State Herter, July 1, 1960, 2 p.m., *FRUS:1958–1960*:VII:2, d188. See also Telegram from the Embassy in France to the Department of State, June 24, 1960, 7 p.m., *FRUS:1958–1960*:VII:2, d186.

115. Message from the Prime Minister to President Eisenhower, undated, FO 371/152100.

116. Draft shown to Caccia in Washington1411 to FO, July 18, 1960, FO 371/152101.

117. Minute by P. E. Ramsbotham, June 21, 1960, FO 371/152100.

118. Washington1435 to FO, July 20, 1960, FO 371/152101.

119. Telegram from the Mission at the UN to the Department of State, July 14, 1960, 3 a.m., *FRUS:1958–1960*:XIV, d123.

120. Circular Telegram from the Department of State to Certain Diplomatic Missions, July 21, 1960, *FRUS:1958–1960*:XIV, d143.

121. UKDel180 to FO, July 14, 1960, FO 371/146696; UKDel182 to FO, July 14, 1960, FO 371/146696.

122. UKDel252 Saving to FO, July 20, 1960, FO 371/146696.

123. Telegram from the Department of State to the Embassy in Belgium, August 2, 1960, *FRUS:1958–1960*:XIV, d160n2. See also de Staercke's explicit but highly confidential warning to the British in UKDel194 to FO, July 27, 1960, FO 371/146696.

124. Telegram from the Department of State to the Embassy in Belgium, August 2, 1960; UKDel189 to FO, July 25, 1960, FO 371/146696.

125. UKDel205 to FO, August 5, 1960; Joseph J. World to Permanent Representatives, August 9, 1960, both in FO 371/146696. For Spaak's public defense of NATO's inaction in the Congo see Brussels Airgram G-69 to Secretary of State, September 21, 1960, DDRS/CK3100216156.

126. Paris341 to FO, December 1, 1960, PREM 11/3780; Paris563 to Secretary of State, August 11, 1960, WHO/OSS/INTL/5/France—Vol. III of III (4)/DDEL.

127. Letter from President de Gaulle to President Eisenhower, August 9, 1960, *FRUS:1958–1960*:VII:2, d191.

128. Paris307 to FO, August 9, 1960, FO 371/152102.

129. Memorandum of Telephone Conversation between President Eisenhower and Secretary of State Herter, August 10, 1960, *FRUS:1958–1960*:VII:2, d192; Memorandum for Files by Eisenhower, August 10, 1960, AWF/Whitman Diary/11/[ACW]Diary August 1960 (2)/DDEL.

130. Memorandum of Conference with President Eisenhower, August 16, 1960, *FRUS:1958–1960*:VII:1, d264.

131. FO3610 to Washington, August 19, 1960, FO 371/152103; Memorandum of Telephone Conversation between President Eisenhower and Secretary of State Herter, August 10, 1960, 12:15 p.m., *FRUS:1958–1960*:VII:2, d192.

132. Shuckburgh to Rumbold (Paris), August 12, 1960, FO 371/152102. Home replaced Selwyn Lloyd in July 1960.

133. Memorandum of Conversation, August 17, 1960, *FRUS:1958–1960*:VII:2, 195; "Note of the Prime Minister's Suggestions to Mr. Merchant about President de Gaulle's Message of August 9 to President Eisenhower," August 19, 1960, DDRS/CK3100501674.

134. Letter from President Eisenhower to President de Gaulle, August 30, 1960, *FRUS:1958–1960*:VII:2, d197.

135. UKDel217 to Washington, September 12, 1960, FO 371/154576; "Revised draft telegram to Sir Frank Roberts," drafted by Macmillan and undated, later sent as FO1003 to UKDel, September 13, 1960, both in FO 371/154576; Jeffrey Glen Giauque, *Grand Designs and Visions of Unity: The Atlantic Powers and the Reorganization of Western Europe, 1955–1963* (Chapel Hill: University of North Carolina Press, 2002), 126–57.

136. "Tripartite Consultation between France, the United States and the United Kingdom," March 10, 1961, NSF/70A/France-General/JFKL.

137. Paris3951 to SecState, March 22, 1961, NSF/70A/France-General/JFKL.

138. "Record of a Conversation in the Marble Room at Rambouillet at 2.45 p.m. on Sunday, January 29, 1961," January 29, 1961, PREM 11/3322. See also "United Kingdom International Policies, in the light of the United Kingdom Economic Position," undated memo by Bishop, June 26, 1961, PREM11/3348.

139. "Memorandum" attached to Macmillan's letter to Kennedy, April 22, 1961, PREM 11/3311.

140. "The Nuclear," Philip de Zulueta to the Prime Minister, undated, PREM 11/3311.

141. Foreign Office [Macmillan] to Washington [Bundy], May 9, 1961, PREM 11/3311, NUAK.

142. Macmillan diary entry for June 11, 1961, *MD:PM*, 391.

143. Constantine A. Pagedas, *Anglo-American Strategic Relations and the French Problem, 1960–1963: A Troubled Partnership* (London: France Cass, 2000), 155.

144. "Friday Afternoon Talks," memorandum of conversation, June 2, 1961, DDRS/CK3100133349.

145. "Note of Points made during the Private Discussion between President Kennedy and Prime Minister Macmillan at Admiralty House from 10:30 a.m.–12:45 p.m. on Monday, June 5, 1961," June 8, 1961, DDRS/CK3100165154.

146. SecState6631 to Paris, June 9, 1962, NSF/71/France-General/JFKL. See also "Pre-September Meeting of the Three Foreign Ministers," memorandum of conversation, July 7, 1961, Bohlen Records/13/Tripartitism, 1959–1961/NARA.

147. Macmillan diary entry for June 11, 1961, *MD:PM*, 391. See also Philip de Zulueta to Prime Minister, November 17, 1961, PREM 11/3338.

148. Paris SECTO 6 to Secretary of State, June 2, 1961, DDRS/CK3100038381.

149. "Friday Afternoon Talks," June 2, 1961.

150. "Meeting with President De Gaulle, 23 July 1962," July 24, 1962, NSF/71A/France-General/JFKL.

151. SSO JCS 539–61, General Norstad SHAPE Paris to Admiral Burke Washington, April 24, 1961, NSF/70A/France-General/JFKL. This was something of a self-fulfilling prophecy, for the French had a deliberate policy of transferring out of Algeria any officers considered unreliable. Thus "ranking officers in NATO, France, and West Germany would be more suspect than those who were based in Algeria." "Situation Appraisal in France as of 30 January 1964: Indications of Anti-Americanism," CIA Intelligence Information Cable, January 31, 1964, NSF/Country/169/LBJL.

152. Memorandum of Conversation, June 1, 1961, 3:30 p.m., *FRUS:1960–1963*:XIII, d107; Paris SECTO 6 to Secretary of State, June 2, 1961; "Extract from a Conversation between the Prime Minister and President de Gaulle which began at 10.30 a.m. on Sunday, June 3," June 4, 1962, PREM 11/3775; "Record of a Meeting at the Palais Schaumberg at 10 a.m., on Tuesday, January 9, 1962," January 9, 1962, PREM 11/3776, NUAK.

153. "Conversation concerning Alleged US Encouragement of General Challe," memorandum for Secretary McNamara, Ivan White, Mr. Bohlen, Mr. Dulles, Mr. McGeorge Bundy, from William P. Bundy, May 6, 1961, NSF/70A/France-General/JFKL.

154. Undated handwritten notes, Bundy/WHSF/33/European Trip, Sept. 1962 (2 of 3)/JFKL.

4. A PROFOUND BITTERNESS

1. "President Kennedy at Independence Hall, 4 July 1962," John F. Kennedy Presidential Library and Museum, http://www.jfklibrary.org/Asset-Viewer/RrjaDhW 5B0OYm2zaJbyPgg.aspx. The speech is often misinterpreted; it is complex because it considers the Atlantic relationship at different possible points in the future. See Rostow, *Diffusion of Power*, 235–38. For interpretations see Sebastian Reyn, *Atlantis Lost: The American Experience with De Gaulle, 1958–1969* (Amsterdam: Amsterdam University Press, 2010), 123–26; James Ellison, *The United States, Britain and the Transatlantic Crisis: Rising to the Gaullist Challenge, 1963–68* (New York: Palgrave Macmillan, 2007), 3. For an overview of the Kennedy era see Thomas Schwartz, "The United States and Western Europe," in *The Diplomacy of the Crucial Decade: American Foreign Relations during the 1960s*, ed. Diane B. Kunz (New York: Columbia University Press, 1994). A more recent overview with attention to NATO is Carolyne Davidson, "Dealing with de Gaulle: The United States and France," in *Globalizing de Gaulle: International Perspectives on French Foreign Policies, 1958–1969*, ed. Anna Locher, Garret Martin, and Christian Nünlist (Lanham, MD: Rowman & Littlefield, 2010). For Kennedy's relations with the major European powers see Nigel John Ashton, *Kennedy, Macmillan and the Cold War: The Irony of Interdependence* (New York: Palgrave Macmillan, 2002); Erin R. Mahan, *Kennedy, de Gaulle and Western Europe* (New York: Palgrave Macmillan, 2002); Granieri, *The Ambivalent Alliance*: Konrad Adenauer, the CDU/CSU, and the West, 1949–1966 (New York: Berghahn Books, 2003), 150–90; Frank A. Mayer, *Adenauer and Kennedy: A Study in German-American Relations, 1961–1963* (New York: St. Martin's, 1996). On strategic issues see Pagedas, *Anglo-American Strategic Relations*; Trachtenberg, *Constructed Peace*, 283–402. On the interplay between these relationships, strategy, and broader visions of Europe see Giauque, *Grand Designs*, 98–238.

2. Gerard C. Smith to Henry Owen, August 9, 1962, Smith/27/MLF Correspondence 1962/DDEL; Smith to Rostow, July 2, 1962, Smith/27/MLF Correspondence 1962/DDEL.

3. On the Berlin crisis the crucial text is Trachtenberg, *Constructed Peace*. See also John P. S. Gearson and Kori N. Schake, *The Berlin Wall Crisis: Perspectives on Cold War Alliances*, Cold War History Series (New York: Palgrave Macmillan, 2002); Paul H. Nitze, Steven L. Rearden, and Ann M. Smith, From Hiroshima to Glasnost: At the Center of Decision: A Memoir (New York: G. Weidenfeld, 1989), 196–208.

4. Gregory W. Pedlow, "NATO and the Berlin Crisis of 1961: Facing the Soviets While Maintaining Unity," in *A City Torn Apart: Building of the Berlin Wall* (Washington, DC: National Archives and Records Administration, 2011), 28–31, https://www.cia.gov/library/publications/international-relations/building-of-the-berlin-wall/building-the-berlin-wall.pdf.

5. Theodore C. Sorensen, *Kennedy* (New York: Perennial Library, 1988), 562.

6. SHAPE LN Washington DC DA992476 to USNMR Paris [Acheson to Norstad], March 24, 1961, DDRS/CK3100328745.

7. "Second Session with Mr. Acheson on NATO," Komer to the President, March 14, 1961, NSF/220/NATO-General/JFKL. The chairman of the policy planning staff Walt Rostow agreed the US "must learn automatically to take into account the Alliance's interests," especially "when we operate outside the North Atlantic Community." "NATO Paper," Acheson from Rostow, March 20, 1961, NSF/220/NATO-General/JFKL.

8. "A Review of North Atlantic Problems for the Future," March 1961, POF/NATO: General, 1961: January–April/JFKLDC.

9. "Western European Area," May 5, 1955, DDRS/CK3100440746.

10. On NATO and Berlin see Kaplan, *NATO 1948.* On the Berlin blockade and airlift see Harrington, *Berlin on the Brink: The Blockade, the Airlift, and the Early Cold War* (Lexington, KY: University Press of Kentucky, 2012). On the Korean War see "U.K. Reaction to U.S. Policy (NSC (5404/1)," May 16, 1955, DNSA/BC000011; "Berlin," November 24, 1958, DNSA/BC00385. On internal US discussion over how to respond to Khrushchev see Memorandum of the Substance of Discussion at a Department of State–Joint Chiefs of Staff Meeting, November 21, 1958, *FRUS:1958–1960*:VIII, d57. "Notes from the State-JCS Meeting at 11:30 Hours on 21 November 1958," November 25, 1958, DNSA/BC00395 is the same meeting as above but verbatim. Memorandum of Telephone Conversation between Secretary of State Dulles and Secretary of Defense McElroy, November 17, 1958, *FRUS:1958–1960*:VIII, d44; Notes of the Secretary's Staff Meeting, November 18, 1958, *FRUS:1958–1960*:VIII, d46; Memorandum of Conversation between President Eisenhower and Secretary of State Dulles, November 18, 1958, *FRUS:1958–1960*:VIII, d47. On the differences between tripartite and NATO responsibility for Berlin see FO to UKDel, "NATO versus Tripartite Responsibility," October 2, 1961, FO 371/160492.

11. Philip de Zulueta to Prime Minister, June 18, 1959, PREM 11/2718; Telegram from the Mission to NATO and European Regional Organizations to the Department of State, November 26, 1958, *FRUS:1958–1960*:VIII, d70. See also London2842 to SecState, November 23, 1958, DNSA/BC00373.

12. Bonn1597 to SecState, January 23, 1959, DNSA/BC00657; Paris2073 to SecState, January 24, 1959, DNSA/BC00666. Regarding recognition of East Germany see Telegram from the Mission to NATO and European Regional Organizations to the Department of State, November 17, 1958, *FRUS:1958–1960*:VIII, d43; "Germany and Berlin," November 18, 1958, DNSA/BC00312; Telegram from the Department of State to the Embassy in Germany, November 17, 1958, *FRUS:1958–1960*:VIII, d41. On softness see Bonn1160 to SecState, December 2, 1958, DNSA/BC00443; Telegram from the Department of State to the Embassy in Germany, November 17, 1958.

13. Norstad to the Chairman, Joint Chiefs of Staff, December 23, 1958, DNSA/BC00551.

14. USCINCEUR Paris France EC 9–10240 to JCS, February 23, 1959, DNSA/BC00810; "Berlin Contingency Planning," May 18, 1960, PREM 11/3005. On the command structure and working groups see Gregory W. Pedlow, "Three Hats for Berlin: Lauris Norstad and the Second Berlin Crisis, 1958–1962," in *The Berlin Wall Crisis: Perspectives on Cold War Alliances,* ed. John P. S. Gearson and Kori N. Schake (New York: Palgrave Macmillan, 2002), and "Allied Crisis Management for Berlin: The Live Oak Organization, 1959–1963," in *International Cold War Military Records and History: Proceedings of the*

International Conference on Cold War Military Records and History Held in Washington, D.C., 21–26 March 1994, ed. William W. Epley (Washington, DC: Office of the Secretary of Defense, 1996); Robert S. Jordan, *Norstad: Cold War NATO Supreme Commander: Airman, Strategist, Diplomat* (Houndmills, Basingstoke, UK: Macmillan, 2000), 148–55; Norman Gelb, *The Berlin Wall* (London: M. Joseph, 1986), 117–19.

15. Live Oak grew to become a "third hat" for the traditionally dual-hatted officer. Pedlow, "Three Hats for Berlin"; Lawrence S. Kaplan, "The Berlin Crisis of 1958–1962: Views from the Pentagon," in Epley, *International Cold War Military Records and History*, 72.

16. Pedlow, "Three Hats for Berlin," 174.

17. Mark Jonathan Rice, "The Alliance City: NATO and Berlin, 1958–1963" (PhD diss., Ohio State University, 2010), 100, 107–9.

18. FO to UKDel, "NATO versus Tripartite Responsibility," October 2, 1961, FO 371/160492.

19. Note to the Prime Minister from T. J. Bligh, September 16, 1959, PREM 11/3005.

20. "Berlin Contingency Planning (D.(59)35 and D.(59)38.)," to the PM from Bligh, December 8, 1959, PREM 11/3005.

21. "In face of H.M.G.'s desire to avoid a showdown with the Americans, these plans remain on the books although there is no commitment to carry them out," undated letter [late February 1961], FO 371/160485.

22. "Berlin Contingency Planning (D.(59)35 and D.(59)38.)," December 8, 1959.

23. Rusk to the President, January 28, 1961, POF/Germany-Security JAN-JUNE 1961/ JFKLDC; "The Berlin Problem in 1961," POF/Germany: Security, 1961: January–June/ JFKLDC. "Imaginative planning" in "Key National Security Problems," February 10, 1961, NSF/303/Policy Planning, 1/61-2/10/61/JFKL. See also "Notes for the President. Subject: Planning Item, NSC Agenda," February 23, 1961, NSF/303/Policy Planning, 2/11/61-5/61/JFKL; "NATO Paper," memorandum for Acheson from Rostow, March 20, 1961, NSF/220/NATO-General/JFKL.

24. This despite repeated calls for consideration of "alternative approaches to the Berlin and German problems" and worry that only one part-time consultant—Henry Kissinger—was thinking about the German issue writ large. "An Illustrative List of National Security Planning Problems Which May Justify Urgent Attention," February 17, 1961, NSF/303/Policy Planning, 2/11/61-5/61/JFKL; "Revised List of National Security Planning Problems," from Komer to Bundy and Rostow, May 15, 1961, NSF/303/Policy Planning, 2/11/61-5/61/JFKL. Acheson did not hold an official position in the Kennedy administration. Schlesinger claims Kennedy specifically sought a hard-line analysis before making his decision. Arthur M. Schlesinger, *A Thousand Days: John F. Kennedy in the White House* (Boston: Houghton Mifflin, 1965), 380. For various interpretations of Acheson's appointment see Lawrence Freedman, *Kennedy's Wars: Berlin, Cuba, Laos, and Vietnam* (New York: Oxford University Press, 2000), 45–49, 62–63; Frank Costigliola, "The Pursuit of Atlantic Community: Nuclear Arms, Dollars, and Berlin," in *Kennedy's Quest for Victory: American Foreign Policy, 1961–1963*, ed. Thomas G. Paterson (New York: Oxford University Press, 1989), 29; Schwartz, "The United States and Western Europe," 121; Rice, "Alliance City," 107–9.

25. "Key National Security Problems," February 10, 1961.

26. "Berlin," Memorandum for the President from Dean Acheson, April 3, 1961, POF/ United Kingdom: Security, 1961: 27 March–April/JFKLDC.

27. "Berlin," April 3, 1961. See also his letter to Lucius Clay, in which he wrote that troops should be built up with "evident and real intent to use them, if necessary, with SAC in support." Acheson to Clay, January 4, 1962, AP/Gen. Corr./6/77. On this issue, and for a slightly different reading, see Trachtenberg, *Constructed Peace*, 291

28. "Berlin," April 3, 1961.

29. On Norstad's reaction to the Kennedy administration's views on war see Trachtenberg, *Constructed Peace*, 289–91.

30. "East-West Issues: Berlin," April 5, 1961, *FRUS:1961–1963*:XIV, d14; "Extract from record of conversation between the CDS + President Kennedy—Washington, April 12, 1961," undated, FO 371/160486. See also Mountbatten's quote in Pedlow, "Allied Crisis Management for Berlin," 103; Trachtenberg, *Constructed Peace*, 289–90.

31. Minutes on jacket CG1016/4G "Berlin Contingency Planning," by J. E. Killick, February 20, 1961, FO 371/160485; "Confidential Annex to C.O.S.(61)21st Meeting Held on Thursday, 23rd March, 1961," FO 371/160485.

32. "Vice Chiefs of Staff March 23: Berlin Contingency Planning," undated, FO 371/160485; "Confidential Annex to C.O.S.(61)21st Meeting Held on Thursday, 23rd March, 1961." Kennedy appeared to approve Acheson's thinking the next day. "The President's Meeting with Prime Minister Macmillan, Washington, April 1961, East-West Issues: Berlin," April 6, 1961, *FRUS:1961–1963*:XIV, d15.

33. Costigliola, "Pursuit of Atlantic Community," 62; Freedman, *Kennedy's Wars*, 62; Kaplan, "Berlin Crisis of 1958–1962," 70. American diplomats believed that Adenauer became "anti-American" after he visited Kennedy in 1961. "Proceedings of the Atlantic Affairs Conference, American Embassy, Luxembourg, November 29–30, 1964," RG59/EUR/DAS/Schaetzel/1/Atlantic Affairs Conference, Luxembourg 11/29-30/64/NARA.

34. "Comparison of 'A Review of North Atlantic Problems for the Future,' with Existing National Security Council Policy," March 28, 1961, NSF/220/NATO-General/JFKL.

35. Murphy to Norstad, March 31, 1961, NP/75/MURPHY, Col. Charles J. V. (2)/DDEL.

36. "NATO Policies and Procedures," UNSNMR SHAPE to SECDEF, NP/96/Assistant Secretary of Defense/ISA (3)/DDEL.

37. Remarkably, in 1959, future secretary of state Dean Rusk complained that friends in Europe told him "public opinion would not accept the additional costs. I find this infuriating when responsible leaders have not even bothered to ask their peoples the relevant question." Rusk to Acheson, December 8, 1959, AP/Gen. Corr./27/341.

38. "View of Italian Ambassador [sanitized] on NATO Strategy," CIA Information Report, June 26, 1961, NSF/220A/NATO-General/JFKL.

39. William Tyler to Acheson, June 16, 1957, AP/Gen. Corr./32/404; "NMR Germany re steps and decisions by FRG," November 12, 1962, NP/49/Germany 1961–1962 (1)/DDEL.

40. "NMR Germany re steps and decisions by FRG," November 12, 1962.

41. Michael Beschloss, *The Crisis Years: Kennedy and Khrushchev, 1960–1963* (New York: Edward Burlingame Books, 1991), 145–46; "The Problem We Face," Memorandum to the President from Rostow, April 21, 1961, NSF/303/Policy Planning, 2/11/61-5/61/JFKL.

42. "Memorandum of Conversation," June 4, 1961, 3:15 p.m., *FRUS:1961–1963*:XIV, d33.

43. On Kennedy and Berlin see Honoré Marc Catudal, *Kennedy and the Berlin Wall Crisis: A Case Study in U.S. Decision Making* (Berlin: Berlin-Verlag, 1980), 151–52; Beschloss, *Crisis Years*, 145–46; "Suggested Remarks before the Meeting on Berlin 4:00 P.M. 17 July 1961," POF/Germany: Security, July 1961/JFKLDC; "Military Planning for a Possible Crisis," Memorandum to the President from McNamara, May 5, 1961, *FRUS:1961–1963*:XIV, d22.

44. "Berlin," Memorandum from Bundy to Rusk, McNamara, and Dillon, July 7, 1961, *FRUS:1961–1963*:XIV, d58; on interdepartmental coordination see Gelb, *Berlin Wall*, 117–19.

45. "Berlin," Memorandum from Bundy to Rusk, McNamara, and Dillon, July 7, 1961.

46. Memorandum to the President from W W R[ostow], July 20, 1961, POF/Germany: Security, July 1961/JFKLDC.

47. Trachtenberg contrasts Kennedy's efforts to "set policy for the West as a whole" with Eisenhower's efforts to act as a broker, especially between British and German allies: see *Constructed Peace*, 304; Beschloss, *Crisis Years*.

48. "Posing the Issues of Negotiations and Our Attitudes to the GDR," Kohler to the Secretary of State, July 17, 1961, POF/Germany: Security, July 1961/JFKLDC.

49. For disagreements in Washington see Memorandum for the President from Arthur Schlesinger Jr., July 30, 1961, POF/Schlesinger, Arthur M., 1961/JFKLDC.

50. "Mr. Spaak's Views on the German Problem," June 9, 1961, POF/Germany: Security, 1961: January–June/JFKLDC.

51. The German statement is from Blankenhorn as retold by Spaak, "Mr. Spaak's Views on the German Problem," June 9, 1961. The German ambassador had insinuated Bonn's worry about war for Berlin to Norstad in July 1961. See Jordan, *Norstad*, 171; "Berlin," Memorandum from Harold Watkinson to the Prime Minister, June 23, 1961, FO 371/160487.

52. UKDel84 to FO, July 10, 1961, PREM 11/3348. See also UKDel83 to FO, July 10, 1961, PREM 11/3348.

53. Catudal, *Kennedy and the Berlin Wall Crisis*, 152, and quote at 161. See also Washington TOPOL 38 to USRO, July 9, 1961, *FRUS:1961–1963*:XIV, d60; UKDel88 to FO, July 12, 1961, PREM 11/3348; Editorial Note, *FRUS:1961–1963*:XIV, d73.

54. "Documents Prepared in Response to NSC Action Memorandum59 of July 14, 1961," July 18, 1961, POF/Germany: Security: Interdepartmental Coordinating Group papers, July 1961/JFKLDC.

55. Notes on Meeting of the Berlin Steering Group, September 7, 1961, *FRUS:1961–1963*:XIV, d143.

56. Paris POLTO 240 to SecState, August 30, 1961, POF/France: Security, 1961: General/JFKLDC. In fact, France was "isolated" as the only NATO ally opposed to responding in some way to Khrushchev. "Berlin," Memorandum of Conversation, August 24, 1961, *FRUS:1961–1963*:XIV, d126.

57. Washington DC to FO, "Berlin: Economic Counter-Measures," August 24, 1961, FO 371/160496.

58. Summary Record of a Meeting of the Council, Paris, October 4, 1961," C-R(61)50, October 12, 1961; "Summary Record of a Meeting of the Council, Paris, October 23, 1961," C-R(61)54, October 23, 1961, NATO; see also the minutes on "The Use of Economic Counter-Measures in the Berlin Crisis, K. W. D. Strong, FO 371/160490. For "fully watertight embargo" see "Possible Economic Counter-Measures," Report by the Committee of Political Advisers, May 29, 1961, C-M(61)45, NATO; "Possible Economic Countermeasures to be taken in the Face of the Berlin Crisis," C-M(61)82, September 29, 1961, NATO.

59. For "sledgehammer" see P. W. Marten [Bonn] to John Killick, May 25, 1961, FO 371/160495; for "bad odour" see Killick to Peter Murray, May 9, 1961, FO 371/160495. See also Christopher Steel to Evelyn Shuckburgh, May 29, 1961, FO 371/160486. The Germans raised the possibility of economic countermeasures at NATO as early as 1960. See "Possible Economic Counter-Measures," AC/119-WP(60)95, November 11, 1960, NATO and "Action Sheet," AC/119-R(60)44, December 8, 1960, NATO.

60. Paris POLTO 240 to SecState, August 30, 1961, POF/France: Security, 1961: General/JFKLDC. "Possible Economic Countermeasures to be taken in the Face of the Berlin Crisis, September 29, 1961; FO to Washington, "Economic Counter Measures," August 25, 1961, FO 371/160946, August 25, 1961; "The Use of Economic Counter-Measures in the Berlin Crisis, K. W. D. Strong; Marten to Killick, May 25; "Summary Record of a Meeting of the Council, Paris, October 31, 1961," C-R(61)56, November 13, 1961, NATO;

"Summary Record of a Meeting of the Council, Paris, December 7, 1961," C-R(61)62, December 19, 1961, NATO.

61. "Draft Minute from the Secretary of State to the Prime Minister," June 29, 1961, FO 371/160487. Shuckburgh was convinced the JCS were "quite aware that operations in question were in themselves militarily unsound." "Politico-Military Discussions," July 11, 1961, PREM 11/3348. Note that Rusk was concerned enough to "make his position clear" to the president that he thought "shooting" must be "an act of last resort." Nonmilitary measures, such as an airlift, or sanctions, should be "exhausted" before any military means. "Even a small probe," Rusk said, "could quickly get out of control." "Record of a Meeting, 4:30 p.m., August 3, 1961," POF/State, 1961: August–September/JFKLDC.

62. BDS Washington GM 199 to Ministry of Defence London, September 7, 1961, DEFE 7/2254.

63. Freedman, *Kennedy's Wars*, 93.

64. For Kennedy's political incentive to take a hard line on communism see Beschloss, *Crisis Years*, 23–25.

65. Gallup polls in July 1961 asked what the United States should do if "Communist East Germany closes all roads to Berlin and does not permit plans to land in Berlin." Of the respondents, 67 percent argued the US and its allies "should fight" for Berlin, and a measly 16 percent said they "should not fight"; 85 percent responded that they were "willing to risk war to keep U.S. Troops in the divided city." "Key Questions and Answers in the Gallup Poll of July 1961," POF/Germany: Berlin Crisis polls, July 1961/JFKLDC; Catudal, *Kennedy and the Berlin Wall Crisis*, 169–70. See other poll figures in Costigliola, "Pursuit of Atlantic Community," 40. American diplomats reported from Europe that the allies thought Washington was "working itself up into a lather somewhat prematurely, and generating its own crisis atmosphere in the process." "Documents Prepared in Response to NSC Action Memorandum59 of July 14, 1961," July 18, 1961, POF/Germany: Security: Interdepartmental Coordinating Group papers, July 1961/JFKLDC.

66. For the Canadian warnings see Moscow to External Affairs, Germany and Berlin, September 15, 1962, and Washington to External Affairs, "Berlin Krolls interview with Khrushchev," September 21, 1962, both in RG25/50341-A-2-40-S/LAC.

67. "Berlin," Memorandum to the PM from Harold Watkinson, June 23, 1961, FO 371/160487.

68. Draft Telegram, FO to Washington, undated [July 1961], FO 371/160487.

69. "Berlin Contingency Planning and Military Staff Talks," July 6, 1961, FO 371/160487. See also "Points Arising from Discussion with General Lemnitzer," note by Chief of the Air Staff [Mills], July 3, 1961, FO 371/160487.

70. Draft Telegram, FO to Washington, [July 1961]; "Berlin Contingency Planning," minute by E. E. Tomkins, July 5, 1961, FO 371/160487; Memorandum from Sir F. Hoyer Miller to Evelyn Shuckburgh, July 13, 1961, FO 371/160487.

71. Draft Minute from the Prime Minister to the Foreign Secretary, undated [June 24, 1961], PREM 11/3348; "weak sister" line from Marten to Killick, May 25, 1961.

72. Draft Minute from the Prime Minister to the Foreign Secretary [June 24, 1961].

73. "Message to Mr. Rusk on Berlin," Home to the Prime Minister, June 30, 1961, PREM 11/3348.

74. Catudal, *Kennedy and the Berlin Wall Crisis*, 175. See also Memorandum of a Meeting on Berlin, July 18, 1961, *FRUS:1961–1963*:XIV, d75; Memorandum from Bundy to Kennedy, July 19, 1961, *FRUS:1961–1963*:XIV, d76; Memorandum of minutes of the National Security Council Meeting, July 19, 1961, *FRUS:1961–1963*:XIV, d77; "Politico-Military Discussions," July 11, 1961. On "general war" see "NATO Policies and Procedures," June 22, 1961, NP/96/Assistant Secretary of Defense/ISA (3)/DDEL.

75. "Berlin," July 27, 1961, FO 371/160487; L. J. Sabatini to Killick, July 28, 1961, FO 371/160487; "Berlin. Record of a Meeting Held in the Minister's Room, Ministry of Defence, on Wednesday, 16th August, 1961 at 3:30 p.m.," FO 371/160490; "Training for Trade Wind," memorandum by E. E. Tomkins, September 19, 1961, FO 371/160492.

76. "Confidential Annex to C.O.S.(61)47th Meeting Held on Tuesday 25th July, 1961," FO 371/160488.

77. The message to de Gaulle was similar to those to Macmillan and Adenauer. Washington 422 to Paris, July 20, 1961, DNSA/BC02200. See editorial note, *FRUS:1961–1963*:XIV, d79. Still, White House advisers worried over the "dearth of political planning" for alternative negotiating positions presented by the Department of State, which remained curiously focused on military plans. Record of Meeting of the Berlin Steering Group, July 20, 1961, *FRUS:1961–1963*:XIV, d78.

78. Memorandum of minutes of the National Security Council Meeting, July 19, 1961. See also Catudal, *Kennedy and the Berlin Wall Crisis*, 176.

79. UKDel to Foreign Office, "Berlin: Mr. Rusk's Statement to the North Atlantic Council," August 8, 1961, FO 371/160488.

80. Although Kennedy referred to "our allies" regarding "costly military preparations," it is clear he meant the Germans. "Record of a Meeting, 4:30 p.m., August 3, 1961," POF/State, 1961: August–September/JFKLDC. See also "Issues to be Settled with General Clay," Memorandum to the President from Bundy, August 28, 1961, POF/Clay, General Lucius D., August 1961–June 1963/JFKLDC.

81. "Memorandum on Statement to the North Atlantic Council in Private Session on Military Build-up, Soviet Motives and Intentions," by the United States Delegation, August 8, 1961, NATO/MPBE.

82. FO to Washington DC [Shuckburgh personal to Caccia], August 17, 1961, FO 371/160490. For more on the assumed "implication for the long-term future of NATO quite apart from Berlin" see Killick to Tomlinson, August 14, 1961, FO 371/160491.

83. "United States of America," attached to Memorandum from J. Sagne to Secretary General, JS.104/61, August 19, 1961, NATO/MPBE.

84. "Memorandum on Statement to the North Atlantic Council in Private Session on Military Build-up, Soviet Motives and Intentions," by the United States Delegation, August 8, 1961, NATO/MPBE; "Very much in the dark" in UKDel111 to FO, August 21, 1961, DEFE 7/2253.

85. "North Atlantic Council. Berlin," August 23, 1961, FO 371/160490; "(1) Berlin Negotiations and (2) Possible Reprisals," Memorandum for the President from Bundy, August 14, 1961, POF/Bundy, McGeorge, 1961/JFKLDC. See also Fabian Rueger, "Kennedy, Adenauer and the Making of the Berlin Wall, 1958–1961" (PhD diss., Stanford University, May 2011), 241; "France and NATO," note to the Prime Minister, April 4, 1966, PREM 13/1043.

86. See Memorandum of Conversation between President Eisenhower and Secretary of State Dulles, November 18, 1958, *FRUS:1958–1960*:VIII, d47; on de Gaulle see Cyril Buffet, "De Gaulle, the Bomb and Berlin: How to Use a Political Weapon," in *The Berlin Wall Crisis: Perspectives on Cold War Alliances*, ed. John P. S. Gearson and Kori N. Schake (New York: Palgrave Macmillan, 2002).

87. For allied reaction to the troop movement see FO to Washington DC [Shuckburgh personal to Caccia], August 17, 1961. On Tuchman and miscalculation see Sorensen, *Kennedy*, 513; Freedman, *Kennedy's Wars*, 56; Beschloss, *Crisis Years*, 19, 87.

88. Bonn to FO, "Allied access to East Berlin," August 30, 1961, FO 371/160491.

89. Berlin to FO, "Allies access to East Berlin," September 1, 1961, FO 371/160491.

90. See Memorandum for the President from McNamara, August 24, 1961, POF/Clay, General Lucius D., August 1961–June 1963/JFKLDC, and "Issues to be Settled with

General Clay," August 28, 1961; Washington DC to FO, "Berlin: General Clay," August 31, 1961, FO 371/160491; Catudal, *Kennedy and the Berlin Wall Crisis*, 133. For "deep disquiet" see Ann Tusa, *The Last Division: A History of Berlin, 1945–1989* (Reading, MA: Addison-Wesley, 1997), 335–36.

91. Berlin564 to FO, November 7, 1961, FO 371/160573.

92. Hood to Tomkins, October 20, 1961, FO 371/160574; Ashe to Hood, FO 371/160574.

93. Washington2981 to FO, FO 371/160574.

94. Bonn1197 to FO, November 9, 1961, FO 371/160574. On this confusion see Jordan, *Norstad*, 175–78. Clay seemed willing to go beyond his authority. Raymond L. Garthoff, "Berlin 1961: The Record Corrected," *Foreign Policy* 84 (Autumn 1991). See also note by E. E. Tomkins, November 23, 1961, FO 371/160574. See also Steel to Shuckburgh, November 7, 1961, FO 371/160574; Record of a Conversation with the Chief of the Imperial General Staff, Norstad, and General Stockwell at SHAPE, by Evelyn Shuckburgh, August 9, 1961, FO 371/160488.

95. Lauris Norstad Oral History, OH-558, DDEL, 171.

96. See Trachtenberg, *Constructed Peace*, 298–99.

97. "Summary Record of a Meeting of the Council, Paris, August 23, 1961," C-R(61)39, August 29, 1961; "North Atlantic Council. Berlin," memorandum of meeting by UKDel, August 23, 1961, FO 371/160490.

98. Washington2086 to FO, August 26, 1961, DEFE 7/2253. See also Telegram from the Department of State to London, August 26, 1961, *FRUS:1961–1963*:XIV, d129.

99. Pedlow, "Three Hats for Berlin," 184–85.

100. Pedlow, 184–85; Trachtenberg, *Constructed Peace*, 302; Jordan, *Norstad*, 187–89.

101. Norstad, OH-558, DDEL, 142.

102. Pedlow, "Three Hats for Berlin," 184–85.

103. Quotes from the Norstad oral history in Pedlow, 188

104. Quoted in Trachtenberg, *Constructed Peace*, 302.

105. Freedman, *Kennedy's Wars*, 104.

106. UKDel to FO, "Instructions to SACEUR," September 12, 1961, FO 371/160492; Washington2072 to FO, DEFE 7/2253; Ramsbotham to Sabatini, October 18, 1961, FO 371/160492.

107. "Memorandum to NAC on Draft Instructions to General Norstad SACEUR," from the United Kingdom Delegation, September 1, 1961, NATO/MPBE; "Memorandum and Comments on Draft Instructions to SACEUR," by the Secretary General, September 2, 1961, NATO/MPBE.

108. "Memorandum to NAC on Draft Instructions to General Norstad SACEUR," September 1, 1961.

109. "Memorandum on the relationship between Live Oak and NATO Planning," September 2, 1961, NATO/MPBE.; "Summary of meeting between Secretary General and General Heusinger Chairman of the Military Committee on 31st August at 3 pm," NATO/MPBE.

110. All quotes from "Memorandum on Draft Instructions to General Norstad SACEUR," September 2, 1961, NATO/MPBE. See also "Considerations on ambassadorial steering group's draft instructions to SACEUR," Casardi to the Secretary General, September 19, 1961, NATO/MPBE; Pedlow, "Three Hats for Berlin," 188; Freedman, *Kennedy's Wars*, 104.

111. UKDel to FO, September 22, 1961, FO 371/160492; Hood to Shuckburgh, September 27, 1961, FO 371/160494. See also "Memorandum. North Atlantic Council. The Ambassadorial Steering Group. Council Meeting: Friday, September 22, 1961," FO 371/160493; "Summary Record of a meeting of the Council, Paris, September 22, 1961,"

C-R(61)46, September 22, 1961, NATO; "Note for Sir Evelyn Shuckburgh," from Tomlinson, undated, FO 371/160493.

112. "Although we have not said so specifically to our Allies," wrote D. R. Ashe, "Berlin Counter Measures," November 23, 1961, FO 160575. On the acceptability of the proviso to the Chiefs of Staff Committee see "Comments on the Draft Instructions to NATO Supreme Allied Commanders," Annex to Chiefs of Staff Committee, "Instructions to NATO Supreme Allied Commanders: Note by the Secretary," September 27, 1961, FO 371/160492.

113. "Meeting of the Secretary General with the Permanent Representatives of France, the United States and Germany and the Acting Perm. Rep. of the UK, on 2 Sept. 1961," by G. Vest, September 4, 1961, NATO/MPBE; Bonn912 to FO, September 8, 1961, FO 371/160491. On American warnings see Kissinger's conversation with Adenauer in Telegram from Bonn to SecState, February 17, 1962, *FRUS:1961–1963*:XIV, d298.

114. While Eisenhower expected the Soviets could withstand an economic embargo for twelve months, West Berlin "could be choked in 2 weeks." Memorandum of Discussion at a Special Meeting of the National Security Council, March 5, 1959, *FRUS:1958–1960*:VIII, d201. See also Burke to Twining, April 10, 1959, DNSA/BC01131; "Military and Non-Military Counter-measures in the Berlin Crisis," May 21, 1959, DNSA/BC01292.

115. Bonn912 to FO, September 8, 1961.

116. On Schelling see Freedman, *Kennedy's Wars*, 101; On plans for demonstrative use see Letter from Kennedy to Norstad, October 20, 1961, *FRUS:1961–1963*:XIV, d185; Memorandum of Conversation, May 4, 1962, EUR/RPM NATO Affairs/1/NATO 1. Policy. Plans. 1962/NARA; "Berlin Contingency Planning: The Preferred Sequence of Military Action in a Berlin Conflict," Secretary General to Permanent Representatives, PO(62)593, September 17, 1962, NATO; "Notes on the President's Meeting with General Norstad, January 25, 1962, 2:30–3:45 pm," January 27, 1962, NSF/220A/NATO; General Meetings between the President and General Norstad, 7/61–1/62/JFKL; "Memorandum: North Atlantic Council. Berlin Military Planning. Private Session: February 23, 1962. Briefing by General Norstad," February 2, 1962, DEFE 7/2255. On allied worries see "Summary Record of a Meeting of the North Atlantic Council, Paris, September 29, 1961," C-R(61)49, September 29, 1961, NATO; Timothy Andrews Sayle, "Canada, NATO, and the Berlin Crisis, 1961–1962: 'Slow-Boil' or 'Pressure Cooker'?," *International Journal* 62, no. 2 (2013): 255–68.

117. For "test" see Telegram from the Department of State to the United States Delegation to NATO, October 12, 1961, *FRUS:1961–1963*:XIV, d175. On "shadow of a collision" see Washington to FO, October 12, 1961, FO 371/160494.

118. The connection between plans and reality was tenuous. The British calculated that "in the event of really serious attack the Americans and ourselves would react on our own initiative and the Allies would string along. This may sound cynical, but I think it is realistic." See "N.A.T.O. approval of planning by General Norstad," minute by L. Fielding, September 14, 1961, FO 371/160573.

119. Air Marshal Mills in BDS Washington GM 199 to Ministry of Defence, September 7, 1971, DEFE 7/2254; Hood to Tomkins, October 17, 1961, FO 371/160575.

120. Memorandum with Remarks on Draft Instructions to SACEUR, September 2, 1961, NATO/MPBE.

121. Memorandum with Remarks on Draft Instructions to SACEUR, September 2, 1961. "Junta" remark is in "Meeting of the Secretary General with the Permanent Representatives of France, the United States and Germany and the Acting Perm. Rep. of the UK, on 2 Sept. 1961," by G. Vest, September 4, 1961, NATO/MPBE.

122. UKDel to FO, "Directive to General Norstad," September 29, 1961, FO 371/160492; Mason to Ramsbotham, October 5, 1961, FO 371/160494; "Governmental

Decisions to Execute NATO Military Counter-Measures," memorandum by T. A. K. Elliot, October 2, 1961, FO 371/160494; Memorandum of Conversation [Kennedy with quadripartite foreign ministers], September 15, 1961, *FRUS:1961–1963*:XIV, d152; Hood to Shuckburgh, September 27, 1971, FO 371/160494. On "deep water" see "Tripartite/ NATO Relationship. Lord Hood's letter of September 4," undated, FO 371/160491.

123. For Stikker's interpretation see "NATO Planning for Berlin Emergency—the question of Political Authorities," PO/61/809, October 17, 1961, NATO; for the American take on unanimity see Washington2979 to FO, November 7, 1961, FO 371/160574; FO8128 to Washington, November 8, 1961, FO 371/160574; Paris POLTO 380 to Sec-State, September 23, 1961, NSF/222/NATO-General, Cables/JFKL. For the British delegation's shock see UKDel190 to FO, October 13, 1961, FO 371/160573.

124. "Memorandum of Meeting with the President, October 20, 1961–10 AM" by Bundy, POF/Germany: Security, 1961: August–December/JFKLDC.

125. "Standing Group Liaison Office Memorandum by the Standing Group Representative Major General Barry to the Secretary General on Instructions to NATO military authorities—Berlin," LOM 130/61, October 26, 1961, NATO/MPBE.

126. "Summary Record of a Meeting of the Council, Paris, December 14, 1961," C-R(61), January 25, 1962, NATO.

127. Memorandum of Conversation, December 12, 1961, *FRUS:1961–1963*:XIV, d238.

128. "Berlin Counter Measures," by D. R. Ashe, November 23, 1961, FO 371/160575.

129. Quote from "Minutes of Meeting held on Wednesday, 27th September, 1961 at 2.45 p.m. C.O.S.(61)65th Meeting," DEFE 7/2254. See also "NATO Ministerial Meetings: Berlin Contingency Planning," undated [early December 1961], FO 371/160576; "Tripartite/NATO Relationship," minute by L. Fielding, January 4, 1962, FO 371/160576.

130. "Record of a Private Meeting 31/01/1962 in the Secretary General conference room," NATO/MPBE.

131. Letter from the Secretary General to the French Permanent Representative, PO(62)100, February 14, 1962, NATO/MPBE.

132. "Recommendation by the Governments of France, United Kingdom and United States concerning relationships between NATO and the Three Powers in the planning and control of Berlin Contingency Operations," BQD-M-22, February 1962, NATO/MPBE. On the plans see Sayle, "'Slow-Boil' or 'Pressure-Cooker'?"

133. Washington532 to FO, February 20, 1962, PREM 11/3711.

134. Brief on present Soviet policy attached to untitled memorandum by Evelyn Shuckburgh, June 20, 1962, PREM11/3805; "Berlin Contingency Planning: Annex to COS.275/1/3/62," March 1, 1962, DEFE 7/2255.

135. Dean to Hood, November 16, 1966, FO 1042/156.

136. Dean to Hood, November 16, 1966.

137. Dean to Hood, November 16, 1966.

5. THE LIMITS OF INTEGRATION

1. For this argument and periodization see Trachtenberg, *Constructed Peace*.

2. On the Soviet humiliation and then strategic arms buildup after Cuba see William Taubman, *Khrushchev: The Man and His Era* (New York: Norton, 2003), 579; Garthoff, *Détente and Confrontation*, rev. ed. (Washington, DC: Brookings Institution, 1994), 41, 88; Henry Kissinger, *White House Years* (Boston, MA: Little, Brown, 1979), 196–98.

3. This phrase was used by John McNaughton to describe allied worries. Memorandum for Mr. McGeorge Bundy from McNaughton, November 9, 1965, NSF/193/LBJL.

4. Tyler to Millar, January 4, 1960, EUR/OAPMA/Subjects, 1953–1962/17/Germany, vol. 1/NARA. For a broad examination of NATO nuclear strategy and the nuclear strategies of the key allies see Beatrice Heuser, *NATO, Britain, France and the FRG: Nuclear*

Strategies and Forces for Europe, 1949–2000 (New York: St. Martin's, 1997). On flexible response, the first stop should be Francis J. Gavin, "The Myth of Flexible Response: United States Strategy in Europe during the 1960s," *International History Review* 23, no. 4 (December 2001): 847–75. See also Jane E. Stromseth, *The Origins of Flexible Response: NATO's Debate over Strategy in the 1960s* (New York: St. Martin's, 1988); John S. Duffield, *Power Rules: The Evolution of NATO's Conventional Force Posture* (Stanford, CA: Stanford University Press, 1995), 112–76.

5. John Steinbruner, *The Cybernetic Theory of Decision*: New Dimensions of Political Analysis (Princeton, NJ: Princeton University Press, 1974), 200; see also Pascaline Winand, *Eisenhower, Kennedy, and the United States of Europe* (New York: St. Martin's, 1993), 221. For diverse interpretations of the motives behind the MLF proposal see Trachtenberg, *Constructed Peace*, 305; Lawrence S. Kaplan, Ronald D. Landa, and Edward J. Drea, The McNamara Ascendancy, 1961–1965, History of the Office of the Secretary of Defense (Washington, DC: Historical Office, Office of the Secretary of Defense, 2006), 385; Lawrence S. Kaplan, "The U.S. and NATO in the Johnson Years," in *The Johnson Years*, vol. 3, *LBJ at Home and Abroad*, ed. Robert A. Divine (Lawrence: University Press of Kansas, 1994), 121; Sherrill Brown Wells, "Monnet and 'the Insiders': Nathan, Tomlinson, Bowie, and Schaetzel," in *Monnet and the Americans: The Father of a United Europe and His U.S. Supporters*, ed. Clifford P. Hackett (Washington, DC: Jean Monnet Council, 1995). On Germany and nuclear weapons see Mark Cioc, *Pax Atomica: The Nuclear Defense Debate in West Germany during the Adenauer Era* (New York: Columbia University Press, 1988); Catherine McArdle Kelleher, *Germany and the Politics of Nuclear Weapons* (New York: Columbia University Press, 1975); Jeffrey Boutwell, *The German Nuclear Dilemma* (London: Brassey's, 1990), 14–52. See also Ronald J. Granieri, "The Fall and Rise of German Christian Democracy, from Détente to Reunification," unpublished manuscript in author's possession.

6. Steinbruner, *Cybernetic Theory of Decision*, 257.

7. Memorandum of Conversation with Seymour Weiss, Office of Political Military Affairs, Department of State, May 29, 1963, Neustadt/20/Government Consulting Skybolt/Atlantic Affairs. Atlantic Assignment, 1963/JFKL.

8. A. J. P. Taylor, *The Course of German History: A Survey of the Development of Germany since 1815* (New York: Capricorn Books, 1962), 68.

9. For Bowie's report see "The North Atlantic Nations: Tasks for the 1960's," August 1960, EUR/DAS/Schaetzel/3/North Atlantic/NARA. See also "Document 3: Bowie report (extracts)," Marc Trachtenberg, UCLA, http://www.sscnet.ucla.edu/polisci/faculty/trachtenberg/documents/bowie.html and "Memorandum of Conference with the President, August 16, 1960," August 19, 1960, WHO/OSS/State/4/State Department—1960 (August–September) (1)/DDEL. For Norstad's earlier plans for an MRBM force see NATOParis to External 196, January 27, 1961, RG25/50219-AL-2-40 (1.2)/LAC; NATOParis to External 196, January 27, 1961, RG25/50219-AL-2-40 (1.2)/LAC; London No. 3075 to SecState, December 11, 1959, DNSA/NP00604. The purpose of Norstad's plan was widely understood and remembered as a plan to prevent de Gaulle "from doing something foolish" rather than as a military or strategic plan. Acheson to Stikker, December 27, 1960, AP/Gen. Corr./29/375. On the Paris for New York trade see "Memorandum of Conversation," *FRUS:1961–1963*:XIV, d30.

10. Numbered Letter 171 to USSEA from NATODel, "NATO Nuclear Policy—Land-Based MRBM System," January 31, 1961, RG25/50219-AL-2-40 (1.2)/LAC.

11. NATO Paris to External 1054, April 26, 1962, RG25/50219-AL-2-40 (2.2)/LAC.

12. On the general mood see "Memorandum of Conversation with Seymour Weiss. Office of Political Military Affairs, Department of State," May 29, 1963.

13. "Address before the Canadian Parliament," American Presidency Project, UCSB, http://www.presidency.ucsb.edu/ws/?pid=8136.

14. "Visit of Chancellor Adenauer—Some Psychological Factors," Memorandum for the President from Kissinger, April 6, 1961, POF/Germany: Security: Adenauer meeting: General, April 1961/JFKLDC. On the prevalence of psychological allusions in this era see Frank Costigliola, "The Nuclear Family: Tropes of Gender and Pathology in the Western Alliance," *Diplomatic History* 21, no. 2 (Spring 1997): 163–83.

15. Kissinger to Schlesinger, October 3, 1961, Schlesinger/WH-13/Kissinger, Henry 4/19/61–12/2/61/JFKL.

16. Memorandum for McGeorge Bundy from Fred Holborn, October 13, 1961, NSF/74A/Germany/JFKL.

17. "Memorandum of Meeting—5:00–5:30 PM, March 15, 1962," March 16, 1962, NSF/Kaysen/375/NATO—Subjects: Nuclear Deployment/JFKL. For Kennedy's acknowledgment of the dangers of a nuclear Germany see "US-French Divergencies: Berlin, the Nuclear Question and NATO," Memorandum of Conversation, February 28, 1962, NSF/71/France-General/JFKL.

18. "France and Nuclear Weapons: Answer to Eight Questions," Bohlen/26/Ball, George, 1963–1966 correspondence/NARA. For the president's questions see Memorandum for the President from Bundy, June 17, 1962, Neustadt/20/NATO Nuclear Weapons/AID, 2 of 2/JFKL.

19. "Answers to Eight Questions re European Nuclear Matters," Memorandum for the President from McNamara, June 16, 1962, Neustadt/20/NATO Nuclear Weapons/AID, 2 of 2/JFKL. On the power of allied opposition see Draft [of DoD response to eight questions], June 2, 1962, DDRS/CK3100116250.

20. "Some interim conclusions about the responses to the President's eight questions," June 17, 1962, NSF/226/NATO, Weapons, Cables, France, Eight Questions, May 25, 1962, [June 17, 1962]/JFKL.

21. "Defence Policy Statement on Saturday, 5 May [1962] by Secretary McNamara at the NATO Ministerial Meeting in Athens," available in National Security Archive Electronic Briefing Book no. 236, ed. William Burr, http://nsarchive.gwu.edu/nukevault/ebb236/.

22. Paris POLTO 21 to SecState, July 5, 1962, NSF/222/NATO, General, Cables/JFKL. See also "Subject: Initial Reactions to the American Paper on MRBMs," Memorandum for the File, June 18, 1962, NP/113/US REP. NATO (1)/DDEL; "Subject: European Unity: Memorandum of a conversation between the Secretary General and Ambassador Finletter on 30th June, 1962," July 2, 1962, NP/110/SECRETARY GENERAL-NATO (2)/DDEL. The American Embassy in Bonn disagreed with his assumption of a "rapidly emerging West German objective to have atomic weapons in one form or another": Bonn No. 57 to SecState, July 7, 1962, NSF/222/NATO, General, Cables/JFKL. For Kennedy's instructions to Finletter see Department of State TOPOL 1922 to Paris, June 14, 1962, Neustadt/19/Government Consulting—Skybolt/NATO/Atlantic Affairs—NATO Research, 1961/2, 2 of 3/JFKL. On the issue of military necessity Stikker pointed out that the heads of government communiqué of 1957, MC-70, and the requirements in PO(60)437 of April 11, 1960, and MC26/4 all said otherwise. NATO Paris to External 1495, June 21, 1962, RG25/50219-AL-2-40 (5.1)/LAC. For the cost and requirement of Europeans to bear the bulk of it see NATO Paris to External 1439, June 15, 1962, RG25/50219-AL-2-40 (5.1)/LAC.

23. London to External 2313, June 27, 1962, RG25/50219-AL-2-40 (5.1)/LAC. See also London to External 2250, June 22, 1962, RG25/50219-AL-2-40 (5.1)/LAC. For Rusk's pretrip fears see SecSTate 4770 to Paris, May 5, 1961, NSF/70A/France-General/JFKL. On the joint study see Airgram A-322 from London to SecState, June 28, 1962, NSF/226A/NATO, Weapons, Cables, Germany, FRG-French Nuclear Cooperation/JFKL.

24. Bonn no. 3165 to SecState, June 24, 1962, NSF/226A/Franco-German cooperation/JFKL; "Possible Joint French-German Arrangements in Nuclear Weapons field,"

February 26, 1963, POF/Germany: Security, 1963: January–March/JFKLDC; Paris no. 6066 to SecState, June 18, 1962, NSF/226A/Franco-German cooperation/JFKL.

25. Bonn SECTO 48 to SecState, August 8, 1961, *FRUS:1961–1963*:XV, d172. On balance, the evidence available suggests Dulles never made such a pledge: see Trachtenberg, *Constructed Peace*, 341–42; Heuser, "The European Dream of Franz Josef Strauss," 97, "German Nuclear Developments and rebus sic stantibus," July 6, 1962, NSF/226A/NATO Weapons Cables Germany 3/61-9/63/JFKL.

26. Draft [of DoD response to eight questions], June 2, 1962. Relevance to unification negotiations was confirmed by Muller-Roschach, who told Rostow that Schroeder was pro-MLF, because "perhaps above all—it is an essential bargaining card to interest the Russians in German unity, since Schroeder is prepared to surrender a German nuclear role in the context of a German unity negotiation." "Conversations with Germans at APAG Meeting," October 19, 1965, NSF/Subject/24/LBJL. Carstens, even in 1965, considered the pledge "a card" Bonn did "not want to throw away" without improved nuclear arrangements or progress toward reunification." Quoted in Hood to Shuckburgh, July 15, 1965, FO 115/4629. See also the quotes of German officials that connect reunification with a nuclear renunciation in "German Views on Nuclear Sharing—Background Memorandum," undated, EUR/RPM/NATO Affairs/8/Germany II/NARA. For Strauss's comments to Rusk see "Meeting between the Secretary and the German Foreign Minister," Memorandum of Conversation, November 22, 1961, NSF/75/Germany General 2/62/JFKL.

27. London SECTO 60 to SecState, June 25, 1962, POF/State, 1962: June–July/JFKLDC.

28. London SECTO 81 to SecState, June 26, 1962, POF/State, 1962: June–July/JFKLDC.

29. Department of State TOPOL 128 to Paris, July 19, 1962, NSF/222A/NATO, General, Cables/JFKL.

30. Washington DC to External 3351, November 12, 1962, RG25/50219-AL-2-40 (5.2)/LAC. On the bargain see NATO Paris to External 2628, November 12, 1962, RG25/50219-AL-2-40 (5.2)/LAC. See also Philip Nash, *The Other Missiles of October: Eisenhower, Kennedy, and the Jupiters, 1957–1963* (Chapel Hill: University of North Carolina Press, 1997).

31. "A Word on Nassau," Memorandum to the President from W. W. Rostow, December 17, 1963, POF/United Kingdom: Security, 1962: October–December/JFKLDC. See also "A Nassau Track," December 15, 1962, attached to "A Word on Nassau," December 17, 1962. For American policy on the British deterrent see "NATO and the Atlantic Nations," April 20, 1961, *FRUS:1961–1963*:XIII, d100.

32. "Statement on Nuclear Defense Systems," December 21, 1962, in *American Foreign Policy: Current Documents, 1962* (Washington, DC: Government Printing Office, 1966), 635–37; *MD:PM*, 547–48.

33. On lack of planning see "Nassau Follow-Up," Record of Meeting, December 28, 1962, EUR/DAS/Schaetzel/2/Post-Nassau (Miscellaneous Papers)/NARA; "Next Steps," Memorandum of Conversation, January 18, 1963, NSF/171/United Kingdom General/JFKL. Nassau represented the "lack of coherence and clarity" in Kennedy's policy toward NATO. Kaplan, Landa, and Drea, *McNamara Ascendancy, 1961–1965*, 384. On American hopes for French purchases see "Ambassador Bohlen's initial Exchange with French Officials," Draft Memorandum for the Secretary, December 29, 1962, EUR/DAS/Schzetzel/1/France, 1962–1965/NARA. For de Gaulle's refusal and attacks see "Ambassador Bohlen's initial Exchange with French Officials," December 29, 1962, and Paris no. 2804 to SecState, January 15, 1963, NSF/212/Europe-General/JFKL.

34. See also Finletter's remarks quoted in NATO Paris to External 58, January 9, 1963, RG25/50219-AL-2-40 (6.1)/LAC.

35. Eugene Rostow to Gilpatric, January 15, 1963, EUR/DAS/Schazetzel/1/France, 1962–1965/NARA. For German worries regarding command and control requirements

see Bonn to External 19, January 7, 1963, RG25/50219-AL-2-40 (6.1)/LAC. Regarding withdrawal of tactical weapons see NATO Paris to External 58, January 9, 1963, RG25/50219-AL-2-40 (6.1)/LAC. On McNamara's use of Nassau against the Germans see "Nassau Follow-Up," Record of Meeting, December 28, 1962, EUR/DAS/Schaetzel/2/Post-Nassau (Miscellaneous Papers)/NARA.

36. For British and American disputes over the meaning of Nassau and the effects on Germany see "Conversation with Lord Louis Mountbatten—May 20, 1963," May 31, 1963. "Conversation with Michael Cary, Deputy Cabinet Secretary (I am not absolutely sure about the title) [sic] at lunch—May 20, 1963," May 31, 1963, POF/Schlesinger, Arthur M., 1963, May–June/JFKLDC. For disagreements between the US and UK over the meaning of MLF see Memorandum for the President from Bundy, January 12, 1963, POF/Bundy, McGeorge, 1963: January–June/JFKLDC; "Your Talk with the Earl Mountbatten," Memorandum for the President from Bundy, February 6, 1963, POF/United Kingdom: Security, 1963: January–April/JFKLDC; Paris POLTO 1448 to SecState, May 6, 1963, POF/United Kingdom: Security, 1963: May–June/JFKLDC; "Presentation of U.K. attitude to mixed-manned nuclear force," A. R. Moore, July 1, 1963, FO 953/2112. On implications for Anglo-French relations see "Your Conversation with David Ormsby Gore this afternoon," May 15, 1963, POF/United Kingdom: Security, 1963: May–June/JFKLDC.

37. "The Mess in Europe and the Meaning of Your Trip," Memorandum to the President from Ball, June 20, 1963, Bohlen/26/Ball, George, 1963–1966, correspondence/NARA.

38. "General Discussions of NATO Matters," March 27, 1962, EUR/RPM/NATO Affairs/2/NATO 7 Gen. Taylor—Mar 1962/NARA.

39. "Congressional Consultation about MLF," Rostow to the Secretary, December 5, 1963, Ball/26/Misc. Multilateral Force—1963/NARA.

40. "Congressional Consultation about MLF."

41. "The Mess in Europe and the Meaning of Your Trip," June 20, 1963.

42. "The Mess in Europe and the Meaning of Your Trip"; see also "German Rearmament in the Inter-War Period," by A. France, June 12, 1963, Bohlen/26/Ball, George, 1963–1966 correspondence/NARA.

43. "Congressional Consultation about MLF," Rostow to the Secretary, December 5, 1963, Schlesinger/WH-41/Multilateral Force, 1963/JFKL.

44. "A Further Nuclear Offer to General de Gaulle?," memorandum to the President from Ball, August 8, 1963, NSF/226A/NATO, Weapons, Cables, France/JFKL.

45. Memorandum of Conversation, Jean Monnet and Gerard C. Smith, December 18, 1959, PPC/Subjects/151/Europe 1958/NARA. See also Memorandum of Conversation, Monnet and Smith, December 16, 1960, PPC/Subjects/152/Europe Aug.–Dec. 1960/NARA; Memorandum for the Record, December 15, 1961, NSF/220A/NATO-General/JFKL; Finletter to Ball, April 26, 1963, Ball/26/Misc. Multilateral Force—1963/NARA.

46. "Notes on possibility of a German Withdrawal from NATO, pw—S-S-61, INR/REU," undated, NSF/220A/NATO-General/JFKL.

47. "The Crisis of Confidence in West Germany," INR Research Memorandum REU-21, January 3, 1962, NSF/74A/Germany/JFKL.

48. Monnet, for example, was worried about Ruhr industrialists who were "still very interested in Soviet and Chinese orders, the potential magnitude of which they are grossly exaggerating." Memorandum of Conversation, Monnet and Smith, December 16, 1960.

49. "The Crisis of Confidence in West Germany," January 3, 1962.

50. "West German Views Concerning Nuclear Weapons and MLF," Memorandum from William K. Hitchcock to Henry Owen, April 13, 1963, EUR/RPM/NATO Affairs/8/Germany I/NARA

51. "Europe in the '60's," by Cline, May 25, 1963, NSF/214/Europe-General/JFKL. See also "Merchant Memorandum on the MLF," memorandum for Bundy from Schlesinger, Schlesinger/WH-41/Multilateral Force, 1963/JFKL; Bohlen to Ball, August 2, 1963. Bohlen/26/Ball, George, 1963–1966 correspondence/NARA.

52. "The Coming Crisis of the MLF," by Alistair Buchan, June 23, 1964, NSF/Subject/23/LBJL.

53. "Meeting with Chancellor Adenauer—May 17, 1963," May 30, 1963, POF/Schlesinger, Arthur M., 1963: May–June/JFKLDC.

54. "Merchant Memorandum on the MLF," memorandum for Bundy from Schlesinger, Schlesinger/WH-41/Multilateral Force, 1963/JFKL.

55. Hillenbrand to Klein, November 25, 1964, DDRS/CK3100139304.

56. "Memorandum of Conversation with Ambassador Cattani in Rome, January 16, 1963," January 21, 1963, DDRS/CK3100054276.

57. "Schroeder, the German Reunification Proposal, etc." from Klein to Bundy, April 23, 1964, NSF/CF/183/LBJL; "The Right Wing in German Politics," September 29, 1964, NSF/CF/183/LBJL; December 9, 1964. RLG's [Gilpatric's] Notes on 12/9/64 Discussion with Messrs. Dean and McCloy on Problems of Europe and NATO," December 9, 1964, NSF/Committee File, Committee on Nuclear Proliferation/1/LBJL. See also Kissinger to Acheson, December 31, 1964, AP/Gen. Corr./18/226.

58. Memorandum from the Under Secretary of State (Ball) to Secretary of State Rusk, November 17, 1964, *FRUS:1964–1968*:XIII, d49.

59. London SECUN2 to SecState, December 1, 1964, NSF/ITMF/32/LBJL.

60. "Considerations Involving Germany and France Which are Pertinent to Modification of the US Position on MLF," by David Mark, November 4, 1964, NSF/Subject/23/LBJL.

61. Kissinger to Bundy, November 27, 1964/LBJL, NSF/Files of McGeorge Bundy/15/LBJL.

62. "First Thoughts on De-Fusing MLF (if need be)," memorandum for Bundy, November 7, 1964, NSF/CF/206/LBJL.

63. If the vote were held in late 1964, warned an NSC staffer, a "curious collection of liberals, Joint Committee atom-guarders, and neo-isolationists would probably beat the MLF today if there were a totally free, silent, secret vote in the Senate." "NATO Nuclear Policy, memorandum to the President from Bundy, November 8, 1964, *FRUS:1964–1968*:XIII, d46.

64. Memorandum from Bundy to Ball, November 25, 1964, *FRUS:1964–1968*:XIII, d52. For the commentators' criticism see "MLF—An Alternative View," memorandum to the President from Bundy, December 6, 1964, *FRUS:1964–1968*:XIII, d57.

65. "The Wilson Visit and MLF," memorandum of conversation, December 6, 1964, DDRS/CK3100076994.

66. "Memorandum of Conversations with Secretary of Defense, 20 November 1964," November 21, 1964, NSF/CF/206/LBJL.

67. "First Thoughts on De-Fusing MLF (if need be)," November 7, 1964. See also "Note to Mr. Bundy and Mr. Klein" from Neustadt, NSF/CF/206/LBJL.

68. "MLF—An Alternative View," memorandum to the President from Bundy, December 6, 1964, *FRUS:1964–1968*:XIII, d57.

69. Bundy had been urging this since November. "NATO Nuclear Policy," November 8, 1964.

70. "Next Steps on NATO Nuclear Policy and ANF," memorandum for Bundy, December 17, 1964, NSF/AF/35/NATO General, vol. 2/LBJL.

71. Steinbruner, *Cybernetic Theory of Decision*, 309.

72. Bonn 2651 to SecState, January 16, 1965, NSF/Files of McGeorge Bundy/16/LBJL. For Schroeder and McGhee's views see Bonn 2558 to SecState, January 11, 1965, NSF/CF/184/LBJL. For interpretation of the NSAM see Berlin 36 to SecState, July 12, 1965, NSF/CF/182/LBJL.

73. "Atlantic Nuclear Questions: A Point to be made to Foreign Secretary Stewart," Rostow to the Secretary, October 8, 1965, Bator/29/LBJL; see also Berlin 36 to SecState, July 12, 1965.

74. "Meeting with Minister Heinrich Krone—New York, March 25, 1965," Kissinger to Bundy, March 30, 1965, NSF/Files of McGeorge Bundy/15/LBJL. See also the still partially sanitized intelligence report, "West Germans Views on Nuclear Sharing," December 10, 1965, Bator/29/MLF/ANF (Multilateral Force/Atlantic Force)/LBJL. For tensions with France see Bonn 2651 to SecState, January 16, 1965, NSF/Files of McGeorge Bundy/16/LBJL.

75. "Erhard and De Gaulle at Rambouillet," from Klein to Bundy, NSF/CF/184/LBJL. See also "A Possible George Ball MLF Speech," memorandum for the President from Bundy, February 2, 1965, NSF/Subject/23/LBJL.

76. "The Case for a Strong American Lead to Establish a Collective Nuclear System that would Help Save the Western World from Repeating an Old Mistake," undated, NSF/AF/39/LBJL.

77. December 9, 1965, "The Case Against Offering the Germans Ownership in Nuclear Hardware," December 9, 1965, Bator/29/LBJL; see also attached document: "A Proposal for Nuclear Consultation," October 27, 1965; George W. Ball Oral History/LBJL, 13; "Interview with Mr. McGeorge Bundy on 20th January, 1970," Nunnerley Papers/1/Transcripts—Ball-Douglas-Home/JFKL.

78. Bonn 4985 to SecState, June 23, 1965, NSF/CF/185/Germany, vol. 8, 4/65–7/65," LBJL. See also Andrew Priest, "From Hardware to Software: The End of the MLF and the Rise of the Nuclear Planning Group," in *Transforming NATO in the Cold War: Challenges beyond Deterrence in the 1960s*, ed. Andreas Wenger, Christian Nuenlist, and Anna Locher (London: Routledge, 2007).

79. NATO resumed discussion of a nuclear committee after McNamara's suggestion. See "Resumption of Discussion of Nuclear Questions," Secretary General to Permanent Representatives, PO(65)360, June 29, 1965, and "Nuclear Problems," Secretary General to Permanent Representatives, PO(65)411, July 21, 1965, both in NATO.

80. Text of a Paris POLTO 832 to State, "Primary Objective Special Committee of Defense Ministers," November 21, 1965, NSF/AF/39/NATO, Special Committee of Defense Ministers in Paris (Sec. McNamara)/LBJL.

81. Paris POLTO Circular 18 to SecState, November 27, 1965, NSF/AF/39/NATO, Special Committee of Defense Ministers in Paris (Sec. McNamara)/LBJL.

82. "Initial Statement of the SecDef," November 20, 1965, NSF/AF/39/NATO, Special Committee of Defense Ministers in Paris (Sec. McNamara)/LBJL.

83. Draft State-Defense Message to Cleveland, November 15, 1965, NSF/AF/39/NATO, Special Committee of Defense Ministers in Paris (Sec. McNamara)/LBJL.

84. "Various Nuclear Matters," October 11, 1965, RG59, EUR/DAS/Schaetzel/1/Britain," NARA; "German Veto on Nuclear Weapons Use on Their Soil by US or Other Troops," December 13, 1965, Bator/29/MLF/ANF (Multilateral Force/Atlantic Force)/LBJL.

85. Memorandum for the President from McNamara, July 27, 1966, NSF/CF/186/LBJL.

86. "France and NATO," October 8, 1965, *FRUS:1964–1968*:XIII, d106.

87. "Meeting with the President, 1:15 p.m., Thursday, June 23. Talking Points," June 23, 1966, Bator/28/LBJL.

88. Bator to Bill Moyers, April 12, 1966, Bator/28/LBJL.

89. Record of Meeting with President Johnson, December 17, 1966, *FRUS:1964–1968*:XIII, d106, 231.

90. "Interview—Mr. Robert McNamara. Thursday February 27th, 1970," Nunnerley Papers/1/Transcripts—John—Norstad/JFKL.

91. Ivo Daalder's account of NATO's post-1968 nuclear strategy begins where this account leaves off. Ivo H. Daalder, *The Nature and Practice of Flexible Response: NATO Strategy and Theater Nuclear Forces since 1967* (New York: Columbia University Press, 1991).

92. "West Germans Views on Nuclear Sharing," December 10, 1965, Bator/29/MLF/ANF (Multilateral Force/Atlantic Force)/LBJL.

93. "German Attitudes on Nuclear Defense Questions," October 20, 1965, EUR/RPM/NATO Affairs/6/Defense Affairs NATO 1963–1965, DEF 12 Nuclear Germany/NARA.

94. Memorandum for the Secretary of Defense drafted by Col. Hoover and Mr. Barber, April 5, 1966, Bator/28/LBJL.

95. "Schaetzel-McGhee Exchange on MLF," attached to Memorandum for the Secretary of Defense drafted by Col. Hoover and Mr. Barber, April 5, 1966. See also McGhee's comments in George McGhee Oral History/LBJL, 14–15.

96. "Plans for December NATO Ministerial Meeting and Related Matters," November 16, 1966, CFPF, 1964–1966/3271/NATO 3 Meeting Sessions, 1/1/66/NARA.

97. Memorandum for the Secretary of Defense drafted by Col. Hoover and Mr. Barber, April 5, 1966.

98. "Western Europe looks at Germany," INR Memo REU-30, August 6, 1965, DDRS/CK3100383557.

6. THE NEW TRIPARTITISM

1. EmbParis to External 511, March 9, 1966, RG24/S-2-5100-7F(1)/LAC. See also Paris 4867 to SecState, February 11, 1966, DDRS/CK3100312987; Paris 5900 to SecState, March 16, 1966, DDRS/CK3100075379; Telegram from the Embassy in France to the Department of State, February 25, 1966, *FRUS:1964–1968*:XII, d54.

2. Dean to Hood, November 16, 1966, FO 1042/156. Intriguingly, after de Gaulle had launched an attack on the idea of an Anglo-American continental commitment in 1948, the American correspondent Joseph Alsop had warned de Gaulle's closest advisers that if de Gaulle were to return to power and continue talking like this, "the United States would abandon France and center its policy on building up Germany." Joseph W. Alsop to Dean Acheson, January 9, [1949], AP/Gen. Corr./1/8.

3. Jean Monnet to Acheson, November 23, 1962, AP/Gen. Corr./23/288.

4. Dean to Gore-Booth, July 8, 1966, FO 371/190723.

5. Paris177 to FO, July 17, 1963, FO 371/173435.

6. Bohlen to Bundy, March 2, 1963, NSF/Bundy/16/LBJL.

7. Frédéric Bozo, *Two Strategies for Europe: De Gaulle, the United States, and the Atlantic Alliance* (Lanham, MD: Rowman & Littlefield, 2001), 143–53; Garret Martin, "Towards a New Concert of Europe: De Gaulle's Vision of a Post-Cold War Europe," in *Visions of the End of the Cold War in Europe, 1945–1990*, ed. Frédéric Bozo et al. (New York: Berghahn Books, 2012), 94–97. Martin also sees de Gaulle's "clear agenda to overcome the Cold War." Another excellent account is Marie-Pierre Rey, "De Gaulle, French Diplomacy, and Franco-Soviet Relations as Seen from Moscow," in *Globalizing de Gaulle: International Perspectives on French Foreign Policies, 1958–1969*, ed. Anna Locher, Garret Martin, and Christian Nünlist (Lanham, MD: Rowman & Littlefield, 2010).

8. Tyler to Bohlen, September 18, 1964, DDRS/CK3100020950. See also Paris751 to FO, November 23, 1963, FO 371/173437; Paris758 to FO, November 25, 1963, FO 371/173437; Butler to Barnes, December 10, 1963, FO 371/173437.

9. "Note on Franco-American Relations" [undated; enclosure to Airgram No. 1 from Paris, 1–1920], Yarmolinsky/Subject/32/France-NATO, 1963–1967/JFKL.

10. Paris888 to FO, December 3, 1964. This British cable is in NSF/CF/160/LBJL.

11. Record of a Meeting at the Chateau de Champs at 10:30 a.m. on Sunday, June 3, 1962, PREM 11/3775. This was not mere posturing—see "for Records" [handwritten notes by the Prime Minister], June 7, 1962, PREM 11/3775. Dictated note, December 27, 1962, PREM 11/4230; Harold Macmillan to Foreign Secretary, May 16, 1962, PREM 11/3775.

12. "Notes of Points Made in Discussion at Chequers on May 19, 1962," May 19, 1962, PREM 11/3775.

13. "Transcript of telephone conversation between President Kennedy and Prime Minister Macmillan," January 19, 1963, POF/United Kingdom: Transcripts of Kennedy-Macmillan phone calls, 1963/JFKLDC.

14. February 4, 1963. "A Positive Policy after Brussels," February 4, 1963, Philip de Zulueta, PREM 11/4220.

15. Note to the PM, March 1, 1963, PREM 11/4220. See also the attached telegram FO 2167 to Washington, February 27, 1963.

16. "Notes for use at Meeting of Ambassadors in London Monday March 11, 1963," March 10, 1963, FO 146/4619.

17. "Future Policy in Europe," from Lord Privy Seal, Annex A to Note to the PM, March 1, 1963, PREM 11/4220.

18. "Britain and Europe," CIA Special Report, June 11, 1965, DDRS/CK3100365333.

19. UKDel236 to FO, June 26, 1963, FO 371/173435.

20. Shuckburgh to Barnes, July 29, 1965, FO 371/184424; Paris 1496 to SecState, NSF/AF/37/NATO Messages, vol. 1/LBJL.

21. C. B. E. Burt-Andrews to Air Marshal J. H. Lapsley, November 25, 1964; Burt-Andrews to Lapsley, December 10, 1964, both in FO 371/179064.

22. On the de Gaulle-Eisenhower correspondence see "Views of President Charles de Gaulle Regarding the United States, Europe and NATO; and Italian Reaction," memorandum for the Director of Central Intelligence, March 10, 1964, NSF/CF/169/LBJL; "Response to General de Gaulle's Memorandum of September 17, 1958," Tyler to the Under Secretary, February 3, 1964, NSF/CF/169/LBJL; Paris 5263 to SecState, May 6, 1964, NSF/CF/169/LBJL; SecState 337 to Paris, June 20, 1964, NSF/CF/170/LBJL.

23. Harold Wilson, *The Labour Government, 1964–1970: A Personal Record* (London: Weidenfeld & Nicolson, 1971), 244. See also "Withdrawal of French Naval Forces from NATO," E. J. W. Barnes, June 18, 1963, FO 371/173435.

24. "France and NATO," minute by Barnes, February 17, 1964, FO 371/179064.

25. London 5571 to SecState, May 18, 1965, NSF/CF/207/LBJL. For more warnings see Circular Telegram from the Department of State to the Posts in the NATO Capitals, June 10, 1965, *FRUS:1964–1968*:XIII, d89. See also Paris POLTO 1701 to SecState, May 25, 1965, NSF/CF/171/LBJL; "France and NATO," May 13, 1965, EUR/DAS/Schaetzel/1/Britain/NARA.

26. "The EEC and the NATO Crises," Tuthill to Bator, October 19, 1965, DDRS/CK3100489563. See also Telegram from the Mission to NATO and European Regional Organizations to the Department of State, November 16, 1965, *FRUS:1964–1968*:XIII, d110; Telegram from the Department of State to the Mission to the European Communities, November 24, 1965, *FRUS:1964–1968*:XIII, d112; Telegram from the Department of State to the Embassy in Belgium, January 29, 1966, *FRUS:1964–1968*:XIII, d127.

27. Barclay to Hood, June 25, 1965, FO 115/4628; "U.S. NATO Ambassadors' Conference in The Hague," memorandum for the record, October 27, 1965, NSF/AF/35/NATO General, vol. 2/LBJL.

28. Shuckburgh to Hood, June 18, 1965, FO 115/4628.

29. "Sir E. Shuckburgh's Report on Conversation about U.K. and Future of NATO," D. V. Bendall, June 25, 1965, FO 115/4628. See also Hood to Shuckburgh, June 22, 1965, FO 115/4628.

30. Patrick Dean to Harold Caccia, April 24, 1965, FO 115/4628. Note that this is a repetition of Rusk's earlier comments in Minute by M. N. F. Stewart, April 23, 1965, FO 115/4628.

31. Reilly to Sir Paul Gore-Booth, May 8, 1965 FO 115/4628.

32. Minute by J. B. S. Pedler, May 24, 1965, FO 146/4625.

33. "France and NATO," June 5, 1965, NSF/CF/208/LBJL. Johnson's NSC staff agreed with the British position. "France and NATO," Klein to Bundy, June 10, 1965, NSF/Name File/4/LBJL.

34. "France and NATO, by Hood, June 22, 1965, FO 115/4628; Minute by P. E. Ramsbotham, July 9, 1965, FO 146/4625; Memorandum of Conversation, June 16, 1965, *FRUS:1964–1968*:XIII, d90.

35. "France and NATO," draft NSAM September 25, 1965, DDRS/CK3100313726; "U.S. Policy on the Problem of France and NATO," Memorandum for Bundy from Ball, October 4, 1965, DDRS/CK3100277964; "France and NATO," Memorandum of Conversation, October 8, 1965, 11 a.m., *FRUS:1964–1968*:XIII, d106. The Bureau of Intelligence and Research supported Bundy's argument. See "De Gaulle's 'Attack' on the Atlantic Alliance," REU 41.1, September 30, 1965, DDRS/CK3100422958.

36. Dusseldorf DEPT 14 to SecState, July 23, 1964, NSF/CF/184/Germany/LBJL.

37. "France and NATO," October 8, 1965; "Ferguson Report," Klein to Bundy, July 8, 1965, NSF/CF/163/LBJL.

38. "France and NATO," October 8, 1965.

39. Letter from President de Gaulle to President Johnson, March 7, 1966, *FRUS:1964–1968*:XIII, d137.

40. Telegram Paris to SecState 5382, March 2, 1966, DDRS/CK3100491992.

41. "NATO Session," March 17, 1966, NSF/Komer/1/LBJL; Telegram from Bohlen to the Secretary of State, March 3, 1966, *FRUS:1964–1968*:XIII, d56; Bonn to SecState 2925, March 21, 1966, DDRS/CK3100068055; "France-NATO," March 6, 1966, DDRS/CK3100046869; "NATO and France," Department of State Policy Planning Council, May 6, 1964, DDRS/CK3100009269.

42. Memorandum from the President's Deputy Special Assistant for National Security Affairs (Bator) to President Johnson, March 7, 1966, *FRUS:1964–1968*:XIII, d138. See also Memorandum from the President's Acting Special Assistant for National Security Affairs (Komer) to President Johnson, March 16, 1966, 6:30 p.m., *FRUS:1964–1968*:XIII, d143.

43. Paris to SecState 5048, March 20, 1966, DDRS/CK3100161246.

44. Memorandum for the President (from Bator), "Your letter to DeGaulle," March 18, 1966, 9 a.m., DDRS/CK3100023835.

45. Memorandum of Conversation, August 21, 1966, *FRUS:1964–1968*:XIII, d196.

46. For different perspectives see Schaetzel to Acheson, December 11, 1967, and Schaetzel to Acheson, May 22, 1967, both in AP/Gen. Corr./28/357; Paris to SecState 6078, March 21, 1966, DDRS/CK3100486192; Thomas Alan Schwartz, *Lyndon Johnson and Europe: In the Shadow of Vietnam* (Cambridge, MA: Harvard University Press, 2003), 110.

47. Cabinet Conclusions, CC(66)17, March 10, 1966, CAB 128/41.

48. "The International Consequences of General de Gaulle's Policy," attached to Letter no. 59 from the Secretary of State to Evelyn Shuckburgh, April 13, 1966, FO 146/4632. See also Cabinet Conclusions, CC(66)17, March 10, 1966, CAB 128/41; "France and NATO," note to the PM, March 11, 1966, PREM 13/1043.

49. "France and NATO," Healey to the PM, March 23, 1966, PREM 13/1043.

50. "France and NATO," note to the PM, April 4, 1966, PREM 13/1043.

51. Memorandum by Schaetzel, sent to Acheson, "Closer European Collaboration as one Objective of the France/NATO Crisis," April 11, 1966, EUR/DAS/Schaetzel/3/Acheson/NARA.

52. "France-NATO," Bruce to the Secretary of State, March 8, 1966, Bator/27/LBJL; London to SecState 4437, March 19, 1966, DDRS/CK3100075523; Paris to SecState 6407, March 10, 1966, DDRS/CK3100070888; Paris to SecState 6078, March 21, 1966; "The Political Atmosphere," NATO/G-3, scope paper, December 7, 1966, *FRUS:1964–1968*:XIII, d223.

53. "1966–67 SHAPE Finds a New Home," 2017, Supreme Headquarters Allied Powers Europe, https://www.shape.nato.int/page1463252.

54. London to SecState 4437, March 19, 1966, DDRS/CK3100075523.

55. "The NATO Crisis in its Political Setting," CIA Intelligence Memorandum, April 2, 1966, NSF/CF/178/LBJL.

56. "Britain and Europe," CIA Special Report, June 11, 1965, DDRS/CK3100365333. On Wilson's change of direction see Miriam Camps, *European Unification in the Sixties: From Veto to the Crisis* (New York: McGraw-Hill, for the Council on Foreign Relations, 1966), 141–42, 57–61; Helen Parr, "Anglo-French Relations, Détente and Britain's Second Application for Membership of the EEC, 1964 to 1967," in *European Integration and the Cold War: Ostpolitik-Westpolitik, 1965–1973*, ed. N. Piers Ludlow (London: Routledge, 2007), 82.

57. "Britain and Europe and the NATO Crisis," May 31, 1966, PREM 13/1044.

58. Note for the Record, May 6, 1966, PREM 13/1044. Belgian desires for Britain to take the lead in NATO reported in London 5028 to SecState, April 26, 1966, NSF/177/France-NATO Dispute, vol. 2, 3/66–4/66, LBJL.

59. Minute by State Secretary Carstens, January 27, 1966, *AAPD*:1966:1, 100, 102.

60. Paris 5412 to SecState, March 2, 1966, DDRS/CK3100160894.

61. Paris 5541 to SecState, March 7, 1966, DDRS/CK3100068008.

62. "Military Consequences of a Forced French Withdrawal from Germany," from Wolf Lehman, April 5, 1966, RG59/EUR/GER/FRG/1/De Gaulle and NATO—Pol. 3–1966. Factual/NARA.

63. "Problem Created by NATO Crisis in Regard to Status of French Forces in Germany," INR memorandum REU-30, April 6, 1966, DDRS/CK3100050741.

64. Washington DC to External 997, April 1, 1966, RG24/S-2-5100-7F(1)/LAC.

65. Bonn to External 277, March 22, 1966, RG24/S-2-5100-7F(1)/LAC.; Bonn447 to FO, April 7, 1966, PREM 13/1043.

66. Bonn 2726 to SecState, March 7, 1966, DDRS/CK3100075346.

67. Bonn 2726 to SecState, March 7, 1966; see also Bonn420 to FO, April 4, 1966, PREM 13/1043.

68. Bonn434 to FO, April 6, 1966, PREM 13/1043.

69. Bonn 3120 to SecState, April 4, 1966, DDRS/CK3100068067.

70. Washington1528 to FO, May 14, 1966, FO 371/190716.

71. See Sten Rynning, *Changing Military Doctrine: Presidents and Military Power in the Fifth Republic* (Westport, CT: Praeger, 2002), 54–55.

72. The process was described later in Washington DC to External 1729, May 10, 1967, S-2-5102-2(1), RG24/LAC.

73. Robert Schaetzel of the Department of State quoted in Washington DC to External 1111, April 14, 1966, S-2-5100-7F(1), RG24/LAC. See also Roberts to Hood, November 26, 1966, FO 1042/156.

74. On the crisis see Gregory F. Treverton, *The Dollar Drain and American Forces in Germany: Managing the Political Economics of Alliance* (Athens: Ohio University Press, 1978); Wightman, "Money and Security: Financing American Troops in Germany and the Trilateral Negotiations of 1966–67," *Rivista Di Storia Economica* 5, no. 1 (February 1988): 26–77; Hubert Zimmermann, *Money and Security: Troops, Monetary Policy and West Germany's Relations with the United States and Britain, 1950–1971* (Washington, DC: German Historical Institute and Cambridge University Press, 2002), 209–38; Schwartz, *Lyndon Johnson and Europe*, 115–32, 43–59; Helga Haftendorn, *NATO and the Nuclear Revolution: A Crisis of Credibility, 1966–1967* (Oxford: Clarendon, 1996), 203; Gavin puts the crisis in larger perspective of American financial and economic policy. Francis J. Gavin, *Gold, Dollars, and Power: The Politics of International Monetary Relations, 1958–1971* (Chapel Hill: University of North Carolina Press, 2004).

75. Haftendorn, *NATO and the Nuclear Revolution*, 203.

76. American officials had, even before the French withdrawal, believed that tripartite—that is US-UK-FRG—coordination and agreement was necessary for NATO's survival. See "The EEC and the NATO Crises," Tuthill to Francis Bator, October 19, 1965, DDRS/CK3100489563; "Atlantic Policy After the German Election," June 25, 1965, NSF/AF/52/LBJL. For consequences of failure to reach such an agreement see "S/P Consultants' Discussion of Atlantic Affairs," undated, NSF/CF/163/LBJL.

77. Handwritten notes re: UK Defense Review, January 27, 1966, Bator/25/Europe, LBJL; see also London 2886 to SecState, December 21, 1965, NSF/CF/209/UK7/LBJL.

78. "The United Kingdom Defence Review: Aide Memoire by Her Majesty's Government," undated, Bator/24/US-UK Defense Review 1/27/66/Letter to PM/LBJL.

79. Bator to the President, July 18, 1966, Bator/17/LBJL.

80. "The Economic Situation," Memorandum to Cabinet, July 18, 1966, and Memorandum for the President from McNamara, NSF/CF/209/LBJL.

81. Memorandum from the Assistant Secretary of State for Congressional Relations (MacArthur) to Secretary of State Rusk, September 1, 1966, *FRUS:1964–1968*:XIII, d199; "The Mansfield Resolution," memorandum for Mr. Rostow, January 26, 1967, NSF/Name File/6/LBJL; Cleveland to Rostow, February 8, 1967, DDRS/CK3100083689; Phil Williams, *The Senate and US Troops in Europe* (London: Macmillan, 1985), 139–48. See Johnson's worry of a "showdown in this country" in Summary Notes of the 569th Meeting of the National Security Council, May 3, 1967, 12:30 p.m., *FRUS:1964–1968*:XIII, d251.

82. "McNamara–von Hassel Conversation No. 2 in Paris, 26 July 1966," Bator/20/Offset (US/UK/FRG)/LBJL.

83. Memorandum for the President from McNamara, July 27, 1966, Bator/20/Offset (US/UK/FRG)/LBJL.

84. "Full Reply to Chancellor Erhard's Last Letter," memorandum for the President from Bator, August 4, 1966, Bator/17/ Meeting with President on Birth of Trilaterals 8/24/66 Reply to Erhard 7/5 Letter to PM/LBJL; Telegram from the Department of State to the Embassy in Germany, September 8, 1966, *FRUS:1964–1968*:XIII, d203. Treverton, *Dollar Drain*, 171.

85. "Lunch Conversation with German Minister Georg von Lilienfeld," August 4, 1966, NSF/CF/186/LBJL.

86. "Further Reply to Erhard Letter of July 5: Two Major Decisions," August 12, 1966, Bator/20/Offset (US/UK/FRG)/LBJL.

87. "Further Reply to Erhard Letter of July 5: Two Major Decisions," August 12, 1966.

88. Quotes from "Elements of a Proposal to Prevent BAOR Drawdowns in Germany and Europe," August 18, 1966, Bator/17/LBJL. See also "British Plans for Military Cutbacks in Europe," August 17, 1966, NSF/CF/210/LBJL.

89. "The Choices in Europe," memorandum by E. Hamilton, August 19, 1966, Bator/20//Offset (US-UK-FRG)/LBJL.

90. "Last Minute Information for your European Policy Meeting at 6:30 this Afternoon," August 24, 1966, Bator/17/ Meeting with President on Birth of Trilaterals 8/24/66 Reply to Erhard 7/5 Letter to PM/LBJL.

91. "The Choices in Europe," August 19, 1966; "Last Minute Information for your European Policy Meeting at 6:30 this Afternoon," August 24, 1966, Bator/17/LBJL; "UK Financial Problem with BAOR. Action Memorandum," Leddy to the Secretary, August 23, 1966, DDRS/CK3100521078.

92. Bonn 2368 to SecState, NSF/CF/186/LBJL.

93. Johnson to Wilson, [August 26, 1966], *FRUS:1964–1968*:XIII, d198.

94. Sir John Hackett, the commanding officer of the BAOR, and Frank Roberts, worried that if the Germans commanded the northern front, the Germans might, "for some nationalistic reason or in support of German reunification, create a NATO-Bloc confrontation which might not otherwise arise": Bonn 2423 to SecState, August 27, 1966, Bator/20/Offset (US/UK/FRG)/LBJL.

95. "Memorandum for the Record," by Walt Rostow, September 29, 1966, NSF/CF/210/LBJL.

96. For "clock" see Department of State 44741 to London, Bonn, and Paris, September 10, 1966, NSF/CF/210/LBJL. On the prime minister's needs see "Memorandum for the Record," by Walt Rostow, September 29, 1966, NSF/CF/210/LBJL. For cabinet views see Cabinet Conclusions, CC(66)44, September 1, 1966, CAB 128/41/44. For German worries and Erhard's reaction to the idea of talks see Bator to the President, September 8, 1966, Bator/20/Offset (US/UK/FRG)/LBJL and "Copy of LONDON 1924, Sept. 7, 1966," September 7, 1966, NSF/CF/210/LBJL; Bonn 2951 to SecState, September 9, 1966, Bator/17/ Meeting with President on Birth of Trilaterals 8/24/66 Reply to Erhard 7/5 Letter to PM/LBJL; Bator to the President, September 9, 1966, Bator/20/Offset (US/UK/FRG)/LBJL.

97. "Erhard Visit: Offset and troop levels," Memorandum for the President from Leddy, September 19, 1966, Bator/20/Offset(US/UK/FRG), LBJL; see also Rostow to the President, September 2, 1966, buck slip on undated letter from Birrenbach to Kissinger sent August–September 1966, NSF/CF/187/LBJL.

98. For the American intelligence on Erhard's position see [title and author sanitized], September 16, 1966, NSF/CF/187/LBJL.

99. Bonn 3361 to SecState, September 19, 1966, Bator/20/ Offset (US/UK/FRG)/LBJL.

100. On efforts to prop up Erhard see "Johnson-Erhard Meeting: Presidential Visit to Europe," Leddy to the Secretary, September 12, 1966, Bator/21/Erhard Visit, September 1966/LBJL; "Erhard Visit: Offset and troop levels," September 19, 1966; "Erhard Visit. Scope Paper," from Wyle, September 20, 1966, Bator/21/Erhard Visit, September 1966/LBJL. On Johnson's refusal to budge and McNamara's line see "Your 10:00 AM Meeting on the Erhard Visit," memorandum for the President from Bator, September 21, 1966–9:30 p.m., Bator/21/Erhard, September 1966/LBJL. See also "Action to Forestall Precipitate British Action on Forces in Europe," Leddy to the Secretary, September 25, 1966, Bator/20/Offset (US/UK/FRG)/LBJL.

101. Circular Telegram 5292 to all NATO Capitals from the Department of State, October 4, 1966, DDRS/CK3100190666.

102. Message from President Johnson to Prime Minister Wilson, undated [sent October 1, 1966], *FRUS:1964–1968*:XIII, d208.

103. Walt Rostow to Rainer Barzel, October 16, 1966, Bator/17/LBJL.

104. NATOParis to External 2133, October 6, 1966, S-2-5102-2(1)/LAC.

105. "Tripartite Talks; NATO; French Troops in Germany," October 12, 1966, RG59/EUR/GER/FRG/1/Negotiations with the French, 1966. POL 3/NARA; NATOParis to External 2344, October 24, 1966, RG24/S-2-5102-2(1)/LAC; Schwartz, *Lyndon Johnson and Europe*, 145. See also Dirk Stikker to Jack McCloy, October 11, 1966, AP/Gen. Corr./29/375.

106. "Trilateral Talks; NATO," October 14, 1966, DDRS/CK3100002203; "Foreign Exchange Cost of British Forces in Germany," from Gore-Booth to the Earl of Longford, February 1, 1967, FCO 41/117; NATO Paris to External 2133, October 6, 1966, B.N.W. to Dr. Arnold, undated, NATOParis to External 2172, October 11, 1966, and NATOParis to External 2211, October 14, 1966, all in RG24/S-2-5102-2(1)/LAC.

107. On the implications of McCloy's appointment see Schwartz, *Lyndon Johnson and Europe*, 144. For efforts to move against him see George Thomson to Sir Patrick Dean, February 1, 1967, FCO 41/117; Eugene Rostow Oral History/LBJL, 29.

108. Memorandum from Llewellyn E. Thompson to McCloy, October 24, 1966, RG59/EUR/RPM/Trilateral/1/Assessment Sov. Threat to We. Europe by Ambassador Thompson. EVMcAullife—1966/NARA.

109. "Conference with General Wheeler at State Department—October 25, 1966," October 25, 1966, RG59/EUR/RPM/Trilateral/1/Conversation Bet. Gen. Wheeler & Mr. McCloy. 10/25/66/NARA.

110. "Trilateral Talks. (US-UK-FRG), McCloy Memo 6," October 18, 1966, DDRS/CK3100192838; "Trilateral Talks," memorandum for the Secretaries of State, Treasury, and Defense, the Director Central Intelligence, and Walt Rostow, October 27, 1966, Bator/17/Trilateral Talks, Oct.–Dec. 1966/LBJL. For the outline of issues and fundamental questions McCloy wished to discuss see "Issues for Tripartite Talks," October 19, 1966, RG59/EUR/RPM/Trilateral/1/Issues, 1966/NARA. Morton Halperin prepared the American answers to these questions for McCloy. See "Answers to Questions Posed by United States in Trilateral Talks," October 24, 1966, Bator/17/Trilateral Talks, Oct.–Dec. 1966/LBJL.

111. "Telegram from the Mission to NATO and European Regional Organizations to the Department of State," October 22, 1966, *FRUS:1964–1968*:XIII, d213. See also Schwartz, *Lyndon Johnson and Europe*, 145.

112. Carstens to Erhard, October 21, 1966, *AAPD*:1966:2, 1427.

113. Department of State 83122 to London, Bonn, Paris, November 10, 1966, DDRS/CK3100521713; Minute by Carstens, November 14, 1966, *AAPD*:1966:2, 1516.

114. CAP 66982 [Rostow to the President], November 13, 1966, Bator/19/LBJL; Minute by Carstens, November 14, 1966, *AAPD*:1966:2, 1516; "Statement made by State Secretary CARSTENS on foreign exchange offset problem (unofficial text)," November 9, 1966, Bator/17/LBJL.

115. "Draft Memorandum to the President from Mr. McCloy, with the support of the Secretaries of State, Treasury and Defense," November 9, 1966, Bator/19/LBJL.

116. CAP 66982, November 13, 1966.

117. Circular from Reute, December 5, 1966, *AAPD*:1966:2, 1583; Minute by Ambassador Schnippenötter, January 4, 1967, *AAPD*, 1967:1, 23.

118. CAP 66982, November 13, 1966; "Guidance for Tripartite Meeting on November 25, 1966," undated, late November 1966, Bator/17/Trilateral Talks, Oct.–Dec. 1966/LBJL. See also Circular from Reute, December 5, 1966.

119. Record of a meeting between Kiesinger and McCloy, December 16, 1966, *AAPD*:1966:2, 1650.

120. "Memorandum of meeting with Strauss, the German Finance Minister, December 17, 1966 from 9:00 a.m. to 1:00 p.m. in Dusseldorf," by McCloy, December 22, 1966, DDRS/CK3100470070.

121. "Memorandum of meeting with Strauss, the German Finance Minister, December 17, 1966 from 9:00 a.m. to 1:00 p.m. in Dusseldorf," December 22, 1966; Bonn 9959 to SecState, February 25, 1967, NSF/CF/188/LBJL; "Chancellor Kiesinger's Remarks on American Policy," [source sanitized], April 21, 1967, NSF/CF/199/LBJL; Walt Rostow to the President, April 25, 1967, DDRS/ CK3100117579.

122. On the row in the British Cabinet over the extension see London 5885 to SecState, January 24, 1967, NSF/CF/210/LBJL. On Roberts efforts in Germany to forestall a German cabinet decision see "Tripartite Talks and Offset," Barnes to Hood, January 25, 1967, FCO 41/117; see also London 5885 to SecState, January 24, 1967.

123. "Notes for Meeting with Secretary of State for Defence: Implications of the Withdrawal of British Troops from the Continent," undated [late January, 1966], FCO 41/117; "Tripartite Talks and Offset," Barnes to Hood, January 25, 1967, FCO 41/117.

124. "U.S. Position in Trilateral Negotiations and Instructions to McCloy," memorandum for the President from Rostow and Bator, November 22, 1966, at 5:30 p.m., Bator/17/Trilateral Talks, Oct.–Dec. 1966/LBJL.

125. "Redeployment of Certain US Forces from Europe," Draft Presidential Memorandum from McNamara to the President, January 19, 1967, DDRS/CK3100096939.

126. "Military Redeployments from Europe," memorandum for the Secretary of Defense, February 2, 1967, DDRS/CK3100725075; "Conclusions and Recommendation," a section of McCloy report to Johnson of November 21, 1966, DDRS/CK3100211986; "Draft B" [of memorandum for the president by Eugene Rostow], October 24, 1966, Bator/17/LBJL; "Force Levels in Europe," memorandum for the President, February 23, 1967, DDRS/CK3100212022.

127. "Redeployment of Certain US Forces from Europe," Draft Presidential Memorandum from McNamara to the President, January 19, 1967.

128. "Political Effects of NATO Troop Reductions," part of McCloy's submission to Johnson of November 21, 1966, DDRS/CK3100212003.

129. "U.S. Position in the Trilateral Negotiations," memorandum for the President from Bator, February 23, 1967. DDRS/CK3100480725.

130. "U.S. Position in the Trilateral Negotiations," February 23, 1967.

131. "Results of the Meeting with the President of Feb. 24, 1967" [Bator's undated notes of the meeting], DDRS/CK3100233106.

132. "Talking Points—Force Levels in Europe," February 27, 1967, DDRS/CK3100054480.

133. Memorandum for the record, March 2, 1967, Bator/18//Trilaterals—McCloy Meeting with the President, March 1, 1967/LBJL.

134. Memorandum for the record, March 2, 1967.

135. For Wilson's position see Michael [unclear] to R. E. Parsons, March 3, 1967, FCO 41/119; CAP 67104 [Rostow to the President], March 5, 1967, NSF/CF/210/LBJL; Roberts to Gore-Booth, March 6, 1967, FCO 41/120. For Kiesinger's see "Telegram from the President's Special Assistant for National Security Affairs (Rostow) to President Johnson, in Texas," March 6, 1967, *FRUS:1964–1968*:XIII, d239.

136. Roberts to Gore-Booth, March 6, 1967.

137. "Tripartite Talks," to PUS from Thomson, March 9, 1967, FCO 41/120.

138. Washington650 to FO, March 2, 1967, FCO 41/119; Washington687 to FO, March 6, 1967, FCO 41/119.

139. Washington667 to FO, March 4, 1967, FCO 41/119; Washington687 to FO, March 6, 1967.

140. "U.S. Monetary Ideas," Barnes to Sir P. Gore-Booth, March 8, 1967, FCO 41/120; Washington687 to FO, March 6, 1967.

141. Washington650 to FO, March 2, 1967.

142. "U.S. Monetary Talks," March 7, 1967. For British worries about the plan see Washington667 to FO, March 4, 1967; "U.S. Monetary Ideas," Barnes to Sir P. Gore-Booth, March 8, 1967, FCO 41/120; "International Economic Arrangements: U.S. (Rostow) Proposals," March 15, 1967, FCO 41/121.

143. "Your 12:45 p.m. Meeting with John McCloy on the trilaterals," memorandum for the President, March 8, 1967, Bator/18/LBJL. See also Zimmermann, *Money and Security*, 220; Wightman, "Money and Security," 54.

144. "Meeting with President, March 9, on Trilaterals," Leddy to the Secretary, March 8, 1967, Bator/18/LBJL.

145. "Your 12:45 p.m. Meeting with John McCloy on the trilaterals," March 8, 1967.

146. "Record of President's March 9 Meeting with Messrs. Rusk, McNamara, Fowler, McCloy, Walt Rostow, and Bator," March 9, 1967, DDRS/CK3100233128. For the records of a March 13 trilateral meeting where McCloy urged finding a solution to the short-term problem see "Record of a Meeting between Mr. George Thomson, M.P., Mr. McCloy and Herr Duckwitz at the Foreign Office at 6 p.m. on 13 March, 1967," undated, FCO 41/121; Gore-Booth to Roberts, March 8, 1967, FCO 41/120.

147. McCloy to Johnson, March 22, 1967, Bator/18/Trilateral, April 15–May 15, 1967/ LBJL; Department of State 161070 to Bonn, London, and Paris, March 23, 1967, NSF/ CF/187/LBJL.

148. "Final Report on Trilateral Talks," undated [April–May 1967], *FRUS:1964–1968*:XIII, d249.

149. Ultimately, the French eviction of NATO forces and this agreed minute led to a major overhaul and reorganization of American forces in Europe, REDCOSTE and REFORGER/CRESTED CAP.

150. Reported by the Canadian delegation in Washington DC to External 1648, May 3, 1967, S-2-5102-2(1)/LAC.

151. "Trilaterals—Status Report," memorandum for the President, March 17, 1967, 3:30 p.m., DDRS/CK3100550713.

152. On secrecy and leaks see Hood to Burrows, March 6, 1967, FCO 41/119; Washington DC to External 1310, April 6, 1967; External to Washington DC DL920 (repeated to London), April 6, 1967, and NATOParis to External 1310, April 6, 1967, all in S-2-5102-2(1)/LAC. For allied frustrations see NATOParis to External 1004, April 28, 1967, S-2-5102-2(1)/LAC; Paris 15055 to SecState, March 29, 1967, NSF/CF/173/LBJL.

7. AN ALLIANCE FOR PEACE

1. Brussels 1087 to SecState, March 10, 1966, DDRS/CK3100068041.

2 Adam Yarmolinsky to Francis Bator, June 21, 1966, Bator/28/NSAM 345—Part II, June 1966/LBJL.

3. "Acheson on the January Debacle," February 2, 1963, NSF/212A/ Europe, General 2/1/63-2/6/63/JFKL.

4. On the Harmel Report see Helga Haftendorn, "The Harmel Report and Its Impact on German Ostpolitik," in *The Making of Détente: Eastern and Western Europe in the Cold War, 1965–75*, ed. Wilfrid Loth and Georges-Henri Soutou (New York: Routledge, 2008); Haftendorn, *NATO and the Nuclear Revolution*; Andreas Wenger, "Crisis and Opportunity: NATO's Transformation and the Multilateralization of Détente, 1966–1968," *Journal of Cold War Studies* 6, no. 1 (Winter 2004): 22–74. The lead-up to the Harmel Report is recounted in Anna Locher, Crisis? What Crisis?: NATO, De Gaulle, and the Future of the Alliance, 1963–1966, (Baden-Baden: Nomos, 2010).

5. George F. Kennan, Russia, the Atom, and the West (London: Oxford University Press, 1958), 88; George F. Kennan, "Disengagement Revisited," *Foreign Affairs* 37, no. 2 (January 1959): 187–210.

6. "A New Look at Our European Policy," April 22, 1959, RG59/PPC/Subject Files/151/Europe 1959/NARA.

7. "De Gaulle: Where Do We Stand Now?," memorandum for the President from Schlesinger, January 30, 1963, Schlesinger/WH-34/France, General 9/61–10/63/JFKL.

8. "A New NATO Policy (the 'McCone Plan')," Memorandum for McCone from Cline, March 21, 1963, and "An Alternative US Policy Toward NATO," undated, both in NSF/221/NATO, General 7/62–11/63/JFKL.

9. On the 1950s see "Problems of East-West Trade," June 29, 1962, AC/127-D/71, NATO. For "phenomenal" see Garthoff, *Détente and Confrontation*, 140.

10. "Problems of East-West Trade," June 29, 1962; "Problems of East-West Trade. Note by the Chairman," February 22, 1961, AC/127-WP/70, NATO; "Meeting of Experts on East-West Trade. Note by the Chairman," October 2, 1961, AC/127-D/81, NATO. On export controls in this period see Michael Mastanduno, *Economic Containment: CoCom and the Politics of East-West Trade* (Ithaca, NY: Cornell University Press, 1992).

11. "Problems of East-West Trade. Note by the Chairman," February 22, 1961.

12. "The Application of Western Economic Strength to the East-West Conflict," Note by the United States Delegation, October 10, 1962, AC/214(A)-WP/6, NATO.

13. "Western Economic power in relation to the East-West Conflict," Note by the United Kingdom Delegation, October 9, 1962, AC/214(A)WP/5, NATO.

14. "Use of Western Economic Strength in the East-West Conflict," Note by the German Delegation, October 16, 1962, AC/214(A)WP/10, NATO.

15. "Meeting of National Officials on NATO Countries' Trade Policies Towards the European Satellite Countries," June 8, 1964, AC/127-D(160)Draft, NATO.

16. "Summary record of a meeting of the Council, held at Permanent Headquarters, Paris, XVIᵉ, on Wednesday, 11th November, 1964, at 4.15 p.m.," November 18, 1964, CR(64)49, NATO.

17. "Suggestions Arising out of N.A.T.O. Report on East/West Relations," B. L. Crowe to Mr. Rhodes, January 31, 1967, FCO 41/19; see also Rhodes minute of February 6 and Wilde minute of February 20 on this document.

18. "East-West Relations," Secretary General to the Permanent Representatives, February 1, 1965, PO/65/56, NATO.

19. "France and NATO," note to the PM, March 11, 1966, PREM 13/1043. Wilson annotated the note: "I very much agree with all this."

20. "France and Nato," PM to the Foreign Secretary, PM's Personal Minute No. M11/66, March 15, 1966, PREM 13/1043.

21. Brussels 1087 to SecState, March 10, 1966.

22. "France and Nato," March 15, 1966.

23. "France and NATO, (OPD(66)44)," Burke Trend to PM, PREM 13/1043. See also Brussels 1087 to SecState, March 10, 1966.

24. Cleveland to Acheson, June 24, 1966, RG59/EUR/DAS/Schaetzel/3/Acheson/NARA.

25. "Constructive Action: Part II: Eastern Europe and the Soviet Union," undated, RG59/EUR/DAS/Schaetzel/3/Acheson/NARA.

26. "NATO and German Reunification," Draft Memo from Leddy to Acheson, April 21, 1966, RG59/EUR/FRG Records/1/De Gaulle and NATO—Pol. 3–1966 New Structure for NATO/NARA.

27. Brussels 1087 to SecState, March 10, 1966.

28. Cleveland to Acheson, June 24, 1966, RG59/EUR/DAS/Schaetzel/3/Acheson/NARA.

29. "Memorandum: Atlantic Cohesion and East-West Relations," by Zbigniew Brzezinski, NSF/AF/53/State Department, Policy Planning, vol. 7/LBJL; "Meeting with the President, 1:15 p.m., Thursday, June 23. Talking Points," June 23, 1966, Bator/28/LBJL.

30. *Public Papers of the Presidents of the United States, Lyndon Johnson: Containing the Public Messages, Speeches and Statements of the President, November 22, 1963 to January 20, 1969*, vol. 3, bk. 2 (Washington, DC: Government Printing Office, 1967), 1126–27. For the background of the speech, including domestic political motives, see Thomas A. Schwartz, "Moving beyond the Cold War: The Johnson Administration, Bridge-Building, and Détente," in *Beyond the Cold War: Lyndon Johnson and the New Global Challenges of the 1960s*, ed. Francis J. Gavin and Mark Atwood Lawrence (Oxford: Oxford University Press, 2014), 86.

31. Telegram from Secretary of State Rusk to the Department of State, December 16, 1966, *FRUS:1964–1968*:XIII, d229.

32. "European Impressions," Edward W. Doherty to Owen, June 12, 1967, NSF/AF/53/LBJL. Haftendorn notes that the Harmel Report opened avenues for German *Ostpolitik*. Haftendorn, "The Harmel Report and Its Impact on German Ostpolitik." But clearly the emerging German policy made the efforts to discuss détente in NATO more pressing.

33. "East-West Relations in NATO," Memorandum to the Secretary from Cleveland, RG59/CFPF, 1964–1966/3271/NATO 3 Meeting Sessions, 1/1/66/NARA.

34. "Extract from C-R(66)71" of a meeting held on December 16, 1966, NATO/Harmel. See also "Future Tasks of the Alliance," by the UK delegation at NATO, April 8, 1967, FCO 41/211.

35. The Belgian proposal was "put forward basically in response to growing pressure of public opinion." Christian Chapman to the Secretary General, GAS/67/6, January 13, 1967, NATO/Harmel. See report of Belgian views in London 5028 to SecState, April 26, 1966, NSF/177/France-NATO Dispute/LBJL. See also "Harmel Exercise 1967," by Adam Watson, undated, FCO 41/215; Burrows to Barnes, January 12, 1967, FCO 41/210; Hague to External 74, February 7, 1967, RG24/S-2-5100-7-6(1)/LAC. It is incomplete to argue that the Harmel Exercise gave a voice to NATO's smaller powers, as per Locher, *Crisis? What Crisis?* and Kaplan, "U.S. and NATO in the Johnson Years," 135–36. Or that Johnson "moved the alliance" toward a policy of détente, as per Thomas Schwartz, *Lyndon Johnson and Europe*, 46. Johnson, according to Rusk, took little interest in the exercise. Dean Rusk, Oral History IV, LBJL, 14. Any American enthusiasm for the idea went only so far as Washington saw an opportunity to control détente and inform the allies of the risks of unmitigated exchange with the East. For others, like the British, there was hope that the study "might encourage some of the more reticent allies"—no doubt including the Americans—"that steps towards détente can be safely taken." UKDel650 to FO, December 4, 1966.

36. Brussels to External 144, February 3, 1967, RG24/S-2-5100-7-6(1)/LAC. There was very little enthusiasm for the Harmel Exercise. See FO1674 to Brussels, December 9, 1966, FO 1042/156. See also "The Future of the Alliance Study (The Harmel Study)," paper prepared by EUR, October 16, 1967, NSF/AF/60/LBJL. For more on British distaste for the idea see "Wise Men" Exercise, Extract of conversation between Leddy and Hood in Washington, undated, FO 1042/156; Tomkins to Hood, November 28, 1968, FO 1042/156. On British concerns about economic matters see UKDel650 to FO, December 4, 1966. On American refusal to discuss the German question see Washington3367 to FO, December 9, 1966, FO 1042/156. On American and German hesitancy to discuss military matters see "Belgian Proposal for Experts Study of Future of NATO ('Wisemen')," background paper for Brosio visit, November 14, 1966, DDRS/CK3100339744; "Future Tasks of the Alliance: Record of a meeting with the Special Group on Friday 17 March [1967]," March 20, 1967, FCO 41/210. The Dutch did not take the initiative seriously at first. Bonn1810 to FO, December 12, 1966, FO 1042/156; Carran to Hood, December 8, 1966, FO 1042/156. For allied depression about Belgian efforts see Burrows to Barnes, January 11, 1967, FCO 41/210.

37. "The Future of the Alliance Study (The Harmel Study)," October 16, 1967.

38. UKDel500 to FO, December 11, 1967, FCO 41/214.

39. UKDel23 Saving to FO, November 25, 1967, FCO 41/214.

40. "NATO Studies of European Security, the German Problem and Arms Control," Watson to Hood, November 14, 1967, FCO 41/214; see also Watson to Burrows, October 19, 1967, FCO 41/213.

41. "Record of a Conversation at a Luncheon Given by the United States' Minister, in the American Embassy, on Thursday, 14 September, 1967," September 15, 1967, FCO 41/212.

42. Telegram from the Mission to NATO and European Regional Organizations to the Department of State, December 17, 1966, *FRUS:1964–1968*:XIII, d232. Burrows made similar arguments to the Right Honourable George Brown, December 22, 1967, FCO 41/215.

43. "Mr. Eugene Rostow's Visit—Harmel Exercise," Watson to Hood, September 12, 1967, FCO 41/212; "Harmel Exercise 1967," undated.

44. Barnes to Millard, May 23, 1967, FCO 41/211. Similar arguments are made in "The NATO 'Harmel' Exercise," Memorandum for Mr. Rostow, October 2, 1967, DDRS/ CK3100133443; Record of Discussion at the 23d Meeting of the Senior Interdepartmental Group, October 19, 1967, *FRUS:1964–1968*:XIII, d271. The idea that NATO hindered, rather than helped, the relaxation of tensions was still strong years after Kennan had given his Reith lectures. See the first source in this note and Belgian views in London 5028 to SecState, April 26, 1966, NSF/177/France-NATO Dispute/LBJL.

45. NATOParis to External 434, February 22, 1967, RG24/S-2-5100-7-6(1)/LAC.

46. See "The NATO 'Harmel' Exercise," October 2, 1967, for a breakdown of the groups. For more on the groups and their subjects see Telegram from the Department of State to the Embassy in France, September 6, 1967, *FRUS:1964–1968*:XIII, d264.

47. For French reactions see "Harmel Exercise (Part 1 of 3)," memorandum of conversation, September 25, 1967, *FRUS:1964–1968*:XIII, d266. On the effect of de Gaulle's veto see NATOParis to External 1601, July 14, 1967, RG24/S-2-5100-7-6(1)/LAC. The less generous understanding of subgroup 2's purpose was another Belgian political need: to provide an "outlet for Monsieur Spaak's energies in this field." "Harmel Exercise 1967," undated.

48. "The Future of the Alliance Study (The Harmel Study)," October 16, 1967.

49. John Vernon to Director of Information, JV(67)314, June 22, 1967, NATO/ Harmel.

50. Letter from Deputy Under Secretary of State for Political Affairs (Kohler) to the British Assistant Under Secretary of State (Watson), July 13, 1967, *FRUS:1964–1968*:XIII, d260.

51. A. G. Kühn to A.S.G.(P.A.), January 9, 1967, RS/67/4, January 9, 1967, NATO/ Harmel.

52. "Future Tasks of the Alliance," by the UK delegation at NATO, April 8, 1967, FCO 41/211.

53. NATOParis to External, May 16, 1967, RG24/S-2-5100-7-6(1)/LAC.

54. "Address by the Honorable Eugene Rostow, Under Secretary for Political Affairs, before the American Chamber of Commerce. Brussels, Belgium, April 14, 1967," April 15, 1967, White House Aides, Bellinger/13/LBJL.

55. Christian Chapman to the Secretary General, January 13, 1967. See similar conclusions in "Record of Meeting in the Office of the Secretary General, 25th February 1967, at 10.30 a.m.," NATO/Harmel.

56. Schaetzel to Acheson, April 2, 1967, AP/Gen. Corr./28, folder 357.

57. Letter from Deputy Under Secretary of State for Political Affairs (Kohler) to the British Assistant Under Secretary of State (Watson), July 13, 1967.

58. "Harmel Exercise (next steps)," J. H. A. Watson, May 23, 1967, FCO 41/211.

59. "The Future Security Policy of the Alliance (Report of Subgroup 3)," by Kohler, October 6, 1967, NATO/Harmel.

60. See "Harmel Exercise (Part 1 of 3)," September 25, 1967, 4:30 p.m., *FRUS:1964–1968*:XIII, d266.

61. Watson to Barnes, May 15, 1967, FCO 41/211.

62. Burrows to Barnes, January 26, 1967, FCO 41/210.

63. A. Alacakaptan to ASG for Political Affairs, GAS/67/6, January 3, 1967, NATO/ Harmel. See also Memorandum from the Counselor of the Department of State (Bowie) to Secretary of State Rusk, October 16, 1967, *FRUS:1964–1968*:XIII, d270. For British views about changes in the Soviet Union see Memorandum of Conversation, "Harmel Exercise (Part 1 of 3)," September 25, 1967.

64. Tomkins to Hood, October 5, 1967, FCO 41/213. On plans for NATO and disarmament see "Harmel Exercise (Part 1 of 3)," September 25, 1967; NATOParis to External 2128, September 27, 1967, RG24/S-2-5100-7-6(2)/LAC.

65. NATOParis to External 1601, July 14, 1967, RG24/S-2-5100-7-6(1)/LAC; "The Future of NATO," Barnes to Hood, FCO 41/214.

66. "The NATO 'Harmel' Exercise," Memorandum for Mr. Rostow, October 2, 1967, DDRS/CK3100133443.

67. For "expendable" see Parsons to Millard, September 27, 1967, FCO 41/212. For de Gaulle and Couve de Murville's view see UKDel303 to FO, September 26, 1967, FCO 41/212. On the German worries see NATOParis to External 2219, October 6, 1967, RG24/S-2-5100-7-6(2)/LAC. For British worries about the Common Market see Burrows to Hood, September 21, 1967, FCO 41/212; Burrows to Hood, September 21, 1967, FCO 41/212.

68. Telegram from the Mission to NATO to the Department of State, November 23, 1967, *FRUS:1964–1968*:XIII, d277.

69. External DL3538 to NATO, November 21, 1967, RG24/S-2-5100-7-6(2)/LAC. For fears regarding Congress see Burrows to Hood, September 21, 1967, FCO 41/212.

70. External DL3767 to NATO, December 21, 1967, RG24/S-2-5100-7-6(2)/LAC.

71. Memorandum of conversation between Victor Kompletov, Counsellor of the Embassy of the USSR, and Richard N. Ullman, NSC Staff, December 4, 1967, NSF/Fried Files/2/LBJL.

72. Memorandum of Conversation, December 18, 1967, *FRUS:1964–1968*:XIII, d282.

73. "Crisis Management Aspects of the Invasion of Czechoslovakia," Report by the Council Operations and Exercise Co-ordinating Working Group, C-M(68)42, September 25, 1968, NATO.

74. "Crisis Management Aspects of the Invasion of Czechoslovakia," September 25, 1968; "NATO and Czechoslovakia," Barnes for D. Greenhill, September 10, 1968, FCO 41/444.

75. "A Military Analysis and Assessment of the Warsaw Pact Invasion of Czechoslovakia," DPC/D(68)30, September 26, 1968, and "Analysis of Recent Soviet Actions in Czechoslovakia from a Military Point of View," MCM-70–68(Revised), September 23, 1968, both in NATO.

76. "A Military Analysis and Assessment of the Warsaw Pact Invasion of Czechoslovakia," DPC(68)30, September 26, 1968, NATO.

77. Minute of the [Cabinet] Meeting, September 5, 1968, Cabinet Papers/14/LBJL.

78. Ginsburgh to Rostow, August 15, 1968, DDRS/CK3100510797. For the "flash" cable see Department of State 224681 to US Mission NATO, all NATO Capitals, US Mission Berlin, USUN, August 20, 1968, DDRS/CK3100155333.

79. UKDel56 Saving to FO, September 2, 1968, FCO 28/57.

80. "Material for Use in the SIG Meeting, October 4, Concerning Contingency Planning in Europe," Leddy to the Under Secretary, October 1, 1968, NSF/AF/59/LBJL.

81. These worries set off a flurry of rumors, reporting, and intelligence reports; for high-level discussions of these issues see the previous notes for this paragraph and "Talking Points on Czechoslovakian Situation for Use at Cabinet Meeting, Thursday, 22 August 1968," memorandum for the Secretary of Defense from Paul Warnke, August 21, 1968, DDRS/CK3100049733; UKDel56 Saving to FO, September 2, 1968, FCO 28/57; Minute of the [Cabinet] Meeting, September 5, 1968; "Will the Russians try to remove Ceausescu?," Smith to Maitland, September 6, 1968, FCO 28/57; FO7055 to Washington, October 2, (N) [1968], FCO 28/57; Rostow to Johnson with attached memorandum by Kramaemer, October 3, 1968, NSF/CF/189/LBJL; "Czechoslovakia," C. M. James (Paris) to C. S. R. Giffard, October 11, 1968, FCO 28/57; Telegram from the Department of State to the Mission to NATO, October 16, 1968, *FRUS:1964–1968*:XIII, d333; Cabinet Conclusions, November 22, 1968, CAB.

82. "Material for Use in the SIG Meeting, October 4, Concerning Contingency Planning in Europe," October 1, 1968.

83. Summary Record of Meeting of the Council, CR(68)50, October 11, 1968, NATO.

84. "Czechoslovakia," James to Giffard, October 11, 1968.

85. "Political implications of the Czechoslovakian Crisis," report by the Chairman of the political committee at senior level, CM(68)43, September 26, 1968, NATO.

86. "Czechoslovakia," James to Giffard, October 11, 1968. For NATO's assessment of Eastern European reactions to the Soviet invasion see "Political Assessment of the Implications of the Czechoslovak Crisis" [prepared by F. A Warner, UKDel], undated [September 1968], FCO 28/57.

87. "Czechoslovakia," James to Giffard, October 11, 1968. See also Telegram from the Embassy in France to the Department of State, September 2, 1968, *FRUS:1964–1968*:XII, d83.

88. "Talking Points on Czechoslovakian Situation for Use at Cabinet Meeting, Thursday, 22 August 1968," August 21, 1968.

89. "Political Assessment of the Implications of the Czechoslovak Crisis," undated [September 1968], FCO 28/57.

90. Bonn 2032 to SecState, August 27, 1968, DDRS/CK3100058049. See also Cable from Rostow to the President, September 2, 1968; "Further Comments on Possible NATO and EDC Initiatives," memorandum by Miriam Camps, September 3, 1968, DDRS/CK3100475152. On Kiesinger's plans for a NATO summit see Cable from Rostow to the President, CAP82344, September 2, 1968, DDRS/CK3100072901.

91. "Further Comments on Possible NATO and EDC Initiatives," memorandum by Miriam Camps, September 3, 1968, DDRS/CK3100475152.

92. Summary Notes of the 590th NSC Meeting, September 4, 1968, 5:00–7:25 p.m., DDRS/CK3100195752. On delayed reductions see London 12398 to SecState, September 5, 1968, NSF/CF/212/LBJL.

93. Summary Record of Meeting of Council, CR(68)50, October 1, 1968, NATO.

94. Bonn to SecState 17480, September 28, 1968, NSF/CF/189/LBJL.

95. John Leddy Oral History/LBJL, 8.

96. "American Attitudes towards NATO," Barnes for Lord Hood, November 8, 1968, FCO 41/444.

97. George Ignatieff, The Making of a Peacemonger: The Memoirs of George Ignatieff (Toronto: University of Toronto Press, 1985), 206.

98. Rostow to Johnson, July 24, 1968, DDRS.

99. "Further Comments on Possible NATO and EDC Initiatives," memorandum by Miriam Camps, September 3, 1968, DDRS/CK3100475152; Telegram from the Mission

to NATO to the Department of State, October 5, 1968, *FRUS:1964–1968*:XIII, d331; "Implications of Czechoslovakia for European Security," memorandum of conversation, September 10, 1968, DDRS/CK3100070868; Memorandum of Conversation between Birrenbach and Rusk, September 9, 1968, and "European Policy," memorandum of conversation, NSF/CF/189/LBJL.

100. Wilson, *Labour Government,* 554.

101. Quoted in "The Eurogroup in NATO," *Survival* 14, no. 6 (1976): 291.

102. "French Intention to Revive European Defense Community Concept during De Gaulle's September Visit to Bonn," CIA Intelligence Information Cable, September 13, 1968; see also Rostow to Johnson, September 14, 1968, NSF/CF/189/LBJL. For American views on British thinking about the EDC see "Intelligence Memorandum No. 2049/68," November 4, 1968, *FRUS:1964–1968*:XIII, d334.

103. "NATO and Czechoslovakia," Burrows to Stewart, Letter No. 39, December 16, 1968, FCO 41/450.

104. London 12398 to SecState, September 5, 1968.

8. BUSTING EUROPE

1. "Meeting between Sec. Laird and MOD Schmidt," May 24, 1971, Laird/C17/Documents 288–289/GFL.

2. Memorandum from Secretary of Defense Laird to President Nixon, November 9, 1971, *FRUS:1969–1976*:XLI, d74.

3. Cromer to the Prime Minister, April 23, 1973, PREM 15/1362.

4. "National Intelligence Estimate," December 4, 1969, *FRUS:1969–1976*:XLI, d27. Similarly, see Washington130 to FCO, December 28, 1971, FCO 82/71.

5. "United States: First Impressions: No Longer God's Own Country?," Cromer to Douglas-Home, July 21, 1971, FCO 82/55.

6. "NSSM-83: Key Issues of European Security" [draft], August 13, 1970, Laird/C15/Documents 177/GFL. On détente and political affiliation see Hans-Peter Schwarz, "Atlantic Security Policy in an Era without Greater Alternatives," in *America and Western Europe: Problems and Prospects*, ed. by Karl Kaiser and Hans-Peter Schwarz (Lexington, MA: Lexington Books, 1977), 192–93. On NATO as a forum for discussing détente see "US-Soviet Diplomacy on European Security," Sonnenfeldt to Kissinger, January 8, 1970, NSC/667/Europe—European Security Issues (U.S. and Soviet Diplomacy) Jan. 70 [February 1969–January 1970]/RNL. See also "Point Paper of the Secretary of Defense: Strategic Issues in NATO in the '70's," attached to "Talking Paper for the Secretary of Defense and the Chairman of the Joint Chiefs of Staff NSC Meeting 28 January 1970," Laird/Documents 88–89/C14/GFL.

7. "Record of conversation between the Foreign and Commonwealth Secretary and the Secretary-General of NATO at the Foreign and Commonwealth Office at 4 p.m. on Monday, 13 July, 1970," PREM 15/349. See also "Memorandum of Conversation [at the Foreign Office, London]," June 25, 1971, 10:15 a.m.–11:50 a.m., NSC/HAK/ 62/UK Memcons (originals)/RNL. For examples of nefarious Soviet offers see "US-Soviet Diplomacy on European Security," January 8, 1970.

8. General Brief: Strategic Arms Limitation Talks, July 31, 1969, FCO 7/1431. Note that Mutually Balanced Force Reduction (MBFR) talks had begun without a clear plan in mind. See "Record of a Conversation between the Foreign and Commonwealth Secretary and the United States Secretary of State at the State Department, Washington at 5.00 p.m., on Tuesday, 27 January [1970]," FCO 7/1823. Similarly, see British worries about "forfeit[ing] the support of the young" in "Talks with Dr Kissinger in Washington, 10 August 1972, CSCE, MBFR, SALT," Brimelow to Wiggin, August 14, 1972, FCO 82/193. See also Snyder, "The United States, Western Europe, and the Conference on Security

and Cooperation in Europe, 1972–1974," in Mattias Schulz and Thomas A. Schwartz, *The Strained Alliance: U.S.-European Relations from Nixon to Carter* (NY: Cambridge University Press, 2010), 258–59.

9. "Record of a Conversation between the Foreign and Commonwealth Secretary and Dr Henry Kissinger at the Foreign and Commonwealth Office at 4.00 pm on 14 September 1972," FCO 82/197.

10. Memorandum of Conversation [at the Foreign Office, London], June 25, 1971. See also Excerpt of Kissinger background briefing, attached to letter from Crowe to de Courcy Ireland, September 29, 1970, FCO 7/1809.

11. For "only possible" see "Egon Bahr on Ostpolitik," Brimelow to Drinkall, March 31, 1973, PREM 15/1579. For Bahr's conversation with Kissinger see Trachtenberg, *Cold War and After*, 173, 185n9.

12. "Visit by Willy Brandt's Emissary, Egon BAHR," Memorandum for the President from Kissinger, October 20, 1969, DNSA/KT00071. See also "Herr Brandt's Foreign Policies," November 25 1971, PREM 15/1572; "Ostpolitik and its Risks," December 22, 1970, PREM 15/1579; "Herr Brandt's 'Ostpolitik,'" February 1, 1971, PREM 15/1579.

13. "Visit by Willy Brandt's Emissary, Egon BAHR," October 20, 1969.

14. Memorandum of Conversation [at the Foreign Office, London]," June 25, 1971.

15. See "Ostpolitik and its risks," December 30, 1970. For more references to imperial and Nazi Germany see "Herr Brandt's Foreign Policies," November 25 1971, PREM 15/1572; Minutes of a National Security Council Meeting, January 28, 1970, *FRUS:1969–1976*:XLI, d29.

16. "Talking Paper for the Secretary of Defense and the Chairman, Joint Chiefs of Staff (NSC-NSSM 83 Meeting on 14 October 1970)," Laird/C15/Documents 177/GFL.

17. "Herr Brandt's Foreign Policies," November 25, 1971. Sir Alec had disclaimed his earldom in 1963 and was no longer Lord Home.

18. "Extract from Record of Meeting between PM + Pres. Nixon 17.12.70," PREM 15/1579.

19. For "a lot of crap" see "Notes on NSC Meeting 13 February 1969," DNSA/KT00003. Kissinger considers the implications of parity in Minutes of a National Security Council Meeting, October 14, 1970, *FRUS:1969–1976*:XLI, d49. For a good overview of strategic trends see "Foreign Policy Considerations, 1969–1975," by Charles E. Bohlen, undated [spring 1969], NSC/Name/808/Bohlen, Charles E. [June 1969–August 1971]/RNL.

20. Minutes of a National Security Council Meeting, October 14, 1970.

21. George Kennan, "Defense of the Free World," in *Decline of the West? George Kennan and His Critics*, ed. Martin F. Herz (Washington, DC: Ethics and Public Policy Center, Georgetown University, 1978), 28.

22. Pompidou's illustration in Henry Kissinger, *Years of Upheaval* (Boston, MA: Little, Brown, 1982), 167, and Georges-Henri Soutou, "Georges Pompidou and U.S.-European Relations," in Trachtenberg, *Between Empire and Alliance: America and Europe during the Cold War* (Lanham, MD: Rowman & Littlefield, 2003), 181.

23. Freeman to the Secretary of State, June 26, 1969, FCO 7/1427. For Kissinger's similar worries see Minutes of a National Security Council Meeting, October 14, 1970. See also "NSC Meeting on U.S. Strategies and Forces for NATO," memorandum for the President from Kissinger, undated [November 1970], NSC/Inst/H-029/NSC Meeting—NATO and MBFR 11/19/70/RNL.

24. Minutes of a National Security Council Meeting, November 19, 1970, 10 a.m., *FRUS:1969–1976*:XLI, d53.

25. The study considered chances for victory if the United States did not respond to a Soviet invasion with strategic nuclear attack. Minutes of National Security Council Review Group Meeting, June 16, 1970, *FRUS:1969–1976*:XLI, d42.

26. Minutes of a National Security Council Meeting, October 14, 1970.

27. Kissinger, *White House Years*, 393–95. For consideration of increasing costs and debates over allied defense spending see "Notes on NSC Meeting 13 February 1969," DNSA/KT00003; "NSC Meeting on U.S. Strategies and Forces for NATO," memorandum for the President from Kissinger, undated [November 1970], NSC/Inst/H-029/NSC Meeting—NATO and MBFR 11/19/70/RNL; Minutes of a National Security Council Meeting, October 14, 1970; "Issues for the January 16 DPC Ministerial Meeting," Memorandum for the Deputy Secretary of Defense, January 16, 1969, Laird/C13/Document 1/GFL; Kissinger, *White House Years* 79–80, 94; "US/FRG Meeting," October 23, 1968, Laird/C13/Documents 9–10/GFL. In the Nixon years, the European allies moderately increased their defense spending, but it went little appreciated by American officials. See Memorandum from the Assistant Secretary of Defense for Systems Analysis (Tucker) to Secretary of Defense Richardson, January 30, 1973, *FRUS:1969–1977*:XXXV, d2; Memorandum of Conversation, October 4, 1973, *FRUS:1969–1977*:XXXV, d25; Memorandum of Conversation, April 23, 1974, *FRUS:1969–1977*:XXXV, d37.

28. Minutes of a National Security Council Meeting, October 14, 1970. See also David Packard's comments in Minutes of a Combined Senior Review Group and Verification Panel Meeting, October 28, 1970, 10:35 a.m.–noon, *FRUS:1969–1976*:XLI, d51.

29. "Mutual and Balanced Force Reductions between NATO and the Warsaw Pact," August 26, 1970, NSC/Inst/H-047/SRG—US Strategies and Forces for NATO, 8/31/70/RNL.

30. Minutes of a National Security Council Meeting, November 19, 1970.

31. For Clifford's remarks see "US/FRG Meeting," October 23, 1968, Laird/C13/Documents 9–10/GFL. For evidence of Nixon's views see "President's Talking Points NSC Meeting on NATO November 19, 1970," NSC/Inst/H-029/NSC Meeting—NATO and MBFR 11/19/70/RNL.

32. "US Forces Committed to NATO," September 10, 1970, Laird/C15/Documents 165–168/GFL; "NATO with a Reduced American Presence," September 23, 1969, NSC/HAK/15/Planning Staff: Europe/RNL.

33. French worries recorded in Paris963 to FCO, October 23, 1969, FO1116/4; for German concern see "Visit by Willy Brandt's Emissary, Egon BAHR," October 20, 1969; British concerns in "NATO: Annual Review for 1968: Summary," January 2, 1969, FO1116/1. For "radicals" and "appeasers" see "Impressions on European Attitudes, May 1970," Memorandum for Mr. Kissinger from Helmut Sonnenfeldt, May 22, 1970, NSC/667/Europe General thru May 1970 [January 1969–May 1970]/RNL.

34. "Minutes of a Combined Senior Review Group and Verification Panel Meeting," October 28, 1970.

35. Washington2022 to FCO, July 6, 1970, FCO 7/1809.

36. "European Defence Improvement Programme," Carrington to the Prime Minister, November 8th, 1971, PREM 15/1370, NAUK.

37. Minutes of a Legislative Interdepartmental Group Meeting, May 13, 1971, *FRUS:1969–1976*:XLI, doc 62.

38. Memorandum for the Record, May 13, 1971, *FRUS:1969–1976*:XLI, d63.

39. Minutes of NSC Meeting on Defense Strategy, memorandum of conversation, August 13, 1971, DNSA/KT00332.

40. For "blue chip" see Minutes of a Legislative Interdepartmental Group Meeting, May 13, 1971; "SRG Meeting Issues at the NATO Ministerial Meeting: NSSM 121," May 10, 1971, NSC/Inst/H-057/SRG Meeting NSSM 121 NATO 5/14/71/RNL; "McGeo. Bundy/Kissinger," May 12, 1971, 11:30 a.m., DNSA/KA05605; "Geo. Ball/Kissinger," May 12, 1971, 10:20 am, DNSA/KA05602; "Katzenbach/Kissinger," May 12, 1971, 4:18 p.m., DNSA/KA05623; "Dean Acheson," May 12, 1971, 3:45 p.m., DNSA/KA05622.

On the connection to Mutually Balanced Force Reduction talks see "Memorandum from the Deputy Assistant to the President for Legislative Affairs (Korologos) for the President's Files," March 8, 1973, *FRUS:1969–1977*:XXXV, d7; "Conversation among President Nixon and Republican Congressional Leaders," March 20, 1973, *FRUS:1969–1977*:XXXV, d13.

41. Memorandum for the Record, May 13, 1971.

42. Senator Stennis, May 20, 1971, 8:17 a.m., DNSA/KA05737. See also "Senator Ribicoff, May 19, 1971, 6:58 pm," DNSA/KA05729. Nearly simultaneously, a similar debate was unfolding in the German Bundestag. "General Goodpaster/Mr. Kissinger," June 2, 1971, 3:20 p.m., DNSA/KA05843.

43. United States: Annual Review for 1969," January 20, 1970, FCO 7/1803; "Anglo/United States Relations," Brief by Foreign and Commonwealth Office, September 23, 1970, FCO 7/1810.

44. "Neo-Isolationism," letter from Cromer to Sir Alec Douglas-Home, July 15, 1972, FCO 82/54.

45. "Anglo/United States Relations," September 23, 1970.

46. McCluney to Simcock, July 27, 1971, FCO 82/54; "Isolationism in the US," Overton to Hankey, July 23, 1971, FCO 82/54.

47. For Nixon's rhetorical support for Europe see for instance "Your Meeting with Franco Maria Malfatti, President of the Commission of the European Communities (EC)—April 8 at 12 noon—12:45," April 7, 1971, NSC/322/European Common Market, vol. 2, 1971–1972/RNL. On worries over EEC enlargement see "The United Kingdom Application to Join the E.E.C.," September 22, 1969, FCO 7/1427; "U.S. Attitude on Britain's Membership of E.E.C.," December 16, 1969, FCO 7/1427; Washington to FCO3137, November 14, 1969, FCO 7/1427; Washington2022 to FCO, July 6, 1970.

48. "Initiation of Formal U.S. Consultations with the European Community," memorandum for the president from Kissinger, November 13, 1970, NSC/322/European Common Market, vol. 1, 1969–1970/RNL. For European perceptions of Connally's appointment see "The Making of American Foreign Policy," November 12, 1971, FCO 82/66; "US/European Relations," undated, FCO 82/64; "The United States and the EEC," October 15, 1971, PREM 15/261.

49. John B. Connally, remarks at the International Conference of the American Bankers Association, Munich, May 28, 1971, Department of State *Bulletin*, July 12, 1971, 42–46.

50. Vining to Hancock, August 5, 1971, FCO 82/55. On German opinions see unnumbered telegram to Bonn, undated [July 1971], FCO 82/57.

51. Overton to Hankey and Bottomley, November 11, 1971, FCO 82/57. See also Cromer to Tickell, October 21, 1971, PREM 15/261.

52. For Trend's suspicions see "SALT," May 7, 1971, PREM 15/289. Allied worries revolved around Soviet pressure to negotiate on Forward Based Systems (FBS). FBS lacked any clear definition but generally included the tactical aircraft the Americans had deployed in Europe or on aircraft carriers in the Mediterranean, but it did not include the thousands of smaller "tactical" nuclear weapons assigned to NATO forces. "SALT," Douglas-Home to PM, May 10, 1971; "Strategic Arms Limitation Talks (SALT)," Trend to PM, Ref. A09588, April 29, 1971, PREM 15/289. For debate in NATO see "Implications for Anglo-U.S. Relations of Britain's European Policies," FCO 7/1427; Heath's June 2 notes on UKDelNATO 208 to FCO, May 27, 1971, PREM 15/289.

53. "United States: Annual Review for 1971," Cromer to the Secretary of State for Foreign and Commonwealth Affairs, January 5, 1972, FCO 82/176.

54. For British frustration see Washington No. 3781 to FCO, November 12, 1971, FCO 82/65. Nixon, recognizing that this series of policies had alienated his NATO allies, held private meetings with Heath, Pompidou, and Brandt in December 1971. Regarding efforts

to prevent the further deterioration of relations see Cromer to Greenhill, October 29, 1971, FCO 82/64. For allied fears that the Americans would gain benefits from détente but prevent their allies from doing the same see "Interrelationship of Issues Between the US and W Europe," PREM 15/1540. For frustrations with the Nixon-Kissinger style of diplomacy see FCO No. 2879 to Washington2879, FCO 82/65; Overton to Hankey, January 26, 1972, FCO 82/176; "The Making of American Foreign Policy," November 12, 1971; 1972, FCO 82/184; Cromer to Greenhill, December 20, 1972, FCO 82/185; Cromer to Greenhill, May 11, 1973, FCO 82/268.

55. Cromer to Greenhill, February 25, 1972, FCO 82/179. See also Overton to Hankey, January 26, 1972; "United States: Annual Review for 1971," January 5, 1972.

56. "Triangular Politics: The White House, China and Russia," Cable to Overton, February 28, 1972, FCO 82/179; "Record of Discussions with Dr. Kissinger at Washington on 28th July, 1972," FCO 82/194; C. Gordon Bare, "Burden-Sharing in NATO: The Economics of Alliance," *Orbis* 20, no. 2 (Summer 1976): 426.

57. For "resolve" see Memorandum from Secretary of Defense Laird to President Nixon, November 9, 1971. Luns views in Telegram from Secretary of State Rogers to the Department of State, May 31, 1972, *FRUS:1969–1976*:XLI, d81; see also UKDelNATO2 savings to FCO, March 30, 1972, FCO 82/187. For reaction to US-USSR agreement see marginalia on "Discussions with Dr. Kissinger," Trend to the Prime Minister, Ref. A02332, August 4, 1972, PREM 15/1362. For European views on US intentions and the implications of MBFR see "MBFR," Memorandum for the President from the Secretary of Defense, October 19, 1971, Laird/C18/Documents 349–352/GFL. Pompidou's worries recorded in "The United States and the EEC," by C. C. C. Tickell, October 15, 1971, PREM 15/261.

58. "MBFR," November 1, 1972, Laird/C19/Documents 457–465/GFL.

59. "Bermuda Meeting Between the Prime Minister and President Nixon, 20–21 December 1971: Steering Brief—Third Draft," FCO 82/66; "Memorandum of Conversation," September 11, 1972, *FRUS:1969–1976*:III; d100.

60. Memorandum of Conversation, September 11, 1972. See also Information Memorandum from the Assistant Secretary of State for European Affairs (Hillenbrand) to Secretary of State Rogers, November 15, 1971, *FRUS:1969–1976*:XLI, d75; "Currency Crisis; Nuclear Understanding; MBFR; NATO," memorandum of conversation at the British Embassy, March 5, 1973, NSC/HAK/62/UK Memcons (Originals)/RNL; "Personal Record of a Discussion in the British Embassy, Washington DC, on 19th April, 1973," PREM 15/1359; "Record of Conversation at the British Embassy, Washington, on 5 March 1973," PREM 15/1365.

61. Memorandum of Conversation [in the Ambassador's Office], January 16, 1973, NSC/HAK/62/UK Memcons (Originals)/RNL. See also "More European Policy Being Made on the Run," memorandum for Kissinger from Sonnenfeldt, February 4, 1970, NSC/667/Europe General thru May 1970 [January 1969–May 1970]/RNL.

62. For "no more toasts" and connections between Vietnam and NATO see "The President's Meeting with General Goodpaster," February 15, 1973, GFL/VL; Memorandum of Conversation, Thursday, February 15, 1973, 1:00 p.m., GFL/VL; "Relations between Europe and the United States," Extract Record of Conversation PM/Federal Chancellor at Schloss Gymnich on Thursday 1/3/73," PREM 15/1540.

63. A massive NSC study launched in late 1972 and discussed by senior staff in 1973 concurred with Nixon's assessment that there was no reasonable policy option besides NATO. The beneficiary of any other policy would be the USSR. Memorandum from Helmut Sonnenfeldt of the National Security Council Staff to the President's Assistant for National Security Affairs (Kissinger), January 29, 1973, *FRUS:1969–1976*:E15:2, d4; "SRG Meeting, January 31, 1973, NSSM 164: Relations with Western Europe," Memorandum

for Kissinger from Sonnenfeldt, January 30, 1973, NSC/Inst/H-066/SRG Meeting—Europe (NSSM 164) 1/31/73/RNL; Minutes of Senior Review Group Meeting, January 31, 1973, *FRUS:1969–1976*:XLI, d88.

64. Memorandum of Conversation [in the Ambassador's Office], January 16, 1973.

65. "Relations between Europe and the United States, Extract Record of Conversation PM/Federal Chancellor at Schloss Gymnich on Thursday 1/3/73."

66. "Unholy alliance" was an American term passed to the British. "US/Europe," Overton to Head of WOD, June 15, 1973, FCO 82/285. See also "Neo-Isolationism," letter from Cromer to Sir Alec Douglas-Home, July 15, 1972, FCO 82/54.

67. "The US and Europe," Cromer to Greenhill, January 19, 1973, FCO 82/281; Memorandum of Conversation [in the Ambassador's Office], January 16, 1973.

68. Minutes of Senior Review Group Meeting, January 31, 1973; Memorandum of Conversation [in the Ambassador's Office], January 16, 1973.

69. On the impracticality of the idea see "NSSM 164: United States Relations with Europe," John Morse to Sonnenfeldt, January 2, 1973, NSC/Inst/H-066/SRG Meeting—Europe (NSSM 164) 1/31/73/RNL; Memorandum from Helmut Sonnenfeldt of the National Security Council Staff to the President's Assistant for National Security Affairs (Kissinger), January 29, 1973, *FRUS:1969–1976*:E15:2, d4. On the possible backfiring of the plan see Minutes of Senior Review Group Meeting, January 31, 1973; "SRG/CIEP Meeting on Europe," memorandum for Kissinger from Sonnenfeldt, January 30, 1973, NSC/Inst/H-066/SRG Meeting—Europe (NSSM 164), January 31, 1973/RNL.

70. Memorandum from President Nixon to the President's Assistant for National Security Affairs (Kissinger), March 10, 1973, *FRUS:1969–1976*:E15:2, d9.

71. For various ideas and efforts to reorder the relationship before the speech see "Personal Record of a Discussion in the British Embassy, Washington DC, on 19th April, 1973"; "US Policy Towards Europe," Overton to Wiggin, May 21, 1973, FCO 82/284. On Nixon's urgency see Cromer to the PM, April 23, 1973, PREM 15/1362. For Kissinger's hurry see "Discussion with Dr. Kissinger," Trend to the PM, Ref. 104029, April 24, 1974, PREM 15/1359. See also Washington986 to FCO, March 19, 1974, FCO 41/1469.

72. "The Year of Europe: Address by Henry Kissinger (April 23, 1973)," Department of State *Bulletin*, May 14, 1973, 592–98.

73. Washington to FCO 1370, April 23, 1973, FCO 82/282. American efforts to link Kissinger's speech to the Roosevelt-Churchill Atlantic Charter revealed a tin ear for history. See "The Atlantic Charter," Goulding to Wiggin, May 7, 1973, FCO 41/1185; "The Atlantic Charter," Tickell to Wiggin, May 4, 1973, FCO 41/1185; Willy Brandt, *People and Politics: The Years 1960–1975*, trans. J. Maxwell Brownjohn, (Boston: Little, Brown, 1978), 311–12; Edward Heath, *The Course of My Life: My Autobiography* (London: Hodder & Stoughton, 1998), 492; Cromer to Brimelow, May 8, 1973, FCO 82/283; "US/European Relations Etc," Wiggin to McLaren, August 24, 1973, FCO 41/1186; Cromer to Brimelow, May 8, 1973.

74. Cromer to Brimelow, May 8, 1973.

75. "Reactions to Dr Kissinger's Speech," Crowe to Overton, May 4, 1973, FCO 82/283; Trend to PM, Ref. A04075, May 3, 1973, PREM 15/1541.

76. Washington 1822 to FCO, June 11, 1973, FCO 82/285; Cromer to Brimelow, May 8, 1973.

77. "The Year of Europe, UK SLBMs; SALT Principles; MBFR," Memorandum of Conversation, May 10, 1973, NSC/HAK/62/UK Memcons HAK London Trip (Originals)/RNL.

78. "Next Steps in the Year of Europe," Memorandum for the President from Kissinger, May 11, 1973, NSC/HAK/64/Exchanges with the UK—other/RNL. See esp.

"Memorandum of Conversation [in the Foreign Minister's office, Quai d'Orsay]," May 17, 1973, NSC/HAK/56/French Memcons (Originals) Peter Rodman January–May 1973/RNL; Minutes of Defense Program Review Committee/Senior Review Group Meeting, May 25, 1973, *FRUS:1969–1976*:E15:2, d18.

79. "Draft Declaration of Principles on US/European Relations," June 18, 1973, FCO 41/1185.

80. "United States—European Relations and the Kissinger Declaration," July 6, 1973, PREM 15/1542; "President Nixon's Message of July 26 to the Prime Minister," Speaking Notes, undated [late July 1973], PREM 15/1543; Paris578 to FCO, July 26, 1973, PREM 15/1543.

81. The British were not willing to risk French irritation by disagreeing over the Andersen incident, for they wanted French acquiescence on other matters in the EEC. "Draft Declaration of Principles on US/European Relations," June 18, 1973.

82. Memorandum of Conversation, July 30, 1973, *FRUS:1969–1976*:E15:2, d27; Memorandum of Conversation, September 25, 1973, *FRUS:1969–1976*:E15:2, d34.

83. "Record of Meeting at 3.30 P.M. on 30 July, 1973 at the White House, Washington DC, State Secretary Frank and Kissinger," PREM 15/1545; "State Secretary Frank and Kissinger," August 3, 1973, PREM 15/1544.

84. Memorandum of Conversation, July 30, 1973.

85. Brimelow described the meeting to Jobert; see Jobert's reaction in "Record of Conversation between Sir Thomas Brimelow and the French Minister of Foreign Affairs at the Quai d'Orsay on 29 August 1973," PREM 15/1546.

86. For the British take on Kissinger's outburst see Armstrong to Prime Minister, September 18, 1973, PREM 15/1546. Kissinger's explanation of Watergate's effect on foreign policy is in Memorandum of Conversation [on the *Sequoia*], August 3, 1973, NSC/1027/Memcons April–Nov 1973, HAK and Presidential/RNL; Sykes to Brimelow, August 13, 1973, PREM 15/1545.

87. "Record of a Discussion at the Old Executive Building Washington DC on Thursday 1 February 1973 at 4.00 pm," PREM 15/1359; "SRG/DPRC Meeting on NATO Security Issues and Atlantic Charter, Friday, May 25, 1973," memorandum for Dr. Kissinger from Phil Odeen, NSC/Inst/H-067/SRG/DPRC Meeting—NATO Security Issues May 25, 1973/RNL.

88. "Defense Procurement and MFN," President's Meeting with GOP Leadership, September 27, 1973, GFL/VL. See also Kissinger's remarks in Memorandum of Conversation, August 9, 1973, *FRUS:1969–1977*:XXXV, d20.

89. "Record of a Discussion at the Old Executive Building Washington DC on Thursday 1 February 1973 at 4.00 pm."

90. Washington2053 to FCO, July 1, 1973, FCO 41/1185; "Record of a Discussion at Camp David on Friday 2 February 1973 at 4.00 pm," PREM 15/1365.

91. "Record of a Discussion at Camp David on Friday 2 February 1973 at 4.00 pm"; "Year of Europe; SALT Principles, MBFR; Nuclear Treaty; Middle East," Memorandum of Conversation [in Sir Burke Trend's Office,] May 10, 1973, NSC/HAK/62/UK Memcons HAK London Trip (Originals)/RNL.

92. "Year of Europe; SALT Principles, MBFR; Nuclear Treaty; Middle East," May 10, 1973.

93. "SRG/DPRC Meeting on NATO Security Issues and Atlantic Charter," Friday, May 25, 1973.

94. Washington2053 to FCO, July 1, 1973. Schlesinger lodged a similar complaint. See Memorandum from Philip Odeen of the National Security Council Staff to the President's Assistant for National Security Affairs (Kissinger), June 9, 1973, *FRUS:1969–1976*:E15:2, d22.

95. "US/European Relations: Finance and Defence," Tickell to Brimelow, July 24, 1973, FCO 41/1186; Memorandum from Philip Odeen of the National Security Council Staff to the President's Assistant for National Security Affairs (Kissinger), June 9, 1973.

96. "Summary Note of Main Points Discussed between Lord Carrington and Dr. Schlesinger at Annapolis on the morning of 1 August 1973," FCO 41/1187.

97. The matter came up for consideration, periodically, throughout the Cold War. Cromer to Greenhill, February 25, 1972, FCO 82/179.

98. "Extract from Record of Mtg—PM/Pompidou—16.11.73 after lunch," PREM 15/2089.

99. "Record of a Mtg PM and German cabinet 29 May 1973 (extract)," PREM 15/1936.

100. Paris1129 to FCO, August 30, 1973, FCO 82/286; Bonn895 to FCO, August 17, 1973, PREM 15/1545. For Bahr and Brandt's firm opposition to European defense see "Record of a Mtg PM and German cabinet 29 May 1973 (extract)." For more on Brandt's views see Bonn1065 to FCO, October 3, 1973, FCO 82/287; for Bahr, "Herr Egon Bahr," Goulding to James, November 13, 1973, FCO 41/1191.

101. "Record of Conversation between Sir Thomas Brimelow and the French Minister of Foreign Affairs at the Quai d'Orsay on 29 August 1973." For more on the French position see "Minutes of a Meeting held at 10 Downing Street on Wednesday 20 June 1973 at 10.30 am," FCO 41/1185; also "Note for the Record," undated [July 2, 1973], Robert Armstrong, PREM 15/1542. The British were wary but ultimately believed American claims about the seriousness of congressional pressure. Washington 1822 to FCO, June 11, 1973, FCO 82/285; Minute by Hankey on "US/Europe Relations: US Policy and Attitudes," July 2, 1973, FCO 82/285.

102. For "free ride" see "US-European Relations," Memorandum of Conversation [Kissinger and "wise men"], November 28, 1973, NSC/1027/Memcons April–Nov 1973, HAK and Presidential/RNL; Memorandum of Conversation, November 23, 1973, GFL/VL.

103. Kissing used variations on the phrase; this specific iteration appears in "Visit of French Defense Minister Galley; Strategic Programs," August 17, 1973, GFL/VL.

104. Transcript of Telephone Conversation between President Nixon and the President's Assistant for National Security Affairs (Kissinger), August 9, 1973, *FRUS:1969–1976*:E15:2, d31.

105. Memorandum of Conversation, September 5, 1973, GFL/VL.

106. On the American-German alliance see "Visit of French Defense Minister Galley; Strategic Programs"; August 17, 1973; "Record of Conversation between Sir Thomas Brimelow and the French Minister of Foreign Affairs at the Quai d'Orsay on 29 august 1973," PREM 15/1546. On expectations of close Anglo-American cooperation despite British admission to Europe see Memorandum of Conversation [in the Ambassador's Office], January 16, 1973; Conversation between President Nixon and the President's Assistant for National Security Affairs (Kissinger), February 3, 1973, *FRUS:1969–1976*:E15:2, d6. Also Memorandum of Conversation, November 23, 1973, GFL/VL.

107. Memorandum of Conversation, September 5, 1973, GFL/VL.

108. "French Nuclear Discussion," August 9, 1973, GFL/VL. See also "Visit of French Defense Minister Galley; Strategic Programs," August 17, 1973. Trachtenberg has pointed out that while Kissinger's goals here are obscure, they were a part of his effort to "bust" Europe. Trachtenberg, *Cold War and After*, 220–21. For the broader context of the Anglo-American nuclear negotiations in this period see Thomas Robb, "Antelope, Poseidon or a Hybrid: The Upgrading of the British Strategic Nuclear Deterrent, 1970–1974," *Journal of Strategic Studies* 33, no. 6 (2010): 797–817, and Helen Parr, "The British Decision to Upgrade Polaris, 1970–4," *Contemporary European History* 22, no. 2 (May 2013): 253–74.

109. The French offered a new draft of a possible Atlantic declaration, this time with a reference to the need for a substantial and continued American troop commitment in Europe. UKDelNATO636 to FCO, October 5, 1973, FCO 82/287; UKDelNATO630 to FCO, October 3, 1973, FCO 41/1189.

110. A phrase coined by US Representative Chet Holifield, "Record of Conversation 'Over the Port' at HM Embassy, Washington, on 27 June," FCO 41/1185.

111. "Transatlantic Relations," Cromer to Brimelow, October 2, 1973, FCO 41/1189; Cromer to Greenill, October 3, 1973, FCO 82/306.

112. Kissinger, *Years of Upheaval*, 708–9; BDS Washington to MODUK, October 31, 1973, FCO 41/1179.

113. UKDelNATO669 to FCO, October 16, 1973, FCO 41/1178. Rumsfeld's remarks led to enormous confusion. See "The Middle East and the Alliance," October 31, 1973, FCO 41/1178; "The Middle East and East/West Economic Relations," October 24, 1973, FCO 41/1178.

114. For "Warsaw Pact" see "The Middle East and East/West Economic Relations," October 23, 1973, FCO 41/1178. Brandt was so outraged he leaked the matter to the press. See "Hella Pick's Article on the Middle East," October 26, 1973, FCO 41/1178.

115. Cromer to Peck, November 12, 1973, FCO 41/1179. On the delay in notifying NATO see "NATO, Kissinger and the Middle East," November 17, 1973, FCO 41/1179; Washington3539 to FCO, November 8, 1973, FCO 41/1179.

116. "The President—Secretary Kissinger," October 25, 1973, HAKTelcons/StateFOIA/VL.

117. "US-European Relations," November 28, 1973. See also Memorandum from the President's Deputy Assistant for National Security Affairs (Scowcroft) to President Nixon," December 10, 1973, *FRUS:1969–1976*:E15:2, d41.

118. "Bipartisan Leadership Meeting, November 27, 1973, GFL/VL. "Secretary's Staff Meeting, October 25, 1973," October 29, 1973, DNSA/KT00869.

119. "Mr. Sonnenfeldt/Secretary Kissinger," December 4, 1973, 6:05 p.m., HAK-Telcons/StateFOIA/VL.

120. "Memorandum of Conversation," December 9, 1973, *FRUS:1969–1976*:E15:2, d40.

121. "Memorandum of Conversation," December 9, 1973. To analysts in the NATO countries, the recent Soviet buildup of military forces seemed to reveal that Moscow was preparing a capability to wage a blitzkrieg-style war into Western Europe. See John S. Duffield, *Power Rules: The Evolution of NATO's Conventional Force Posture* (Stanford, CA: Stanford University Press, 1995), 207.

122. "French Policy Towards the Atlantic Alliance," Peck to Wiggins, December 20, 1973, FCO 82/289; "The Present State of Franco/Soviet Relations and their Effect on Pompidou's Position," James to Wiggin, December 18, 1973, FCO 82/289.

123. "U.S.-European Relations; Superantelope," January 17, 1974, GFL/VL.

124. "Remarks at a Working Dinner of the Washington Energy Conference," February 11, 1974, available at the American Presidency Project (http://www.presidency.ucsb.edu/ws/index.php?pid=4347).

125. "The President—Secretary Kissinger," February 14, 1974, 6:15 p.m., HAKTelcons/StateFOIA/VL.

126. "Hal Sonnenfeldt. Secretary Kissinger," March 5, 1974, 9:06 a.m., HAKTelcons/StateFOIA/VL.

127. UKDelNATO108 to FCO, March 4, 1974, FCO 41/1469.

128. "Kissinger Trip to the Soviet Union," Memorandum of Conversation, March 11, 1974, GFL/VL.

129. Memorandum of Conversation, March 11, 1974, *FRUS:1969–1976*:E15:2, d52.

130. "Kissinger Trip to the Soviet Union," Memorandum of Conversation, March 11, 1974, GFL/VL; Memorandum of Conversation, March 11, 1974; Memorandum of Conversation, March 8, 1974, GFL/VL.

131. Memorandum of Conversation, March 8, 1974.

132. "The President / Sec. Kissinger," March 15, 1974, 11:00, HAKTelcons/StateFOIA/VL.

133. "Question-and-Answer Session at the Executives' Club of Chicago," March 15, 1974, available at the American Presidency Project, http://www.presidency.ucsb.edu/ws/?pid=4386.

134. Washington944 to FCO, March 15, 1974, PREM 16/419; Washington1069 to FCO, March 25, 1974, PREM 16/419.

135. Memorandum from the President's Deputy Assistant for National Security Affairs (Scowcroft) to President Nixon, March 24, 1974, *FRUS:1969–1976*:E15:2, d55.

136. "Gen. Scowcroft / Sec. Kissinger," March 14, 1974, HAKTelcons/StateFOIA/VL.

137. "Record of a Conversation between the Prime Minister and the Secretary of State, Dr. Henry Kissinger, at 10 Downing Street on Thursday 28 March 1974, at 4.00 pm," PREM 16/419.

138. Memorandum of Conversation, March 19, 1974, GFL/VL.

139. Washington1069 to FCO, March 25, 1974.

140. "The US Draft Alliance Declaration," March 26, 1974, FCO 41/1469.

141. For a full account of the French policy see Soutou, "Georges Pompidou," 189–90.

142. "Prime Minister's Visit to Brussels: 25/26 June: Steering Brief," PREM 16/11; FCO 1374 to Washington, June 21, 1974, PREM 16/11.

143. "Your Visit to Brussels, June 25–27, 1974," Kissinger to the President, undated, NSC/HAK/53/NAC Summit Brussels NSC—Mr. Rodman/RNL.

144. "Prime Minister's Visit to Brussels: 25/26 June: Steering Brief," PREM 16/11.

145. "Note of a Meeting held at the United States Embassy, Brussels, on Wednesday 26 June 1974 at 3.40 pm," PREM 16/11.

146. FCO 1374 to Washington, June 21, 1974, PREM 16/11.

147. "Your Visit to Brussels, June 25–27, 1974," Kissinger to the President, undated.

148. "Prime Minister's Visit to Brussels: 25/26 June: Steering Brief," PREM 16/11.

149. Muirhead to Callaghan, July 3, 1974, FCO 41/1472.

150. Michael Howard, "NATO and the Year of Europe," *Survival* 17, no. 1 (1974): 21.

151. Callaghan to the Prime Minister, PM/74/20, March 26, 1974, PREM 16/92.

152. "Secretary of State's Visit to Bonn," Minute by Head of Chancery, Bonn, PREM 16/392.

9. LEADERLESS MEN

1. "NATO Annual Review for 1976," January 4, 1977, FCO 46/1475.

2. UKDelNATO410 to FCO, November 2, 1976, FCO 46/1366.

3. "NATO Annual Review for 1976," January 4, 1977. See also "Summit Preparation—A Progress Report," memorandum for the President, April 15, 1977, DDRS/CK3100144138.

4. "Medium and Long-Term Problems for NATO," September 10, 1976, FCO 46/1366.

5. Vance's remarks to NATO in UKDelNATO441 to FCO, December 9, 1977, PREM 16/1781 and Callaghan's in "Extract from telecon between PM and Pres. Carter on 17 April 78," PREM 16/1781. See also Meeting of the Special Coordination Committee, July 7, 1977, DDRS/CK3100585003.

6. "Comprehensive Review of European Issues," Presidential Review Memorandum/NSC-9, March 1, 1977, NSC/Inst/27/Presidential Review Memorandum/NSC-9 [1]/JCL.

7. "Managing Russia," July 1979, FCO 46/1964.

8. "East-West Relations over the Next Few Years," [July 24, 1979], FCO 46/1962.

9. Sykes to Killick, September 30, 1976, FCO 46/1366.

10. "NATO: Annual Review for 1975," January 7, 1976, FCO 46/1359; see also "NATO—New Methods of Propulsion in the 80s," [December 21, 1978].

11. "Significant Actions, Secretary and Deputy Secretary of Defense (Week of 5–11 March, 1977), memorandum for the President, March 11, 1977, DDRS/CK3100502863. On the Long-Term Defense Plan see Duffield, *Power Rules*, 212–21.

12. Policy Review Committee Meeting, July 8, 1977, CK3100144176, DDRS; "PRC Meeting on PRM 10—Friday, July 8, 1977, at 10:00 a.m.," July 6, 1977, DDRS/CK3100152016.

13. "Prime Minister's Meeting with Dr Z Brzezinski: 27 September 1977," Brief No. 11, "American Thinking on the Defence of Europe," PREM 16/1911.

14. "West German Foreign Minister Requests Clarification of Continuing US Debate over NATO Strategy," Cable to White House, August 20, 1977, DDRS/CK3100578661.

15. Walter Pincus, "Neutron Killer Warhead Buried in ERDA Budget," *Washington Post*, June 6, 1976, 1.

16. On Congress, nuclear safety, and modernization see "Secretary Schlesinger and Secretary Mason Plenary Discussion," September 24, 1975, *Euromissiles*:II:A, Washington138 to FCO, May 11, 1976, FCO 46/1374. On Congress and possible nuclear withdrawal see "Neo-Isolationism," Renwick to Logan, September 30, 1981, FCO 46/2594. For the state of American and NATO nuclear planning in the Ford years see William Burr, "A Question of Confidence: Theater Nuclear Forces, US Policy toward Germany, and the Origins of the Euromissile Crisis, 1975–1976," in *The Euromissile Crisis and the End of the Cold War*, ed. Leopoldo Nuti et al. (Stanford, CA: Woodrow Wilson Center Press with Stanford University Press, 2015). For "integrated quietly" see "European Attitudes toward the 'Neutron Bomb,'" memorandum for the President, July 25, 1977, DDRS/CK3100516281.

17. "Enhanced Radiation Weapons," September 19, 1977, PREM 16/1576.

18. "The USSR: Regional and Political Analysis," CIA report RP ASU 77-021, August 4, 1977, DDRS/CK3100193725.

19. Memorandum for the President from the Secretary of State and the Secretary of Defense, signed September 23 and September 16, 1977, respectively, DDRS/CK3100567206.

20. Washington4173 to FCO, September 24, 1977, PREM 16/1911; Washington4161 to FCO, September 23, 1977, PREM 16/1576. Brzezinski later said pressing for an early decision was a mistake. "Dr. Brzezinski's Call on the Prime Minister, 27 September 1977," PREM 16/1911.

21. "Enhanced Radiation Warheads," note by the PM (Callaghan), September 21, 1977, PREM 16/1576; "Prime Minister's Meeting with Dr Z Brezinski [*sic*]: 27 September 1977," PREM 16/1911. For Owen's concerns see "Enhanced Radiation Warheads (ERWs)," September 22, 1977, PREM 16/1576. For trade unions, etc., see "Enhanced Radiation Weapons," September 15, 1977, PREM 16/1576. For "educate public opinion" see UKDelNATO332 to FCO, September 27, 2977, PREM 16/1576.

22. Washington no 4993 to FCO, November 22, 1977, PREM 16/1576; UKDel-NATO333 to FCO, September 27, 1977, PREM 16/1576.

23. See Brzezinski's comments in Washington4161 to FCO, September 23, 1977, and in Zbigniew Brzezinski, *Power and Principle: Memoirs of the National Security Advisor, 1977–1981* (New York: Farrar, Straus & Giroux, 1983), 302. The Germans point to the need for sharing political costs in UKDelNATO332 to FCO, September 27, 2977, PREM 16/1576.

24. "Enhanced Radiation Weapons," from the PM's Private Secretary, October 24, 1977, PREM 16/1576; Bonn46 to FCO, January 19, 1978, PREM 16/1570.

25. The FRG Security Council recommended the trade. See "NSC Weekly Report #36," Memorandum for the President from Brzezinski, November 11, 1977, DDRS/

CK3100099286. On American thinking on a trade, and Carter's specific idea of a broader nuclear deal, see Special Coordination Committee Meeting, November 16, 1977, DDRS/CK3100543830; Memorandum for Zbigniew Brzezinski and David Aaron from James Thomson and Victor Utgoff, November 14, 1977, DDRs/CK3100554305.

26. "SALT II Negotiations," Main Points of Anglo/US Official Talks on 31 January [1978], PREM 16/1570.

27. Washington1054 to FCO, March 13, 1978, PREM 16/1577; Washington1107 to FCO, March 15 1978, PREM 16/1577.

28. For "prepared" see "Note of a Conversation between the Prime Minister and Mr Jay in the House of Commons on 1 February 1978," February 2, 1978, PREM 16/1570; for "major row" see "Enhanced Radiation / Reduce Blast Warheads (DOP(78)7)," to the Prime Minister from Clive Rose, March 20, 1978, PREM 16/1577. Owen's position is in "Extract from the Record of a Meeting between the Foreign and Commonwealth Secretary and the US Secretary of State at the US Mission to the United Nations, New York, at 1200 Noon on Sunday 12 February 1978," PREM 16/1570.

29. "Your Meeting on ERW Tonight," memorandum for Brzezinski, March 20, 1978, DDRS/CK3100107238.

30. "Your Meeting on ERW Tonight," March 20, 1978.

31. Brzezinski, *Power and Principle*, 304–5.

32. Bonn (UK) Flash TELNO2 to Washington of March 22, 1978, PREM 16/1577. State Department officials, at first, assured the allies the president's position had not changed. Washington no 1176 to FCO, March 20, 1978, PREM 16/1577.

33. White House SITTO 102 (Cherokee cable) to Rick Inderfurth for Dr. Brzezinski, April 1, 1978, DDRS/CK3100090657.

34. "Extract from minutes of Nuclear Defence Policy Mtg. of 3/4/78," PREM 16/1577.

35. "The FRG and ERWs," memorandum to the PM, April 6, 1978, PREM 16/1577. See also Note to the PM from Owen, April 1, 1978, PREM 16/1577.

36. Washington1395 to FCO, April 4, 1978, PREM 16/1577.

37. Strauss quoted in Bonn257 to FCO, April 8, 1978, PREM 16/1577. Genscher denied the quote. Bonn259 to FCO, April 11, 1978, PREM 16/1577. See also "ERWs: Presentational Aspects," to the PM, PREM 16/1577; "Addition Information Items," memorandum for Brzezinski from the Situation Room, April 19, 1978, DDRS/CK3100712229.

38. For "a President" see "US Foreign Policy," April 17, 1979, FCO 46/1995. For "leaderless men" see Bonn259 to FCO, April 11, 1978. For "sea change" see "A German Perception of US Foreign Policy," April 3, 1979, FCO 46/1998.

39. "Extract from the Prime Minister's Mtg with Chancellor Schmidt, Long Gallery, Chequers, 24-4-78," PREM 16/1571.

40. Schmidt's speech was published as Helmut Schmidt, "The 1977 Alistair Buchan Memorial Lecture," *Survival* 20, no. 1 (January–February 1978): 2–10.

41. "Extract from the Prime Minister's Mtg with Chancellor Schmidt, Long Gallery, Chequers, 24-4-78."

42. Americans concerns noted in Meeting of the Special Coordination Committee, July 7, 1977, DDRS/CK3100585003; Schmidt's in "Extract from PM's Meeting with Chancellor Schmidt at Bonn on 12 March 1978," PREM 16/1570.

43. "Record of a Conversation between the Prime Minister and Chancellor Schmidt in the Federal Chancellery, Bonn, on 19 October 1978 at 0935," PREM 16/1572. For Schmidt's worries about SALT see "Extract from PM's Meeting with Chancellor Schmidt at Bonn on 12 March 1978."

44. "US Nuclear Policy," August 30, 1978, FCO 46/1826; "US Foreign Policy," April 3, 1979, FCO 46/1995.

45. "Note of a Meeting Held at 10 Downing Street on Friday 17 November 1978 at 10.00 am," subject: "Grey Area Nuclear Delivery Systems," PREM 16/1984; "II. Salt/Grey

Areas," September 29, 1978, PREM 16/1911; "NATO's Theatre Nuclear Forces," Mulley to the PM, MO 13/1/34, June 9, 1978, PREM 16/1571; for "Western pawn" see Helmut Schmidt, *Men and Powers: A Political Retrospective*, trans. Ruth Hein (New York: Random House, 1989), 190.

46. See "Task Force 10: Modernisation of Theatre Nuclear Forces," Michael Quinlan to David E. McGiffert (ISA/OSD), January 9, 1978, FCO 46/1825.

47. On the range of possible TNF postures considered by NATO see "Alternative Theater Nuclear Force Postures," paper submitted to NPG High Level Group, February 7, 1978, FCO 46/1825. See also Kristina Spohr Readman, "Conflict and Cooperation in Intra-Alliance Nuclear Politics: Western Europe, America and the Genesis of Nato's Dual-Track Decision, 1977–1979," *Journal of Cold War Studies* 13, no. 2 (2011): 39–89; Ivo H. Daalder, *The Nature and Practice of Flexible Response: NATO Strategy and Theater Nuclear Forces since 1967* (New York: Columbia University Press, 1991).

48. "Theatre Nuclear Force Modernization; Task Force 10 Record of NPG High Level Group Meeting, Held at Los Alamos, 16/17 February 1978," FCO 46/1825. For a similar British analysis see "NATO's Theatre Nuclear Forces," Mulley to the PM, MO 13/1/34, June 9, 1978.

49. "Chancellor Schmidt and Grey Area Systems," June 23, 1978, PREM 16/1571.

50. On the location, by percentage, of NATO's nuclear weapons see "UK Record of High Level Group Meeting Held in Brussels—16/17 October 1978," FCO 46/1828. For early German arguments against sole-hosting the weapons see "European/American Relations," October 26, 1978, FCO 46/1685. Schmidt quoted in "Record of a Conversation Between the Prime Minister and Chancellor Schmidt in the Federal Chancellery, Bonn, on 19 October 1978 at 0935," PREM 16/1572.

51. For "careful preparation" see "Modernisation of Theatre Nuclear Forces—Work of the NATO High-Level Group," annex to MO 13/1/34, December 19, 1978. See Callaghan's confusion in "Cruise Missiles," October 26, 1978, PREM 16/1984. The Americans were the least sensitive to the controversy. See "Record of a Conversation between the Prime minister and Dr. Brzezinski in the Imperial Hotel, Blackpool on Wednesday 4 October at 1000 hours," 1978, PREM 16/1911, and "SCC Meeting on PRM-38, August 23," Briefing Memo for the Secretary from Ericsson and Vest, August 16, 1978, Document 2, NSA EBB 301.

52. See efforts to achieve secrecy in "Possible Quadripartite Meeting about Grey Area Systems etc" to PM, October 30, 1978, PREM 16/1984; Washington4261 to FCO, October 26, 1978, PREM 16/1984. For "vital" see "Grey Area Systems," Memorandum A08327 to the PM from Hunt, November 16, 1978, PREM 16/1984.

53. "Extract from Four-Power Discussions in Guadeloupe 5/6 January 1979: Second Session, on Friday 5 January 1979 at 1630 hours," PREM 16/1984. For more on the summit see Kristina Spohr, "Helmut Schmidt and the Shaping of Western Security in the Late 1970s: The Guadeloupe Summit of 1979," *International History Review* 37, no. 1 (2013): 167–92.

54. For "watershed" see "Grey Areas," Memorandum A09126 March 8, 1979, PREM 16/1984. For "the right thing" see "Long-Range Theater Nuclear Forces and Gray Areas," memorandum for the President, February 13, 1979, DDRS/CK3100543617. The German cabinet's thinking is reported in "Grey Area Systems: Modernisation and Arms Control," Memorandum A08918 to the PM, February 8, 1979, PREM 16/1984, and "Note of a Meeting Between the Secretary of State and the German Minister of Defence in the FRG Delegation, Brussels on Monday 14th May 1979 at 5.30 pm," PREM 19/15.

55. For "expose" see "TNF Arms Control Objectives/Principles," Memorandum by David Gompert, April 5, 1979, *Euromissiles*:2:B. For "Cuba-in-reverse" see "Policy Review Committee Meeting," May 14, 1979, DDRS/CK3100147800, and Harold Brown's comments to NATO in UKDelNATO73 to FCO, May 17, 1979, PREM 19/15. The slow change

in the American position occurred for a number of political and strategic reasons: see Spohr Readman, "Conflict and Cooperation in Intra-Alliance Nuclear Politics"; Daalder, *Nature and Practice of Flexible Response*, 181. "Long-Range Theatre Nuclear Forces," Pym to the Prime Minister, September 17, 1979, PREM 19/15.

56. "TNF Modernization—US Diplomacy, Your Role and the Schmidt Visit," Vance and Brown to the President, May 9, 1979, DDRS/CK3100108807; "Additional Information Items," Memorandum for Brzezinski, September 28, 1979, DDRS/CK31006838718; FCO143 to Certain Missions, November 20, 1979, PREM 19/15. On the mix of local and Soviet support for the antinuclear movement see Holger Nehring and Benjamin Ziemann, "Do All Paths Lead to Moscow? The NATO Dual-Track Decision and the Peace Movement—a Critique," *Cold War History* 12, no. 1 (2012): 1–24. Lawrence Wittner puts the opposition to LRTNF in the broader context of the disarmament movement. Lawrence Wittner, *Toward Nuclear Abolition: A History of the World Nuclear Disarmament Movement, 1971–Present* (Palo Alto, CA: Stanford University Press, 2003).

57. "Record of Discussion between the Defence Ministers of the United Kingdom, France and the Federal Republic of Germany at the Rathaus, Hamburg, on Monday 15th October Beginning at 3pm," 1979, FCO 46/1989; Bonn758 to FCO, December 7, 1979, FCO 28/3697; "Brezhnev's Speech on 6 October: Some Preliminary Comments," October 8, 1979, FCO 28/3694.

58. "Extract from record of discussion between PM and Chancellor Schmidt," October 31, 1979," PREM 19/15.

59. On the importance of election cycle see "Note of a Meeting Between the Secretary of State and the German Minister of Defence in the FRG Delegation, Brussels on Monday 14th May 1979 at 5.30 pm." For the smaller powers' concern and the larger powers' responses see "Report on Consultations with Belgian, Dutch and Italian Governments," March 20, 1979, *Euromissiles*:3:A; Garthoff, *Détente and Confrontation*, and Bonn to FCO 804, December 20, 1979, TAO; On the Dutch and the withdrawal of one thousand weapons see "Telephone conversation between the President and Chancellor Schmidt of FRG mostly on TNF," October 30, 1979, DDRS/CK3100480229.

60. John R. Galvin, *Fighting the Cold War: A Soldier's Memoir* (Lexington: University Press of Kentucky, 2015), 356.

61. Some Americans would later claim that the arms control half of the "Dual-Track" was simply political cover for a modernization program. Cyrus Vance, *Hard Choices: Critical Years in American Foreign Policy* (New York: Simon & Schuster, 1983), 392; Garthoff, *Détente and Confrontation*, 947; Daalder, *Nature and Practice of Flexible Response*, 197. Schmidt thought the solution to the TNF problem was arms control. See "Chancellor Schmidt and Grey Area Systems," undercover of Walden to Cartledge, June 23, 1978, PREM 16/1571, and "Record of a Conversation between the Prime Minister and Chancellor Schmidt in the Federal Chancellery, Bonn, on 19 October 1978 at 0935," PREM 16/1572; Schmidt, *Men and Powers*, 189. David Owen's preference for arms control is noted in "NATO's Theatre Nuclear Forces," Owen to the PM, PM/78/47, May 30, 1978, PREM 16/1571. Carter had hoped ERW would offer an arms control solution to the SS-20; see also his remarks at Guadeloupe, both above. For the communiqué see "Special Meeting of Foreign and Defence Ministers (the 'Double-Track' Decision on Theatre Nuclear Forces), Chairman: Mr. J. Luns," December 12, 1979, http://www.nato.int/cps/en/natolive/official_texts_27040.htmt.

62. On "delicate package" see "The Arc of Crisis and the Transatlantic Relationship," April 28, 1980, FCO 46/2179. Brzezinski's suggestion that the United States might use nuclear weapons in Southwest Asia drove Schmidt to distraction. "Partial Record of a Meeting between the Prime Minister and the Chancellor of the Federal Republic of Germany, Herr Schmidt, at No. 10 Downing Street on Monday 25 February 1980," PREM

19/136. The Europeans worried that the war in Afghanistan, succeeding as it did the 1979 Iranian Revolution and seizure of the American Embassy in Tehran, might cause the Americans to take rash action in the Middle East and Central Asia and risk the start of regional war. "Chancellor Schmidt's Visit to Moscow," to Gladstone to Ferguson, April 23, 1980, FCO 46/2317. Lack of consultation on Afghanistan, including over the Olympic boycott, was a major source of tension. Memorandum from the Secretary of State, February 25, 1980, DDRS/CK3100097002. On NATO and Poland see "Poland—Effect of Intervention on Threat to NATO," memorandum for Brzezinski to Aaron from Thomson, December 11, 1980, DDRS/CK3100580311, and, more generally, Andrea Chiampan, "'Those European Chicken Littles': Reagan, NATO, and the Polish Crisis, 1981–2," *International History Review* 37, no. 4 (2014): 682–99. Allied relations remained strong despite these crises, according to Piers Ludlow, "The Unnoticed Apogee of Atlanticisim?," in *European Integration and the Atlantic Community in the 1980s*, ed. Kiran Klaus Patel and Kenneth Weisbrode (New York: Cambridge University Press, 2013), esp. at 19.

63. On "Party of Peace" and "cake and eat it" see "Wehner," Bullard to Wright, FCO 46/1998; see also "US/German Relations," April 18, 1979, FCO 46/1998. On fear of Schmidt giving in, and Carter being brusque to the point of rude, see undated teletype, DDRS/CK3100726528. For the German domestic political battle over the LRTNF deployment see Jeffrey Herf, *War by Other Means: Soviet Power, West German Resistance, and the Battle of the Euromissiles* (New York: Free Press, 1991).

64. For Haig's remarks see Bonn155 to FCO, February 23, 1980, 1981, FCO 46/2601; for Apel's, see "FRG Defence Policy," February 24, 1981, FCO 46/2601.

65. UKDelNATO398 to FCO, November 20, 1981, FCO 46/2601.

66. For "dead wrong" and "serious problem" see "Neutralism in Western Europe," June 26, 1981, FCO 46/2765. Schmidt quoted in Bonn 4153 to SecState, December 9, 1981, DDRS/CK3100548091.

67. "A Public Affairs Campaign to Support and Follow Up President Reagan's Trip to Europe, June 2–11," Strategy Paper prepared by USICA, undated, DDRS/CK3100533003. See also Holger Nehring, "The West German and the U.S. Peace Movements," in *European Integration and the Atlantic Community in the 1980s*, ed. Kiran Klaus Patel and Kenneth Weisbrode (New York: Cambridge University Press, 2013), 19.

68. Reagan quoted in Washington2421 to FCO, August 14, 1981, FCO 46/2713; Hitchens in "Excerpt from the *New Statesman*," March 6, 1981, FCO 46/2741.

69. For the American presentation to NATO on Soviet Active Measures (still partly redacted) see "Soviet "Active Measures" in the West and the Developing World," paper circulated by Lawrence Eagleburger at NATO, September 11, 1981, FCO 46/2783. See also UKDelNATO342 to FCO, September 16, 1981, FCO 46/2783; "Reinforced Political Committee on Reciprocity/Active Measures," October 27, 1981, FCO 46/2783. For information on forged documents (including copies) see "The Affair of the Forged US Telegram," December 30, 1980, FCO 46/2766; "Forged US Top Secret Documents," January 9, 1981, FCO 46/2766. On Soviet approaches to Social Democrats see the Eagleburger paper and "Transatlantic Relations and European Public Opinion," September 13, 1981, FCO 46/2594. Brezhnev quoted in David Holloway, "The Dynamics of the Euromissile Crisis, 1977–1983," in Nuti et al., *Euromissile Crisis*, 20. See also Gerhard Wettig, "The Last Soviet Offensive in the Cold War: Emergence and Development of the Campaign against NATO Euromissiles, 1979–1983," *Cold War History* 9, no. 1 (2009): 79–110.

70. Walter Z. Laqueur, "Hollanditis: A New Stage in European Neutralism," *Commentary*, August 1, 1981.

71. "Anti-Nuclear Sentiment and Pacifism in NATO Europe," July 16, 1981, FCO 46/2765; "The Netherlands and ?Neutralism [*sic*]," Note by C. R. Budd, July 24, 1981, FCO 46/2765.

72. On Belgium see "Anti-Nuclear Sentiment in Belgium," British Embassy Brussels to Mallaby, July 31, 1981, FCO 46/2765, and Vincent Dujardin, "From Helsinki to the Missiles Question: A Minor Role for Small Countries? The Case of Belgium (1973–1985)," in *The Crisis of Détente in Europe: From Helsinki to Gorbachev, 1975–1985*, ed. Leopoldo Nuti (New York: Routledge, 2009), 72–85. On Italy see Maria Eleonora Guasconi, "Public Opinion and the Euromissiles Crisis," in Nuti et al., *Euromissile Crisis*, 270. On Germany see "Anti-Nuclear Sentiment and Pacifism in NATO Europe," July 24, 1981, FCO 46/2765. For the British paper see "Transatlantic Relations and European Public Opinion," September 13, 1981. The British conclusions were echoed by other NATO officials. See "The Challenge to the Alliance: Security Policy in Democracy," paper presented by Horst Ehmke, deputy chairman of SPD parliamentary group, at "Internationale Wehrkundetagung," Munich, February 10–12, 1984, Burns/V16/1983–84: E(1)/GFL.

73. For "worryingly" see "Nuclear Weapons Policy and Public Opinion," January 26, 1981, FCO 46/2759; for polling data see "CND: Public Opinion Surveys," August 21, 1981, FCO 46/2765.

74. "Nuclear Weapons: Public Attitudes," Douglas Hurd to the Secretary of State, FCO 46/2741.

75. Professor Kurt Biedenkopf (floor leader in the North Rhine–Westphalian Parliament) to Dr. Fred Luchsinger of the *Neue Zuercher Zeitung*, July 15, 1981 (embassy translation, October 26, 1981), Burns/V2/1981–82 B(1)/GFL. For "forget" see "U.S. Ambassador to NATO Abshire's Speech to the Evangelische Akademie, Hannover," James Lane to Ambassador Burns, November 18, 1983, Burns/ V15/ 1983–84: A(1)/GFL.

76. "Nuclear Weapons Policy and Public Opinion," January 26, 1981, FCO 46/2759.

77. "Nuclear Issues," Nott to the PM, October 20, 1982, PREM 19/979.

78. "Nuclear Weapons Policy and Public Opinion," January 26, 1981.

79. Ronald Reagan, "Remarks to Members of the National Press Club on Arms Reduction and Nuclear Weapons, November 18, 1981," American Presidency Project, http://www.presidency.ucsb.edu/ws/index.php?pid=43264.

80. For pressure from Schmidt see Bonn 24153 to SecState, December 9, 1981, DDRS/CK3100548091; for pressure from Carrington see SecState 053702 to London, March 11, 1981, DDRS/CK3100555893; for allied understanding that the American position was an effort to "placate allies" see "US Foreign Policy," March 21, 1981, PREM 19/1152; NAUK. Thanks to Susie Colbourn for this reference.

81. Wittner, *Toward Nuclear Abolition*, 134.

82. Jonathan Schell, *The Fate of the Earth* (New York: Alfred A. Knopf, 1982), 4. For reference to Schell's book see "U.S. Ambassador to NATO Abshire's Speech to the Evangelische Akademie, Hannover," November 18, 1983.

83. Holloway, "Dynamics of the Euromissile Crisis," 22.

84. For Gorbachev's position on disarmament see Melvyn P. Leffler, *For the Soul of Mankind: The United States, the Soviet Union, and the Cold War* (New York: Hill & Wang, 2007), 374–76; V. M. Zubok, *A Failed Empire: The Soviet Union in the Cold War from Stalin to Gorbachev* (Chapel Hill: University of North Carolina Press, 2009), 288. Thatcher quoted in Margaret Thatcher, *The Downing Street Years* (London: HarperCollins, 1993), 471. For European concern see Daalder, *Nature and Practice of Flexible Response*, 253.

85. Rogers quoted in Steven L. Rearden, *Council of War: A History of the Joint Chiefs of Staff, 1942–1991* (Washington, DC: Military Bookshop, 2012), 460. Galvin, however, supported the treaty, on the basis that the reduction to zero required the Soviets to give up more missiles. Galvin, *Fighting the Cold War*, 356. For Scowcroft see Miller Center, "Interview with Brent Scowcroft," http://millercenter.org/president/bush/oralhistory/brent-scowcroft. For dislike of INF Treaty among European leaders see Daalder,

Nature and Practice of Flexible Response, 255–57. On public opinion and the INF Treaty see German public opinion polling data in Thomas Risse-Kappen, "Anti-Nuclear and Pro-Detente? The Transformation of the West German Security Debate," in *Debating National Security: The Public Dimension*, ed. Hans Rattinger and Don Munton (New York: P. Lang, 1991), 290.

86. For "central political symbol" see "Background Information for Short-Range Nuclear Forces (SNF) Briefing)," undated [March 29, 1989], Scowcroft/91120/1/BPL. On NATO's plans for SNF through the 1980s see USNATO to SecState 9698, February 7, 1989, NSC/PA/8900706/BPL.

87. USNATO 7875 to SecState, September 11, 1987, DDRS/CK3100682668; "Intervention for the Second Day of NATO Summit," undated, DDRS/CK3100475981.

88. Shultz's observation in "Visit of West German Foreign Minister Hans-Dietrich Genscher in Capacity of European Community (EC) Presidency," January 21, 1988, Shultz to the President, January 20, 1988, DDRS/CK3100475123. Shultz's views of public opinion are supported by evidence in Risse-Kappen, "Anti-Nuclear and Pro-Detente?," 269. On SNF killing Germans only see "Short-Range Nuclear Forces and NATO's 'Comprehensive Concept,'" Memorandum for the President from Brent Scowcroft, undated, Scowcroft/91120/02/BPL. For "increasingly smitten" see "Meeting with West German Chancellor Helmut Kohl," from Colin L. Powell, February 17, 1988, DDRS/CK3100700215.

89. USNATO to SecState 9698, February 7, 1989, NSC/PA/8900706/BPL.

90. On the German coalition see "Meeting with Manfred Woerner, Secretary General of NATO," May 29, 1989, 9:00 a.m.–9:30 a.m., NSC/PA/8904368/BPL, and USNATO to SecState 9698, February 7, 1989, NSC/PA/8900706/BPL. For concern about the German position see "Talking Points for the President's Telephone Call to Prime Minister Thatcher on SNF," under cover of memorandum from Zelikow to Scowcroft, April 21, 1989, Scowcroft/91120/03/BPL, and Daalder, *Nature and Practice of Flexible Response*, 283–84.

91. For "domestic security consensus" see "Dealing with the Germans," Memorandum for the President from Scowcroft, August 7, 1989, Scowcroft/91120/04/BPL. For American concerns about the outsize influence of the FDP see James Baker's comments in "Meeting with Manfred Werner, Secretary General of NATO," May 29, 1989. For uncertainty about Kohl see Letter from Sir J. Fretwell to Sir C. Mallaby, May 18, 1989, *DBPO*:3:7, d15. For a German perspective on strains in American-German relations caused by the SNF issue see Frank Elbe and Richard Kiessler, *A Round Table with Sharp Corners: The Diplomatic Path to German Unity* (Baden-Baden: Nomos, 1996), 16.

92. The resident's remarks are in "Meeting with Manfred Woerner of NATO," Memorandum of Conversation, April 12, 1989, NSC/PA/8902548/BPL; for Scowcroft's point that NATO had to solve SNF quickly see "Meeting with Ciriaco De Mita, Prime Minister of Italy," May 27, 1989, 10:10 a.m.–11:45 a.m., NSC/PA/8904368/BPL.

93. James A. Baker, *The Politics of Diplomacy: Revolution, War, and Peace, 1989–1992* (New York: G. P. Putnam's Sons, 1995), 82–83, 90–91; Mary Elise Sarotte, *1989: The Struggle to Create Post–Cold War Europe* (Princeton, NJ: Princeton University Press, 2009), 26–27; "mischief" in George Bush and Brent Scowcroft, *A World Transformed* (New York: Alfred A. Knopf, 1998), 114. The CIA had assumed in 1988 that Moscow wished to "impede NATO's force modernization plans." SNIE 11-16-88 CX, November 1988, "Soviet Policy during the Next Phase of Arms Control in Europe (Key Judgments Only)," in *At Cold War's End: US Intelligence on the Soviet Union and Eastern Europe, 1989–1991*, ed. Benjamin B. Fischer (Reston, VA: Central Intelligence Agency, 1999).

94. "Meeting with NATO Secretary General Manfred Werner," Scowcroft to the President, February 9, 1990, Scowcroft/91116/03/BPL.

95. Baker, *Politics of Diplomacy*, 91.

96. "Dealing with the Germans," Memorandum for the President from Scowcroft, August 7, 1989. On Congress, etc., see "Meeting with NATO Secretary General Manfred Werner," Scowcroft to the President, February 9, 1990. For a similar formulation by British officials see Sir C. Mallaby to Sir G. Howe, April 10, 1989, *DBPO*:3:7, d7.

10. PROMISES ARE NEVER ENOUGH

1. Heads of State and Government participating in the meeting of the North Atlantic Council, "London Declaration on a Transformed North Atlantic Alliance," NATO, http://www.nato.int/docu/comm/49-95/c900706a.htm.

2. For an account of the meeting see ADST Foreign Affairs Oral History Project, "[Oral History Interview with] Robert M. Beecroft," www.adst.org/OH%20TOCs/Beecroft,%20Robert%20M.toc.pdf.

3. Letter from Mr. Powell (No. 10) to Mr Wall, February 24, 1990, *DBPO*:3:7, d313.

4. Bush and Scowcroft, *World Transformed*, 53. On changes in Eastern Europe see NIE 11/12-9-88, May 1988, "Soviet Policy toward Eastern Europe under Gorbachev," in Fischer, *At Cold War's End*.

5. "The NATO Summit," Memorandum for the President from Scowcroft, March 20, 1989, Kanter/CF00779/22/BPL.

6. For skepticism about Gorbachev see Robert M. Gates, *From the Shadows: The Ultimate Insider's Story of Five Presidents and how they won the Cold War* (New York: Simon & Schuster, 1996), 375–78, 80–89, 404, 73–75. Scowcroft and Gates discussed their views of Soviet policy and history in Miller Center oral histories. See "Interview with Robert Gates," Miller Center, University of Virginia, https://millercenter.org/the-presidency/presidential-oral-histories/robert-m-gates-deputy-director-central; "Interview with Brent Scowcroft," Miller Center, University of Virginia, http://millercenter.org/president/bush/oralhistory/brent-scowcroft.

7. Bush and Scowcroft, *World Transformed*, 12. See Scowcroft's assessment in "The NATO Summit," Memorandum for the President from Scowcroft, March 20, 1989.

8. USNATO to SecState 540, May 14, 1989, Kanter/CF00779/22/BPL.

9. "Interview with Brent Scowcroft"; ADST Foreign Affairs Oral History Project, "[Oral History Interview with] David Michael Adamson," http://www.adst.org/OH%20TOCs/Adamson,%20David%20Michael.toc.pd.

10. Bush and Scowcroft, *World Transformed*, 114.

11. "[Oral History Interview with] Robert M. Beecroft."

12. Beecroft's worries were evident in 1983; see "German Democracy: How Tender a Flower," June 29, 1983, Burns/V15/1983–84: B(1)/GFL. On the Greens and the threat to NATO see "Otto Schily on the Greens," January 18, 1985, Burns/V25/1984–85: S(2)/GFL.

13. Wolfgang Donsbach, Hans Matthias Kepplinger, and Elisabeth Noelle-Neumann, "West Germans' Perceptions of NATO and the Warsaw Pact: Long-Term Content Analysis of *Der Spiegel* and Trends in Public Opinion," in *Debating National Security: The Public Dimension*, ed. Hans Rattinger and Don Munton (New York: P. Lang, 1991), 260–62.

14. According to Assistant Secretary of State Richard Burt, "German After the Election," March 1, 1983, Burns/V11/1982–83—K(4)/GFL.

15. "The NATO Summit," Memorandum for the President from Scowcroft, March 20, 1989.

16. "The NATO Summit," March 20, 1989.

17. George Bush, "Remarks to the Citizens of Mainz, Federal Republic of Germany, May 31, 1989," http://www.presidency.ucsb.edu/ws/?pid=17085.

18. Gates, *From the Shadows*, 461–62.

19. Gates; Baker, *Politics of Diplomacy*, 91.

20. Bush to Lubbers draft letter attached to "NATO Summit Initiative—Letters to Allied Leaders," Memorandum to the President from Scowcroft, undated, Kanter/CF00779/22/BPL.

21. "NATO Summit," for Robert Gates from Zelikow through Blackwill and Kanter, April 13, 1989, Kanter/CF00779/22/BPL.

22. North Atlantic Council, "Declaration of the Heads of State and Government Participating in the Meeting of the North Atlantic Council, May 29–30, 1989," NATO, http://www.nato.int/docu/comm/49-95/c890530a.htm.

23. Letter from Sir J. Fretwell to Sir C. Mallaby, May 18, 1989, *DBPO*:3:7, d16; for a similar sentiment by Woerner see "Meeting with Manfred Werner, NATO Secretary General," October 11, 1989, 2:00–3:00 p.m., NSC/PA 8909134/BPL.

24. "GDR Crisis Contingencies," November 6, 1989, Blackwill/CF00182/20/BPL.

25. Hurd quoted in Sarotte, *1989*, 4.

26. "U.S. Diplomacy from the New Europe," for the President from Brent Scowcroft, December 22, 1989, Scowcroft/91116/02/BPL.

27. "Meeting with Wilfried Martens, Prime Minister of Belgium," May 28, 1989, NSC/PA 8904368/BPL. See also Sir A. Acland (Washington) to FCO, January 30, 1990, *DBPO*:3:7, d231.

28. "Your Meetings in Brussels with NATO Leaders, December 3–4," for the President from Brent Scowcroft, undated, Scowcroft/91116/01/BPL.

29. For concerns about a German Peace Conference see "Your Breakfast with Kissinger: Managing the German Question," for Scowcroft from Hutchings to Blackwill, January 26, 1990, Blackwill/CF00182/20/BPL, repeated in "A Strategy for German Unification," for the President from Scowcroft, NSC/PA/9000922/BPL. For Thatcher's concerns see Letter from Mr Powell (No. 10) to Mr Wall, February 10, 1990, *DBPO*:3:7, d286.

30. "U.S. Diplomacy for the New Europe," for the President from Brent Scowcroft, December 22, 1989, Scowcroft/91116/02/BPL. Bush administration concerns about Europe closely mirror those held by Nixon and Kissinger. See "Presidential Speech on Western Europe," for Brent Scowcroft from Rodman and Blackwill, April 11, 1989, Scowcroft/91117/2/BPL; "Deputies Committee Meeting to Review Economic Issues in NSR 5: US–Western Europe Relations Wednesday, March 22, 3:00 P.M., WHSR," for Gates from Hutchings and Deal through Blackwill, March 21, 1989, Zelikow/CF01468/01/BPL.

31. "United States Policy toward Eastern Europe," for Brent Scowcroft from Robert L. Hutchings through Robert D. Blackwill, December 16, 1989, Scowcroft/91125/03/BPL. See also "Meeting with Manfred Woerner, Secretary General of the North Atlantic Treaty Organization," February 24, 1990, NSC/PA 9001053/BPL; "U.S. Policy in Eastern Europe in 1990," for the President from Scowcroft, Scowcroft/91125/03/BPL; "Your Meetings in Brussels with NATO Leaders, December 3–4," undated.

32. For Scowcroft's views see "U.S. Diplomacy for the New Europe," for the President from Brent Scowcroft, December 22, 1989. On Rosenfeld see "U.S. Policy in Eastern Europe in 1990," for the President from Scowcroft, Scowcroft/91125/03/BPL.

33. See Roland Dumas remarks quoted in Sir E. Fergusson (Paris) to Mr Hurd, February 2, 1990, *DBPO*:3:7, d246.

34. Letter from Sir C. Mallaby (Bonn) to Mr Weston, January 24, 1990, *DBPO*:3:7, d221. See also Extracts from Conclusions of a Meeting of the Cabinet held at 10 Down[ing] Street on 1 February 1990 at 9.30 a.m.," *DBPO*:3:7, d236.

35. Sir A. Acland (Washington) to FCO, January 30, 1990, *DBPO*:3:7, d231.

36. "Letter from Mr Powell (Strasbourg) to Mr Wall, December 8, 1989, *DBPO*:3:7, d165.

37. "Preparing for the Six Power German Peace Conference," Memorandum for the President from Scowcroft, [draft under cover of February 14, 1990, memorandum], Blackwill/CF00192/20/BPL. See Mitterrand quoted in Bush and Scowcroft, *World Transformed*, 211. "Your Breakfast with Kissinger: Managing the German Question," January 26, 1990. See also "Scope Paper—Your Bilateral with Chancellor Kohl," for the President from Brent Scowcroft, Scowcroft/91116/01/BPL; Letter from Sir C. Mallaby (Bonn) to Sir J Fretwell, November 8, 1989, *DBPO*:3:7, d95; Letter from Mr Powell (No. 10) to Mr Wall), January 31, 1990, *DBPO*:3:7, d233; Minute from Mr Powell (No. 10) to Mrs Thatcher, February 9, 1990, *DBPO*:3:7, d277.

38. The Soviets—and some Germans—floated an idea for a "French solution" for Germany in NATO, whereby the Federal Republic might remain party to the North Atlantic Treaty but, like de Gaulle and France in the 1960s, remove its forces from SACEUR's command. In this plan (which Gorbachev himself would later suggest), the Americans saw a Soviet ploy to reduce NATO's military to a "shell" and to put pressure on the Germans to push for the withdrawal of American troops from NATO, too. "Preparing for the Six Power German Peace Conference" [draft under cover of February 14, 1990, memorandum]; Sir A. Acland (Washington) to FCO, February 24, 1990, *DBPO*:3:7, d307; Bush and Scowcroft, *World Transformed*, 274.

39. Sir C. Mallaby (Bonn) to Mr Hurd, February 1, 1990, *DBPO*:3:7, d238.

40. See Kristina Spohr, "Germany, America and the Shaping of Post–Cold War Europe: A Story of German International Emancipation through Political Unification, 1989–90," *Cold War History* 15, no. 2 (2015): 9; Philip Zelikow and Condoleezza Rice, *Germany Unified and Europe Transformed: A Study in Statecraft* (Cambridge, MA: Harvard University Press, 1995), 44. For the nuances of Genscher's thinking see Mr Hurd to Sir C Mallaby, March 12, 1990, *DBPO*:3:7, d330.

41. Quoted in Sarotte, *1989*, 104.

42. Even Genscher's foreign policy advisers recognized "Genscherism was a synonym for the new politics of 'appeasement.'" Elbe and Kiessler, *Round Table with Sharp Corners*, 16–17. See Rice quoted in Alexander von Plato, *The End of the Cold War? Bush, Kohl, Gorbachev, and the Reunification of Germany*, trans. Edith Burley (New York: Palgrave Macmillan, 2015), 1553.

43. Baker's notes of the conversation read: ". . . NATO—*whose juris. would not move *eastward!" The "one inch" was inserted by Baker in a letter to Kohl. Quoted in Sarotte, *1989*, 110–11.

44. See Kristina Spohr, "Precluded or Precedent-Setting? The 'NATO Enlargement Question' in the Triangular Bonn-Washington-Moscow Diplomacy of 1990–1991," *Journal of Cold War Studies* 14, no. 4 (Fall 2012); Mary Elise Sarotte, "Not One Inch Eastward? Bush, Baker, Kohl, Genscher, Gorbachev, and the Origins of Russian Resentment toward NATO Enlargement in February 1990," *Diplomatic History* 34, no. 1 (January 2010).

45. Zelikow and Rice, *Germany Unified*, 184.

46. Zelikow and Rice, 189.

47. See Sarotte, "Not One Inch Eastward?," esp. at 140.

48. For a full review of the controversies and literature on the matter see Joshua R. Itzkowitz Shifrinson, "Deal or No Deal? The End of the Cold War and the U.S. Offer to Limit NATO Expansion," *International Security* 40, no. 4 (Spring 2016).

49. For British concern see Sir A. Acland (Washington) to FCO, February 24, 1990.

50. "Meetings with German Chancellor Helmut Kohl," undated (February), 1990, Scowcroft/91116/03/BPL.

51. "Meetings with German Chancellor Helmut Kohl," undated (February), 1990.

52. "First Meeting of the European Strategy Steering Group," for Robert Gates from Condoleezza Rice through Blackwill and Kanter, February 21, 1990, Scowcroft/91116/03/BPL.

53. "Meetings with German Chancellor Helmut Kohl," undated (February), 1990.

54. For Baker's view of this as a straight quid pro quo see Zelikow and Rice, *Germany Unified*, 173.

55. "Meetings with German Chancellor Helmut Kohl," undated (February), 1990.

56. Bush and Scowcroft, *World Transformed*, 250–58.

57. George Bush, "Joint News Conference Following Discussions with Chancellor Helmut Kohl of the Federal Republic of Germany," American Presidency Project, http://www.presidency.ucsb.edu/ws/?pid=18188.

58. "Telephone Conversation with President Mikhail Gorbachev of the Soviet Union," February 28, 1990, https://bush41library.tamu.edu/files/memcons-telcons/1990-02-28--Gorbachev.pdf. See also Zelikow and Rice, *Germany Unified*, 216–17.

59. Letter from Mr. Powell (No. 10) to Mr Wall, February 24, 1990.

60. "Preparing for the Six Power German Peace Conference" [draft under cover of February 14, 1990, memorandum].

61. Baker, *Politics of Diplomacy*, 198.

62. Zelikow and Rice, *Germany Unified*, 227.

63. Zelikow and Rice, 193.

64. See Blackwill's comments quoted in Sir A. Acland (Washington) to FCO, February 24, 1990.

65. Mr Hurd to Sir C. Mallaby (Bonn), March 12, 1990, *DBPO*:3:7, d334.

66. "Meeting with Manfred Woerner, Secretary General of the North Atlantic Treaty Organization," February 24, 1990; Sir A. Acland (Washington) to FCO, January 30, 1990, *DBPO*:3:7, d231; Bush and Scowcroft, *World Transformed*, 269.

67. See Hurd quoted in Sir R. Braithwaite (Moscow) to FCO, April 11, 1990, *DBPO*:3:7, d374. See also Thatcher's comments recorded in Letter from Mr Powell (No. 10) to Mr Wall, June 8, 1990, *DBPO*:3:7, d411.

68. A detailed account of the summit is in Bush and Scowcroft, *World Transformed*. See also Leffler, *For the Soul of Mankind*, 446.

69. Hannes Adomeit, "Gorbachev, German Unification and the Collapse of Empire," *Post-Soviet Affairs* 10, no. 3 (1994): esp. at 226.

70. On domestic criticism of Gorbachev and Shevardnadze see "Preparing for the Six Power German Peace Conference" [draft under cover of February 14, 1990, memorandum].

71. Zelikow and Rice, *Germany Unified*, 283; Bush and Scowcroft, *World Transformed*, 292.

72. Mary Elise Sarotte, "Perpetuating U.S. Preeminence: The 1990 Deals to 'Bribe the Soviets Out' and Move NATO In," *International Security* 35, no. 1 (Summer 2010): 113; Zelikow and Rice, *Germany Unified*, 263.

73. Minute from Sir P. Cradock to Mrs Thatcher, June 19, 1990, *DBPO*:3:7, d423. Vladislav M. Zubok explains the importance to Gorbachev of promised changes to NATO: "With His Back against the Wall: Gorbachev, Soviet Demise, and German Unification," *Cold War History* 14 (2014), no. 4: 619–45.

74. Sir A. Acland (Washington) to FCO, January 30, 1990.

75. "Special NATO Foreign Ministers Meeting: Scenario Brief," RG25/27-4-NATO-12/LAC.

76. David Abshire to Brent Scowcroft, May 2, 1990, Wilson/CF00293/09/BPL.

77. "Meeting with Manfred Woerner, Secretary General of the North Atlantic Treaty Organization," February 24, 1990; "[Oral History Interview with] David Michael Adamson."

78. "Your Meeting with Your Counterparts on the NATO Summit, Tuesday, June 19, at 5:00 pm," for Scowcroft from Zelikow through Blackwill and Kanter, Wilson/

CF00290/08/BPL; Message to Prime Minister Thatcher from President Bush, via Cabinet Channels, July 1, 1990, Koch/CF01333/015/BPL.

79. "London Declaration"; Bush and Scowcroft, *World Transformed*, 301.

80. "Qs and As for President's Press Conference, July 6, 1990," Wilson/CF00290/008/BPL; Message to Prime Minister Thatcher from President Bush, July 1, 1990.

81. "Objectives for Our Strategic Dialogue with the French," Memorandum for Scowcroft from Zelikow and Basora, October 9, 1990, Zelikow/CF01468/009/BPL.

82. "NATO Liaison: General Principles for Development," by Stephen Flanagan, May 14, 1991, Lowenkron/CF01526/007/BPL.

83. Zelikow and Rice, *Germany Unified*, 466n78.

84. Mr Budd (Bonn) to Mr Hurd, July 17, 1990, *DBPO*:3:7, d434. The Americans were not pleased that Kohl made concessions without consultation. Minute from Mr West to Mr Wall, July 23, 1990, *DBPO*:3:7, d438.

85. Mr Hurd to Sir M. Alexander (UKDEL NATO), July 18, 1990, *DBPO*:3:7, d435.

86. "NATO as a 'Political' Organization," Rodman to Scowcroft, March 26, 1990, NSC/APNSA/9001935/BPL.

87. "Seminar on Germany: Summary Record," Enclosure in No. 3, *DBPO*:3:7, d507.

88. "Our Goals in CSCE," Memorandum for Scowcroft from David C. Gompert, October 22, 1990, NSC/PA/9008391/BPL.

89. SecState 349766 to USNATO, "guidance for NATO Strategy Review Group," October 16, 1990, Wilson/CF00293/01/BPL.

90. For worries Gorbachev might be maneuvered into using force, or replaced, see "Seminar on Germany: Summary Record," and "Meeting with Prime Minister Brian Mulroney of Canada," April 10, 1990, Rostow/CF01329/10/BPL. On Lithuania's importance to Moscow see "Lithuania: Points to Register," May 3, 1990, Brussels, Belgium, in RG25/27-4-NATO-12/LAC.

91. SecState 349766 to USNATO, "guidance for NATO Strategy Review Group," October 16, 1990.

92. "Enhancing the Political Role of NATO," March 14, 1990, Rice/CF00720-1/07/BPL.

93. Letter from Mr. Powell (No. 10) to Mr Wall, February 24, 1990.

94. UKDelNATO 450 to FCO, September 10, 1990, PREM 19/3081.

95. "Summary of Conclusions: European Strategy Steering Group, November 29–30, 1990," November 30, 1990, Wilson/CF00293/002/BPL.

96. "The Security of the East European Democracies," Memorandum for Scowcroft from Rodman, June 21, 1990, Rostow/CF01329/09/BPL.

97. "Enhancing the Political Role of NATO," March 14, 1990.

98. "Enhancing the Political Role of NATO."

99. "Military-to-Military Contacts with Eastern Europe," August 1990, Scowcroft/91125/09/BPL. See also "The Security of the East European Democracies," June 21, 1990.

100. "Military Exchanges with Eastern Europe," Memorandum for Scowcroft from Hutchings through Basora and Kanter, August 16, 1990, Scowcroft/91125/09/BPL.

101. "Your Meeting of the European Strategy Steering Group on Monday, October 29, from 3:00 to 5:00 pm," for Gates from Zelikow, October 26, 1990, Wilson/CF00293/004/BPL.

102. "Your Meeting of the European Strategy Steering Group," October 26, 1990.

103. "America's Postwar Agenda in Europe," issue paper for European Strategy Steering Group Meetings, March 11–12, 1991, March 8, 1991, Zelikow/CF01468/005/BPL.

104. "Draft Summary of Conclusions: European Strategy Steering Group, March 11–12, 1991," Wilson/CF00293/17/BPL.

105. "Draft Summary of Conclusions." Coincidentally, on the second day of the ESSG meeting, a Policy Planning staffer penned a note speculating on the possibility of NATO enlargement. The memorandum is quoted in part in Sarotte, "Perpetuating U.S. Preeminence," 118.

106. "Security Consultations at NATO," for Kanter, Gordon, and Fry from Wilson, February 1, 1991, Wilson/CF00286/012/BPL.

107. Robert L. Hutchings, *American Diplomacy and the End of the Cold War: An Insider's Account of U.S. Policy in Europe, 1989–1992* (Washington, DC: Woodrow Wilson Center Press and Johns Hopkins University Press, 1997), 288.

108. On French motivations see "Summary of Conclusions: European Strategy Steering Group, November 29–30, 1990," November 30, 1990, Wilson/CF00293/002/BPL. For French fears of Germany in a nonfederated Europe see "Binding Germany In," Draft Paper by the Policy Planning Staff, June 15, 1990, *DBPO*:3:7, d419.

109. "Your Meeting of the European Strategy Steering Group on Thursday, November 29, at 1:00 p.m.," for Gates from Zelikow through Gompert and Gordon, November 28, 1990, Wilson/CF00293/03/BPL; for strain see "Draft Summary of Conclusions: European Strategy Steering Group, March 11–12, 1991," Wilson/CF00293/17/BPL.

110. "Draft Summary of Conclusions: European Strategy Steering Group, March 11–12, 1991."

111. "NATO and European Integration," draft memorandum for the President from Scowcroft, undated, Wilson/CFL00293/19/BPL.

112. "Our Goals in CSCE," Memorandum for Scowcroft from David C. Gompert, October 22, 1990, NSC/PA/9008391/BPL; "Meeting with Manfred Woerner, Secretary General of the North Atlantic Treaty Organization," February 24, 1990.

113. Note from Kanter on "Memo to the President on the European Pillar," for Scowcroft from Gompert, March 5, 1991, Wilson/CF0293/19/BPL.

114. "European Pillar Discussions," for Scowcroft from Gompert, October 3, 1991, Gompert/CF01301/19/BPL; "NATO and European Integration," draft memorandum for the President from Scowcroft, undated.

115. Mitterrand quoted in Frédéric Bozo, *Mitterrand, the End of the Cold War, and German Unification*, trans. Susan Emanuel (New York: Berghahn Books, 2009), 319. "Joint Statement: US-German Views on the New European and Trans-Atlantic Architecture," US Department of State Dispatch, vol. 2, no. 19, May 13, 1991.

116. "Your Visit to the NATO Summit in Rome, November 7–8, 1991," Memorandum for the President from Baker, November 5, 1991, Wayne/CF01099/BPL.

117. USNATO 4044 to SecState, September 9, 1991, Chellis/CF01436/01/BPL.

118. "The President's Meeting with Secretary General of NATO Manfred Woerner," October 11, 1991, Lowenkron/CF01526-2/21/BPL.

119. "Enhancing Relations with Central and Eastern Europe," undated, briefing book for "North Atlantic Council Ministerial Meeting, Brussels, December 17–18, 1990," R25/27-4-NATO-12-Fall-1990/LAC.

120. For Eastern European interests see "The President's Meeting with Secretary General of NATO Manfred Woerner," October 11, 1991.

121. "The Rome Summit and NATO's Mission," undated, Holl, CF01397/BPL; "Your Visit to the NATO Summit in Rome, November 7–8, 1991," for the President from Baker, November 5, 1991, Wayne/CF01099/BPL.

122. USNATO 4044 to SecState, September 9, 1991.

123. USNATO 6121 to SecState, November 15, 1991, Wayne/CF01099/BPL. Hutchings, *American Diplomacy*, 289, 92.

124. USNATO 5516 to SecState, November 29, 1991, Chellis/CF01436/10/BPL.

125. Warsaw 18786 to SecState, November 22, 1991, Chellis/CF01436/10/BPL.

126. On the deal with France see Bozo, *Mitterrand*, 355. For "biggest supporters" see "Your Visit to the NATO Summit in Rome, November 7–8, 1991," Memorandum for the President from Baker, November 5, 1991. See also the remarks of Hungarian foreign minister quoted in USVienna 2336 to SecState, December 6, 1991, Chellis/CF01436/09/BPL.

127. "The Rome Summit and NATO's Mission," undated.

128. "Expanding Membership in NATO," Rostow/CF01329/05/BPL.

129. Hutchings, *American Diplomacy*, 290–92.

130. "Developing Criteria for Future NATO Members: Now is the Time," to Ross and Zoellick from Flanagan through Holmes, May 1, 1992, Lowenkron/CF01526-1/13/BPL.

131. "Memorandum: Atlantic Cohesion and East-West Relations," by Zbigniew Brzezinski, NSF/Agency/ 53/State Department, Policy Planning, vol. 7/LBJL.

132. "Developing Criteria for Future NATO Members: Now is the Time," May 1, 1992.

133. "Implications for NATO of Expanded WEU Membership," Lowenkron to Gompert, March 20, 1992, Lowenkron/CF01526-1/13/BPL. For American emphasis on integrated command see "Expanding Membership in NATO," Rostow/CF01329/05/BPL.

134. "Implications for NATO of Expanded WEU Membership," March 20, 1992.

135. "Developing Criteria for Future NATO Members: Now is the Time," May 1, 1992.

136. "NATO Membership," Niles to Zoellick, April 27, 1992, Lowenkron/CF01526-1/13/BPL.

137. "NATO Membership," Niles to Zoellick, April 27, 1992.

CONCLUSION

1. "Memorandum: Atlantic Cohesion and East-West Relations," by Zbigniew Brzezinski, NSF/Agency/53/State Department, Policy Planning, vol. 7/LBJL; Minutes of Meeting of Working Group, August 16, 1948, *DCER*:14, d386.

2. This account draws heavily on James M. Goldgeier, "NATO Expansion: The Anatomy of a Decision," *Washington Quarterly* 21, no. 1 (Winter 1998): 85–103. See also *Not Whether but When: The U.S. Decision to Enlarge NATO* (Washington, DC: Brookings Institution Press, 1999); James M. Goldgeier and Michael McFaul, *Power and Purpose: U.S. Policy toward Russia after the Cold War* (Washington, DC: Brookings Institution Press, 2003).

3. Quoted by George F. Will, "'A Dog in That Fight'?," *Newsweek*, June 11, 1995, http://www.newsweek.com/dog-fight-183518.

4. "NATO and the Bosnian Crisis," Memorandum for Scowcroft from Lowenkron and Holl, July 2, 1992, NSC/Wayne/CDF01099/BPL.

5. Edgar Buckley, "Invoking Article 5," *NATO Review*, Summer 2006, http://www.nato.int/docu/review/2006/issue2/english/art2.html.

6. Philip H. Gordon and Jeremy Shapiro, *Allies at War: America, Europe, and the Crisis over Iraq* (New York: McGraw-Hill, 2004).

7. "Transcript of Defense Secretary Gates's Speech on NATO," *Wall Street Journal*, June 10, 2011.

8. Cf. Robert Kagan, *Of Paradise and Power: America and Europe in the New World Order* (New York: Alfred A. Knopf, 2003).

9. Patrick Stephenson, "Confessions of a NATO Speechwriter," *ForeignPolicy.com*, May 1, 2016, http://foreignpolicy.com/2016/05/01/nato-speeches-rasmussen-russia-afghanistan-trump.

10. "Conclusions from Continental Tour, 1955," October 1955, Basil Liddell Hart papers, LH/11/1955/7, LHCMA.

11. Josh Rogin, "Europe's Convinced U.S. Won't Solve Its Problems," *Bloomberg-View*, February 13, 2016, https://www.bloomberg.com/view/articles/2016-02-13/europe-s-convinced-u-s-won-t-solve-its-problems.

12. Washington2053 to FCO, July 1, 1973, FCO 41/1185.

13. Killick to Sykes, December 21, 1976, FCO 46/1366.

14. Judy Dempsey, "NATO's European Allies Won't Fight for Article 5," *Strategic Europe, Carnegie Europe*, June 15, 2015, http://carnegieeurope.eu/strategiceurope/?fa=60389.

15. "Anti-Nuclear Sentiment and Pacifism in NATO Europe," to Mallaby, July 13, 1981, FCO 46/2765.

16. David A. Shlapak and Michael W. Johnson, *Reinforcing Deterrence on NATO's Eastern Flank*, RAND Research Report, 2016, https://www.rand.org/content/dam/rand/pubs/research_reports/RR1200/RR1253/RAND_RR1253.pdf.

17. One of the most forceful statements of American frustration with European allied spending on NATO was made by Robert Gates, secretary of defense to Barack Obama. "Transcript of Defense Secretary Gates's Speech on NATO," *Wall Street Journal*, June 10, 2012, http://blogs.wsj.com/washwire/2011/06/10/transcript-of-defense-secretary-gatess-speech-on-natos-future/.

18. "United States: First Impressions: No Longer God's Own Country?," Cromer to Douglas-Home, July 21, 1971, FCO 82/55.

19. See the transcript attached to Tim Haines, "Trump: NATO Is Obsolete and Expensive, 'Doesn't Have the Right Countries in It for Terrorism,'" *Real Clear Politics*, March 27, 2016, http://www.realclearpolitics.com/video/2016/03/27/trump_europe_is_not_safe_lots_of_the_free_world_has_become_weak.html.

20. Susan B. Glasser, "Trump National Security Team Blindsided by NATO Speech," *Politico*, June 5, 2017.

21. "Most Americans Support NATO Alliance," Michael Smith, *Gallup News* online, February 17, 2017.

22. The first suggestion in this sentence is Brzezinski's; see Goldgeier, "NATO Expansion."

23. "Transcript of Defense Secretary Gates's Speech on NATO."

24. Alex Danchev and Daniel Todman, eds., *War Diaries, 1939–1945: Field Marshal Lord Alanbrooke* (London: Weidenfeld & Nicolson, 2001), 680.

Index

Abshire, David, 229
Acheson, Dean
  and advent of North Atlantic Treaty, 16
  on beginnings of NATO, 22
  and Berlin crisis, 80–82, 86–87, 97, 283n27
  on détente, 152
  and French withdrawal, 125, 126
  on German support for NATO, 130
  on NATO and nuclear weapons, 82–83
  and Nuclear Planning Group, 116
  on politicians, 5
  studies American policy toward NATO, 78
Achilles, Theodore, 2, 16
Adenauer, Konrad, 26, 43, 55, 107, 109–13
Afanassievsky, Nikolai, 216
Afghanistan, 205, 243, 325n62
Africa, tripartite talks concerning, 58, 60–61.
  See also Algeria
Ailleret, Charles, 130
el-Alamein, Viscount Montgomery of, 6, 7, 18,
  30, 54, 274n12
Algeria, 46, 48, 59, 61, 281n151
Alphand, Hervé, 56, 57, 58, 59–60, 73–74
al-Qaeda, 243
Alsop, Joseph, 297n2
Ambassadorial Working Group, 93, 94
Andersen, Knud Borge, 179–80
Andréani, Jacques, 163
Anglo-American alliance, 36–50, 271n99
Anglo-American Nassau agreement, 108–9
antinuclear sentiment, 9, 167, 191–92, 202,
  207–11, 219
apathy, 232, 239
Arab-Israeli War (1973), 184–85
army, European, 18–19, 25
Atlantic Community, 76, 77–78, 85, 99
Atlantic Declaration, 179–80, 182, 188,
  319n109
atomic cooperation, 61–63
atomic stockpile, 43–44, 45. *See also* nuclear
  weapons and capabilities

Backfire bomber, 200
Baghdad Pact, 10*fig.*, 45
Bahr, Egon, 170, 196

Baker, James, 214, 225–26, 227, 242, 330m43
Ball, George, 109–10, 113, 115, 116
Barnes, John, 159
Bator, Francis, 126, 133–34, 141, 144, 145
Bay of Pigs, 84
Bech, Joseph, 35
Belgium
  antinuclear sentiment in, 207
  and Congo crisis, 69–72
  and détente, 152, 154–55, 307n35
  NATO headquarters moved to, 127
Berlin and Berlin crises, 76–77
  allied doubts about US intentions
    concerning, 89–90
  American strong-arm tactics in, 94–99
  blockade and airlife, 14, 78
  and construction of Berlin Wall, 90–92
  and flexible response, 82–84
  importance of, 80–82, 283n27
  NATO's role and allied concerns regarding,
    86–89, 286n61
  public opinion concerning, 286n65
  relationship between NATO and, 77–80
  strategy for, 84–86, 92–94
Berlin Wall, 90–92, 222–23
Bevin, Ernest, 11, 12, 13, 15
Bidault, Georges, 25
Bilderberg, 5
Boegner, Jean-Marc, 64
Bohlen, Charles "Chip," 14
bonds, and offset crisis, 144–45
Boon, Henry, 124
Bosnia, 243
Bowie, Robert, 102–3, 159
Bradley, Omar, 20–21
Brandt, Willy, 154, 170, 189–90
Brentano, Heinrich von, 34
Brezhnev, Leonid, 188, 197, 207
Brosio, Manlio, 116, 118, 135, 151, 157–58, 169
Bruce, David, 19, 55, 56, 275n28
Brussels Treaty (1948), 13, 16, 17
Brussels Treaty (1954), 25, 26, 119, 121, 123
Brzezinski, Zbigniew, 153, 159, 194–95, 197,
  198, 199, 238, 241
Buchan, Alistair, 112